Praise for Peter W. Rodman's

Presidential Command

"Outstanding. . . . On target. . . . Timely. . . . Rodman's experience in five of the presidencies he discusses, and his lucid style, keep the focus on reality and the narrative lively. . . . [His] studiously even-handed and balanced style makes his zingers even more telling when they explode on the page, and he is especially acute assessing Republican administrations in which he served."   —*National Review*

"Fascinating and insightful."   —*Richmond Times-Dispatch*

"Surprisingly fun. . . . Rodman moves along briskly, mixing insidery dish with lucid analysis."   —Bloomberg News

"This masterful series of studies, by one of America's most gifted and sensitive national security analysts, merges a scrupulous taste for clarity with a broad and humane vision of the American national interest. It is enlightening, penetrating and always fascinating."
    —Philip Bobbitt, author of *Terror and Consent*

"[*Presidential Command*] brings to bear the qualified judgment of someone who in many cases was actually there. . . . [Rodman] has bequeathed his country a priceless legacy. One can only hope that administrations present and future will make good use of it."
    —*The American Spectator*

"Pungent, provocative, perspicacious. . . . An incisive, in-depth, and often firsthand examination of the successes and failures of the last seven administrations."   —*Tulsa World*

"Invaluable. . . . Rodman casts a cold light on a number of established clichés about foreign policy conflicts. . . . But at its heart this book is about more than foreign policy. In the end, *Presidential Command* is about the central problem of democratic government today in all fields of policy."   —*The Weekly Standard*

"Telling. . . . Rich in detail."   —*The National Interest*

"Rodman [had] a close-up look at the process of governmental decision making—and the bureaucratic elbowing that the process usually entails. . . . His rankings of presidential performance pack interest."
                    —*St. Louis Post-Dispatch*

"Observers of the new Obama administration and its inaugural moves in foreign affairs should find lessons in Rodman's experienced outlook."   —*Booklist*

"Peter Rodman was incisive, wise, and fair and these qualities are reflected in his revealing, timely, and truly important account of how our recent presidents both succeeded and failed in exercising strategic 'command' over U.S. foreign policy."   —Zbigniew Brzezinski

Peter W. Rodman

Presidential Command

Peter W. Rodman was a senior fellow in foreign policy at the Brookings Institution in Washington, D.C. He served as deputy assistant to the president for national security affairs, as director of the State Department's Policy Planning Staff, as special assistant to Henry Kissinger in the White House, and, most recently, as assistant secretary of defense of international security affairs (2001–2007). Rodman is the author of *More Precious than Peace*. He died in August 2008.

ALSO BY PETER W. RODMAN

More Precious than Peace:
The Cold War and the Struggle for the Third World

PRESIDENTIAL COMMAND

POWER, LEADERSHIP, AND THE
MAKING OF FOREIGN POLICY FROM
RICHARD NIXON TO GEORGE W. BUSH

Peter W. Rodman

Vintage Books
A Division of Random House, Inc.
New York

146119709

CONTENTS

INTRODUCTION
Henry A. Kissinger

A kind Providence caused Peter Rodman's life and mine to intersect more than four decades ago. Peter was assigned to me as a tutee in 1965 at Harvard. He was part of my life ever since. It will be an emptier and less joyful world without him.

Peter wrote a brilliant undergraduate thesis. I was so impressed with him that, even as he decided to go to law school, I offered him a position as research assistant should he decide against practicing law. As it turned out, I had become President Nixon's national security adviser by the time Peter took up the offer.

Peter started work as my personal assistant. In a short time, his duties developed to supervising the assembly of documents and information relevant to the many negotiations taking place simultaneously, to see to it that an accurate record of these meetings existed, and to distill them together with his colleagues—mostly in their twenties—into recommendations for the next phase. He also helped me write speeches.

No one worked more closely with me than Peter. He sat at my side during every negotiation and was part of the team designing their tactics and strategy.

Public service was Peter's vocation. From the moment he joined my staff and for nearly four decades afterward, five presidents, from Richard Nixon through George W. Bush, benefited from his understated wisdom, his unselfish dedication, and his wry wit, as director of the Policy Planning Staff at the State Department, as presidential assistant, and as assistant secretary of defense for international security affairs. His principal weakness was a passionate attachment to the Boston Red Sox—incomprehensible for a Yankee fan.

Peter grew up during a time when America's exceptionalism had turned on itself. It was inevitable that America would learn that there were limits even to the "shining city on the hill." But the process was painful. Throughout our history, every problem recognized as a problem had proved soluble. Vietnam proved obdurate.

The so-called greatest generation that saw us through the confrontation with Fascism and Japan had been sustained by a moral consensus and unambiguous objectives. Hence, Peter had to work on policies that were challenged not so much for their prudence as for their motive. In the 1960s and 1970s, the intellectual community, mourning the assassination of a president with whom it had identified, and perplexed by an impasse to which its own theories had contributed, interpreted its frustrations as a moral failure of the American system and experience. Dialogue evaporated and eventually turned into a kind of intellectual civil war.

Peter transcended the passions of a turbulent time. He did so by his integrity, his special kind of innocence, which caused even his intellectual adversaries to feel that they learned from him, even when they could not bring themselves to share his conclusions.

In an increasingly narcissistic age, while many of his contemporaries analyzed themselves and their motives with rapt fascination, Peter helped sustain the nation by unobtrusive commitment to the cause of freedom fought in the trenches of the bureaucracy and the battlefields of diplomacy. Peter sought fulfillment, not glory. He served to do, not to be.

Not for Peter was the debate between idealism and realism. He had seen that the key governmental decisions were close, 49.5 to 50.5 percent, and that serious people were seeking to solve them. A grasp of circumstances was essential. Yet, by themselves, experts of circumstance inspire paralysis, not direction. Events cannot be shaped, or challenges overcome, without faith in fundamental values. The highest task of a public servant is to take his or her society from where it is to where it has never been. This implies the courage to face complexity, the character to act when the outcome is still ambiguous. For Peter, the issue of courage did not arise because he perceived no alternative to pursuing his duty. And character was inherent, requiring no affirmation.

Peter was much too modest to have put his role into words as these. The fact remains that the nation has lost one of its sentinels, all the more indispensable for never having made that claim for himself.

IT WOULD NOT SERVE Peter's memory to leave him as an abstract figure on a pedestal. It was the good fortune of Peter's associates that he was as warm a human being as he was selfless. Excessive deference was not his defining trait. At diplomatic lunches, Peter did not let note-taking interfere with his voracious appetite, eating with his left hand while scribbling with his right. On one occasion, an ambassador noticed that Peter stopped taking notes, though not eating, while I attempted a humorous point. "Don't you record the secretary's jokes?" the diplomat wanted to know. "Yes," Peter replied. "The first time."

Peter had a wicked sense of humor. One of his specialties was to pro-duce spoofs of option papers. One such effort concerned John T. Downey, who had been imprisoned in China since the early 1950s. After Nixon's opening to Beijing, I asked Chou En-lai to release Downey on compassionate grounds so that he could see his mother one last time. When Ford became president, Peter concocted a spoof option paper with the following theme: Chou En-lai had released Downey based on our representation that his mother was dying. The mother did not die, generating a credibility problem for the United States. The president, according to Peter, therefore had the following options, in ascending order of severity: (a) he could apologize for Mrs. Downey's survival and offer unspecified compensation, (b) he could send Downey back to China, (c) he could turn the whole matter over to the CIA to terminate Mrs. Downey.

Shortly after Ford had succeeded Nixon, I slipped Peter's memoran-dum into a number of genuine option papers Ford was considering in my presence. When Ford came to Peter's paper, I noticed he grew red in the face, saying "no" with increasing vehemence until it was nearly a shout at the last option.

Another masterpiece of Peter's, concocted in collaboration with Bill Hyland and Winston Lord, was an apocryphal memorandum, based on a standard form developed by Bob Haldeman, preparing Nixon for an encounter with the Almighty.

BEYOND ALL THE NATIONAL PROJECTS on which we worked together and the books and articles on which he helped me as researcher and editor, I feel the loss of a surrogate son. I loved Peter, above all, for his values, his loyalty, and his utter decency. Peter treasured his parents; he adored his wife, Véronique, whom he met while he helped with my memoirs; he was proud of his two children; and he was devoted to his husky, who, though a female, was called "George." It is always unnatural when what we expect to be the succession of generations is reversed in this manner. And Peter still had so much left to do.

As we part from Peter, he takes with him a piece of our lives. He leaves us the pride of having shared part of the way with a genuinely moving personality, who, in the process, gives us a deeper perspective on what it all meant. All whose lives he touched—whatever our previous or continuing differences—are united by our affection for Peter and our gratitude for what he contributed to the intellectual and moral content, and, above all, the nobility of our life.

—As delivered at Peter W. Rodman's memorial service,
October 10, 2008

AUTHOR'S NOTE

This book has a modest objective, and makes a few simple points. It is not an institutional history of the national security policy-making process. Others have written excellent accounts of the origins and history of the National Security Council (NSC) system and the role of the White House national security adviser. I have learned from their efforts (and list some of them in the end notes). Even less is this intended as a complete account of the tumultuous history of American foreign policy in the period covered.

But I lived through some of that history, and this book conveys my personal perspective on how presidents have responded to one of their toughest tests—how they establish their control and policy direction of the sprawling bureaucracy that is the U.S. government. I have been able to watch, at close range, the interaction of policy, politics, and personalities that determined whether they succeeded or failed. Though it is not a complete history, it is a collection of observations, impressions, examples, and conclusions by someone who was inside the process. The comparative perspective also sheds useful light on the present. In five of these administrations—those of Richard Nixon, Gerald Ford, Ronald Reagan, George H. W. Bush, and George W. Bush—I served in various positions in the White House, State Department, or Defense Department. In two Democratic administrations—those of Jimmy Carter and Bill Clinton—I did not serve, but I have included my assessments of their experience for the continuity of the story. The problems that arise are not confined to administrations of one party or the other, and the issues are not partisan.

The reader will notice that I appear in the narrative myself on occasion, Zelig-like, in different places, either describing a personal observation of people I saw in action or describing an episode or issue I was involved in. At the end of this Author's Note I have listed the positions I held throughout this period, in case there is confusion about what my vantage point was at various times. But I can summarize my story here. Henry Kissinger was my teacher at Harvard College when I was an innocent nineteen-year-old senior. Little did I know then how far my tutoring at his hands would take me. He invited me to join him in the White House in 1969; I did so in the summer after graduating law school and remained his special assistant through the Nixon-Ford period. Then I left the government with him to assist him with his memoirs. I rejoined the government in the third year of the Reagan administration. After three years at the State Department Policy Planning Staff under Secretary of State George Shultz, I returned in 1986 to the NSC staff where I remained through the end of Reagan's term and for most of the first two years of George H. W. Bush. Republicans being fortunate, a third tour came for me under George W. Bush, this time in the Pentagon as assistant secretary of defense for international security affairs. I cannot claim to have been an eyewitness to every presidential action I describe. What I can claim is to have seen much and to have formed an educated judgment about many other things.

THE BOOK CONVEYS a few simple points—lessons, if you will—about how presidents can best maintain their personal control and policy direction. They are summed up in the last chapter, but the themes are threads that run throughout the book. They have to do with the inescapable necessity for presidents to be personally and systematically engaged, lest feuds between cabinet agencies fester or bureaucracies remain unresponsive to presidential preferences. These may seem obvious points, yet the account of seven presidencies that follows includes a perhaps surprising number of negative examples that demonstrate the price that is paid when their importance is not understood.

No organization chart will tell you how an administration works in practice. In our system, intangibles reign—most importantly the personality of the president. Presidents in turn come to rely most on individuals whose judgment (and loyalty) they have most confidence in. In some instances power gravitates to personalities who seize it; in other cases, personal ambitions only provoke reactions. Sometimes tensions develop between a president and his closest White House advisers. Not every policy failure is the result of a faulty process; conversely some great successes (Nixon's China initiative, for example) have come from highly irregular procedures.

Each of the recent presidents, we will see, exemplifies a different approach—and a different set of problems. This cumulative experience is rich in lessons for future presidents seeking to give effect to their electoral mandate. How should they manage cabinet dissent and cabinet rivalries? Which qualities should they look for—and watch out for—when they choose their key cabinet secretaries and White House advisers? What is the proper role of the White House national security adviser and NSC staff? Is there a trade-off between collegiality and policy discipline? When is it possible to delegate, and when does a president have an inescapable responsibility to take charge?

I hope to put the current debates in the perspective of longer experience, and guide future presidents to get the lessons right.

Peter W. Rodman—Positions Held

• August 1969–January 1977: Special assistant to the assistant to the president for national security affairs (White House/NSC staff)

• March 1983–March 1986: Member, then director, of the Policy Planning Staff (Department of State)

• March 1986–January 1987: Deputy assistant to the president for national security affairs (foreign policy)(White House/NSC staff)

• January 1987–September 1990: Special assistant to the president for national security affairs and NSC counselor (White House/NSC staff)

• July 2001–March 2007: Assistant secretary of defense for international security affairs (Department of Defense)

Presidential Command

CHAPTER ONE

Bureaucracy, Democracy, and Legitimacy

THERE IS A FAMOUS STORY of President Abraham Lincoln, taking a vote in a cabinet meeting on whether to sign the Emancipation Proclamation. All his cabinet secretaries vote nay, whereupon Lincoln raises his right hand and declares: "The ayes have it!"

The story is apocryphal, but it well captures the truth of Lincoln's relations with his cabinet. That cabinet included supremely ambitious men, substantial political figures in their own right, several of whom had sought the presidency in 1860 and remained convinced that they, not the country lawyer from Illinois, should be sitting in his chair. Yet Lincoln came to dominate this "team of rivals" and seized the responsibility that was inescapably his.

Such a story brings a smile when the president under discussion is the most revered political leader in the history of the republic. But our modern political culture and sensibility are more ambivalent. When less revered presidents make controversial decisions, what do we really believe about presidential authority? How do we feel, for example, about Richard Nixon overruling the dissent of both his secretary of state and his secretary of defense to order military escalations that he thought essential to prosecute the Vietnam War? What do we think of Ronald Reagan pursuing what he thought was a strategic opening with Iran, over the objection of his chief cabinet officers? With respect to the very public anguish of Secretary of State Colin Powell and his State Department over George W. Bush's decisions on Iraq, do we identify with Bush or with Powell? How often do we read in the press about White House "interference" in the work of experts in the departments and agencies, and complaints that their work is being "politicized"? One part of our brain seems to side with the permanent government. In the age of the whistle-blower, what do we really think about a president's authority to decide and carry out policies with which subordinates disagree? The answer should not depend simply on one's own policy or partisan preferences. There ought to be neutral principles, not only to guide the public discourse but also to guide presidents. The modern trend, especially since the United States emerged from World War II as a global power, has been to expand the White House staff and institutions like the National Security Council (NSC) precisely to enable more centralized control, or at least better central coordination, over an expanding policy community. That policy community includes traditional cabinet departments with an international role (State, Defense, Treasury), other institutions (the Central Intelligence Agency, the uniformed military, and agencies in charge of trade and foreign aid policy), and departments and agencies only recently playing an important role in foreign policy (the departments of Justice and Homeland Security, the Federal Bureau of Investigation, and the Drug Enforcement Administration). But like a law of physics, presidential efforts to strengthen control over this expanding community only stimulate the countertrends that are at work—powerful centrifugal forces in Congress, in the media, and in the Executive Branch itself.

The subject of this book is not the question of presidential prerogative vis-à-vis Congress. Library shelves are already filled with books on the two "co-equal" branches, and especially the ancient debate over war powers. The issue here is presidential control over the Executive Branch.

Congress's role, however, is an enormously important factor. As scholar Richard Neustadt has expressed it, the Constitutional Convention of 1787 did not, as commonly thought, create a system of separated powers. "Rather, it created a government of separated institutions *sharing* powers." Presidents undoubtedly have more freedom of action in the national security realm than in making domestic policy. Nonetheless, cabinet secretaries and their departments have obligations to Congress by statute; they are beholden to Congress for the final disposition of their budgets and their testimony is a duty. Cabinet secretaries are thus inevitably responsive, at least in part, to Congress as well as to the president. But that only restates the problem.

Neustadt recounts that President Harry Truman in 1952, contemplating the possibility that Dwight Eisenhower would be elected to succeed him, predicted that the eminent general would have problems adjusting: "'He'll sit here,' Truman would remark (tapping his desk for emphasis), 'and he'll say, "Do this! Do that!" *And nothing will happen.* Poor Ike—it won't be a bit like the Army. He'll find it very frustrating.'" Truman's own experience was: "I sit here all day trying to persuade people to do the things they ought to have sense enough to do without my persuading them. . . . That's all the powers of the President amount to."

That was Neustadt's analysis as well. His answer was to counsel presidents and would-be presidents on how to maximize their power to persuade. His classic book *Presidential Power*, first published in 1960, explained that a president's success depended on expanding and husbanding his personal political leverage and prestige, his mastery of tools of influence that convince his subordinates that what the president wants them to do comports with their own personal and bureaucratic interests. Neustadt graded presidents according to their "power sense"—their instinct for maintaining their personal political power; he thought Franklin Roosevelt and Harry Truman had this "power sense," but Eisenhower did not. His book was seized upon by the new administration of John F. Kennedy as a primer on how to strengthen presidential control. However, the centrifugal forces have only strengthened since then—to the point where Neustadt, in an edition of his book twenty years later, felt compelled to go out of his way to debunk the notion of the "imperial presidency" that had become fashionable in some circles in the interim. As late as 1990, even after the Reagan presidency, Neustadt was still preoccupied with what he saw as the weakness of the office: "Weakness is still what I see: weakness in the sense of a great gap between what is expected of a man (or someday a woman) and assured capacity to carry through." Part of this weakness resides in the expansion of the modern bureaucracy and the increasing difficulty of a single individual's asserting systematic control over it.

Concepts of Legitimacy

Our Constitution, on the face of it, seems unambiguous about who is in charge of the Executive Branch: "The executive power shall be vested in a President of the United States of America" (Article II, section 1). But, as usual, a closer reading of our founding document reveals a more complex picture. Passages in section 2 of the same Article II refer specifically to the "executive departments" and to Congress's power to authorize the heads of those departments to appoint subordinates. The president's authority over the civilian establishment is less explicit than his authority as commander in chief of the armed forces. The renowned constitutional scholar Edward S. Corwin concluded that the phrase "executive power" is a "term of uncertain content."

While the United States may have a cabinet, we do not have a cabinet system, which is what the British have. The cabinet at Westminster is "the government"—the body of ministers (what we would call cabinet secretaries) headed by the prime minister, who is in theory only the "first among equals." This institution evolved in the seventeenth and eighteenth centuries as the leadership of the Parliament, which extracted from the monarch the right to form his government. In parallel it became the leadership body of the political party that held the parliamentary majority. As such it embodied the distinctive characteristic of parliamentary government—what British scholar Walter Bagehot called the "nearly complete fusion" of the executive and legislative powers.

An important element of this system is the theory of the cabinet's collective responsibility. Certainly the personal role and power of the prime minister have grown considerably over the last century and a half, and many would argue that prime ministerial government has eclipsed the cabinet. But there are occasional reminders that the system has nowhere near evolved into presidential-style government. When Winston Churchill assumed office during the great crisis of May 1940, in the first three weeks he was nearly outvoted in the war cabinet by a faction that wanted to pursue a negotiation with Hitler. Even more recent prime ministers who have achieved extraordinary political dominance have discovered that, when political fortunes ebb, the party asserts its collective will. Just ask Margaret Thatcher and Tony Blair.

There have been a few attempts in the United States over the years to limit presidential authority in a manner suggestive of British cabinet-style arrangements, but they were short-lived exceptions that prove the rule:

> • John Quincy Adams took a vote at a cabinet meeting on at least one occasion and bowed to the majority when he was outvoted. But Adams, chosen as president in 1824 by the House of Representatives after not receiving even a plurality of either the electoral or popular vote, was one of our weakest presidents. Among other things,

he adamantly refused to consider party affiliation when making government appointments. For "power sense," Professor Neustadt would have graded him an F.

• When the National Security Council was created in 1947, there were those who saw it as a way of pressing presidents to make decisions in a more collegial framework. The British system was viewed as a model. This was a reaction to FDR's freewheeling management style and to doubts whether Harry Truman was up to the job. As we shall see, Truman, acutely sensitive to any challenge to his constitutional prerogative, eluded the trap.

• When Richard Nixon was engulfed by the Watergate scandal, one of the arguments he used in his defense was that removal from office before the end of his term would alter our political system in the direction of a parliamentary system, eroding a crucial pillar of the president's constitutional independence. The argument did not convince. When his political support finally collapsed in early August 1974, it was a delegation of senior Republican Party leaders who came to see him; they could not force him to resign, but only seek to persuade him that resignation was best for the country and for the party. This he agreed to.

• An implication that the top man might not be fully up to the job may have played a role in the 1980 discussions about Ronald Reagan's taking on ex-President Gerald Ford as his running mate, with Henry Kissinger slated once again to be secretary of state. Reagan and Ford permitted their close advisers to hold a series of secret meetings at the Republican National Convention on this idea—which some dubbed a "co-presidency"—before the two principals agreed to drop it.

Our constitutional structure thus seems strong enough to withstand attempts to turn it into something it isn't.

IF ONE SOURCE of presidential authority is constitutional legitimacy, a second is democratic legitimacy. Our political system puts itself through great convulsions every four years to elect a president (though it seems more and more a never-ending process). Presumably we do this on the premise that something important is at stake in the election, namely the authority to determine the direction of national policy for the next four years. It is generally assumed that we are choosing the individual we want to set the policies that the Executive Branch will carry out. That is what the phrase "popular mandate" refers to. Democratic legitimacy is also democratic accountability.

This calls to mind another major difference from the British system, and indeed from European and most other systems. An American president today has around three thousand so-called political appointments to make to key positions in the government, several layers down into the bureaucratic machinery. These include not only cabinet secretaries, but deputy secretaries, under secretaries, and assistant secretaries. These several layers give the president a considerable ability to put his or her political stamp on the policies that will emerge from this machinery. When a new president enters office, especially if a change of political party is involved, the turnover is huge and the transition tumultuous.

Both political parties in this country have cadres of people to bring into government with the advent of a new administration. They come from private business, the academic and policy think tank community, and congressional staffs, and thus have a claim to professionalism as well as to responsiveness to the elected president's philosophy. Many who enter at senior positions have served at lower levels in prior administrations of the same party, and thus come with experience as well.

Britain, and most other countries, have nothing resembling this. The permanent civil service populates ministries up to much higher levels of the government. Even when a general election sweeps a new party into office, the incoming political leadership consists of cabinet ministers, a few other members of Parliament who serve as junior ministers in each department, and a handful of other assistants—perhaps 100 to 120, all together, in Britain. The rest are civil servants whom they meet when they arrive. Even in the prime minister's office, the cabinet tradition severely constrains a new prime minister's freedom to bring in more than a few personal advisers in any field.

One advantage of this system is continuity. When an election brings a change of leadership, the new political team, small as it is, is easily in place in a matter of days. The principle is that the civil servants shift their loyalties immediately to the new leaders and in the most professional manner help them implement whatever changes of policy are directed. The disadvantage is that the permanent government may not be as amenable to effective political control as the theory holds.

Political control over the bureaucracy may be one of the most significant challenges to modern democratic government in the twentieth and twenty-first centuries. The American system addresses this from two directions—by the presidential power over personnel and by congressional oversight. Especially when the two branches are controlled by opposite parties, no one can doubt the vigor of congressional oversight over the bureaucracy—certainly no one who has testified to a congressional committee in such circumstances. In parliamentary systems, in contrast, the very "fusion" of the executive and legislative branches gives the whip hand to the government; parliamentary inquiries into alleged executive malfeasance are notoriously weak.

The British in their inimitable way have immortalized these truths in a cultural masterpiece, namely two television series produced by the BBC entitled *Yes Minister* and *Yes Prime Minister*. The first series recounts the career of a bumbling politician, James Hacker, who becomes a cabinet minister. He immediately encounters his would-be helpmeet, Sir Humphrey Appleby, the permanent secretary, or career head of the department. Sir Humphrey's real preoccupation is to insure that bright ideas from the minister do not disrupt the routine of existing policies or of civil service control. "He'll be house-trained in no time," Sir Humphrey assures two civil service colleagues. He deftly manages to steer his minister away from various shoals of policy innovation, all the while convincing Hacker that he, the minister, is totally in charge and that the outcomes comport exactly with his wishes (hence the title of the show).

In the sequel, Hacker has by some freak accident of history stumbled into 10 Downing Street as prime minister; Sir Humphrey accompanies him. Issues of foreign policy and defense now broaden the agenda, and Sir Humphrey is able to collude with civil service colleagues in the Foreign and Commonwealth Office and Ministry of Defence where necessary. At one point, a difference of view with the prime minister over how to vote on a United Nations resolution elicits the Foreign Office observation: "The PM must realize that as far as Foreign Affairs are concerned his job is to confine himself to the hospitality and ceremonial role."

If this rings all too true to an American who has served in the U.S. government, it is because the American system—despite the vaunted three thousand appointees—has not solved the problem of presidential political control over our own bureaucracy. As we shall see, our cabinet departments, too, have a life and culture of their own. This can produce a number of different phenomena. Professionals in a department, whether career or "political," often develop more of a loyalty to their cabinet secretary, with whom they work day to day, than to a president who is a more remote figure across town. To a remarkable degree, a president comes to be viewed by the professionals as an interloper in policies that their departments are immersed in on a daily basis. Career officials also know that political appointees come and go while they will remain and their own career advancement is determined mainly by their permanent institutions. In the British system, departmental parochialism has been mitigated somewhat by the "generalist" tradition of rotating civil servants among departments; in the U.S. system, in contrast, most civil servants tend to spend their careers in a single department. Even political appointees come to absorb much of the institutional culture. "Where you stand depends on where you sit," is an old Washington adage. Nixon aide John Ehrlichman once said of political appointees: "We only see them at the annual White House Christmas party; they go off and marry the natives."

This has a significant influence over how policies are originated and implemented. As many scholars have noted, the nature of society and politics in America, much more so than in Europe, fosters an egalitarian culture even in hierarchical organizations; the culture fosters two-way flows of information and ideas, not just top-down. One result is that policy recommendations often "bubble up" from lower levels, and political leaders often find themselves (as Dean Acheson once put it) in a "judicial" mode weighing what advice comes from below.

Henry Kissinger in his memoirs refers to one result of the strength of the bureaucracy. Whether or not specific ideas flow in both directions, ultimately these institutions are not likely to be sources of bold innovation:

> [A] large bureaucracy, however organized, tends to stifle creativity. It confuses wise policy with smooth administration. A complex bureaucracy has an incentive to exaggerate technical complexity and minimize the scope or importance of political judgment; it favors the status quo, however arrived at, because short of an unambiguous catastrophe the status quo has the advantage of familiarity and it is never possible to prove that another course would yield superior results. It seemed to me no accident that most great statesmen had been locked in permanent struggle with the experts in their foreign offices, for the scope of the statesman's conception challenges the inclination of the

expert toward minimum risk. . . . Ultimately there is no purely organizational answer; it is above all a problem of leadership.

"A camel is a horse designed by a committee" is another old Washington adage.

The pivotal figures in the system are the cabinet secretaries. As Kissinger has observed, a cabinet secretary has a strategic choice to make:

> [H]e can see himself as the surrogate of the head of the organization [i.e., the president], taking on his shoulders some of the onus of bureaucratically unpopular decisions. Or he can become the spokesman of his subordinates and thus face the chief executive with the necessity of assuming the sole responsibility for painful choices.

Earlier administrations were conscious of the same problem. John Kennedy's special counsel Theodore Sorensen, in a public lecture in 1963, candidly pointed out that a typical cabinet secretary "was not necessarily selected for the President's confidence in his judgment alone—considerations of politics, geography, public esteem, and interest-group pressures may also have played a part, as well as his skill in administration."

Kennedy's national security adviser, McGeorge Bundy, in his post–White House reflections, was more scathing:

> The unending contest between the Presidency and much of the bureaucracy is as real today as ever, and there has been no significant weakening in the network of triangular alliances which unite all sorts of interest groups with their agents in the Congress and their agents in the Executive Branch. . . . [T]he Executive Branch remains woefully short of first-class executive agents of the President. . . . The Cabinet role which I am trying to describe . . . in its relation to the White House . . . must be at once highly autonomous and deeply responsive. It is political, but only in the President's interest. It is managerial, but only on the President's terms. . . . At a test—unless he means to resign—the Secretary should always be the President's agent in dealing with the bureaucracy, not the other way around.

The basic argument for this kind of Secretary is simply that no other instrument can give the Presidency control over its own branch of government.

Charles G. Dawes, an early-twentieth-century statesman who served as vice president, budget director, and ambassador, has been quoted as observing: "The members of the Cabinet are a President's natural enemies."

Richard Nixon's first term was one possible paradigm for dealing with this problem. This was the era in which Nixon and his assistant Henry Kissinger pulled the reins of policy into the White House (as we shall describe in Chapter 3). This was a system of maximum centralization of personal control in the president's hands, and maximum coherence of policy, but they came at the price of maximum demoralization of the rest of the government. This method achieved a number of major successes, but in the end it is not a model to be emulated. Kissinger, who served as secretary of state under Nixon and Ford after nearly five years in the White House, concluded, having experienced it both ways, that a strong secretary of state enjoying the confidence of the president is the better model:

> A foreign policy achievement to be truly significant must at some point be institutionalized; it must therefore be embedded in permanent machinery. No government should impose on itself the need to sustain a tour de force based on personalities. . . . If the President does not trust his Secretary of State he should replace him, not attempt to work around him by means of the security adviser.

All of these Executive Branch officials serve at the president's pleasure, and, as Kissinger suggests, replacing them is a presidential prerogative. In short, and in theory, he can fire them. But that is not so easy in practice. If Nixon's problem was an unwillingness to fire people, Gerald Ford's experience, as we shall see, illustrates the pitfalls of firing people. The excruciating dilemma of whether or when to replace cabinet officers, we shall also see, is one of the burdens that confronted George W. Bush over Iraq.

Thus, every administration must balance a trade-off between coherence and discipline in presidential policy on the one hand, and bureaucratic collegiality on the other. The hard choices that this poses will be a recurring theme in this book. George H. W. Bush, we shall see, did a good job of reconciling coherence and collegiality, but other presidents considered here had a harder time of it.

WHILE CONSTITUTIONAL LEGITIMACY and democratic legitimacy underpin presidential prerogative, prudence levies its own requirements. There seems to be a third, informal, concept of legitimacy, which relates to the way decisions are made and can be measured by the bureaucratic acceptance that follows (or doesn't follow) when an important agency of the government is overruled. Professor Neustadt's recommendation of persuasion is the ideal. But what if it can't be done? If differing points of view persist, the president may have to overrule *somebody*; consensus may not be attainable (or even desirable, if it only masks hard choices that must be made). And presidents have the right—like Abraham Lincoln—to overrule a consensus of all their subordinates.

What is it that enables presidents to do this without mutiny, without rancorous charges of "cabals" and insufficient consultation? If there is such a notion of procedural legitimacy, how is it defined? How is it reconciled with the president's constitutional supremacy in his branch of government, and with the system's need for consistent personal leadership? The formal, collegial structures of modern policy-making, centered in the National Security Council process, are part of the answer, but different presidents use this mechanism in different ways.

Alexander Hamilton is well known as the champion of a strong presidency; it was his essay No. 70 in *The Federalist* that argued for "energy in the Executive." Yet in 1800, Hamilton put forward the prudential case for a president's close consultation with his cabinet. This was, to be sure, in the context of a bitter feud with the incumbent president, his political rival John Adams, but the eloquence is familiar and the advice stands on its own:

> A President is not bound to conform to the advice of his ministers. He is even under no positive injunction to ask or require it. But the Constitution presumes that he will consult them; and the genius of our government and the public good commend the practice.
>
> As the President nominates his ministers, and may displace them when he pleases, it must be his own fault if he be not surrounded by men who, for ability and integrity, deserve his confidence. And if his

ministers are of this character, the consulting of them will always be likely to be useful to himself and to the state.

Hamilton contrasted Adams with his illustrious predecessor: "Very different from the practice of Mr. Adams was that of the modest and sage Washington. He consulted much, pondered much, resolved slowly, resolved surely."

CHAPTER TWO

The Modern Setting

Harry Truman's Council

The growth of the White House staff and Executive Office of the President, including mechanisms like the National Security Council, is the product not only of the growth of the Executive Branch but also of the tension between the president and the cabinet. The NSC, consisting of the president, vice president, and senior cabinet-level advisers, was created by the National Security Act of 1947 "to advise the President with respect to the integration of domestic, foreign, and military policies relating to the national security so as to enable the military services and the other departments and agencies of the Government to cooperate more effectively." In other words, it was meant as a coordinating mechanism, and it has served this purpose well for several presidents since then.

For our purposes, however, both the creation of the NSC and its later history are instructive for the bureaucratic tug-of-war they involved. Some of those participating in establishing the NSC had in mind a restraint on the president's ability to act unilaterally; strong presidents changed it into something very different. An "NSC system" has developed, consisting of the council together with a supporting staff and subcommittees. But how it works and how important it is in any administration are a function of how the president chooses to exercise power. It is the modern setting for the continuing struggle of presidents to control their bureaucracy.

There is a conventional narrative that a Republican Congress foisted the National Security Council on a reluctant President Harry Truman as a kind of posthumous revenge against Franklin Roosevelt's solo policy-making during the war. This narrative is, for the most part, off the mark. In fact, the need for a better mechanism for coordinating national

security policy was a bipartisan insight shared by the Truman administration and Congress; creation of the NSC was not a matter of serious
political controversy. The most important debates about the NSC's role
and structure took place within the Executive Branch.

Despite the great reverence for Franklin Roosevelt in the Truman
administration, there was indeed a reaction to what one historian has
called the "administrative chaos" of the Roosevelt era. Many of
those who helped shape the 1947 act were envious of the British, whose
Committee of Imperial Defence (CID), established in 1904, had
the mission of "obtaining and collating for the use of the Cabinet all
the information and expert advice required for shaping national
policy in war, and for determining the necessary preparations in peace."
Chaired by the prime minister and including the relevant ministers,
the CID was technically a subcommittee that reported to the full cabinet. But in wartime it effectively turned itself into a war cabinet. It also
was aided by a permanent secretariat and various subcommittees of its
own.

The United States, in contrast, had entered World War II with only
the most rudimentary means of interagency coordination. As war
approached, FDR's secretary of state, Cordell Hull, took the initiative to
organize a Standing Liaison Committee composed of the under secretary of state, the chief of naval operations, and the army chief of staff.
But this group was more a forum for exchanging information than a
body for coordinating and directing policy; nor did it grapple with big
policy issues. It disbanded in 1943.

FDR's improvisational management style compounded the problem—
for example, famously giving the same assignments to different staffers
without their knowing, playing off their competition in order to stimulate creativity and, not incidentally, keep the reins of power firmly in his
own hands. "You know I am a juggler," he told Henry Morgenthau in
May 1942, "and I never let my right hand know what my left hand does."
In running the war, FDR dealt directly with his commanders and
service chiefs, or left it to key White House aides such as Harry Hopkins and Admiral William Leahy to handle day-to-day coordination. He
reserved major strategic decisions to himself. Secretary of State Hull
was virtually excluded.

The 1942 landing in North Africa, for example, was ordered by Roosevelt over the strong objection of Army Chief of Staff General George C.
Marshall and of Marshall's chief planner, Brigadier General Dwight D.

Eisenhower. For strategic reasons, Roosevelt wanted an early Allied counterstroke against Hitler; his commanders thought it a dissipation of effort. (Eisenhower, but not Marshall, later conceded that the president was right.) A key document in which the president conveyed his views to Marshall is signed, "Roosevelt, C-in-C [Commander-in-Chief]"—the only occasion he is known to have done this—to hammer home who was in charge.

Only in late 1944 was a senior committee set up to do important coordinated planning. The State-War-Navy Coordinating Committee (SWNCC), at the assistant secretary level, worked on postwar plans for the occupation of Germany, Austria, and Japan as well as other topics like aid to China. By 1945, also, the secretaries of state, war, and navy had begun holding weekly meetings. Truman, in office only three months when he met at Potsdam with Josef Stalin and Winston Churchill in July, praised the work of the SWNCC in preparing him for the meeting, and before leaving Potsdam he let the three departments know that he liked this system and wanted it to continue.

Another reason the NSC idea was not hugely controversial is that it was caught up in a much bigger battle over unification of the armed services—arguably the most important component of the reforms enshrined in the National Security Act of 1947. Until that act, the secretary of the navy and his Department of the Navy had full cabinet status, equal to that of the secretary of war (that is, the Army). Champions of the Navy worried that unification—including creation of a new secretary of defense above all the services—spelled subordination of the Navy. Some of them became advocates of the new council because they hoped that the gods of unification could perhaps be appeased by a forum that insured better coordination at a more exalted level of national policy-making, obviating the need for consolidation at lower levels.

Truman, in the end, turned the tables on the Navy. By the end of the process he had pocketed the National Security Council *and* gotten unification of the services, as he had long personally favored. The main issue of contention was: What kind of council? This was the subject of intense negotiations between 1945 and 1947. Some of its early advocates consciously modeled their proposed National Security Council after the British CID, hoping to incorporate some of the collective quality of the British cabinet system. Their theory was that presidential deliberations and decisions made in that framework would be more collective in nature, restraining Rooseveltian impetuosity. Some of Truman's staff are on record as strongly suspecting that an additional motivation was an assumption that the former haberdasher from Missouri, thrust so abruptly into the presidency, was not capable of carrying the burdens of the office without that kind of support.

It was the Bureau of the Budget that weighed in to protect presidential prerogative. This organization, part of the Executive Office of the President since 1939, not only has the job of coordinating departmental budget submissions for the president and assisting him in presenting his national budget to Congress; by that very task it is also a key management arm of the presidency with respect to departmental programs. (President Nixon renamed it the Office of Management and Budget— today's OMB—in 1970, broadening its role as an instrument of presidential control over the government.) During the lengthy negotiation over the National Security Act, the various cabinet departments and military services all knew, or thought they knew, where their interests lay; the only body that zeroed in on the presidential interest was the Budget Bureau.

Key bureau officials alerted Truman to the traps. They squelched a proposal to name the secretary of defense as the stand-in for the president at NSC meetings in the latter's absence, and to house the NSC staff and secretariat in the Pentagon. Budget Bureau officials insured, in addition, that the purely advisory role of the NSC was emphasized throughout the bill and that the president would be clearly free to attend or not as he chose—so as not to be a prisoner in any way of the forum. By 1949, after amendments to the law and a further executive reorganization, it was the vice president who presided in the president's absence, and the staff and structure were formally absorbed and housed in the Executive Office of the President, not the Pentagon.

Truman understood fully what was at issue. In his memoirs, he recounts, with a tinge of sarcasm:

> There were times during the early days of the National Security Council when one or two of its members tried to change it into an operating super-cabinet on the British model. . . . There is much to this idea— in some ways a Cabinet government is more efficient—but under the British system there is a group responsibility of the Cabinet. Under our system the responsibility rests on one man—the President. To

change it, we would have to change the Constitution, and I think we have been doing very well under our Constitution. We will do well to stay with it.

At least one historian has wondered why the State Department did not play a more prominent role in all these interagency negotiations over the role and structure of the NSC system. Especially given the later experience of the 1970s, when White House national security advisers Henry Kissinger and Zbigniew Brzezinski overshadowed the secretary of state in foreign policy, it might have been foreseen that the new NSC system had large ramifications for the department. In fact, George C. Marshall, now Truman's secretary of state, did see many of these impli cations. When he was shown a draft in early 1947, he responded with a passionate memorandum to the president on February 7 that warned against several sections of the bill, including the new council. Marshall predicted it would introduce "fundamental changes in the entire question of foreign relations"; it would give the military establishment a role of "predominance" in foreign policy and would "dissipate the constitutional responsibility of the President," who would become an "automaton" of the council.

Marshall's reaction helped persuade the White House to take over from the Pentagon the negotiations with Congress regarding the draft bill. But there was no sustained involvement by State in the deliberations. Perhaps this was in part because Marshall could count on the Budget Bureau to fix the most obnoxious features of the original plan— namely, the Defense Department's attempts to control the council. For State, presidential control was one thing; Pentagon control would have been truly anathema. In addition, once the new NSC was up and running, the State Department's Policy Planning Staff under George Kennan managed to gain the primary role in drafting the papers and setting the agenda for NSC meetings. Neither the NSC staff nor any staff in the Office of the Secretary of Defense had yet developed the institutional capacity to compete with the substantive quality of State's work. Military representatives on the NSC staff tried their hand at broad, muscular global strategy papers on such topics as "Position of the United States with Respect to Soviet-Directed World Communism." (This was before the era of generals and admirals with Ph.D.s in international relations from major American universities.) In contrast, Kennan and his staff proposed more concrete agenda items such as (to take an example from May 1948): "Dhahran, Tsingtao, Austrian Treaty, Japan, Philippines, and Italian Colonies." Papers on these were more useful, and most NSC meetings were devoted to such specific subjects.

The State Department's problem was more long-term in nature—gradually losing its leadership position as other departments (Defense, Treasury) strengthened their own international roles. The State Department was (and remains) organized in a way that, on its face, suits it for the leadership role in the national security community. It has a bureau of political-military affairs, and it has traditionally had the lead role on policy and budgets with respect to security assistance, police training, and other international political-military issues. It has an under secretary for economic affairs and a bureau devoted to economic and business issues. Nonetheless, other cabinet departments have been less and less willing to submit to State's direction.

Don K. Price, respected dean of the Harvard Graduate School of Public Administration, testified to Senator Henry Jackson's national security subcommittee in 1961 that the State Department simply was not well equipped for leadership over other departments when the United States became a world power and needed to integrate all these different strands of national policy:

> The situation we got into at the end of World War II was that a nation that in the 1920's and 1930's had managed to stay pretty isolationist and maintain a Foreign Service that was interested only in very restricted political functions had to take on a tremendous range of military and economic responsibilities and propaganda responsibilities all over the world. The Department of State was consequently not equipped in the slightest degree to take on the direction of those responsibilities.
>
> I think this is what forced the creation by statute of interdepartmental machinery at the Cabinet level to deal with strategy and international security affairs.

The State Department had "abdicated its primacy," Price continued, and could win it back only by years of building up the "necessary personnel and institutional habits." Over the postwar decades, as we shall see, there have been strong secretaries of state who have indeed reasserted some dominance over broad international policies—Acheson, John Foster Dulles, Kissinger, for example. But this seems mainly to have been a function of personalities at the top—of the intellectual and physical energy of the cabinet secretary and the support of the president for this arrangement. At other times, State has been outperformed by the NSC staff, or the civilians in the Pentagon, or other cabinet departments.

IRONICALLY, while President Truman had asked Congress to create a National Security Council, he never fully overcame his sensitivity with respect to how it might affect his constitutional prerogatives. At the NSC's very first meeting, on September 26, 1947, Truman used the occasion to emphasize in characteristic fashion that it was "*his* council and that he expected everyone to work harmoniously without any manifestations of prima-donna qualities." It was decided not to establish any set schedule for NSC meetings, but to arrange them as required. Of the fifty-seven NSC meetings held from this first meeting until the Korean War (June 1950), Truman himself attended only twelve. He was determined to preserve his freedom of action, as he took pains to stress in his memoirs:

> I used the National Security Council only as a place for recommendations to be worked out. Like the Cabinet, the Council does not make decisions. The policy itself has to come down from the President, as all final decisions have to be made by him.
>
> A "vote" in the National Security Council is merely a procedural step. It never decides policy. That can be done only with the President's approval and expression of approval to make it an official policy of the United States.

Truman had two outstanding secretaries of state in George Marshall and Dean Acheson, and he tended to deal with them directly rather than through the formal NSC mechanism. He also dealt directly, outside of NSC channels, with his secretary of defense, and continued to rely as well on the Bureau of the Budget. The man he chose as executive secretary of the council, retired Rear Admiral Sidney Souers, was a trusted poker-playing friend. Truman also relied on close White House political assistants, first Clark Clifford and later Averell Harriman, to keep watch over national security affairs.

When the Korean War began in June 1950, however, Truman quickly saw value in the orderly processes of the NSC; he began to attend its meetings more frequently and he took steps to streamline its structure.

In wartime, more systematic preparation and deliberation are imperative, and the formality and staff structure enabled this. Of the seventy-
one council meetings from June 28, 1950, through January 9, 1953,
Truman attended and presided at sixty-two of them (or 87 percent).
Truman's jealous guarding of his prerogative was not directed solely
at the new council. Whatever his regard for George Marshall and Dean
Acheson, Truman often found himself railing at the indiscipline of the
State Department. State's opposition to his decision to recognize the
new state of Israel in 1948 triggered this tirade in his memoirs:

> Every President in our history has been faced with this problem: how
> to prevent career men from circumventing presidential policy. . . .
> And it has happened in the Department of State. . . . I wanted to
> make it plain that the President of the United States, and not the sec-
> ond or third echelon in the State Department, is responsible for mak-
> ing foreign policy, and, furthermore, that no one in any department
> can sabotage the President's policy. The civil servant, the general or
> admiral, the foreign service officer has no authority to make policy.
> They act only as servants of the government, and therefore they must
> remain in line with the government policy that is established by those
> who have been chosen by the people to set that policy.

One of Truman's most famous legacies is the image of the thirteen-
inch-long painted glass sign stating THE BUCK STOPS HERE, the gift of a
friend, which sits to this day on his desk at the Truman Library in Independence, Missouri. Truman wins a fairly good grade from Professor
Neustadt with respect to husbanding his presidential authority. Where
FDR did this out of an instinct for personal power, Truman did it out of
an acute consciousness of the duties of the office. Moreover, says
Neustadt, Truman "loved to make decisions"—unlike Eisenhower, who
he says tried to keep away from them, and FDR, who inclined to defer
them. Using a term that George W. Bush would later employ, Neustadt
says that Truman's image of the office "made him sensitive to anything
that challenged his position as decider and proposer."

This image of Truman should not be taken, as it sometimes is, to
mythological heights. Contrary to Neustadt, there is evidence that like
many other presidents he actually did prefer to have his senior subordinates present him a consensus recommendation if possible. "He likes
things to run smoothly," said one intimate. "He doesn't like his advisers

to disagree." Indeed, the fateful decision in the Korean War in October–November 1950 to permit General Douglas MacArthur to charge northward toward the Chinese border—which provoked Chinese military intervention—may have been the product of too much collegiality around the National Security Council table. Acheson's memoirs refer to the deep uneasiness then about where MacArthur's strategy was leading, but which no one was willing or able to express in categorical terms to the president. "I have an unhappy conviction," Acheson wrote, "that none of us, myself prominently included, served him as he was entitled to be served." The result was not only a military disaster but a step toward Truman's confrontation with and dismissal of MacArthur, which was one of the biggest domestic political crises of his presidency.

That decision to authorize MacArthur's northward offensive deserves particular attention; it was a major blunder by an administration that has been justly praised for its wisdom and creativity in shaping America's global policy after World War II. The point worth noting is not the irony that Truman, so often hailed as a great "decider," was the prisoner of a seeming bureaucratic consensus, a sin usually attributed (unfairly) to Eisenhower. Rather, the event raises a question that will recur in this book: To what extent was this a failure of *process*, as opposed to simply a failure of policy judgment? One analyst calls it an example of "groupthink," or an object lesson in Peter Drucker's maxim that "the first rule in decision making is that one does not make a decision unless there is disagreement." Acheson had the same view. "[T]o decide," he wrote, "one must know the real issues. These have to be found and flushed like birds from a field. The adversary process is the best bird dog."

On the other hand, there are examples suggesting that while that kind of adversarial process may be necessary, it may not be sufficient. In the Vietnam case fifteen years later, there was a prominent and articulate dissenter, George W. Ball. President Lyndon Johnson heard Ball's views often, but the prevailing judgment of the president and his other advisers was that the risks that Ball called attention to were manageable or were outweighed by risks on the other side of the argument. And in the case of the Iraq War, President George W. Bush heard dissents from Secretary of State Colin Powell and was aware of analyses that called attention to risks involved in overthrowing Saddam Hussein. Not only the CIA, but also Secretary of Defense Donald Rumsfeld sent his own memorandum listing things that could go wrong. Yet Bush, like LBJ, had to make his own assessment of competing risks that are always much clearer in hindsight than before the fact. The process of weighing competing risks is not a science; nor is it made easier by counting votes among advisers. Smoking out divergent and dissenting opinions is an excellent starting point, but as we explore this question through later administrations, we need to allow for the possibility that to search for a *procedure* that assures the right decision is to pursue a mirage.

Eisenhower's "Hidden Hand"

President Dwight Eisenhower was a believer in orderly procedure, and he faulted both Roosevelt and Truman for neglecting it. Truman, he jibed, "didn't know any more about government than a dog knows about religion." In his memoirs Eisenhower wrote: "Organization cannot make a genius out of an incompetent. . . . On the other hand, disorganization can scarcely fail to result in inefficiency and can easily lead to disaster." This was a lesson he absorbed from his military career. Richard Nixon, who watched him closely for eight years as his vice president, described the "team" concept and "staff system" as they worked:

> Having chosen his Cabinet and staff on the basis of each man's ability to handle his job, he had confidence in the men working for him, trusted them, and delegated authority to them. Finally, though, in the staff system, he received the essence of the problem, the thinking that went into it, and the recommended solution. And then he either approved the decision, rejected it and substituted his own, or sent the problem back for further study.

Eisenhower institutionalized the NSC process, setting up a schedule of weekly meetings. Over his two terms, the council met 366 times; he presided at 329 of them, or about 90 percent.

During his time in the White House, this desire for orderly process led to a conventional caricature of Eisenhower as a weak leader, a prisoner of rigid staff procedures, dependent on the consensus of his advisers, inarticulate, even a bumbler. This was the widely held view among liberal journalists and intellectuals. It was propagated most vigorously by his predecessor, Harry Truman. One pungent example:

> In 1959, when Castro came to power down in Cuba, Ike just sat on his ass and acted like if he didn't notice what was going on down there,

why, maybe Castro would go away or something. Of course what happened, the Russians didn't sit on their ass, and they got him lined up on their side, which is what you have to expect if you've got a goddam fool in the White House. He was probably waiting there for his Chief of Staff to give him a report, and he'd initial it and put it in his out basket. Because that's the way he operated.

Truman was contemptuous of Eisenhower for having a chief of staff at all: "I said to him, 'The President of the United States is his own chief of staff. . . . [T]he people of the United States . . . don't elect you to sit around waiting for other people to tell you what to do.'" A more elegant version of the same theme was put forward by Richard Neustadt, whose book *Presidential Power* was published during Eisenhower's last year in office. As we touched upon earlier, Neustadt believed that Eisenhower's desire to be "above politics" weakened his hand in what is an inherently political game, and that he failed to develop the "power sense" necessary to preserve his personal leverage.

By the late 1960s, however, a revisionist view of Eisenhower began to appear in some circles of those who had disparaged him. It began with an article by liberal writer Murray Kempton in *Esquire* magazine in September 1967 entitled, "The Underestimation of Dwight D. Eisenhower"; three years later, Garry Wills included a fresh assessment of Eisenhower in a biography of Richard Nixon (*Nixon Agonistes*). This change of attitude may have come in part because, amidst the turmoil of the late 1960s, the relative tranquillity of the 1950s began to look in retrospect like a not inconsiderable achievement. But both Kempton and Wills were also influenced by a unique inside account that Nixon published in 1962. Nixon recounted among his "six crises" the chilling experience of Eisenhower's hinting in both 1952 and 1956 at Nixon's removal from the ticket. In 1952 it was because of the supposed scandal over an alleged slush fund, and in 1956 it was a more opaque suggestion by Eisenhower that, nevertheless, caused Nixon great anguish. Nixon's overall assessment of his patron is the portrait of a shrewd, cold, even calculating leader who treated his vice president at arm's length and is without doubt the dominating figure of the era. In a classic Nixonian turn of phrase, Nixon calls Eisenhower "a far more complex and devious man than most people realized, and in the best sense of those words." From Richard Nixon, this is, if not high praise, then at the very least an authoritative assessment by one battle-hardened practitioner of politics of the handiwork of another. Eisenhower does not come across as one who was unconscious of his personal political power or of how to use it. Nixon goes on:

> Not shackled to a one-track mind, he always applied two, three, or four lines of reasoning to a single problem and he usually preferred the indirect approach where it would serve him better than the direct attack on a problem. His mind was quick and facile. His thoughts far outraced his speech and this gave rise to his frequent "scrambled syntax" which more perceptive critics should have recognized as the mark of a far-ranging and versatile mind rather than an indication of poor training in grammar.

Kempton and Wills also both cite an episode in Eisenhower's own memoirs in which, just before a presidential news conference during the Quemoy-Matsu crisis in the Taiwan Strait in 1955, his press secretary, James Hagerty, advised him that the State Department preferred that he not comment on the delicate issue. "'Don't worry, Jim,' I told him as we went out the door of my office, 'if that question comes up, I'll just confuse them.'" This anecdote, minor as it is, seemed to both Kempton and Wills first of all to bespeak a healthy self-awareness and, second, to confirm Nixon's observation that Eisenhower's much derided syntax at news conferences might not indicate such a deficient intelligence after all.

A full-blown revisionist assessment came in 1982 when Princeton professor Fred I. Greenstein published *The Hidden-Hand Presidency*, a book that fleshed out, on the basis of memoirs and newly opened archives, that indeed Eisenhower was a much more dominant figure in his administration than the caricature had it. Greenstein portrays a leader who exploited his "above-politics" image as a deliberate political strategy to maximize his influence; thus by choice, not lack of ability, he eschewed the image of the "skilled, tough politician" that is Neustadt's model. "Artlessness and art" is Greenstein's description of Eisenhower's style. Where Truman had a desk ornament proclaiming THE BUCK STOPS HERE, Eisenhower had one displaying the Latin motto *Suaviter in modo, fortiter in re* (pleasantly in manner, powerfully in deed).

The most important point is that NSC meetings were hardly the only means by which Eisenhower operated. Whatever the regularity of NSC procedures, a State Department official history of the National Security Council dismisses the idea that the president was a prisoner of them:

> In fact, Eisenhower was actively in command of his administration, and the NSC system met his instincts and requirements. There is substance in the criticism that the Eisenhower NSC became to some extent the prisoner of a rigidly bureaucratic process, but the criticism misses the point that Eisenhower and [Secretary of State John Foster] Dulles did not attempt to manage fast-breaking crises or day-to-day foreign policy through the NSC apparatus. An examination of several of the major foreign policy problems that confronted the Eisenhower administration reveals that the NSC system was used to manage some and was virtually bypassed in others. . . . Crisis situations . . . such as the Suez crisis of 1956, the off-shore island [Taiwan Strait] crises of 1955 and 1958, and the Lebanon crisis of 1958, were typically managed through telephone conversations between Eisenhower, Dulles, and other principal advisers, and through small meetings with the President in the White House.

The Suez crisis may have been the clearest example of Eisenhower's personal dominance. Eisenhower felt strongly that the British-French-Israeli attempt to seize the Suez Canal by force was objectionable on moral, legal, and political grounds; he wanted the United States to be respected in the Middle East as a mediator and friend of the Arab world, not to be tarred with the colonialist brush. He insisted on significant U.S. political and economic pressure on the three allies to force them to halt their military action. One analyst records that, after Foster Dulles was hospitalized for colon cancer in late October:

> Eisenhower took personal charge of the Middle East crisis by supervising his State Department and United Nations delegations directly from the Oval Office, holding consultations with his military and intelligence brass, and conducting intensive diplomatic maneuvering with cables and transatlantic phone calls to pressure [British Prime Minister Anthony] Eden and the French to disengage.

The recently published transcript of one such telephone conversation with Eden during the peak of the fighting reveals an insistent president ("Anthony, this is the way I feel about it . . .") succeeding in imposing his will on an exhausted prime minister ("We are going to cease firing tonight").

There is evidence to suggest that both Foster Dulles and his brother, CIA director Allen Dulles, were rooting for the three allies to succeed in seizing the canal before the U.S. pressure kicked in. While the crisis was under way, Allen Dulles sent a message via his station chief in London that the British should either accept a cease-fire or go ahead with the invasion: "Either way, we'll back 'em up if they do it fast." After the crisis was over, a bedridden Foster Dulles, at Walter Reed Army Hospital, stunned visiting British and French leaders by asking: "Why did you stop? Why didn't you go through with it and get [Egyptian president Gamal Abdel] Nasser down?" "If ever there was an occasion when one could have been knocked down by the proverbial feather, this was it," one of the visitors (Selwyn Lloyd) later wrote. It might have been some consolation to the Dulles brothers to know that, a decade later, Eisenhower told at least two interlocutors that he had changed his mind about Suez. It had been his biggest foreign policy mistake, he concluded; U.S. policy in 1956 had only strengthened Nasser as a radical force in the Middle East and weakened the will of our best allies. But at the time, he was without doubt the driver of a very different policy.

Eisenhower's institutionalization of the NSC system included one change that was to grow in significance in future years. It was he who created the post of special assistant to the president for national security affairs. The man he chose was Robert Cutler, who had been a Boston banker, wartime aide to George Marshall, and adviser to the Truman NSC; Cutler's background and conduct of the office established the "honest broker" paradigm later exemplified by Brent Scowcroft in the administrations of Gerald Ford and George H. W. Bush. However, for all the formality of the Eisenhower machinery, the very creation of the position was another step in the strengthening of the president's hand over it.

Kennedy and Johnson

The inauguration of John F. Kennedy in 1961 brought with it two further milestones in the evolution of these institutions—one admirable, the other less so. The less admirable one is the continuation of the pattern of incoming presidents repudiating the practices of their predecessors, sometimes on the basis of politicized misimpressions of what exactly those practices were. We have seen that creation of the NSC under Truman was in part a rebuke to FDR. Then Eisenhower revamped the NSC system as a rebuke to both Truman and FDR. Kennedy carried this to a new level in reaction to the perceived deficiencies of Eisenhower. And we shall see in later chapters that Kennedy was not the last in this chain.

Learning lessons from the experiences of one's predecessors, positive and negative, is a healthy thing—indeed it is the very purpose of this book. But the rejection of one's predecessor's arrangements should derive from some dispassionate analysis of what works the best; it should not be a political reflex. Astute observers such as I. M. Destler, Leslie Gelb, and Anthony Lake have pointed out the disservice that politicization of these matters can do to the national interest, especially when it is based on misperception and overreaction. The day may come when our political leaders will outgrow this habit. But that day may not come soon: The misadventures of George W. Bush's administration will undoubtedly lead his successors to emphasize changes in management methods and practices. Let us hope they will be the right ones.

Kennedy and his team accepted completely the then conventional view of Eisenhower as a poor leader. They agreed with Neustadt's portrayal of Ike as imprisoned in procedures and weak with respect to husbanding his political leverage over his government. Kennedy told a British television audience in April 1961 that the staff system "[o]ccasionally, in the past, I think . . . has been used to getting a pre-arranged agreement which is only confirmed at the President's desk, and that I don't agree with." As we saw in the quotations from Sorensen and Bundy in Chapter 1, the Kennedy team also came into office with considerable doubts about the competence, intellectual caliber, and loyalty of the cabinet departments.

The result was an emphasis on personal presidential authority, flexibility, and control. Journalist Charles Bartlett, a close friend of the new president, wrote in early 1961:

> The Eisenhower concept was that the bulging Federal Government could only be held in shape with a tight and precise organization at the top. Mr. Kennedy's emerging philosophy is that the gangling structure responds less to organization than to highly personalized leadership.

Sorensen explained in 1963 that:

> The parochialism of experts and department heads is offset in part by a President's White House and executive staff. These few assistants are the only other men in Washington whose responsibilities both enable and require them to look, as he does, at the government as a whole.

The Kennedy administration therefore reverted to a loose, Rooseveltian model of White House staffing, dismantled key pillars of Eisenhower's formal NSC structure, and beefed up the White House national security staff—all with the goal of strengthening the president's personal freedom of action and power of decision. The NSC met as a body less often—only sixteen meetings in the first six months of the Kennedy administration. Another important change was the streamlining and recasting of the role of the special assistant to the president for national security affairs and the NSC staff. Eisenhower had two senior men dealing with these matters: Robert Cutler (succeeded by Gordon Gray), dealing with NSC policy issues, and also Colonel Andrew Goodpaster, who as staff secretary served Eisenhower in a more personal capacity handling day-to-day national security matters including intelligence. These two functions were now combined in Bundy; he was also formally designated as director of the NSC staff. The staff was reduced to twelve substantive officers. No longer was it a large group of sixty-odd civil servants representing their departments and managing a bureaucratic process; though smaller, it was now a staff of bright young academics dedicated to the president's vision. In Bundy's telling phrase in a 1961 letter to Senator Henry Jackson, the NSC staff was now "essentially a Presidential instrument."

Many of the deliberate efforts to dismantle the Eisenhower structure were later reversed by Nixon and not revived by later presidents. But the more lasting legacy of the Kennedy model was the milestone it represented in the further strengthening of presidential control. We have seen these ideas gestating in previous administrations, but the concept of the NSC staff as a *presidential* staff was truly born then, as was the idea of a White House national security adviser and staff with the mission of giving the president independent advice, helping him direct the bureaucracy, and devoted to protecting his interests. Bundy was praised as scrupulously fair in insuring that the president heard the full range of views. But the institution that he and his aggressive staff embodied had been significantly changed.

The small size of the NSC staff in the Kennedy period reflected, paradoxically, a hope that the State Department could be prodded to take charge of implementation and coordination of policy now that Eisenhower's elaborate machinery was dismantled. But State seemed incapable of stepping up to the task. The failed invasion of Cuba at the Bay of Pigs in April 1961 only reinforced the trend of centralization in the White House. Kennedy and his inner circle concluded that the fiasco came, in large part, from excessive deference to departments and agencies that gave poor advice. "The first lesson was never to rely on the experts," wrote Arthur Schlesinger, Jr. Not only were the military and the CIA found wanting, but also State. In a memorandum to the president in June 1961, his staff delicately described its efforts to encourage more energy at State without trampling on departmental prerogatives:

> [T]he White House–NSC group has gradually encouraged the growth of responsible self-reliance in the Departments, and especially in the Department of State. . . . Quietly, but persistently, White House men have pressed for activity and energy. . . . Criticism of the sort lately leveled at White House men for work in Latin America is wildly beside the point; the President's men have sometimes filled vacuums as best they could, but they have never tried to take over the work of men who showed energy and ability of their own.

Toward the end of 1962, after both the Bay of Pigs and the Cuban missile crisis, McGeorge Bundy would sadly conclude in a private note to the president that "[t]he State Department has not proved to be as effective an agency of executive management as we hoped, and above all, it has not shown the capacity for interdepartmental coordination which we hoped to force upon it." A "bowl of jelly" was the president's own assessment, according to Sorensen.

One response was what Schlesinger euphemistically calls a "blood transfusion [at State] from the White House" at the end of 1961. This effectively purged Chester Bowles as Dean Rusk's deputy and implanted men considered Kennedy loyalists—George Ball, George McGhee, Averell Harriman, Walt Rostow, Fred Dutton. Experience had provided "convincing evidence," says Schlesinger, "that the President required people in the State Department whose basic loyalty would be to him, not to the Foreign Service or the Council on Foreign Relations." Dean Rusk himself was an enigma to the Kennedy White House.

They saw him as personally intelligent, hardworking, and loyal to the president. But they also saw him as passive, unimaginative, and unable to give strong leadership to his department. Arthur Schlesinger recorded that at White House meetings Rusk would "sit quietly by, with his Buddha-like face and half-smile," not forcefully asserting his views. Rusk answered back many years later, saying in a book of reminiscences that he kept his thoughts to himself whenever Arthur Schlesinger was in the room since he knew Schlesinger was a notorious gossip at Georgetown cocktail parties.

White House control was strengthened in other ways. One important step after the Bay of Pigs was to shift the physical location of McGeorge Bundy's office. From the elegant Executive Office Building across West Executive Avenue, where his predecessors had resided since the 1940s, Bundy moved into the basement of the West Wing, a short run up the stairs to the Oval Office. It was a sacrifice of elegance for proximity—a sacrifice that presidential aides are usually willing to make, if not kill for. Another major step was to create the Situation Room, also in the West Basement, so that the White House could receive and send classified communications on its own and not be dependent on the departments to do so. During the Bay of Pigs crisis, decisions on naval and aircraft movements had been relayed from the Cabinet Room to the Pentagon over unclassified telephone lines. State Department historians have concluded ruefully: "More than anything else, the Sit[uation] Room allowed Bundy and his NSC staff to expand their involvement in the international activities of [the] foreign affairs community and become, in essence, 'a little State Department.'"

The Cuban missile crisis of October 1962 saw the Kennedy team revert to some degree to a more structured approach, just as the Korean War had led Truman to a greater appreciation of the National Security Council. Kennedy formally created an "Executive Committee" of the NSC (which journalists later nicknamed "ExComm"), intended as a streamlined and personalized NSC, to conduct the most important deliberations during the crisis. (ExComm's core membership consisted of fifteen top officials from State, Defense, CIA, and the White House, plus Attorney General Robert Kennedy, United Nations ambassador Adlai Stevenson, and outsiders such as Dean Acheson, John McCloy, and Robert Lovett.) ExComm proved so useful for coordinating policy during the Cuban crisis that, until it was formally disbanded in March

1963, it was given other topics to work on, such as policies toward Brazil, the Congo, Europe and NATO, and South Asia. But Bundy successfully argued against its continuation or reactivation, believing that it was not so well suited to lesser issues or for forward planning.

For our present purposes, the Cuban missile crisis is also notable for another reason. A crucial dimension of the crisis's resolution was kept well compartmented from the collegial deliberations of ExComm— namely Robert Kennedy's closely held secret communications with Soviet ambassador Anatoly Dobrynin. This is our introduction to the presidential "backchannel," which became famous—and controversial— in the context of Nixon and Kissinger's secret communications with other governments that bypassed the State Department. Private presidential channels have ample precedent, going back at least to Woodrow Wilson and his confidant Colonel Edward House, or FDR and Harry Hopkins. But in the modern period, in any discussion of good governance, the pros and cons of such irregular procedures inevitably come to be debated. Special channels sometimes offer presidents greater "secrecy and despatch," two qualities that the framers of our Constitution saw as indispensable to diplomacy and to presidential management of it. But there are always complications of one kind or another when regular procedures are bypassed.

Robert Kennedy's channel to Dobrynin did not exclude the cabinet secretaries; Rusk and Defense Secretary Robert McNamara were both part of the small Oval Office team that approved the messages passed. A more serious issue with respect to backchannels has to do with substance—that is, whether the messages passed in the special channel are consistent with what is going on in regular channels. In the case of Reagan's irregular overtures to Iran in the mid-1980s, the message conveyed was in sharp contradiction to U.S. policy at the time, which was to tilt against Iran in the Iran-Iraq War because of the ideological and geopolitical threat posed by Iran after its revolution. Of the many objections posed to this enterprise by Secretary of State George Shultz and Defense Secretary Caspar Weinberger, this to me was the weightiest— namely the policy incoherence that it embodied (see Chapter 6). As for Nixon and Kissinger, the products of their backchannels were surfaced soon enough: The China breakthrough was announced when it happened in July 1971; Kissinger's secret Paris negotiations on Vietnam were disclosed in a speech by Nixon in January 1972. On other issues such as Berlin or strategic arms limitation, understandings reached in

Kissinger's private channel to Dobrynin were quickly introduced by both parties into the official negotiations then going on.

The full extent of the compromise arrangement that settled the Cuban missile crisis—namely the explicitness of President Kennedy's promise to remove U.S. missiles from Turkey within four to five months after Moscow's removal of its missiles from Cuba—was denied in public and kept secret for more than two and a half decades until it leaked from the Soviet side. The secrecy could be justified as important to alliance management—so as not to show that the United States would sacrifice the interests of NATO or its ally Turkey in a bilateral bargain with the Soviet Union. (The U.S. missiles in Turkey were in fact obsolete, and Kennedy had ordered the State Department months before to begin consultations on their removal.) But the public refusal of such a "deal" was also an important part of the Kennedy administration's claim to have remained faithful to its alliances. Administration officials publicly rebuked Adlai Stevenson shortly after the crisis ("Adlai wanted a Munich") for having advocated what the president privately approved. In 1989, Sorensen publicly admitted that, in what historian John Lewis Gaddis wryly calls an example of "custodial historiography," he had taken it upon himself to censor Robert Kennedy's famous posthumously published memoir of the crisis, *Thirteen Days*, to edit out any suggestion that the president had approved such an explicit trade.

FOR HIS PART, Lyndon Johnson inherited and retained John Kennedy's team but the procedures worked somewhat differently. As Walt Rostow has described it:

> Johnson's advisory system for national security policy was built initially around Rusk, McNamara, and Bundy. As a colleague, he had seen these men at work for almost three years. He admired each of them. As a matter of principle, he sought continuity with Kennedy's administration.

Johnson's system proved to be less White House–centered, however, and gave more of a role to his cabinet officers. Like Kennedy he preferred small informal meetings, considering them a more congenial forum for candid discussion and decision, and—very importantly—for minimizing the risk of leaks. By early 1964 he had settled on a new format—the Tuesday lunch. In attendance were the president, Rusk,

McNamara, and Bundy (later succeeded by Rostow). Lunches were scheduled irregularly at first. But, especially as the Vietnam War heated up, the attendants met almost every Tuesday. Johnson convened some 160 Tuesday lunches over the course of his presidency. Eventually this, too, came to be caricatured by Johnson's successors.

Richard Nixon and Henry Kissinger, as we shall see, had a low opinion of the Tuesday lunches, and Nixon in his 1968 campaign went so far as to attribute serious foreign policy failures to this departure from the discipline and regularity of Eisenhower's NSC. Walt Rostow makes a good case, however, that the Tuesday lunches were in fact a "rather conventional and orderly bureaucratic procedure . . . conducted in a deceptively informal setting." An agenda was prepared; presidential decisions were recorded and transmitted to concerned departments "with full formality." Yet the informal setting encouraged "extraordinary candor," Rostow argued: "Clashing, exploratory, or even frivolous views could be expressed with little bureaucratic caution and with confidence no scars would remain. It was a deadly serious but somehow intensely human occasion."

While the Tuesday lunches may have served the president well as a collegial forum for deliberation, the system still lacked a mechanism for monitoring implementation. Johnson, like Kennedy, looked to the State Department to take the primary role in this. In March 1966, a presidential directive officially—yet again—assigned to the secretary of state the responsibility for overall direction, coordination, and supervision of U.S. government activities overseas. The directive created the Senior Interdepartmental Group (SIG), chaired by the under secretary of state (a title later changed to deputy secretary), with Interdepartmental Regional Groups (IRGs) supporting it, each chaired by the assistant secretary of state responsible for the relevant region.

This was the system that Richard Nixon inherited.

CHAPTER THREE

Richard Nixon

I T WAS AN IRONIC SETTING for plotting a revolution. The Pierre
Hotel is an elegant New York landmark overlooking Fifth Avenue
and Central Park, its upper stories offering a spectacular panorama of
the city. Built in 1930, the Pierre had begun by the late 1960s to let some
of its elegance fade, though not its reputation for exclusiveness and lux-
ury. Its guests included some of the Hollywood elite—Cary Grant,
Audrey Hepburn, Elizabeth Taylor. From November 1968 to January
1969, it was the scene of a real-life historical drama, as the transition
headquarters of President-elect Richard Nixon.

It was here, on the Pierre's thirty-ninth floor, that Nixon had his first
conversations with Henry Kissinger, the forty-five-year-old Harvard professor he had chosen as his White House assistant for national security
affairs. The two men hardly knew each other; they had met once
before at a New York cocktail party a year earlier. But Nixon had read
Kissinger's writings and had judged, correctly, that they shared a
strategic- and geopolitical-minded view of the world. In these first discussions, Nixon talked of the changes he planned to make in American
foreign policy—and in how that policy was made. Kissinger recorded on
his yellow pad a blunt edict he received from his new boss: "Influence
of State Department establishment must be reduced."

In the previous chapter we saw presidents Harry Truman and John
Kennedy lament the State Department's unresponsiveness to presidential authority. Richard Nixon took this assessment a large step further.
He had the same view of State Department stodginess, having watched
the department as vice president during the eight years of the Eisenhower era. He also believed he had suffered personal slights at the

hands of the East Coast Foreign Service establishment when he was vice president, and even more when he traveled abroad as a private citizen after his political career seemed in ruins. If the Kennedy crowd thought the department was too conservative, Nixon had the opposite perspective. In 1968 he was inheriting not only the Vietnam War but the social transformations that were following in its train. If Nixon was predicting that the antiwar mood spreading in our culture would soon make its way into our foreign policy elite, he was correct.

In short, by his own account, he came into the White House fundamentally convinced that "Washington is a city run primarily by Democrats and liberals." Thus he "urged, exhorted, and finally pleaded" with all his new cabinet appointees, repeatedly, "to move quickly to replace holdover bureaucrats with people who believed in what we were trying to do. [He] warned that if they did not act quickly, they would become captives of the bureaucracy they were trying to change." This was his attitude to the entire federal bureaucracy, not only the State Department, and it would be reflected in some extraordinary measures such as his asking for the resignations of his entire administration following his reelection victory in 1972. We will trace the ramifications of that episode later in this chapter.

Nixon also shared Kissinger's critique of the national security decision-making process they were inheriting from Kennedy and Johnson. Nixon deplored its seeming lack of rigor, its informality, and what he considered its negative results. In a campaign radio address in late October 1968, he pointedly recalled his own attendance (and sometimes chairmanship) of the National Security Council during Eisenhower's eight years of peace. Citing the wars in Vietnam and the Middle East, he went so far as to blame "most of our serious reverses abroad since 1960" on Kennedy's and Johnson's dismantling of the NSC system that they had inherited from Eisenhower and Nixon.

Nixon was taking on Eisenhower's mantle, and identifying it with the National Security Council, but in fact he had something different from Eisenhower's model in mind:

> When Eisenhower selected Foster Dulles as his Secretary of State, he wanted him to be his chief foreign policy adviser, a role Dulles was uniquely qualified to fill. From the outset of my administration, however, I planned to direct foreign policy from the White House.

The New NSC System

In 1961, in its famous examination of the presidential decision-making process, Senator Henry Jackson's national security subcommittee had emphasized an important truth:

> Each President will have his own style of doing business—the product of his nature and experience. Each President therefore needs great freedom to adapt his office and procedures to suit the peculiarities of his style. . . . He can use the [National Security] Council as little, or as much, as he wishes. . . . [The Council is] the President's instrument [and] exists only to serve the President.

In designing a new system to meet Nixon's requirements, Kissinger turned to now General Andrew Goodpaster, who had served as President Eisenhower's staff secretary but in 1968 was deputy U.S. commander in Vietnam. Initially agnostic himself on the question of State's proper role in the structure, Kissinger was stunned by the vehemence of not only Goodpaster but Eisenhower himself on the subject. Goodpaster took Kissinger along to visit Eisenhower at Walter Reed Army Hospital. The old man—bedridden, emaciated by his cumulative heart ailments, immobilized by a pacemaker, and having only a few months to live—expressed himself with surprising forcefulness: The system had to be pulled into the White House, he emphasized; the Pentagon would never accept interagency coordination under State Department control. For all his admiration for Dulles, Eisenhower said he had always kept control of the NSC machinery in the White House. Goodpaster later recalled:

> I recommended strongly and Henry agreed that the [senior] interdepartmental groups should be chaired by someone from the White House. The State Department tried to fight this. . . . Nixon stood fast and said, no, the chairing would be done—in other words the agenda would be set—by somebody from the White House. So, the die was cast.

To flesh this out, Kissinger turned to two men—Morton Halperin, a young former Harvard colleague who had recently served as one of Robert McNamara's civilian "whiz kids" in the Pentagon, and

Lawrence Eagleburger, a junior foreign service officer assigned by the State Department. Halperin and Eagleburger drafted a nine-page, single-spaced "Proposal for a New National Security Council System," which Kissinger presented to Nixon at the end of December in Key Biscayne, Florida. Nixon was scheduled to meet there on December 28 with his new cabinet designees William P. Rogers (State) and Melvin Laird (Defense) to discuss the new arrangements. Unbeknown to them, however, the president-elect had reviewed the paper the day before—and already approved it.

The Kissinger memorandum cited the strengths and weaknesses of the Eisenhower system, and set about to offer up a new system that improved upon it. It recommended that the National Security Council meet regularly, as the "principal forum for issues requiring interagency coordination." Below the level of the council, the assistant to the president for national security affairs would chair an NSC Review Group, which would insure that papers presented to the full council properly framed the issues for the president. An Under Secretaries Committee (chaired by State) would handle implementation and follow-up of certain issues, and the Johnson administration's assistant secretary–level Interdepartmental Regional Groups (IRGs, also chaired by State) would continue, but both these committees would become "sub-organs" of the NSC. An expanded NSC staff would monitor the day-to-day business of the cabinet departments, prepare NSC agenda papers, and do longer-range studies.

An innocuous-sounding but very pregnant "note" in the middle of the December 27 memorandum declared: "The elaborated NSC machinery [in this paper] makes the continued functioning of the existing Senior Inter-Departmental Group unnecessary." The SIG, created in 1966, had been the last effort of the Kennedy-Johnson team to give the State Department the leadership role in coordinating and integrating national policy. The memorandum proposed to abolish it, putting the Kissinger-chaired Review Group in its place.

The State Department professionals fought a tenacious rearguard action to change Nixon's mind before inauguration day. The distinguished senior diplomat U. Alexis Johnson, tapped by Nixon to be under secretary of state for political affairs, did his best to argue the matter with Kissinger—and simultaneously to explain to his new boss, William Rogers, a foreign policy novice, why all this was important from the department's point of view. Johnson in his memoirs tells of hurried conversations in elevators with Rogers and Rogers's deputy-to-be Elliot Richardson to explain the "bureaucratic theology" that was involved, "with which, of course, they were entirely unfamiliar." Johnson's effort was in vain. Over the course of the first year, Nixon ordered other NSC subcommittees to be set up—focusing, for example, on crisis management, strategic arms control, and defense programs—and all were chaired by Kissinger. Every administration since Nixon has retained some version of the White House–centered system he put in place.

Another feature of Nixon's system was his insistence on being presented with policy options. The Key Biscayne memorandum stressed this, and Nixon highlighted it in public statements. A lengthy report sent to Congress on U.S. foreign policy after a year in office devoted a full chapter to his new NSC system. In it, Nixon declared:

> I do not believe that Presidential leadership consists merely in ratifying a consensus reached among departments and agencies. The President bears the Constitutional responsibility of making the judgments and decisions that form our policy. . . . I refuse to be confronted with a bureaucratic consensus that leaves me no options but acceptance or rejection, and that gives me no way of knowing what alternatives exist.

This emphasis on being presented with options was one of the most important features of the Nixon system. It was not really a matter of organization, but it was a central demand he made of the process. Perhaps there was some residual sensitivity that his mentor Eisenhower was still, in those days, often accused of being a prisoner of bureaucratic consensus. In any case, Nixon saw it—correctly—as a vital element of presidential control. Not every president works this way; many chief executives, before and since, have found it more comfortable to encourage their cabinet colleagues to agree on a recommendation. Nixon—his determination to dominate the process only reinforced by his suspicions of the bureaucracy's loyalty—was insistent on making the choices himself. His NSC staff had the task of forcing the bureaucracy to present policy issues in this way; if this effort was unavailing, as it often was, the staff spent much of its time writing its own memoranda to the president laying out, as fairly as it could manage, what the choices were, and the pros and cons. Not only was Nixon not afraid of choosing among sharply conflicting recommendations; he was, as we shall see, fully capable of overruling his cabinet secretaries when they agreed among themselves.

Thus, under Richard Nixon the history of the National Security Council and the NSC system reached its climactic point. The institution that Harry Truman had been wary of as a possible infringement on his presidential prerogative had become, through the changes wrought by first John Kennedy and then Richard Nixon, an instrument of presidential control.

But this is only part of the story. There is much that the institutional history does not explain. The replacement of the SIG by the Review Group has become part of the folklore, perceived as a great victory for Kissinger that established his power; it has even been referred to as the *"coup d'état* at the Hotel Pierre." But Kissinger himself is skeptical of this assessment. The SIG episode, he has written, was "important less in terms of real power than in appearance and in what it foretold about the President's relations with his principal advisers"—as "the first of seemingly unending skirmishes" between Nixon and Rogers, which Rogers invariably lost. Kissinger concluded:

> [I]n the final analysis the influence of a Presidential Assistant derives almost exclusively from the confidence of the President, not from administrative arrangements. My role would almost surely have been roughly the same if the Johnson system had been continued.

Even the Nixon system was designed, on the face of it, as a collaborative bureaucratic process, albeit with the White House in the lead. Morton Halperin stresses that it worked that way at the beginning:

> The [interagency] system was not a fraud, and was not intended to be mainly a camouflage for the secret work being done for the President by Henry Kissinger. It was taken seriously by Richard Nixon and Henry Kissinger and was meant to be taken seriously by the bureaucracy.

Halperin points to some useful early interagency papers done on Vietnam, the Middle East, and strategic forces. Indeed, Nixon and Kissinger continued for the first few years to rely on the NSC process to elicit the best thinking that was available in the government.

The question then becomes: What is it that so undermined the president's confidence in the State Department that it led him to build up

Kissinger's role even further? The answer lies in a series of missteps committed by the department in the first two years of the administration, over both the procedure and the substance of policy, which compounded Nixon's suspicions and led him to strengthen White House dominance even beyond the White House–centered bureaucratic process he had started with.

Stumbles by State

For many people at State, the new NSC procedures apparently took some getting used to—particularly Nixon's insistence on policy choices. There is a classic Kissinger joke about how the bureaucracy responds to requests for options. If the president wants options, they offer him three: Option 1 is nuclear war; option 2 is surrender; and option 3 looks strangely like existing policy. Sir Humphrey in *Yes Prime Minister* would understand completely. But, alas, there is a basis for the joke. The historians who compile the invaluable archival series *Foreign Relations of the United States* have included the record of an early meeting of the new NSC Review Group, on February 13, 1969, chaired by Kissinger, on the subject of East-West relations. The account is not based on notes taken by the NSC staff or the State Department representative, as might be expected. Instead it is a summary by a neutral participant (the CIA representative), who could barely conceal his amusement at what he was witnessing. The policy paper presented to the Review Group by the State Department's European affairs bureau did not set forth alternative approaches; it was, rather, an advocacy paper on behalf of existing policy. The CIA observer continued:

> The paper contained some half-hearted gestures toward meeting the options format which Kissinger had requested, but these alternate options were patently straw men, lacking both internal logic and conviction. . . . The State Department view was that . . . in reality . . . there is only one view which "responsible people" can hold regarding policy toward East-West relations, and that view is set forth as Option 3, "Strong Deterrent with Flexible Approach." Gradually during the course of this discussion agreement was reached that Option 3 as stated was so broad that it needed to be articulated in a series of suboptions. As Kissinger put it, "Surely there is divergence between the attitudes expressed by the Arms Control and Disarmament Agency on

the one hand, and those of the Joint Chiefs of Staff on the other. Somewhere between these two outer wings are other defensible positions. The President and the NSC should be given the opportunity to discuss this range."

The State Department's difficulties carried over into substance, not only procedure. Nixon came into office with some clear views on the kind of policy he wanted to carry out, especially with respect to the two dominant issues of the period, U.S.-Soviet relations and the Vietnam War. Contrary to some accounts, Nixon never claimed in his campaign that he had a "secret plan" to end the war; that was media mischief. But he did believe that the United States had not exerted its full leverage to press the Soviet Union to exert leverage over North Vietnam. It followed from this that our diplomacy toward Moscow should feature Vietnam more prominently, and that our policy on issues that seemed to be of interest to the Soviets—especially arms control, expansion of trade, and the Middle East—should not be considered in isolation but treated as linked to other matters we cared about, especially Vietnam.

This was the famous notion of "linkage." Nixon declared in his very first news conference, for example, on January 27, 1969, that arms talks should be conducted in a way that promoted progress on "political" issues. Kissinger used the term "linkage" in a background briefing for reporters on February 6. Nixon sent a letter to secretaries Rogers and Laird and CIA director Richard Helms on February 4 laying out his reasoning in more detail.

Prevailing opinion in Congress, the media, and the State Department, however, favored strategic arms control and East-West trade as the key solvents of international tensions and thus as necessities in their own right. President Johnson had been on the verge of commencing arms talks with the Soviets in August 1968, which were canceled because of the Soviet invasion of Czechoslovakia; Nixon was pressed by his critics—and by his own diplomats—to relaunch them (what later became the Strategic Arms Limitation Talks, or SALT) as soon as possible. Crucial opportunities would be lost, he was told, if he continued to dawdle. Likewise, Congress began pressing for liberalization of U.S.-Soviet trade, and the Soviets were pressing to play a diplomatic role in the Middle East.

But Nixon did not want to be stampeded. He wanted to probe what was possible with the Soviets on Vietnam; he and Kissinger were also concerned that more analytical work needed to be done in the U.S. government (on issues such as verification, weapons capabilities, and U.S. strategic requirements) before we would be ready to begin negotiating on SALT. Nixon also understood that in demonstrating that he could successfully withstand domestic pressures, he was gaining bargaining leverage with the Soviets. For all these reasons, he did not wish to agree immediately to a date for the relaunch of SALT.

In the State Department, the president's letter of February 4 on linkage was assumed—correctly—to have been drafted by Kissinger and his staff; this may have been thought a sufficient reason not to take it too seriously. The fact that Nixon had personally and publicly proclaimed the same doctrine in his news conference (not to mention signing and sending the letter) did not seem to register. For whatever reason, State proceeded to pursue its preferred approach. On March 19, U.S. chief negotiator Gerard Smith reassured his Soviet counterpart that the start of SALT "need not be tied, in some sort of package formula, to the settlement of specific international problems." At an April 7 news conference, Rogers predicted that SALT would begin "in the late spring or early summer." On Rogers's instructions, U.S. diplomats in Moscow suggested dates in June or July. Press leaks to diplomatic correspondents kept the world informed of this movement. Nixon, worn down and preempted by all these pressures, reluctantly agreed in early June to inform the Soviets that we were ready.

Our diplomats displayed a similar impatience over Vietnam. Peace talks had begun in Paris at the end of the Johnson administration; an understanding had been reached, through Soviet mediation, by which the United States halted the bombing of North Vietnam in return for a halt to Communist attacks on major population centers. Early in Nixon's term the Communists resumed their shelling of Saigon and other cities. This did not lessen the eagerness of American diplomats to resume the talks, which also seemed to overtake considerations of what strategy we might pursue. In January 1969, an article written by Kissinger when he was still a Harvard professor appeared in *Foreign Affairs;* it suggested a new approach to the negotiations, namely to concentrate with the North Vietnamese on resolving the military issues (cease-fire, U.S. withdrawal, and return of prisoners of war), while leaving the political future of South Vietnam to a longer-term negotiation between the Communist and non-Communist South Vietnamese. Nixon supported this approach of separating the military and political issues (and it later became the basis of the 1973 Paris Agreement). On March 8, 1969, with the shelling continuing, and without consulting the White House, Rogers called in Soviet ambassador Anatoly Dobrynin, proposed immediate private talks with North Vietnam, and assured him we were willing to talk about political and military issues simultaneously. Kissinger complained bitterly to Nixon's chief of staff, H. R. (Bob) Haldeman, that Rogers's reversal of policy was "disastrous." This episode, as we shall see, played its part in establishing the role of a special White House backchannel to Dobrynin.

Yet another area of East-West relations proved controversial. Nixon had the idea of visiting Romania in the fall of 1969, as part of his around-the-world trip after meeting the Pacific Ocean splashdown of Apollo 11 following its return from the moon. Romania, while remaining a member of the Soviet-led Warsaw Pact, had broken with Moscow earlier in the decade, somewhat as Charles de Gaulle had struck an independent course in the North Atlantic Alliance. Nixon was the first American president to show the flag in Communist Eastern Europe; his Romanian visit in 1969 was followed by trips to Tito's Yugoslavia in 1970 and to Poland in 1972. The point of all these unprecedented visits was to demonstrate that the United States did not concede Soviet dominance in Central or Eastern Europe. This was an especially significant message for the United States to convey in the year after the Soviet invasion of Czechoslovakia and proclamation of the "Brezhnev Doctrine"—the doctrine of Soviet leader Leonid Brezhnev that demanded obeisance to Moscow as sole leader of the "socialist camp."

The State Department quickly leaked its negative view of the Romania enterprise, however. The trip arrangements having been made through White House channels, journalists sympathetic to State were quick to proclaim that the visit was a "disturbing" development and a "blunder." Nixon was accused of recklessness—of being needlessly provocative to the Soviet Union and foolishly endangering SALT and other vital negotiations with Moscow.

Events like these soon altered Kissinger's assumptions about his job. Despite the beefing-up of the NSC system, Kissinger had started out with a rather naïve idea of what his role would be. I remember his saying during the transition that he wanted to focus on basic strategy and long-range planning, and not get dragged into the "cable-clearing" business— that is, the flood of telegrams around the clock back and forth between the State Department and overseas posts, issuing instructions in the name of the secretary of state and reporting back on overseas developments. Yet, Kissinger soon learned that this operational activity *was* our foreign policy. "Tactics turn into strategy," as he later told Haldeman. If Kissinger and his staff did not exert themselves to insure that outgoing instructions reflected the president's policies, all the brilliant strategizing in the West Wing would be overtaken by the reality of the policy being made by the State Department in its cables. In this lay the origin of one of the great melodramas of the Nixon administration—the tug-of-war between Rogers and Kissinger over operational policy.

Throughout 1969, the White House struggled to gain control over important policy cables that State sent out. In June, for example, the State Department issued instructions to U.S. diplomats at the Vietnam peace talks in Paris, including for meetings with Soviet representatives, without clearance by the White House. Kissinger called Attorney General John Mitchell to complain that the Soviets "must think we have lost our minds" on the basis of State instructions contrary to presidential guidance. (Mitchell, like Haldeman, was known to be a close political confidant of Nixon and was thus in a position to reinforce Kissinger's authority.) Mitchell agreed strongly with Kissinger's assessment— "could not be stronger about anything he has run into down there." Nixon thereupon sent a memorandum to Rogers on June 20 reaffirming his instruction that "departmental telegrams be cleared with the White House to insure that I am kept fully abreast of communications on important policy and operational matters of Presidential interest." Rogers replied that "policy" matters, of course, should be cleared with the White House but that he reserved the discretion to decide what "operational" details need not be called to the president's attention. Nixon sent another message to Rogers on June 26 reaffirming his interest in both "policy" and "operational" matters. Problems continued, to the point that Kissinger met on a Saturday morning with Mitchell on July 12, 1969, to go over a long list, compiled by his staff, of State deviations from presidential guidance on U.S.-Soviet relations and Vietnam.

Nixon then tried again. On September 1, while attending a National Governors Conference in Colorado Springs, he issued a more formal directive, this time addressed to Rogers, Laird, and Helms, reaffirming that all public statements and press releases "on matters of known or potential Presidential interest," as well as official communications "with policy implications," must be cleared by the White House. NSC staffers later discovered that the president's Colorado Springs directive was never distributed within the Department of State—indeed, that most directives emanating from the White House were assumed at State to be merely Kissinger products and some were thought even to have been sent out without the president's knowledge. These assumptions were incorrect.

Kissinger's complaints about State continued, leading Nixon to muse in a philosophical vein to Haldeman in October 1969 about Kissinger's "overreactions" and "obsession with *total* compliance and perfection." Haldeman recorded in his diary: "K[issinger] argues that you have to maintain tight discipline on the little things or you can't control the big ones, P[resident] feels you should lose the ones that don't matter and save your strength and equity for the big battles that really count." When, later in the month, another conflict arose having to do with State's contacts with the Soviets on the Middle East, Nixon groused that Kissinger was "obsessed beyond reason with this problem." Haldeman called it a "tough one, because there *is* some real merit to K's concerns about Rogers' loyalty."

Over the next few years the conflicts between the White House and State only multiplied. The controversial U.S. and South Vietnamese military operation against North Vietnamese bases in Cambodia at the end of April 1970, which unleashed passionate protests across the United States, had their reverberations in Foggy Bottom: Fifty foreign service officers and two hundred other officials from State sent a letter to Rogers on May 8 denouncing the president's policy. Periodically, Kissinger's staff would pull together yet another compilation of instances of State's overeagerness in contacts with the Soviets, press leaks disparaging presidential policy, refusals to clear important cables at the White House, and/or efforts to curry favor with Congress at White House expense. This author helped to compile some of them. At various times, Nixon vented to Haldeman his frustration with the behavior of both Kissinger and Rogers, his tentative conclusion that one or the other would have to go, and, ultimately, his desire that someone else (Haldeman or Mitchell) handle it. But the issue for Nixon, in the end, was not personalities but policy. The most damning material in the NSC staff's burgeoning dossiers had to do with examples of real deviations from presidential policy, and Nixon knew he had to back Kissinger. Losing Kissinger would be a "major loss," Nixon commented to Haldeman in September 1970, "and then State and Rogers would run rampant which would be very bad."

At the end of November 1970, Kissinger's deputy, Brigadier General Alexander Haig, sent Haldeman a short memo listing five new items that he considered "indicative of the problems we are having with the Department of State." They included press leaks plausibly attributable to State either disparaging or distancing itself from Nixon's policies. This triggered a series of private conversations between Nixon and Haldeman over the next few days. On December 3, Nixon concluded he "may have to bite the bullet" and fire his old friend Rogers, but he wanted to "put a fully documented case together." Thus, this time it was Nixon who asked for a full dossier on press leaks attributable to State that undercut presidential policy—it was not Kissinger who volunteered it. The next day Nixon repeated his instruction to Haldeman to talk to Rogers:

> making the point that there are two different fights here. One is [between] K[issinger] and Rogers, and that the P[resident], of course, has to side with Rogers on. But the second one is much more important: that's the foreign service vs. the P. There it's unforgivable, and the P is going to have heads rolling. Since Cambodia, they've been taking on the P, leaking, etc. These things don't just happen, and from now on, it's us or them. State can't be told anything, and that's the way it is.

Haig responded to the president's request on December 7, 1970, with what the archivists call "a twenty-three-page detailed description of more than 70 press leaks concerning, among other topics, Southeast Asia, Latin America, the Middle East, Europe, and SALT." Haig's signature, but probably my work.

Nixon later became fond of quoting British statesman William Gladstone to the effect that the first requisite for a prime minister is to be a good butcher—lamenting that he lacked that quality himself. In 1970, abhorring personal confrontations, he postponed any action to discipline or replace his secretary of state. Rogers remained in office three more years.

Exclusively Eyes Only

Nixon resorted to another strategy—conducting operational policy more and more from the White House, relying on Kissinger and the

NSC staff to implement it. This was Nixon's personal rebellion against Richard Neustadt's dictum that presidential power is "the power to persuade." Given Nixon's introversion, he was never likely to attempt to follow that method. Bypassing the rest of the government was procedurally and psychologically much simpler—and also insured a centralization, consistency, and coherence in policy that has rarely been seen before or since.

A symbolic step occurred in the summer of 1970 when Kissinger's office moved upstairs. A renovation and reorganization of the West Wing shifted the White House press corps from its traditional loitering area in the front lobby to what is today the press briefing room, and turned the lobby into a dignified reception area for those visiting the president or other senior officials. This also opened up what became an elegant office on the northwest corner facing onto Pennsylvania Avenue. No longer in the basement, Kissinger—and most of his successors—now resided on the same floor as the Oval Office, and only a few steps away.

Elder statesman Dean Acheson commented on the Kissinger phenomenon in the July 1971 issue of *Foreign Affairs*, in an article written even before the dramatic announcement that month of Kissinger's trip to China. Its title was, significantly: "The Eclipse of the State Department." In it Acheson did not lament, deplore, or complain of what was happening to his beloved department; he acknowledged it and sought to explain it. To Acheson, both the Constitution and much of American history demonstrated the fundamental "fragility" of the secretary of state's position. When President William McKinley ordered the U.S. Navy to take the Philippines and destroy the Spanish fleet, thereby launching the United States into the world as a great power, he did not bother to consult or inform his secretary of state. Woodrow Wilson, once he burst on the stage as a world statesman, saw no reason to share that stage with secretaries of state he did not particularly respect; he was content, in Acheson's words, "to rely upon his own typewriter and the reports of his unofficial ambassador-at-large and collaborator, Colonel Edward M. House of Texas." Franklin Roosevelt distrusted the State Department and ignored Secretary of State Cordell Hull as we have seen. Acheson did not omit to mention John Kennedy's distrust of the department and quest for more personal control over policy. Perhaps his own close relationship with Truman had been the exception:

What has been occurring [Acheson concluded] has not been that the White House advisers have edged the foreign office out of functions being competently performed but that they have been needed to do what is not being done anywhere to the satisfaction of the man responsible, the President.

RELATIONS WITH THE SOVIET UNION, as we have noted, were a priority for Nixon. All U.S.-Soviet negotiations had come to a virtual halt after the Soviet invasion of Czechoslovakia in August 1968, and the Kremlin was wary of Nixon and his reputation as a Cold War hard-liner. Soviet ambassador Dobrynin paid his first courtesy call on President Nixon on February 17, 1969, a month after inauguration. Kissinger had already suggested to Nixon that he invite Dobrynin to set up a confidential channel to the White House. Toward the end of the meeting, Nixon dismissed both Kissinger and the State Department representative from the Oval Office and told Dobrynin he wanted this special channel established through Kissinger. When Secretary Rogers misspoke to Dobrynin on March 8, with respect to the president's Vietnam policy, as noted earlier, Nixon sent Kissinger to see Dobrynin on March 11 to tell him that the Soviets' impression of a change in U.S. policy was "premature." Nixon soon began using the Kissinger-Dobrynin channel to step up diplomatic pressure on the Soviets to press North Vietnam into serious negotiations. In mid-April, Kissinger warned Dobrynin that Vietnam could become a major obstacle to U.S.-Soviet relations and handed him a note, initialed by Nixon, proposing a special negotiating channel between the United States and North Vietnam outside the existing Paris framework. While at that time Nixon was thinking of some distinguished private American as the emissary, this later became Kissinger's own secret talks with the North Vietnamese.

Dobrynin recounts in his memoirs that he was initially taken aback by this "two-tier" method of diplomacy, but soon adapted to it. But while Dobrynin mastered the complexities and delicacies of actually working in two separate channels in Washington, he reports that his boss, Foreign Minister Andrei Gromyko, had a more difficult time on a visit to the United States in the fall of 1969.

The main subject of Gromyko's visit happened to be the Middle East, on which the convolutions in the U.S. government were particularly complex. Secretary Rogers was developing a Middle East peace plan, with Nixon's approval, but Nixon was at the same time somewhat skeptical of the effort and reserving his own judgment. Gromyko, visiting for the United Nations General Assembly, had two conversations over lunch with Rogers and was pleasantly surprised; he concluded that the United States and Soviet Union were close to an agreement on the Middle East. He was so excited he wanted to report this to Moscow. With difficulty, Dobrynin persuaded him to wait:

> Gromyko became very angry: "I came here to negotiate with the secretary of state. I don't want to listen to you."
>
> After the lunch broke up and Gromyko asked me: "What do we do now? What do we send to Moscow?"
>
> "Nothing for the time being," I replied. "Let's wait for a meeting with the president."
>
> Gromyko then became really angry. "What kind of secretary of state is this?" he said.
>
> The next day Gromyko met with Nixon and of course discovered that what Rogers had confusingly told him reflected neither the president's nor Kissinger's policy.

The Kremlin eventually got the hang of it, and Kissinger's back-channel with Dobrynin was to be the vehicle for a number of diplomatic advances. The first came when they broke a procedural impasse on SALT. The Soviets had been pressing hard to stop the anti-ballistic missile (ABM) system that Nixon had proposed to deploy; the American side wanted limits on the rapid Soviet buildup of offensive missiles. Kissinger and Dobrynin hammered out an agreement to discuss limits on both offensive and defensive systems in parallel. This was announced on May 20, 1971—and caught both sides' diplomats by surprise. A few months later came a breakthrough on Berlin. A formal negotiation had begun in early 1970 among the four powers occupying postwar Berlin (the United States, Soviet Union, United Kingdom, and France); it produced an agreement in 1971 that assured Western access to the city and essentially ended the Cold War crises over Berlin that had bedeviled the Truman, Eisenhower, and Kennedy administrations. Progress came fitfully in this complex multilateral negotiation, but was spurred by understandings reached on key points through secret communications among Kissinger, Dobrynin, and West German chancellor Willy Brandt's confidant Egon Bahr. Dobrynin was also aware of Kissinger's secret talks with the North Vietnamese in Paris, and the channel was used occasionally, as we have seen, to try to engage Moscow to press Hanoi. In most negotiations, deadlocks are eventually raised to a higher political level for top leaders to resolve. But it is usually a cumbersome formal process involving interagency negotiations. In the Nixon administration, the backchannel kept the top political levels involved on both sides and facilitated rapid decisions.

The private channels that Nixon authorized Kissinger to set up with Dobrynin were only part of an elaborate diplomatic network that emanated from the White House. Kissinger's secret talks at safe houses in the Paris suburbs with North Vietnamese Politburo member Le Duc Tho—not the official talks at Avenue Kléber downtown—turned out to be the forum in which a Vietnam settlement was reached in January 1973. Nixon in his meetings with foreign leaders in the Oval Office or on trips abroad would tell his interlocutors that any special messages to him should be conveyed through Kissinger. Similar special channels were set up with 10 Downing Street and with the Elysée Palace, to match that with the West German Chancellery, either through their ambassadors in Washington or through the leaders' trusted advisers in their capitals; the common feature was that foreign ministries were generally excluded. White House and NSC staff documents dealing with the sensitive diplomacy received the exuberant classification marking: TOP SECRET/SENSITIVE/EXCLUSIVELY EYES ONLY.

The opening to China, probably the most celebrated product of this process, was also an illustration of how various elements of Nixon's system worked. Nixon had published an article in *Foreign Affairs* in 1967 expressing interest in easing the hostility between the United States and China that was the legacy of the 1949 Communist takeover and the Korean War. On February 5, 1969, just over two weeks into the administration, one of the first of the new National Security Study Memorandums from the White House formally instructed the departments and agencies to study various issues with respect to "Communist China" including "alternative U.S. approaches on China and their costs and risks." This produced an interagency paper by May, which contained useful analyses of China's militant ideology, the Taiwan problem, U.S. trade and travel restrictions, U.N. membership, U.S. interests in Asia, and other issues. But from Nixon's and Kissinger's perspective these analyses, while useful as a catalogue, treated the various concerns "as if they existed in a vacuum." The Soviets and Chinese had just had a series of unprecedented military clashes along their border, and opportunities presented themselves for a more triangular American diplomacy. Nixon had already decided he wanted to signal to the Chinese that we were interested in a rapprochement and that we opposed Soviet aggression against them. The interagency process was proving decidedly unhelpful when it came to these basic questions of strategy. When Nixon's intentions in this direction became widely known—indeed, little of this was secret—delegations of senior State Department diplomats even came to the White House to counsel him against it, since it risked provoking the Soviet Union. They were not thinking the same way he was.

Thus the pattern emerged that Nixon and Kissinger looked to the bureaucracy for technical expertise, but not for strategy. On June 26, the NSC Under Secretaries Committee, chaired by Rogers's deputy Elliot Richardson, was directed to provide detailed recommendations on how the United States might modify the various legal restrictions then in effect on trade, travel, and other intercourse with China. The resulting paper was a useful, indeed indispensable, menu of all the steps one could take. But Nixon reserved for himself the decision on which ones to implement, at what pace, and in what context. Nixon was doing his own signaling to China—not only through some of these unilateral steps to liberalize exchanges, but also through public comments distancing ourselves from Soviet bullying of China, and private comments to heads of state known to have good ties with China's leadership.

Initial contacts with Beijing were made in regular diplomatic channels in 1969 and 1970 through American and Chinese ambassadors in Warsaw. But the State Department weighed the talks down with a detailed agenda of technical issues, and shared the results with at least ten foreign governments. "We'll kill this child before it is born," Nixon sighed. When the breakthrough came, it was through the sensitive Pakistani backchannel. From then on, the contacts were kept secret from the Department of State, and indeed from NSC staff members who had no need to know. Winston Lord, Kissinger's senior special assistant and colleague on the China initiative, tells of the contortions that he went through to maintain different sets of books. When Kissinger set out on an around-the-world trip in July 1971, only some members of his traveling party knew of the secret two-day detour from Pakistan into China. In fact there were three sets of briefing books:

One set for those who were going into China. . . . Another set were for those knowing that people were going into China, but were part of the cover team staying back in Pakistan. . . . And then the third briefing book was for those who didn't even know there was going to be a China leg. And I swear to God, we'd get them all updated and I'd put my head on a pillow, and Kissinger would then wake up and look at it and want it redone again, and I've got to do all three all over again.

There is a common perception that secrecy in the conduct of foreign policy is a conspiracy to conceal blunders and/or criminal behavior. On occasion, perhaps, but that is not the reason the framers of the Constitution were so forthright in recommending "secrecy and despatch" as qualities needed in the Executive Branch for the conduct of diplomacy. Most often, secrecy in negotiations is what enables compromises to be made. If one party's deliberations about possible concessions are leaked, that could doom its domestic support and undermine the whole enterprise; when negotiations are kept confidential until final results can be disclosed (and they certainly should be disclosed), the trade-off of mutual concessions is evident and domestic support more likely to be sustained.

In the China case more broadly, the reason for secrecy had to do with the desire to shield a delicate initiative from the many forces that had an interest in torpedoing it. When Nixon announced to the world on July 15, 1971, that Kissinger had just returned from China, a state that we had treated as hostile for over two decades, the effect was stunning. They had been deathly afraid of premature leaks, which could have been shaped, manipulated, or exploited by various parties that had maximum incentive to sabotage the policy—the Soviet Union, Taiwan, some of Taiwan's American supporters, et al. Controlling the China disclosure meant that Nixon's July 15 announcement could explicitly reassure friends and allies—especially Taiwan, Japan, and South Vietnam—that the United States would consult intensively before Nixon's own trip to China, which did not come until February of the following year. Premature disclosure by another party with a negative spin ("betrayal!") could have turned the July 1971 event into something wholly different from the positive event that the world now remembers. Instead of a dramatically successful initiative, the same Kissinger trip could have been turned into an even more dramatic fiasco. Control over disclosure can be a synonym for control of one's own policy.

Secrecy is not popular, especially among journalists whom it deprives of interesting stories to write. Even among historians, it is common to deplore the Nixon administration's allegedly "compulsive" devotion to secrecy, when it would be difficult to identify a president in this book who did not strive to keep important things secret and rail at leaks. Most of the substantive products of the Nixon administration's backchannel diplomacy, though, have been kindly treated. The American ambassador to Japan, Armin Meyer, who learned of the Kissinger trip only when he heard Nixon's announcement over Armed Forces Radio while sitting in a barber chair in Tokyo, conceded in his memoirs that his initial bitter embarrassment gradually gave way to acknowledgment that the Japanese government, leaky as a sieve, could not have been counted on to keep the initiative secret if it had been informed in advance. John Lewis Gaddis has acknowledged, "To have consulted the Departments of State and Defense, the C.I.A., the appropriate Congressional committees, and all allies whose interests would have been affected *prior* to Kissinger's 1971 Beijing trip would only have ensured that it not take place." Gaddis is similarly charitable toward the contribution of the backchannels during the SALT and Vietnam negotiations.

Perhaps the most massive and famous of all leaks of classified documents came on June 13, 1971, a Sunday morning that saw the opening installment of the *New York Times*'s publication of the Pentagon Papers—a documentary record of American involvement in Vietnam compiled in the Pentagon toward the end of the Johnson administration. Kissinger's deputy, Alexander Haig, briefed Nixon by telephone on what the published documents included, reassuring him that documents of the Nixon administration were better protected:

> H[AIG]: It's the most incredible thing. All of the White House papers; Rostow papers; communications with the ambassadors; JCS [Joint Chiefs of Staff] studies.
>
> P[RESIDENT]: We have been more careful, haven't we? We have kept a lot from State, I know, and enough from Defense.
>
> H: Your White House papers are in very good shape.
>
> P: That's why we don't tell them anything.

Nixon and Kissinger also had a conversation that afternoon, Kissinger calling in from California. Less than two weeks earlier, through the Pakistan channel, the Chinese had formally invited

Kissinger to visit Beijing in July to prepare the way for a trip by Nixon. Savoring this success made up at least in part for the shock of the Pentagon Papers, but it, too, emphasized for these men the necessity as they saw it to keep the rest of the government at arm's length. "Dulles always used to say that he had to operate alone because he couldn't trust his own bureaucracy," Kissinger said. "I just wish that we operated without the bureaucracy," Nixon responded. Kissinger laughed, and Nixon then realized the irony of what he had just said, adding: "We do." "All the good things that are being done," Kissinger said. "Yeah, we do, we do, we do," Nixon repeated.

Nixon's Trade-off

A treatment of the Nixon-Kissinger relationship published by historian Robert Dallek in 2007 makes much of the personalities—the backbiting, sniping, jealousies, insecurities, and tensions among Nixon, Kissinger, and Rogers. Personality disorder is, indeed, its explicit theme. Dallek makes use of the flood of now disclosed transcripts of meetings and telephone conversations that constitute the most intimate chronicle of an administration's inner thoughts that we will ever have. These are conversations (or at least parts of them) that could never have been meant for the historical record or public consumption. Previous administrations managed to keep such exchanges to themselves. It is unlikely that the Kennedy brothers, when they discussed their political opponents in the Oval Office, were reading responsively from the Sermon on the Mount, nor Lyndon Johnson when he conferred with his staff while doing his business on the toilet. But they were wise enough to leave no records of this. By the same token, administrations after Nixon's have undoubtedly learned their lesson and severely cut back the kind of records they keep in the first place. Thus, a few historians' gain is many historians' loss.

The more important point, however, is that preoccupation with personal idiosyncrasies is misleading. Nixon and Kissinger (and Rogers and Laird) were grappling with more profound problems of policy than most administrations are faced with—not only to extricate the country from Vietnam in honorable fashion, but to put in place the main elements of a post-Vietnam foreign policy (U.S.-Soviet relations, China, Middle East peace process) while doing so. Dallek's book has relatively little analysis to offer on the substance of these foreign policy challenges, and much of what it does say is a rather conventional critique from the liberal point of view. The reader is left to conclude that departures from conventional liberal ideas are to be associated with personality disorder.

A richer and more illuminating account is to be found, perhaps surprisingly, in the State Department archivists' product, *Foreign Relations of the United States.* Like an epistolary novel, the documents tell a story that unfolds over the first two years of the administration. The Kissinger memoranda on the creation of the new NSC system are all there. Internal papers of the State and Defense departments record their efforts to push back. The NSC staff periodically compiles memos and press clippings to document State's deviations from presidential policies. State Department officials complain that Kissinger and his staff are having their own meetings with foreign diplomats of which the department was not officially informed. Kissinger's appeals to Nixon, Haldeman, and Mitchell for support are recorded, including vivid excerpts from Haldeman's diaries. Nixon frequently expresses his affection for both Rogers and Kissinger, his frustration at the continual conflicts, and his conclusion that he has to back Kissinger on the substance.

What comes through in this dispassionate record is the tragic aspect. As the story unfolds, all the elements of the train wreck fall into place. The leaders at State are unable to grasp at first that they inhabit not just a new administration, but a new kind of administration. They are used to a world in which presidents set broad lines of policy and leave it to the State Department to implement—indeed, presidents usually ratify broad policies that the professionals originate as well as carry out. Lyndon Johnson's decisions on the Vietnam War were usually the product of a regular bureaucratic deliberation. Even John Kennedy's high-powered NSC staff consisted of only a dozen people, who saw their job as prodding the bureaucracy, not substituting for it. But Richard Nixon was a president who came into the Oval Office after an unprecedented personal immersion in foreign affairs and who wanted not only to initiate broad policy but to control its execution in order to insure it was consistent with what he wanted.

The May 20, 1971, breakthrough on SALT was a watershed bureaucratically as well as in arms control. Until then, the NSC system for interagency deliberation had been working more or less as Nixon intended. It elicited the best information and ideas available in the U.S. government, and empowered Nixon and Kissinger to set the strategy. The secret backchannels gave the White House the option of involving itself directly at key moments in key negotiations. They had the best of both worlds.

But in mid-1971, as the extent of Kissinger's backchannel diplomacy began to be revealed—SALT, Berlin, China, and Vietnam—the documents show the bureaucratic game beginning to change. Instead of constant White House complaints about, or efforts to prevent, State Department actions at variance with the president's wishes, it was increasingly clear that the White House was taking the policy initiative into its own hands. Foreign governments figured out that if there was any inconsistency between what they heard from the White House and from State, the White House view counted. Internal documents show the State Department struggling more and more to keep up with what the president, Kissinger, or the NSC staff were doing. When a Kissinger background briefing to the press made news, Rogers would sometimes complain bitterly to Kissinger and/or to Haldeman if he thought it inconsistent with the policy he was pursuing. When Nixon met with foreign leaders, Kissinger was usually the only other person present (perhaps besides an interpreter). Records of the president's meetings were often not sent to State, or only after a delay. Thanks to creative photocopying, the transcripts we sent to State often omitted sensitive passages—for example, early exchanges with the Soviets about a possible summit meeting.

As the years went by, State's initial incomprehension eventually gave way to a twofold reaction. For Rogers personally, the reaction was one of wounded acquiescence. When the president informed Rogers of the May 20, 1971, accord on SALT, Haldeman had to go over to the State Department afterward to soothe Rogers's hurt feelings. Rogers was clearly upset—not at all by the substance of the accord but by the personal embarrassment: Haldeman recorded that Rogers was afraid of being embarrassed that it would be known that he was not involved. "[I]t was clear," Haldeman concluded, that Rogers "was very worried about the short-term impact on his own image and hadn't yet figured out the long-term implications." Much later, in January 1973, Winston Lord and I were invited by Rogers to accompany him to Paris for the official public signing—by foreign ministers—of the Vietnam agreement that Kissinger had secretly negotiated (and in which Winston and I had participated). Rogers played his ceremonial role with dignity, with consummate courtesy to the two of us, and with no outward sign of the humiliation that this Paris trip embodied.

But for the rest of the bureaucracy, some significant battles continued, especially over SALT, where the complex negotiations still depended on interagency collaboration. Kissinger and his staff continued to try to use the NSC system to elicit information, analysis, and options from the bureaucracy, as the system was designed for; they would then frame the choices for Nixon. But as the departments came to realize the pivotal role of the Kissinger backchannel, the result was not resignation but an ingenious form of revenge. Especially as Nixon's second term began, and the political climate shifted to the right, the departments discovered that they could take hard-line positions without bearing responsibility for achieving them in a negotiation with the Soviets—since that was on Kissinger's shoulders. The bureaucracy suddenly shifted to Nixon's right, when it had been on Nixon's left in his whole first term, and this fed into the national debate on foreign policy, which was itself drifting to the right once U.S. troops were out of Vietnam.

As for Rogers, his personal saga played out into the summer of 1973. Nixon finally sent Haig to tell Rogers in August that the president wished his resignation. Rogers calmly replied to Haig that if the president wanted this, he would have to ask for it himself—which, of course, Nixon was loath to do. Eventually Nixon screwed up the courage to invite Rogers in for the painful conversation. Kissinger recounts: "To everyone's surprise and Nixon's immediate intense relief, Rogers made it easy for his old friend. Without letting Nixon speak he submitted a letter of resignation free of recrimination or argument. It was a classy performance."

Nixon recounts in his memoirs that he had chosen Rogers to be secretary of state because Rogers was "a strong administrator," who "would have the formidable job of managing the recalcitrant bureaucracy of the State Department." If that is what Nixon expected, he miscalculated. The record shows many expressions of Nixon's regard for Rogers; Rogers as attorney general in the Eisenhower administration had stood by Nixon loyally and advised him astutely during the various attempts to drive him from the ticket over allegations of wrongdoing. (And Rogers, a pillar of the legal profession, seems to have been a strong attorney general.) But Nixon, as we have seen, did not want a secretary of state who actually made foreign policy. That was the trade-off: Rogers's mission was to keep the Foreign Service in line and loyally carry out the president's policy—to be "a staff man to the President on foreign policy, not the competitor," as Haldeman once put it in a conversation with Nixon.

The root of the problem is that it was difficult for Rogers to be a "strong" secretary of state when he had no background in foreign policy. This handicap made it harder to impose the president's will on a formidable career service. There is an American tradition of appointing a prominent lawyer as secretary of state. In the early years of the twentieth century, when much of America's international involvement had to do with international law, this was a natural thing. Dean Acheson and John Foster Dulles, two of the strongest secretaries in the post–World War II period, came out of that tradition, but they also had had extensive foreign policy experience before they took command of the State Department. Since 1945, given the scale and scope of our strategic challenges, policy inexperience is a weakness in any cabinet officer whose job is to impose political direction on the bureaucracy. A weak secretary of state is not a competitor of the president, certainly, but by the same token his command over the department is likely to be weak—compounding, not solving, the president's problem of managing the bureaucracy. Nixon's trade-off backfired.

Two of the presidents treated in this book who most effectively performed as "their own secretaries of state"—Nixon and George H. W. Bush—had both been, perhaps not by coincidence, immersed in foreign policy for eight years as vice president and in Bush's case had had other high-level diplomatic and policy experience. Bush picked a strong and loyal individual, James A. Baker III, who while not a foreign policy expert had been a strong treasury secretary (which involves a significant international role) and who, most important, consciously and effectively ran the State Department as an instrument of presidential policy. (See Chapter 7.) Nixon made a poorer choice, soon concluded that the State Department was not responding to his policy direction, and developed an alternative machinery to bypass it.

Naming a strong individual as secretary of state requires a considerable self-confidence on the part of a president. This self-confidence can take two forms. One is a willingness to defer and delegate to the secretary, comfortable in the belief that his or her actions will reflect loyalty to the president and the president's broad wishes. This is the model of Truman and Acheson, Ford and Kissinger. The risk involved in the future is that a president who is not a master in foreign affairs may have a difficult time keeping an energetic secretary under control. The second model is that of presidents who are confident of their own mastery of foreign policy and also confident of their ability to give direction to a strong secretary whom they trust to know what kind of foreign policy they want. This is the model of Eisenhower and Dulles, Bush 41 and James Baker. Nixon's relationship with Kissinger as his secretary of state is another example of this, though it was heavily affected by the complexes of Nixon's first term and by the unprecedented upheaval of Watergate. Nevertheless, the converse—avoiding a strong personality out of fear of being overshadowed, or of having a competitor—is usually a bad choice for a president, compounding the president's problem of bureaucratic control.

Melvin Laird's Pentagon

Melvin Laird of Wisconsin, a distinguished conservative and Republican leader in Congress, was not only an experienced defense expert but a master politician. Back in 1967, planning his run for the White House, Nixon mentioned to former President Eisenhower that he was considering Laird for a role in his campaign. Eisenhower was hesitant; Laird was "the smartest of the lot, but he is too devious." When Nixon, as president-elect, told Eisenhower he had picked Laird as his secretary of defense, the old man repeated his doubts. Nixon reports that Laird then paid a call on Eisenhower, after which Eisenhower "told me he thought I had made a good choice. Flashing his famous grin, he said, 'Of course Laird is devious, but for anyone who has to run the Pentagon and get along with Congress, that is a valuable asset.'" This talent of Laird's would also enable him frequently to outmaneuver Kissinger, the NSC staff, and Nixon's desire to gain some control over defense policy.

Defense policy is a different animal from foreign policy. There is no way for a president to bypass the Department of Defense on military operations, or to set up an alternative mechanism for determining defense budgets and programs. Thus Laird, unlike Rogers, held a lot of the cards. He also remained influential in Congress through his friendship with key committee chairmen. Kissinger says of Laird:

> There was about him a buoyancy and a rascally good humor that made working with him as satisfying as it could on occasion be maddening. . . . Laird accepted bureaucratic setbacks without rancor. But . . . I eventually learned that it was safest to begin a battle with Laird by closing off insofar as possible all his bureaucratic or Congressional

escape routes, provided I could figure them out, which was not always easy. . . . But even with such tactics I lost as often as I won.

Laird, like Rogers, had his initial concerns about the new NSC system that the president-elect and Kissinger were designing during the transition at the Pierre Hotel. But when Kissinger met with Laird over dinner at a hotel in Washington, Laird withdrew his formal objections on the basis of some understandings that he and Kissinger reached relatively easily. One sensitive issue, however, only lightly touched upon in this initial exchange, had to do with the president's direct contacts with the Joint Chiefs of Staff, bypassing the secretary of defense. This was the subject of a written exchange between Kissinger and Laird shortly after inauguration. Kissinger did his best to assure Laird that the secretary of defense would be the addressee of "all official National Security Council communications," but that this routing was "not intended to affect the direct access between the President (and the NSC) and the Joint Chiefs of Staff, nor their statutory role as the principal military advisers to the President and the NSC." This issue remains a delicate one. No commander in chief can relinquish his right of direct communication with his military subordinates, yet if it is done in a way that weakens the standing of the secretary of defense it can do harm to another important principle, that of civilian control of the defense establishment. Empowering rather than weakening the secretary of defense is a key to that principle. Nixon, as we shall see, was to exercise this prerogative in ways that complicated his relations not only with Laird but, ironically, with the military.

The new NSC system included a subcommittee meant to provide interagency (and especially White House) supervision of defense programs and budgets. But Laird successfully fended off the intrusion. In the fall of 1969, the president approved creation of a Defense Program Review Committee (DPRC), intended to review, as he reported to Congress, "the major defense policy and program issues which have strategic, political, diplomatic, and economic implications in relation to overall national priorities." Nixon wanted to be able to review these issues while the defense budget was still in its formative stages, and to have interagency advice on the strategic context (actual and potential threats; criteria for determining requirements; etc.) and on the trade-offs with domestic priorities. He signed a directive in this vein in April 1970 after Laird had dragged his feet for several months in submitting the Pentagon's budget and program plans to interagency scrutiny. Compliance with this directive remained grudging, fitful, and partial.

Withdrawing U.S. troops from Vietnam was the subject of another continuing tug-of-war between the president and his secretary of defense. Nixon's announced strategy in Vietnam had two components: first, Vietnamization, that is, training and equipping the South Vietnamese army so that it could take over combat responsibility from U.S. troops, and second, the negotiating track, that is, the effort to induce North Vietnam to accept a compromise settlement. Nixon all along hoped to be able to remove all U.S. troops by the end of his term—not coincidentally, around the time he would be up for reelection. But his strategy for withdrawing was, as we would say now, conditions-based. He was determined to control the timing and pace of the withdrawals, and the size of withdrawal increments, in accordance with his overall strategy, which included persuading the North Vietnamese of our staying power and maintaining flexibility to use the remaining U.S. troops for significant military operations as long as possible. He also wanted to keep his cards close to his vest, so that the impact of his announcements would not be frittered away by leaks. For example, after a number of short-term, small-increment withdrawals in 1969, to reassure the public that we were on a gradual but clear path to leave, in early 1970 he faced the problem of withdrawals potentially cutting into real fighting strength in Vietnam. (The North Vietnamese, meanwhile, were stepping up their military actions in neighboring Laos and Cambodia.) Kissinger came up with the idea, announced by Nixon on April 20, 1970, of a much larger withdrawal of 150,000 troops, to be spread out over a year. But this was to be back-loaded—keeping the bulk of the designated troops in place for most of 1970. The announcement bought more time with the American public but also preserved strategic flexibility.

Laird was responding to other imperatives, however. As a politician he was sensitive to public and congressional pressures to keep pulling troops out. The uniformed military, as an institution, was happy to be on its way out of Vietnam as well. Nixon's concerns about Hanoi's perceptions or about the blow to U.S. credibility from too fast a withdrawal were matters of broad strategy with which Laird was personally less concerned.* Laird's office was not above leaking its own, more rapid,

---

*A similar phenomenon was to be seen a generation later under George W. Bush with respect to troop withdrawals from Iraq. See Chapter 9.

withdrawal plans to the press, to force Nixon's hand or make clear that delays in getting out were Nixon's fault, not Laird's. This was the classic syndrome of a cabinet secretary insuring that the president, not he, would bear the onus of controversial decisions.

A week before the April 20, 1970, announcement, therefore, Nixon convened a meeting of his NSC principals on the subject but withheld from them that he had already decided on the 150,000/one-year plan. Instead, he solicited recommendations while pretending to be thinking of another small increment as before. While our men on the ground in Saigon, Ambassador Ellsworth Bunker and General Creighton Abrams, were aware of Nixon's thinking and supported it, Rogers and Laird were informed only a few hours before Nixon's speech. Kissinger recounts:

> The maneuvers of Nixon and Laird to steal the credit for each announced troop withdrawal from Vietnam were conducted with all the artistry of a Kabuki play, with an admixture of Florentine court politics of the fifteenth century. . . . But it was a game that Nixon, being less playful, more deadly, and holding the trump cards of the Presidency, rarely lost.

More dramatic clashes with his cabinet secretaries came when Nixon ordered controversial military operations in Indochina, overruling their dissents. The first was the U.S. and South Vietnamese attack on North Vietnamese sanctuaries in Cambodia in the spring of 1970, opposed by both Rogers and Laird; the second was the U.S.-supported South Vietnamese strike against a key node of the Ho Chi Minh Trail in Laos in early 1971, opposed particularly by Rogers. Nixon considered both these operations strategically necessary if the gradual, controlled U.S. disengagement from Vietnam was not to turn into a rout. As we saw, he was husbanding the remaining U.S. troops in order to be able actually to inflict blows on the enemy. In the heated environment of the time, this was a controversial idea.

In March–April 1970, action was forced on Nixon by a North Vietnamese offensive that threatened to overthrow the Cambodian government, which would have expanded the North Vietnamese sanctuary in Cambodia from small base camps along the border to the entire extent of the country. Nixon did not see how the U.S. strategy in Vietnam could survive this. Rogers argued that events in Cambodia were not a serious threat and that little would be gained by a military operation;

Laird supported shallow cross-border operations by the South Vietnamese but his political antennae told him that a major involvement of
U.S. troops would provoke a domestic reaction. Even Kissinger had had
initial doubts about a U.S. ground operation. Laird also claimed that
General Abrams did not support the bigger plan—which Nixon and
Kissinger, having contacted Abrams directly, knew not to be the case. In
the end, Rogers and Laird were not wrong about the domestic controversy, but Nixon—like FDR and the North African campaign—had a
more strategic view and made his lonely (and courageous) decision. The
combination of the Tet Offensive, and the enemy's loss of Cambodia as
a logistics base, virtually ended the war in the southern (and most popu-
lous) part of South Vietnam.

The bitterness of the dissension surrounding the Cambodian operation took its toll on Nixon, however. Press leaks from both departments
distanced their secretaries from the decision amidst the firestorm of
domestic protest, ignited not only by the military escalation but by the
killing of four students by National Guardsmen at a demonstration at
Kent State University a few days later. This painful experience shaped
Nixon's deliberation the following year when General Abrams sent in a
recommendation for a strike against the Ho Chi Minh Trail. Kissinger
recounts:

> Nixon was determined not to stand naked in front of his critics as he
> had the year before over Cambodia. This time he would involve his
> key Cabinet officers in every facet of the decision-making, to force
> them to take some of the heat of the inevitable public criticism.

The decision-making process for the Laos operation proved somewhat less convoluted (though Rogers dissented forcefully). Unfortunately, the South Vietnamese, who in this case did all the ground
fighting, were pushed back by the North Vietnamese and this operation
proved controversial because it failed.

ONE LAST, but not least, dimension of Nixon's relationship with his
Defense Department deserves mention here. One possible reason for the
"buoyancy" that Kissinger observed in Mel Laird is that, it turns out, the
Defense Department was much better informed than the State Department as to what Nixon and Kissinger were up to. The Pentagon had a
three-tiered spying operation going on, targeted on Kissinger's office.

The first tier was Laird's use of the National Security Agency (NSA) and the Defense Intelligence Agency (DIA) to monitor White House backchannel activities. Laird later regaled journalist Seymour Hersh with how one of his first moves as secretary of defense was to call in the two men he had chosen to head these two DoD-run agencies: "I brought them into my office and told them they'd better be loyal to me," Laird says. "If they were, they'd get four stars after four years. . . . And goddamn it," Laird add[ed] with a laugh, "they were loyal." (And sure enough, they both received their fourth stars in September 1972, a few months before Laird left office.) Hersh asserts that Laird thus received "a steady stream of information" on Kissinger's contacts with the Soviets, Chinese, and North Vietnamese. The NSA intercepted backchannel messages; the U.S. Army Signal Corps tracked White House telephone conversations; the Special Air Missions branch of the U.S. Air Force ran the fleet of aircraft that Kissinger used. (Laird reportedly had advance knowledge of Kissinger's secret trip to Beijing by these means.)

The second tier was the famous Yeoman Charles Radford, the young Navy man assigned to the small military office in the NSC staff whose job was to serve as liaison to Chairman of the Joint Chiefs of Staff Admiral Thomas Moorer. It seems the office was not simply a transmission belt for authorized communication but had a more entrepreneurial assignment—that of stealing whatever information it could about Nixon's and Kissinger's activities. During his fifteen months on the job before being caught, Radford told Hersh, he managed to purloin some five thousand documents, through making photocopies or stealing discarded carbons or from notes he took. The liaison office was located across the street in the Executive Office Building, not in the West Wing of the White House. But Radford, an expert stenographer, ingratiated himself with Haig and accompanied Haig on three sensitive missions on which Nixon sent him to talk to leaders in Southeast Asia, such as South Vietnamese president Nguyen Van Thieu. Radford stole documents from burn bags of discarded classified material or on occasion directly from Haig's briefcase, including EYES ONLY reports that Haig sent to the president and Kissinger.

Radford hit the jackpot when he was assigned to accompany the Kissinger party on the round-the-world trip in July 1971 that included the secret detour to China. Not meant to be witting of the China stop— he was in Category 3 of Winston Lord's three categories of briefing books—he found out nonetheless, rummaging through papers in Kissinger's room in Pakistan before the China visit. On the flight home, he delved into Kissinger's document briefcases and took notes on Kissinger's private message to Nixon on his talks with Chinese premier Zhou Enlai.

When the White House uncovered this caper in December 1971, Kissinger and Haig wanted Moorer fired. Nixon demurred, considering Moorer loyal and useful in other respects, and not wanting another scandal damaging to the U.S. military. Radford was quietly reassigned to Salem, Oregon. Nothing leaked until early 1974. According to White House assistant John Ehrlichman, who first investigated the matter, Nixon was happy to leave Moorer in place, with the admiral knowing "we had the goods," and even to reappoint him to another term as chairman. "After this, the admiral was preshrunk," as Ehrlichman put it.

A third, and perhaps even more productive, part of the Pentagon's intelligence-gathering was Chief of Naval Operations Admiral Elmo Zumwalt's private window into Kissinger's front office. Zumwalt and Kissinger got along well, at first, after the brash and innovative admiral became CNO in June 1970. Kissinger trusted Zumwalt to the extent of using Navy communications for some of the early backchannels involving Pakistan and the Berlin negotiations. While Zumwalt maintained his outward cordiality, at some point he concluded that the secretive style of the Nixon-Kissinger White House was not to his liking and Kissinger's worldview was too Spenglerian for his taste. Meanwhile, Zumwalt persuaded Kissinger that he needed more Navy personnel on the NSC staff, and for the next few years Zumwalt sent over a succession of bright young officers for one-year stints as special assistants to Kissinger. Crammed though they were into a tiny closet-sized room between Kissinger's office and Haig's in the West Wing front office, they had an unequaled vantage point on everything going on—discussions of all the most sensitive diplomacy, helping prepare the most secret plans, listening in on Kissinger's telephone conversations with Nixon, Rogers, Dobrynin, and others.

Zumwalt disclosed with some satisfaction to JCS historians in 1990 that "assigning carefully chosen lieutenants to serve as Kissinger's aides" was one of the means by which he obtained information the White House was attempting to deny. "I had my own spies," he told another interviewer. In some cases their reporting was oral and informal. In other cases it may have been more systematic. Seymour Hersh's book on Kissinger quotes several passages from what he calls an "informal journal" kept by an unnamed close Kissinger aide and "carefully shared with at least one senior member of the government outside the White House." Its intimate revelations of goings-on in the front office are the kind of reporting that a young man sent over from the Zumwalt Employment Service would have been in a position to do.

The White House consciously shared much sensitive information with the chairman and the chiefs, to keep them informed of the president's thinking—often on condition that it not be shared with Laird. This caused frequent awkwardness inside the Pentagon when, for example, Laird's deputy David Packard peeked at Moorer's briefing book during an NSC meeting and saw a document with a White House letterhead that he and Laird had not received; the liaison office tried to solve this problem by henceforth snipping off the White House or NSC letterhead from sensitive documents before photocopying them. Zumwalt also met frequently himself with the admirals in charge of the JCS liaison office, as a way of keeping informed.

Zumwalt told the JCS historians he had concluded that the Nixon-Kissinger strategy was "to 'divide and conquer' the bureaucracy by selectively withholding information," and he saw it as his mission to overcome this. Thus was the Defense Department, too, in rebellion against Nixon's effort to centralize control over policy. Students of civil-military relations in a democracy may want to examine this further as an interesting case study. It is not clear whence derives the constitutional or statutory obligation of a president of the United States to share his most sensitive diplomatic strategies with his chief of naval operations—or even, truth be told, his secretary of defense. But it was an ironic result. The liaison office that employed Yeoman Radford had been envisioned by Nixon as a way to cultivate a special relationship with the Joint Chiefs. In Haig's recollection, Nixon wanted them to have direct knowledge of his views so that they would know "what he wanted them to do in a crisis and why he wanted them to do it." We saw above, with respect to Vietnam troop withdrawals and military operations, that direct communication with the commanders insured more accurate White House understanding of their thinking.

Whatever the root causes of this unhealthy situation, it illustrates for a president, among other things, the perils of weakening one's secretary of defense. The military is a career bureaucracy, unique in many ways, to be sure, but also meant to be subordinate to political authority; for this, the president requires a secretary who can be the instrument of this presidential authority. Laird's reluctance to step up to this role made its own contribution to all this—his inclination to be a spokesman for the military's cautious instincts over Vietnam rather than for the president's strategy. But the principle remains, and we can see the price that Nixon paid. There is an analogy with William Rogers: If a president lacks confidence in his cabinet officer, he should replace him, not bypass him. It is hard to imagine Donald Rumsfeld agreeing to serve under an "arrangement" such as that of Nixon and Laird. A president, in his own interest, should be looking for ways to strengthen his secretary of defense, not undercut him.

Nixon and Kissinger

There are many different accounts of the Nixon-Kissinger relationship, some even accurate. They include conflicting accounts of who deserves credit for the administration's achievements with China, the Soviet Union, and the Middle East. Especially while they were in office, there were both admirers and detractors of Kissinger who were convinced that he was exerting a Svengali-like influence over the California politician. Nixon loyalists like William Safire responded with a counterimage of Nixon as the "puppetmaster" manipulating his petulant and insecure "marionette" of a national security adviser. Given the hemorrhage of intimate records, as we have seen, others content themselves with simply portraying the relationship as a dysfunctional one.

What I saw close-up, as a member of Kissinger's staff, was something different. Nixon was not only thoroughly knowledgeable in world affairs; he had the deepest intuition and shrewdest strategic judgment of any modern president. This was coupled with raw personal and political courage. A quintessential loner, withdrawn and awkward—that is, not having by any means the gregarious personality that usually characterizes American politicians, and, on top of that, having seen his career ostensibly destroyed on multiple occasions—he persevered in spite of all in a lifetime career of politics whose indignities he must have hated every waking minute. Thrusting his way back after repeated humiliations, he reached the pinnacle. The life of Richard Nixon was an astonishing display of the sheer force of will.

By the same token, he was no natural executive. For all his strategic insight and conviction, he needed subordinates to shield him from distraction, sustain his morale, and implement his policy preferences (including filtering out the orders he really didn't intend to be carried out). "Nixon distrusted his own impulsiveness," Safire has noted, "and placed Haldeman between himself and the rest of the world as a safety catch on a trigger." Likewise he needed trusted subordinates to impose his policies on a recalcitrant government. He was impatient with detail and allergic to face-to-face disagreements of any kind. His loyalists, who often heard him expound brilliantly on world events, may not have been conscious of how great the distance is between exposition and execution. Therefore he needed not only a Haldeman but a Kissinger. Kissinger provided the specifics of both strategy and tactics. The scores of analytical memoranda that Kissinger provided for Nixon, especially before any important diplomatic mission by either of them, are a much better record of this than informal (and idiosyncratic) telephone conversations. Kissinger was also possessed of a remarkable (and probably unexpected) degree of bureaucratic tenacity. Without a partner with these qualities, Nixon, given his own qualities, would not have had the means to implement his visions.

But Kissinger was no natural executive either. While he had honed his competitive skills in the faculty wars of academia, he had never run or managed anything larger than a Harvard summer seminar for promising mid-career leaders from foreign countries. He had brilliance, intellectual self-confidence, and physical stamina—but in the early days he was socially shy. That is where the NSC staff and structure came in, including a capable deputy in Alexander Haig who smoothed over his rough edges in dealing with the bureaucracy. The new organizational structure did bring more of the reins of power into Kissinger's hands; the enlarged and capable staff gave him a sustained ability to monitor the rest of the government and ride herd on it—or to implement an alternative policy bypassing that government. And his celebrity—the product of a series of diplomatic achievements—as it came gradually, further strengthened his bureaucratic clout.

Thus I saw the Nixon-Kissinger relationship evolve, though not so much in their work method as in the personal intangibles. No simple description captures the relationship amid all the changes. In 1971–1972, after the revelations of Kissinger's role in significant secret diplomacy, the relationship became something very different from what it had been in 1969. Similarly, in 1973, when Nixon was weakened by Watergate and Kissinger's celebrity seemed more and more to come at his expense, it was far different from what it had been in 1971.

At the very beginning, Kissinger was no superstar. He had real reasons to feel insecure as an outsider among Nixon's close-knit political team—a longtime associate of Nixon's rival Nelson Rockefeller; a Republican who socialized with liberals; an intellectual in a crowd of loyalist political operatives. Safire observed that "[t]o the President, he was more deferential than any of us [were]; we excused this on the grounds that he was the newcomer to the group, had never called Nixon by his first name or been made to feel needed by a man struggling to come back." While much was made of the "coup d'état" of the abolition of the SIG, the Kissinger-chaired NSC Review Group that replaced it was composed of deputy and under secretaries and hardly gave him dominance over their superiors, the cabinet officers. His continual complaints to Nixon, Haldeman, and Mitchell about State Department deviations from policy are further evidence of his lack of decisive leverage without their consistent backup. While Kissinger appeared on the cover of *Time* magazine a few weeks after taking office, he remained known mainly to foreign policy specialists and Washington insiders: He spoke to the media exclusively on an anonymous "background" basis—Nixon had given strict orders to that effect—and he did not appear on television until a CBS 60 *Minutes* segment on him in late 1970. He gave no televised news conferences until mid-1972 (his fourth year in office), and delivered no on-the-record policy speeches until his fifth year (a speech on Europe in April 1973).

Before Kissinger went off on any sensitive diplomatic mission, as mentioned, he and his staff prepared a strategy paper and the two men spent hours deliberating on strategy and tactics. Nixon made his preferences clear, but he invariably sent Kissinger off with a broad mandate to use his judgment. There were two important episodes in which Kissinger did exercise his judgment, leading to some short-term, long-distance tensions between the two. In April 1972, before a pre-summit trip by Kissinger to Moscow, Nixon wanted him to stress Vietnam with Brezhnev and not give the Soviets "a goddamn thing—unless we get something on Vietnam." Kissinger, once in Moscow, made a strong pitch on Vietnam but then decided to tempt Brezhnev with a discussion of other issues that magnified the Soviet leader's stake in the forthcoming summit. SALT and the expansion of trade were two of the issues; a third was the fact that Willy Brandt's "Eastern Treaties" (renouncing

West German territorial claims on East Germany, Poland, and the USSR) were hanging by a thread in the Bundestag and Brezhnev wanted American help. Kissinger's approach paid off. A few weeks later, the North Vietnamese launched a major military offensive against the South and Nixon retaliated on May 8 with the biggest U.S. escalation of the war—resuming the bombing of North Vietnam—but Brezhnev's huge stake in the summit (scheduled for May 22) kept him from canceling it.* The successful summit—the first-ever visit by an American president to Moscow—neutralized the antiwar protest in the United States and essentially guaranteed both Nixon's Vietnam strategy for the rest of 1972 and his reelection.

In the fall of 1972, Kissinger's North Vietnamese interlocutor Le Duc Tho began making concessions in the secret Paris talks. Kissinger was convinced that Hanoi saw the impending U.S. election as a deadline, fearing that Nixon could prosecute the war without restraint after reelection. Kissinger in fact thought Hanoi was miscalculating—that pressures on Nixon to end the war would only grow in a second term—but he saw value in squeezing the North Vietnamese up against their self-imposed deadline. Nixon, for his part, was torn. He was by that stage certain to win and did not need a peace agreement for electoral reasons; indeed, he and his political advisers were nervous that a compromise settlement before the election would only alarm his conservative base.

On October 8, bearing out Kissinger's thesis, Le Duc Tho presented to Kissinger in Paris a compromise proposal that for the first time accepted Nixon's preferred framework for a settlement—a solution to the military issues (cease-fire, U.S. troop withdrawal, and return of prisoners), leaving the political conflict to be resolved by the South Vietnamese parties. Hanoi dropped its long-standing demand that the United States turn over the South Vietnamese government to the Communists. "[I]t is the same proposal made by President Nixon himself," Le Duc Tho declared. Kissinger spent four days working out a text that pinned the North Vietnamese down on the key details. Nixon, campaigning, was sent only brief reports of what was transpiring—"more tantalizing than enlightening," as he later put it.

Yet he always backed Kissinger up. In the Vietnam case, Nixon

---

*Brezhnev's canceling the summit would also have left the Americans in bed with the Chinese, whose summit with Nixon had occurred three months earlier. It was a vindication of "linkage," though not exactly as had been anticipated in 1969.

understood that he would have no support for keeping the war going once it was known the North Vietnamese had accepted his proposal for ending it. Whether with foreign leaders or with the bureaucracy, Kissinger's decisive asset was the president's authority—his credible claim to be speaking for the president and his ability to sustain that claim. On the strategies and philosophy of foreign policy the two were intellectual allies. Compare the case of Zbigniew Brzezinski, President Jimmy Carter's national security adviser, who had the same intellectual advantage over a weak State Department but under a schizophrenic president who had no consistent foreign policy philosophy and often split the difference between Cyrus Vance's liberalism and Brzezinski's harder line views. (See Chapter 5.) Moreover, Kissinger was fortunate enough to move to the State Department in 1973, which enabled him to rest on his own institutional base of power when that presidential authority was crumbling over Watergate.

Kissinger at the Department of State

When Kissinger became secretary of state in September 1973, he retained his post as national security adviser; he was not about to permit anyone else even to attempt to get between him and the president as he had done with Rogers. His new deputy in the White House, the trusted Air Force Lieutenant General Brent Scowcroft, managed the interagency process. When Haldeman and Ehrlichman were jettisoned in April as casualties of Watergate, Nixon pulled Kissinger's former deputy Alexander Haig out of the Army and made him White House chief of staff. Kissinger's home base was secure. Haig writes with some relief that Kissinger as secretary of state now outranked him again, "which restored not merely the appearance but also the reality of cordial relations between us."

Some observers have been tempted to speak of the Watergate period as a "Kissinger Presidency" or "Nixon-Kissinger Presidency," but this exaggerates a complicated situation. Kissinger himself acknowledges the unprecedented nature of his stewardship of foreign policy during a collapsing presidency; by accident of history he had achieved a degree of personal stature that enabled him to assert American authority internationally that could compensate in part for the loss of the president's. But the record will show that Nixon had not entirely lost his touch. During the October 1973 Arab-Israeli War, when difficulties mounted in resupplying Israel by indirect means (such as charter aircraft), it was

Nixon who straightforwardly ordered a U.S. military airlift; it was a characteristically bold Nixon decision. And, as we saw, two key moments when Nixon accepted Kissinger's exercise of diplomatic freedom of action occurred during 1972, when Nixon was at the height of his powers.

An event often cited as evidence of Kissinger's abnormal dominance is a meeting he chaired in the White House Situation Room in the late evening of October 24, 1973, toward the end of the Middle East war. Leonid Brezhnev had sent Nixon a message threatening Soviet military intervention to defend Egypt if Israel continued its military advances. The attendees at the meeting—Kissinger, Haig, Scowcroft, Defense Secretary James Schlesinger, Chairman Admiral Moorer, CIA director William Colby—agreed on an increase in the alert levels of U.S. forces worldwide as a deterrent signal to the Soviets, coupled with a stern reply to Brezhnev warning against intervention. It is commonly believed that they implemented these steps without waking the president, who had retired for the evening. This has been treated by many analysts as a virtual collapse of the presidency.

There is no doubt of Nixon's distress and distraction over Watergate during this period; his political career was entering its terminal phase. But the truth about the Situation Room meeting is less dramatic than it has been portrayed. For one thing, Nixon had emphasized to Haig, before he retired, that he wanted a strong response to the Soviets, including alert measures. (The Soviets had been telegraphing their intervention threat during the course of the day, including at the U.N.) In addition, the record suggests that Haig left the Situation Room gathering at various stages of the evening to get Nixon's blessing of what was being discussed.

HENRY KISSINGER was secretary of state for the last ten and a half months of the Nixon presidency, and then for another two and a half years under Gerald Ford. During the remainder of the Nixon period the relationship of the two men can be said to have normalized, in the sense that the bureaucratic contradictions and contortions of the previous period disappeared overnight and foreign policy was henceforth directed by a president via his secretary of state. Much of the personal awkwardness remained, however, compounded by the great transformation that was taking place: Kissinger now had an independent base and international stature; as he continued to achieve successes, it was

Nixon who began to cling to Kissinger's political authority as his own authority waned. Kissinger was awarded a Nobel Peace Prize in October 1973 for his Vietnam negotiation. Following the October Arab-Israeli War, his "shuttle diplomacy" produced landmark agreements between Israel and Egypt (in January 1974) and between Israel and Syria (May 1974), which began the modern Middle East peace process. Nixon could not wait to make his own triumphal tour of the Middle East, which he did in June as soon as the Syrian accord was finished. But the upshot was to convince his domestic opponents of Kissinger's indispensability, not his own.

Kissinger arrived at State with skepticism about the department's capacity to run foreign policy. When he wrote his memoirs after departing the office, his views had not entirely changed. The Department of State, he continued to believe, was not well suited to manage interagency affairs; that was best left to the White House national security adviser. The department's organization still inclined it to inertia, day-to-day responses to cables, and preoccupation with management of its cumbersome internal system of autonomous fiefdoms. Conceptual thinking, especially of a strategic or geopolitical variety, did not come easily to it.

The United States Foreign Service is a true elite—a tiny cadre of only around 6,500 men and women (as of 2008), selected through a process of rigorous examinations and trained to a high level of professional expertise. Overseas posts often involve working in difficult conditions— many more ambassadors have been killed in the line of duty in recent generations than generals and admirals. Yet they are perpetually underfunded by Congress and enjoy none of the popular adulation bestowed on the men and women of our armed forces. Like any other close-knit fraternity enduring hardships together, the Foreign Service has developed a strong esprit de corps only intensified by its shared sense of beleaguerment and underappreciation. This has contributed to the development of a strong institutional culture, which includes a set of institutional predispositions with respect to both the process of policy-making and its substance.

One of the hallmarks of the Department of State is its legendary internal "clearance" procedures. When Kissinger as secretary of state visited Brazil in 1976, the briefing memorandum produced for him had been "cleared" in twenty-five different offices. This is perhaps not surprising given the richness of our relations with Brazil and the necessary contribution of offices dealing with political, economic, security, technology, and nonproliferation affairs, et cetera. But such a process of "policy by committee" necessarily dulls sharp edges and sharp thoughts in its intellectual product. The instinct of many into whose hands the memo passes is to strike or soften any sentence that seems a bit provocative or strong. Multiply that by twenty-five (and undoubtedly that record has been broken since 1976).

But there are also institutional predispositions concerning the substance of foreign policy. The legendary Arabist bias of the Foreign Service had in fact begun to fade in Kissinger's time, as had the traditional WASP dominance of the department's ethnic composition. Kissinger was soon to take charge of Middle East policy in any case. But other regional bureaus still had their cultures and outlooks. The Europeanists, as we have seen, had a protective interest in arms control with the Soviet Union and a jaded view (if one may call it that) of China. Another example was Nathaniel Davis, head of the African affairs bureau, who resigned under Kissinger because of his objection to a covert action program against the Cuban-Soviet military intervention in Angola.

The department as a whole has an institutional bias in favor of negotiation, dialogue, and diplomatic "engagement"; that's what they do for a living. If a problem cannot be solved by these means, then the lead responsibility in the U.S. government is liable to migrate to some other agency (the Pentagon, or CIA) that disposes of cruder instruments of policy. Thus not only policy substance but bureaucratic turf is at stake. State, therefore, can rarely ever bring itself to admit that diplomacy is not working; in its mind, diplomacy is perpetually deserving of "one more chance." Sometimes this seems to degenerate into dialogue for its own sake, without regard to results or strategy or even the leverage that might make dialogue more fruitful.

State is also blessed with being the beat of an unusually knowledgeable corps of journalists. The title of "diplomatic correspondent" still carries the trench-coat aura of sophistication and marks one as part of an elite in the profession. State generally enjoys sympathetic treatment in the media for its endeavors, especially if it is seen to be struggling against more pugnacious elements in the government (in the White House or Pentagon). Leaks from State are thus a familiar and sometimes effective weapon in the bureaucratic wars.

What redeemed the institution in Kissinger's eyes when he arrived there, however, was not only the wealth of expertise within the Foreign Service but its responsiveness to strong and consistent political leadership. The Foreign Service's natural instinct is loyalty to the secretary. While under William Rogers this turned into hostility to the White House (and no little personal animosity toward Kissinger), once he arrived at State this turned in his favor. "In the hands of a determined Secretary," Kissinger wrote, "the Foreign Service can be a splendid instrument, staffed by knowledgeable, discreet, and energetic individuals." The department relished being at the center of the action for a change. While he brought a few of his NSC staff colleagues with him, by far most of his appointments to policy-making positions in the department, especially assistant secretaries, were of career people. In his frenetic diplomacy over the years of his tenure, most of the pivotal players on his team were foreign service officers. Having spent his whole life in foreign affairs, Kissinger was confident enough in his ability to provide firm intellectual direction.

A conservative critic, Ambassador Laurence Silberman, has written that while Kissinger was "astonishingly successful" at controlling the department, this did not constitute "presidential" control over foreign policy precisely because it depended so much on career officers instead of political appointees at policy-making levels. Silberman is probably right as a general matter that bringing in political appointees is a way to insure political direction. But Kissinger was an unusual case; he had the intellectual and physical energy—and closeness to the president—to accomplish the same result. When the transcripts of Kissinger's State Department senior staff meetings are published, they will vividly convey the flavor of his firm direction being given—often in his inimitably acerbic fashion—and reflecting what he knew to be his president's convictions.

In Chapter 7, we will see the contrast with another strong secretary of state, James A. Baker, who took over the department in January 1989 with an equal determination to insure its responsiveness to political direction. Baker's memoirs on this subject echo Kissinger's critique of its institutional biases and weaknesses, and with a strong emphasis on the need to insure loyalty to the president's agenda. Baker came in with a strong team of colleagues who formed an "inner circle" that members of the career service could not easily gain admission to, and resented. Kissinger, for all the coldness with which the Foreign Service greeted him when he arrived, seems to have been more confident in his own ability to use it, guide it, and lead it.

Nemesis

The foreign policy of Richard Nixon's administration comes closest of any modern presidency to what scholar Graham Allison calls the "rational actor" model of decision making. That is, much diplomatic history, and most laymen, are inclined to view governments as unitary actors and attribute to their decisions the kinds of motivations and logical reasoning that are conventionally attributed to individuals. Allison's contribution was to present other models, based on organizational behavior or bureaucratic politics, which portray governmental decisions as the result of many contending forces. The policy-making of the Nixon administration, however, could not have been more opposite to the "government by committee" that characterizes almost every other administration since Franklin Roosevelt. The main elements of the foreign policy of the Nixon administration were largely conceived, and sometimes executed, by a committee of two; hence the endless fascination with the intellectual and personal relationship of those two. Certainly there were bureaucratic forces at work, as we have seen in this chapter. But the White House product was a remarkably coherent and disciplined policy reflecting the consistent strategic purposes of the president and his top aide.*

The extraordinary centralization that Nixon achieved in foreign policy was paralleled by a strenuous effort to centralize domestic policy-making. The significance of this for our purposes lies in the equally strenuous reaction that it caused. There is an intriguing theory of the Watergate scandal, advanced by writer Nicholas von Hoffman, that the demise of Nixon was due to no less than the revolt of the bureaucracy whose power he had striven so assiduously to break in every sphere. We know that Nixon resigned because of accumulating public evidence that he was guilty of a felony, namely obstruction of justice. But von

---

*Nixon's status as an archetype of the "rational actor" should not be deemed contradicted by his advocacy of the "madman theory." Walking along a foggy beach once with Haldeman, Nixon explained that he wanted the North Vietnamese to think he was so obsessed about Communism that he couldn't be restrained and "might do *anything*" to stop the war—"and he has his hand on the nuclear button." Nixon indeed conveyed a formidable image—magnified, it must be said, by his opponents' passionate demonizing of him—and this added to his leverage with the North Vietnamese and others.

Hoffman asks a mischievous question: Since, in his view, *most* of our recent presidents have been rogues and miscreants, why was only Nixon brought down? His answer: Nixon's attempts at centralization had so alienated so many vested interests in the American system—the very "iron triangle" of bureaucracy, Congress, and interest groups that predecessors of his had railed against—that he brought about a coalescence of opponents that not only resisted his plans but seized on his Watergate misdeeds to do him in.

On the domestic policy front, von Hoffman borrows the thesis of Richard P. Nathan that Nixon planned a comprehensive, indeed revolutionary, restructuring of national institutions. Nixon proposed a "New Federalism," including revenue-sharing with the states, to weaken the grip of the federal bureaucracy. He expanded the Bureau of the Budget into the Office of Management and Budget to strengthen its management role. After his reelection in 1972, he accelerated the transfer of trusted White House aides into key sub-cabinet positions in the departments, and he proposed a system of "super-secretaries"—a tight group of four cabinet secretaries who would be given the additional titles of "counsellor to the president" and an oversight role over other cabinet departments. Nixon saw all this as a long-overdue reform to streamline the bloated national government and give expression to a conservative philosophy that now had a mandate from the people after a generation of Eastern establishment liberalism. Nathan, in contrast, calls it a plan for an "Administrative Presidency," a concentration of power that ran counter to the theory and practice of checks and balances that applied, in his view, not only to executive-legislative relations but to the structure of the Executive Branch itself.

Perhaps the most dramatic step was Nixon's demand, announced cold-bloodedly the day after his landslide reelection, for the resignations of every noncareer official in his administration, including all cabinet secretaries and the entire White House staff. He did this to emphasize his desire to start afresh and reassert control in a comprehensive manner now that he had such an overwhelming mandate. But what this accomplished, in von Hoffman's account, was that "many of these 2,000 plus people who should have been Nixon loyalists by all rights were driven to make common cause with the already alienated bureaucracy."

Von Hoffman does not claim that Nixon was really on the verge of such a coup against the Constitution as Nathan seems to believe; rather, the attempt was enough to alienate if not frighten large vested interests but without actually weakening their power. They resisted, then fought back. The "super-secretaries" (aka White House counselors) proved unworkable and were abandoned after five months, partly because of squabbling over turf. The CIA rejected White House efforts to suborn its cooperation in blocking the Watergate investigation on "national security" grounds. Most important, in von Hoffman's words, "[t]he bureaucracy was fighting back in the way it always does against insubordinate superiors. It was leaking." A flood of leaks poured from the government—sensitive details of the FBI's investigation of White House involvement in the Watergate burglary, humiliating leaks about Nixon family tax returns, investigations of close Nixon friends, inquiries into who paid for construction of Nixon's residences at San Clemente and Key Biscayne and into a tax deduction claimed by Nixon for donation of his pre-presidential papers to the National Archives, et cetera, et cetera. The drip-drip-drip of leaks ate away at Nixon's public standing whether real impropriety was discovered or not. And of course, when von Hoffman wrote, it was not even known that Bob Woodward and Carl Bernstein's "Deep Throat" was the associate director of the FBI—a career FBI official disgruntled that a politically malleable outsider had been named J. Edgar Hoover's successor rather than a more qualified career person (such as perhaps himself).

Readers today are in a better position to separate the reality of Watergate from the melodrama. Von Hoffman, as noted, does not believe Nixon was anywhere near a "coup" against the Constitution; on the contrary, he thinks Nixon was vastly overestimating his power when he undertook such a centralization of it. He never had a chance. Professor Neustadt agreed. By the same token, the uproar over Watergate (and Vietnam) spawned a generation of institutional changes that weakened the presidency and strengthened the checks on it. Since then we have lived in an age of legally protected whistle-blowers, a vast expansion of what some would call congressional micromanagement of policy in every field, a web of legislative restrictions on presidential discretion, a strengthened Freedom of Information Act, war powers legislation, and the virtual institutionalization of leaking, including of classified documents. This is Richard Nixon's ironic legacy.

We can be thankful that such violations of legality as were committed in the Nixon era (many of which had precedents in prior administrations) are no longer with us. But what about his efforts to assert presidential control over the execution of *policy*? "The executive power shall be vested in a President of the United States of America," says Article II of the Constitution. There is no reference in the document to disgruntled assistant secretaries and their constitutional right to undermine presidential decisions they disagree with. There are scholars who argue that the bureaucracy *should* be independent of presidential control—that in its own way it is a representative institution, given its links with Congress and interest groups, and therefore it ought to be treated as a fourth branch of government. This theory of the "representative bureaucracy" raises serious problems of its own, however. The rest of us may prefer to let regular elections continue to determine what is representative of public preferences at any given period. The vast expansion of bureaucracy in the twentieth century continues to pose a challenge to the constitutional and democratic mandates of both Congress and the president as they try to impose direction on the bureaucracy in accordance with *their* representative duties.

Nixon's determined attempt to centralize direction over policy seems to have broken a host of unwritten rules, even if the fears of constitutional transgression were overwrought. In our democratic culture some principle of collegiality and participation—some notion of procedural regularity—seems to be a source of legitimacy, in the sense of acceptance by those who are overruled. Nixon, even in exercising authority that no one disputes he had, committed an offense against this concept of legitimacy. The institutions of our government have their weapons, both offensive and defensive, to wield against a president if they choose to go to war; if it comes to that, the media and the public will watch it and enjoy it as sport, and the outcome will usually be decided by the court of public opinion as politicians fight it out. But the rest of us—and future presidents—will want to know what lessons should be drawn.

Legitimacy, we will inevitably find, cuts both ways. A president who asserts authority in ways that seem high-handed or arbitrary—and ends up alone, without allies—will usually pay the political price. Nixon is the object lesson, and it is a lesson of prudence at the very least. At the same time, any president elected by the people with a mandate for change will have no choice but to persist in the struggle that Nixon—and other presidents of both parties—have waged to give effect in our government to the popular will. Nixon's political fate, definitive as it may seem, did not by any means answer all the questions that his tumultuous presidency raised.

CHAPTER FOUR

Gerald Ford

THERE WAS AN UNUSUAL BUSTLE around the Oval Office early on a Sunday morning, November 2, 1975. President Gerald Ford was to fly that morning to Jacksonville, Florida, to meet with visiting Egyptian president Anwar Sadat, an important meeting with an important new partner of the United States. But first, Ford had to squeeze in the unpleasant task of firing his director of central intelligence and his secretary of defense.

CIA director William Colby had run afoul of the White House by delivering voluminous CIA documents, without White House clearance, to congressional committees investigating CIA misdeeds. With Defense Secretary James Schlesinger, the president felt there were clashes of personality as well as policy. Their replacement was meant to be part of a broader reshuffle of top administration personnel, but the newsmagazines had gotten wind of parts of the story and were planning to release the news Sunday night. Ford considered it the honorable course to inform the two men in person before it broke in the press. Hence the meetings early Sunday morning. Colby was scheduled first, at eight, Schlesinger at eight-thirty.

Ford's conversation with Colby was calm, brief, and "not unpleasant," Ford later recorded. He was even sympathetic to Colby, since he blamed the aggressiveness of the congressional investigations on ambitious members of Congress and their proliferating staffs. The meeting ended early, about 8:15. As Colby departed the West Wing through the basement lobby he ran into the arriving Schlesinger, who asked, "What the devil are you doing here at this hour?" Colby, having an inkling of what was in store for Schlesinger, said little and mumbled his goodbyes. In the Oval Office, young deputy chief of staff Dick Cheney was urging

Ford to go easy on Schlesinger. "[G]et that son-of-a-bitch in here so I can fire him," Ford snapped, in a display of anger uncharacteristic of him. The second conversation was much more difficult, as Schlesinger spent nearly an hour trying to talk Ford out of it.

Ford then flew off to Florida to meet with Sadat—the Arab-Israeli conflict presumably a welcome relief. He probably had no idea of the uproar that would follow when the story broke. Without knowing it, Ford had just been through one of the defining moments of his administration.

OFFICIALS WHO WORKED for both Richard Nixon and Gerald Ford are effusive about the differences between them—in personality and in the psychological environment they created at the highest levels of government. Ford was outgoing where Nixon was withdrawn, collegial where Nixon was solitary, trusting where Nixon was suspicious, at ease with himself where Nixon battled a lifetime of resentments and insecurities. "There is no guile, no convolution, no complexity in Gerald Ford," said Brent Scowcroft. "He was comfortable in who he was." Unlike Nixon, Ford had the natural gregariousness of a politician but—not having pursued the presidency as an obsession like so many of those who attain it—he was "immune to the modern politician's chameleon-like search for ever-new identities and to the emotional roller coaster this search exacts," Henry Kissinger observed. Kissinger recalls the revelation and relief of his first conversation with Ford after Ford assumed the office: For the first time in his five-year White House experience, he "left the presidential presence without afterthoughts, confident there was no more to the conversation than what I had heard." There was no hidden agenda, no complex presidential motivation to be divined. Ford had been clear, unafraid to say no, unconcerned about who should receive credit for an initiative. "With Ford, what one saw was what one got."

Historically, Ford casts a modest shadow by contrast with most of his larger-than-life predecessors—the Shakespearean flaws of Nixon, the volcanic presence of Johnson, the charisma and martyrdom of Kennedy, the world-historical figure that was Eisenhower even before he became president, and Franklin Roosevelt. Only Harry Truman was of human scale, and the resemblance is a true one: Like Truman, Ford was thrust by history into an unexpected role in the face of huge challenges (including the final stages of a war), stepped up to his responsibilities, and came to be better regarded by posterity than by contemporaries. In his brief term in office, Ford had important achievements in domestic policy (the beginning of regulatory reform) and in foreign policy (a major step toward Egyptian-Israeli peace; the Helsinki Final Act, which enshrined human rights as a component of relations with the Communist world; creation of what is now the G-7 or G-8 grouping of major powers; and first steps toward majority rule in Southern Africa).

Ford also presided over a cabinet of heavyweights. He was comfortable with the model of cabinet government in which the president trusts that his cabinet officers are loyal to his agenda, and delegates to them:

> What I wanted in my Cabinet were strong managers who would control the career bureaucrats and not become their captives; people who knew how to build support in the Congress and the media. I would leave the details of administration to them and concentrate on determining national priorities and directions myself.

He intended to "restore authority to my Cabinet" and give them "a lot more control," to "reverse the trend" of centralization in the White House staff and Executive Office of the President. Ford's cabinet included Kissinger at State, James Schlesinger at Defense, and William E. Simon at Treasury, whom he inherited from Nixon. At Justice—an institution much bloodied by Watergate—he appointed Edward H. Levi, University of Chicago president, renowned legal scholar, and pillar of integrity. Alan Greenspan was chairman of the Council of Economic Advisers, William T. Coleman became secretary of transportation, John T. Dunlop of Harvard secretary of labor, Carla Hills secretary of housing and urban development.

Ford's legislative experience served him well with respect to many issues of substance, particularly defense and the federal budget. He had served twelve years on the House appropriations subcommittee on the defense budget, and had also dealt with intelligence appropriations. "A President controls his Administration through the budget," he knew. Officials who were used to Nixon's cursory attention were surprised by Ford's mastery of detail. In 1976 he briefed the press himself on the budget. "God, but he is good at this," one bureaucrat marveled. Kissinger found that Ford was more interested than Nixon had been in the tactics and details of his negotiations, not only general objectives.

But the job of a legislator is not the same as the job of a president. Donald Rumsfeld, who had been a colleague and ally of Ford in Congress, commented:

> President Ford came into office with wonderful training and success that didn't suit him for an executive function. He started out functioning basically like a legislator. Every day he was president he got better at being an executive. Within a year he became an exceedingly good executive. He began to delegate effectively, to become more strategic, instead of being consumed with what was in his in-box.

A management style that has been labeled one of "extreme collegiality" was eventually to give way under the pressure of events. At first, Ford wanted no chief of staff, visualizing an office (like his own as House minority leader) in which several senior aides had direct access to the boss, like spokes of a wheel. There would be no gatekeeper, no Haldeman. The exigencies of office broke down this idyllic system within six months; the open door policy meant that up to eight or nine senior aides could walk into the Oval Office, "guarantee[ing] endless discussion and infrequent resolution," in James Cannon's words, and consuming precious presidential time. Ford came around to ask Rumsfeld, who had started out with the humble title of "staff coordinator," to pull the reins into his hands and take on the traditional role of chief of staff. Yet both Rumsfeld and his successor, Dick Cheney, have complained that Ford never gave them the full authority they needed to impose discipline in the White House. A former Nixon staffer commented enviously to Ford's press secretary, Ron Nessen: "With Nixon, you had to try to save him from his worst instincts. With Ford, you have to try to save him from his best instincts."

Ford and Kissinger

When Nixon chose Ford as his vice president in October 1973 to replace the disgraced Spiro Agnew, activating for the first time the procedures of the Twenty-fifth Amendment, he exulted to Kissinger that he had purchased a kind of impeachment insurance: The Congress would easily confirm Ford because they liked him but would never think of him as capable of being president. Kissinger was not so sure, and he may have been right: Ford's selection might only have increased the Democrats' incentive to remove Nixon because they were confident they could defeat Ford in 1976. In any event, Kissinger made it a personal priority to attend to the new vice president and ensure his familiarity with all the foreign policy issues confronting the country. At least once a week, Kissinger or his deputy Brent Scowcroft would walk across the street from the White House to the Executive Office Building and spend an hour or so briefing him thoroughly. Ford appreciated it and was confident he was being kept up to date.

"It would be hard for me to overstate the admiration and affection I had for Henry," Ford has written, and by all accounts he meant it. They had known each other for a decade or so, dating from the time that Professor Kissinger had invited the congressman to Harvard to speak to his graduate seminar on national security policy; the topic was congressional control of the defense budget. He made a good impression on the students and on the professor. They had also encountered each other frequently during Nixon's first term. Ford as vice president gave what has been called a "late-night, highball-lubricated *Air Force Two* interview" to journalist John Osborne at the end of March 1974. He confided to Osborne rather indiscreetly that if he were to become president, he would want Kissinger, a "superb Secretary of State," to stay on.

The frequent Oval Office meetings between the new president and his secretary of state were remarkable, as Kissinger has said, for their lack of psychological undercurrents, complexes, or hidden motivations. Brent Scowcroft took rough notes of these meetings, and when they are declassified they will show a relationship of complete openness and mutual confidence. Kissinger kept nothing back, briefing Ford fully on events and personalities and strategies he was proposing. Ford grasped it easily and expressed his own preferences forthrightly. Where foreign policy issues had domestic political repercussions—for example, in the debate over détente with the Soviet Union, or majority rule in Southern Africa—Ford conveyed his judgment of his political circumstances and their implications. Where there was a congressional dimension, Ford himself was the master and educated his subordinates in the ins and outs and personalities that he knew better than anyone. Rough as Scowcroft's notes were, these records will show a relationship of trust and a fullness of deliberation going to the heart of the most sensitive issues of the period.

This charmed relationship, however, came under pressure from two sources. First was the intensifying domestic debate over policy toward the Soviet Union, especially strategic arms control, a debate that divided Ford's cabinet and generated political pressures targeting Kissinger. The second source was Ford's White House staff, some of whom were convinced that Ford, to achieve full presidential stature, had to achieve a certain independence from his overpowering secretary of state.

This is not the place for a full discussion of the debate over détente with the Soviet Union or strategic arms control. The notable point is that where Nixon and Kissinger had been vilified by the left in Nixon's first term for being too anti-Communist and too hard-line toward the Soviet Union, in the second term the public mood shifted to a greater suspicion of the Soviet Union and both Nixon's and Ford's administrations—to their monumental surprise—came under fire from the opposite direction as too soft. And where Kissinger had often been the beneficiary of public attitudes that treated Nixon as the villain and him, by comparison, as the good guy, now, with Ford the unsullied new president and Kissinger having accumulated enemies and liabilities of his own, Kissinger became more often the principal target of the attacks from both left and right.

The record is clear that as Kissinger pursued the SALT negotiations with the Soviets, he was carrying out Ford's wishes. In the end, an agreement was prevented by deep divisions in the cabinet that reflected the deep divisions in the Republican Party that almost cost Ford the presidential nomination in 1976. When Kissinger visited Moscow in January 1976, Ford at the last minute denied him the instructions that might have made an agreement possible, out of fear that his administration would not survive the rupture that an agreement would cause. At the Republican National Convention in Kansas City in August, Kissinger was such a red flag to the conservatives that Ford's aides tried to keep him away from the convention and accepted a platform plank that came close to repudiating the Ford-Kissinger foreign policy. Meanwhile, I have been told by a Democratic friend that Jimmy Carter's campaign team feared more than almost anything that Ford would sign a SALT II accord with the Soviets in 1976 and therefore be perceived by the public as a much more substantial figure in his own right; it might have made the difference in what turned out to be an extremely close election.

The strategic nuclear problem faced by the United States in the 1970s can be summed up as follows, at the risk of great oversimplification: After the Cuban missile crisis of 1962, the United States halted its production of new intercontinental ballistic missiles (ICBMs), on the assumption that the strategic competition was essentially over. The Soviets, for their part, embarked on a major missile buildup that did not stop when they reached parity with the United States (about 1970); rather, they kept on building. Nixon's SALT I accord of 1972 was a five-year freeze on both sides' numbers, which admittedly locked in a Soviet advantage for five years but also halted the Soviet buildup while our next-generation ICBM, the MX, was to come into production at the end of the five-year period. Yet the American domestic debate in the mid-1970s was preoccupied by the seeming inequality of SALT I—blaming it on the arms control process instead of on the unilateral American decisions that had determined the American strategic program. This critique came not only from conservative Republicans but also from Democratic senator Henry Jackson of Washington state, who was himself running for president and making the critique of détente his main platform.

This campaign against SALT was fueled in large part by leaks to the media from inside the administration that depicted a president and secretary of state too eager to make concessions to the Soviets and too unwilling to demand more concessions from them. The public campaign in turn exerted its pressure on Defense Secretary Schlesinger, who became its champion inside the administration. The media perceived a titanic battle between Kissinger and Schlesinger, two brilliant policy intellectuals from Harvard (both *summas* from the Class of 1950). But Ford had a shrewder perception. When Kissinger at one point in 1975 tried to apologize to Ford for the amount of the president's time consumed by this feuding, Ford shot back: "Jim's fight is not with you but with me. He thinks I am stupid, and he believes you are running me, which he resents. This conflict will not end until I either fire Jim or make him believe *he* is running me." Within a few months, as Kissinger notes, Ford chose the first option.

Ford's reaction teaches an important lesson about bureaucratic infighting. Intramural sparring between cabinet departments is hardly new. In this case, the battle was waged by Defense Department leaks against the State Department; in other administrations, it can be the State Department sniping at Defense. The issue is not the direction, or even the substance, of the attack but how it is bound to be perceived by a president. The motive of such sniping is presumably to reduce political support for the opposing position and thereby influence the president's decisions. The problem is, first of all, that public sniping by one department against another is, on the face of it, a sign of disarray. This is a disservice to a president because it suggests he cannot settle an issue definitively or enforce discipline in his administration. Every White House I have known perceives this. Even more serious is the problem that Ford saw: If the president has already decided on a course, or is eager to continue moving in a certain direction, the attack on the adviser whose advice is prevailing can only be seen by the president as an attack on the decision he has made, as an attempt to undermine his chosen policy. A president is likely to resent this. Bureaucratic snipers should beware—not only that they may not hit their intended target, but that their shots may ricochet badly against themselves.

The second source of pressure against the Ford-Kissinger partnership came from members of Ford's White House staff. Most of this had little to do with the substance of policy; it reflected a desire that Ford demonstrate a certain independence from Kissinger to elevate his own stature. To be sure, there was a policy dimension as Ronald Reagan's attacks on the policy mounted during 1976, which only added to the political incentive to distance Ford from Kissinger. On March 1, 1976, for example, someone persuaded Ford to announce that he was not going to use the term "détente" anymore. The difficulty with this, as we have seen, is that the controversial policies that Kissinger was identified with were also Ford's policies. How to distance oneself from one's own policies is a complex task that Ford's eager staffers never figured out how to do.

The more generic quest for "independence" took the form of wanting Ford to be seen getting advice on foreign policy matters from a wider circle than just Kissinger and his deputy Scowcroft. Various memoirs attribute this idea to Donald Rumsfeld. Ron Nessen reports that some White House aides began telling journalists that Kissinger had too much influence and Ford needed to "assert himself as the manager of foreign policy in both image and reality." Rumsfeld also convened White House meetings at which Ford would be seen giving instructions to Kissinger for speeches he was to give at international conferences. Word was also put out that the frequency of Kissinger's meetings with the president was being reduced.

One episode concerned a speech that Ford delivered at Tulane University on April 23, 1975, a week before Saigon fell to the North Vietnamese army. A few days before flying to New Orleans, Ford had told his staff he wanted to send the students an upbeat message that the war that had so dominated their lives was now essentially over. "Why don't you just say that?" aide Robert Hartmann suggested. A line was put into the speech draft to that effect—but not included in drafts circulated to Kissinger or Scowcroft. Ford announced to the six thousand students in the Tulane field house that "Today, America can regain the sense of pride that existed before Vietnam. But it cannot be achieved by refighting a war that is finished as far as America is concerned." The field house exploded in cheers, and reporters on the aircraft home asked Ford whether Kissinger had been consulted about this language. Ford said, simply, no. White House staffers eagerly heralded this as another Ford "declaration of independence" from Kissinger policies. As a policy matter, it was not ideal for the president to make a dramatic pronouncement that could have the effect of speeding up the unraveling in South Vietnam (especially with a difficult evacuation under way). Kissinger treats it sarcastically in his memoirs as a "typical inside-the-Beltway bureaucratic victory," but does not claim it made a significant difference in Vietnam. Ford does not mention the episode in his memoirs.

As Robert Hartmann writes, "Most of the tales that were told about Kissinger losing favor with the President were more wishful than real." Ford in fact was regularly upset at these leaks. "Goddamn it, I don't want any more of this," he once insisted to his aides, pounding his desk for emphasis and threatening "dire consequences" for anyone leaking anti-Kissinger stories. Ford in his memoirs denounces as "misguided" and "nonsense" the leaks from White House staffers trying to build up his foreign policy credentials at Kissinger's expense, and as "totally inaccurate" the stories that he had overruled his secretary of state on several decisions. The fact was, as Ford says, "there never was a conflict of any significance between us." This was arguably even more true than had been the case under Nixon.

The Tulane speech, though, gives a clue to why the sniping from the White House staff was so persistent. There is a tantalizing episode in the memoir of press secretary Ron Nessen in which Ford declares once again how mad he is at the fighting on the staff. "But he didn't seem mad," Nessen says. "I sense that he was not unhappy at all about the stories describing Ford's control of foreign policy as getting stronger and Kissinger's role as getting weaker." We have already noted the president's abrupt "no" when asked by reporters on *Air Force One* whether

Kissinger had played a role in the Tulane speech. Ford clearly acquiesced in some of these staff-driven displays of "independence," but without intending them to have any substantive significance. That is a difficult line to walk. The problem was not that Kissinger was thin-skinned (which he was), but that the seeming derogation of his authority domestically was bound to erode his international authority to some degree, as well as whet appetites in Washington among those who did want to weaken his clout on substance. This was a problem for the president, not just for Kissinger, assuming (as I do) that their substantive views were close to identical.

The White House staffers failed to see that these gestures were more a reflection of weakness on Ford's part than of strength: Why should a president have to try so hard to assert his superiority over a subordinate? A strong president has no need to. And how can a president separate himself in this way from a subordinate whose views he shares? Recall the remarks of Alexander Hamilton that were quoted in Chapter 1, in his critique of John Adams's neglect of his cabinet secretaries. To paraphrase Hamilton: Since the president appointed these men, presumably he wants them around. And if not, why are they there?

A president who wishes to insure control over a strong cabinet officer should dispense with the feeble gestures of "independence" and insist, instead, on two things: a commonality of views and the subordinate's loyalty. The commonality of views can be had by the kind of intimate conversations that Ford, Kissinger, and Scowcroft had regularly in the Oval Office. The loyalty should be defined, in McGeorge Bundy's terms, as being "the president's man" in the bureaucracy, not the bureaucracy's representative in the cabinet—carrying out the policy the president wants and imposing the president's agenda on the department even if it does not comport with the institution's preferences. That is what insures presidential control over foreign policy.

Ford and Schlesinger

James R. Schlesinger is a brilliant intellectual and administrator, a pioneer in the field of defense economics, who had an extraordinary career serving in the Bureau of the Budget and as head of the Atomic Energy Commission (AEC), the CIA, and the departments of Defense and Energy. He came to President Nixon's attention for his effectiveness at the Budget Bureau and for his deft handling of a nuclear-testing contro-

versy while head of the AEC. Another matter he handled with sensitivity and acumen at the AEC was a secret project, ordered by Nixon, of
cooperation with France over its nuclear weapons program.

These skills notwithstanding, his tenure as Gerald Ford's secretary of
defense, inherited from Nixon, was doomed. Ford let it be known even
while he was vice president that if he should succeed to the highest
office, Schlesinger would not remain. In the indiscreet airborne interview with John Osborne in March 1974, Ford complained especially of
what he saw as Schlesinger's mishandling of relations with Congress. In
his memoirs Ford cites an example that same month (which undoubtedly prompted his comment to Osborne) in which Schlesinger intervened clumsily in a jurisdictional dispute between two powerful House
committee chairmen, magnifying a mini-crisis for the administration
that Ford himself had to repair with his former colleagues. Later, the
problem repeated itself in October 1975 when Schlesinger publicly
denounced House appropriations committee chairman George Mahon
for cutting the defense budget; Ford had enormous respect for Mahon
and, again, considered this a clumsy and counterproductive tactic. Ford
cites other examples, including pressing too hard against budget decisions after the president had made them. In a field—the defense
budget—in which Ford was a master, he found Schlesinger an undisci-
plined student.

In Ford's very first week in office, several major news organizations
carried dramatic stories to the effect that in Nixon's final days,
Schlesinger had instructed the Joint Chiefs of Staff to double-check
with him any orders from the White House to insure against any un-
toward use of the military by Nixon. The defense secretary was quoted
as concerned that a desperate Nixon or his aides might try something
(unspecified), and that some Air Force and Navy officers might have
formed an emotional attachment to Nixon because of his devotion to
U.S. POWs in Indochina. Some stories even said Schlesinger had slept
on a cot in his Pentagon office through the period. Ford was "furious" at
these reports, he recalls; they were an "inexcusable" affront not only to
Nixon but to the U.S. military. He complained to Schlesinger about the
stories but Schlesinger gave no inkling of where they might have come
from. Months later, Ford learned that Schlesinger himself had been the
source, at a lunch he had had with Pentagon reporters. (No such
instruction to the chiefs had in fact been issued, but the Schlesinger
luncheon with reporters was real enough.)

The policy feud with Kissinger has been discussed above—in particular, Ford's increasing irritation with it which focused on Schlesinger. In addition, Ford did not even think Schlesinger was sincere in his hawkish views in the SALT debates: "In reality, the reverse was true. His views often were much more dovish than mine."

Beyond the problems of substance, the president and his secretary of defense had a severe clash of personalities. Ford, the most easygoing of men, admits that Schlesinger's "aloof, frequently arrogant manner put me off. I could never be sure he was leveling with me." Robert Hartmann writes:

> [T]he main thing that Ford didn't like about Schlesinger was Schlesinger. Whenever they talked, even alone, Schlesinger gave him the impression of a bored intellectual saying, "I know you're pretty dumb, but I'll do my best to explain it simply." Ford didn't like the fact that a Cabinet officer couldn't remember to button his shirt collar and cinch up his tie when he came to see the President of the United States.

The problems accumulated. In October 1975, at an informal meeting of Ford's "kitchen cabinet" of friends and advisers, Bryce Harlow, the wise counselor to many Republican presidents, warned Ford that the reports of feuding in the administration had created an impression of "internal anarchy" at the highest levels. He urged: "Now, Mr. President, if you have to fire 'em all, you have got to put a stop to it." As we have seen, Ford had determined at a very early stage that he would replace Schlesinger; the only question was when. Perhaps the surprise is not that it happened but that it took fourteen months to happen. While he gradually made other changes in the Nixon cabinet he inherited, Ford was waiting for an opportunity to revamp his entire national security team.

The "Halloween Massacre"

For several days in the second half of October 1975, Ford was confined to his residence upstairs in the White House nursing a cold and sinus infection. During that period of what Hartmann calls "communing with himself," Ford decided the time was ripe to make a set of changes. On a Saturday morning, October 25, he called Kissinger and Rumsfeld into the Oval Office, sat them down in the sofas in front of the fireplace, and informed them of what he had decided to do: Not only was Schlesinger to be fired, but Colby was to be replaced as CIA director:

> The only way I could feel comfortable with my own team, I said, was to fire Schlesinger, ask Colby to submit his resignation, bring [George H. W.] Bush back to be director of the CIA, send Rumsfeld over to Defense, take away one of Kissinger's two hats and upgrade both Cheney and Scowcroft.

Kissinger and Rumsfeld were both caught by surprise. While Kissinger suspected that Rumsfeld had inspired the reshuffle in order to further his own ambitions, Ford has insisted convincingly that he came up with the idea himself, keeping both men in the dark. Rumsfeld indeed tried to talk him out of it (as did Kissinger). Kissinger was concerned that conservative critics would blame him for the loss of their hero Schlesinger, and that the reduction in his own status would impair his effectiveness.

In parallel with Kissinger and Rumsfeld, there were other acts to this drama. Ford and his vice president, Nelson Rockefeller, had their own conversation a few days later in which Ford suggested to Rockefeller that he (Ford) would be in a stronger position to head off a struggle with Reagan for the GOP nomination if Rockefeller were not on the ticket. Rockefeller, a former governor of New York (and longtime mentor of Kissinger), was a moderate Republican who was anathema to the conservatives. In a moment painful for both men, because Rockefeller had been a model of loyalty, Rockefeller withdrew his candidacy. Meanwhile, George H. W. Bush, then our envoy in Beijing, reluctantly accepted the CIA job as a matter of duty, believing it would end his political career—including giving up his chance to be Ford's running mate in 1976. (Some suspected Rumsfeld had engineered that, too.)

Whether in the best of circumstances Ford could have pulled off this complicated reshuffle, with the many interlocking controversies it contained, is a difficult question. In the event, it was blown sky-high by the press leak of the Kissinger-Schlesinger portions of the change a week after Ford's Oval Office conversation with Kissinger and Rumsfeld but before Schlesinger, Colby, et al. had been told. This forced Ford, gentleman that he was, to call Colby and Schlesinger into the Oval Office early on a Sunday morning to give them the hard news personally, as we have seen.

The leak led to a major uproar. As we discussed in the last chapter with respect to Richard Nixon's ferocious desire to control the disclosure of the opening to China, controlling the disclosure can be synonymous with determining the nature of the event. Never has the point been better proved than by the example of Ford's loss of that control in this case. Instead of a familiar kind of reshuffle to bring in fresh faces and complete the process of replacing Nixon holdovers, explained publicly in terms that the White House would have had time to think through and prepare, it came through as a hasty improvisation, abrupt and heavy-handed, to be explained by dark personal ambitions. The media dubbed it the "Halloween Massacre." The president, asked by reporters why he had done it, responded in vague terms about "wanting my own team"—undoubtedly trying to avoid saying demeaning things about Schlesinger or Colby in public. But pundits were thereby left free to speculate on the motives of the individuals involved, often inaccurately as well as contradictorily, agreeing mainly on the proposition that the whole affair showed Ford's incompetence. Even the sympathetic John Osborne wrote scathingly (and very wrongly) that the president's explanations "and the events they concern show Gerald Ford to be intensely egoistic behind that humble façade of his, capable of an inhuman cruelty stupidly evinced, and desperately anxious to establish and prove himself as a national leader in his own right."

The firing of James Schlesinger, in particular, had significant political consequences. Conservatives were in an uproar, believing, as Kissinger predicted, that he had engineered it; the controversy over SALT only intensified. Kissinger told Schlesinger in an awkward telephone conversation after the event: "I think you and I could have held this thing together . . . perhaps only you and I." Schlesinger agreed. Indeed, a year earlier, Kissinger and Schlesinger had agreed on a SALT proposal that led to a framework agreement between Ford and Leonid Brezhnev at a summit meeting in Vladivostok.

When Rumsfeld replaced Schlesinger at the Pentagon, the State-Defense deadlocks simply reappeared, with Rumsfeld apparently unable or unwilling to make similar compromises as Kissinger and Schlesinger might have done. Schlesinger, a technocrat, had been thrust into playing a political role he may never have intended; Rumsfeld, a political figure with a political future, was inevitably caught up in the battle within the GOP and sought to protect Ford (and himself) from the growing challenge from the right. But the firing of Schlesinger only inflamed the right and singed not only Kissinger, but Ford. The departure of Rockefeller from the ticket, meant to head off the challenge from Ronald Reagan, failed utterly to do so.

Nixon, as we saw, did not have the stomach to fire people, and in part for this reason allowed dysfunction to persist in his administration. Ford, ironically, seeking to be decisive and to put in a cabinet team that he thought would work smoothly—and having the grace to dismiss people in person—saw what he did with the best of intentions blow up in his face. A noble attempt at cabinet government went badly awry. The premature leak had a lot to do with it; the scheme, in the end, may just have been too ambitious, with too many moving parts and too many political pitfalls that were not foreseen.

Later events suggest, however, that the problem bedeviling the Ford administration was not just a matter of congenial personalities or lack thereof, but institutional problems reflecting presidential weakness. The SALT stalemate in the administration persisted because the widening gulf in the Republican Party was more than an unelected president, facing a formidable challenge for the nomination, could bridge. A different dimension of institutional weakness, that vis-à-vis Congress, was reflected in the parallel events that had led to the departure of CIA director Colby.

Congress and the Intelligence Investigations

William Colby, like James Schlesinger, had had a distinguished career that propelled him to the top of his profession. Colby's quiet dignity and gray demeanor belied his extraordinary courage as a young Office of Strategic Services officer parachuting into Nazi-occupied France and Norway, and his leadership of a tough counterintelligence campaign against the Viet Cong in South Vietnam. Nixon had named Colby, a CIA professional, to be the agency's next director in May 1973 when Schlesinger was shifted from CIA to Defense. The promotion was deserved; the timing proved disastrous for both Colby and his agency. Vietnam and Watergate having generated a climate of endless scandal and political warfare fueled by tendentious leaks, the intelligence community was to be the next target.

In May 1973—the same month that Nixon nominated Colby to be Schlesinger's successor—press stories about the involvement in Watergate of ex-CIA figure Howard Hunt led Schlesinger to ask agency employees to report to him fully "on any activities now going on, or that have gone on in the past, which might be construed to be outside the legislative charter of this Agency." One week later, a memorandum landed on his desk with the whimsical title, "Family Jewels," attached to a 693-page compendium of CIA activities dating back to 1959 that could arguably have conflicted with the agency's charter, the National Security Act of 1947. Schlesinger and Colby conferred and agreed that the agency's congressional oversight committees should be notified of the compiled record—along with a firm pledge never to repeat such violations—so that it would not derail Colby's confirmation hearing.

In the climate of the time, merely to compile such a record was to do the leakers' homework for them. By December 1974, a few months into Ford's presidency, journalist Seymour Hersh telephoned Colby excitedly and said he had "a story bigger than My Lai" (the Vietnam atrocity story for which Hersh had won a Pulitzer Prize); it had to do with illegal CIA activities in the United States. Colby immediately recognized what he calls "disjointed and distorted accounts of several items" in the "Family Jewels" collection, and did his best to counter the exaggerations and distortions in what Hersh was telling him. On December 22, *The New York Times* splashed Hersh's three-column story on its front page, the lead paragraph of which accused the CIA of a "massive illegal domestic spying intelligence operation during the Nixon Administration against the antiwar movement and other dissident groups in the United States." When the predictable uproar ensued, Colby called the president to promise him a truthful account and assure him that nothing illegal was occurring on his watch.

Shortly afterward, Colby received a phone call from his predecessor, Schlesinger, during whose tenure the "Family Jewels" had been compiled. The two agreed that the article as published was a "distorted concoction of partial truths"; they also sheepishly realized that while Colby had briefed the key committee chairmen about the "Family Jewels" when they had been compiled, neither President Nixon, nor Ford, nor Kissinger "had ever been apprised" of the project. In a phone conversation with Kissinger on December 23, Colby informed Kissinger blandly that "I bundled them together and briefed my two chairmen on it, and I let the skeletons sit quietly in the closet, hoping they would stay there."

The hyped story of "domestic spying" was in fact the climax of an autumn of intelligence leaks, including allegations about the Nixon administration's efforts to block leftist Salvador Allende from becoming president of Chile in 1970 and charges that it played a role in the military coup that brought Allende down in September 1973. Other charges in the press had to do with assassination plots by the U.S. government against foreign leaders. (Extraordinarily enough, Ford himself had inadvertently generated the latter excitement by hinting, at a supposedly off-the-record luncheon with *New York Times* editors, that the intelligence investigations triggered by Hersh could do harm by opening up even more sensitive historical subjects, such as assassinations.) As a result, both houses of the Democratic Congress set up special select committees to examine the charges—in the Senate, chaired by Frank Church of Idaho, in the House under Otis Pike of New York.

Ford, in the vain hope of heading off a demagogic stampede, had already set up his own bipartisan commission under Vice President Rockefeller to look into the charges and make recommendations. But Congress ignored it, and as the congressional investigations accelerated, Ford became more and more alarmed that "some members of Congress wanted to dismantle the CIA" or "eliminate covert operations altogether." He insisted, for his part, that any investigations "had to be conducted with both discretion and dispatch to avoid crippling a vital national institution." Therefore he wanted to determine the strategy by which his administration responded to the inquiries—in Kissinger's words, "to develop some criteria by which to define transgressions and confine investigations to those subjects" and to devise "some procedure to prevent future abuses while preserving essential intelligence activities." It is in fact the norm in such situations for the White House to take charge of how the Executive Branch responds to controversial congressional investigations, if only to determine whether and when to invoke executive privilege. That is a matter of presidential prerogative. While usually the White House lawyers and congressional relations experts convene meetings with their counterparts from the concerned departments and agencies, such controversies are political at their core, and presidents invariably wish to decide for themselves how much political capital to expend and how to manage the broad strategy for the Executive Branch.

Colby had a different approach. Having prepared, at Ford's instruction, a summary report on the "Family Jewels," Colby wanted to hand it over right away to the Senate committee when he testified there in mid-

January 1975. Ford instructed him to keep it classified. Colby then delivered an opening statement virtually identical to the memorandum he had done for Ford, and agreed with the committee to release it as a public statement. Colby writes that he was "privately delighted" that the statement was published, believing it an effective rebuttal to the "misconceptions fostered by Hersh's article," but realized on his drive back from the Hill that he had not forewarned the White House of any of this: "[S]o I stopped there to give Brent Scowcroft a copy of the statement the Committee had released; the substance was well known to them, but the fact of its public release was a new bombshell."

More broadly, Colby considered that the CIA was no longer a creature of the Executive Branch exclusively; he subscribed to the view that "in 1975 the center of political power had moved to Congress and . . . the CIA's survival depended on working out satisfactory rather than hostile relations there." Therefore he unilaterally pledged to the committees his full cooperation with respect to documents and testimony, and issued a directive to CIA employees formally absolving them of their secrecy oaths with respect to testimony before Congress. In September 1975, after the House committee began publishing secret documents over administration objections, Ford prohibited the release of any additional classified material to the committee until it gave assurances about respecting their secrecy. Colby circumvented the order by "loaning" the material to the committee.

The congressional investigations were a two-ring circus. The Church Committee in the Senate respected the ground rules with regard to handling sensitive documents, but it was overeager when it came to issues of substance. One focus was on the exciting topic of U.S. government assassination plots against foreign leaders. Perhaps disappointed when it discovered that Nixon, Ford, and Kissinger were not involved in assassinating anybody, and that the most recent such plots had occurred under John and Robert Kennedy, the committee nevertheless stretched its definitions to include in its report an episode that had occurred in Chile when the Nixon administration (like the Johnson administration before it) sought by covert action to prevent Allende's coming into power. In October 1970, a group of anti-Allende military officers had hatched a plot to abduct the army commander, General René Schneider. Nixon (on Kissinger's advice) specifically disapproved this kidnapping plot; the officers went ahead anyway, bungled it, and killed Schneider by accident. While the Church Committee had to admit that no one in the

U.S. government authorized the assassination of Schneider, it managed to stretch the incident into a detailed thirty-page section of a report devoted precisely to the subject of U.S. government assassination plots.

The contortion act in the Senate was outmatched by the flaming-hoop and knife-throwing act on the House side. Even Colby deplored it as a "pretty awful mess." The Pike Committee looked into a variety of alleged "intelligence failures" including historical case studies, and—even juicier—events in the Nixon and Ford administrations such as the Middle East war of October 1973 and the Cyprus crisis of 1974. Particularly egregious in Colby's eyes was its insistence on declassifying, over his objections, a reference to the Egyptian army's improved communications security before the 1973 war. The U.S. ability (or inability) to intercept foreign military communications is usually treated as an especially sensitive secret. The entire Pike Committee report, containing this and much other sensitive intelligence information, was leaked to CBS newsman Daniel Schorr, who promptly delivered it to *The Village Voice*.

Kissinger was furious at Colby throughout this ordeal, needling him at one point (referring to his Catholicism): "Bill, you know what you do when you go up to the Hill? You go to confession." In his memoirs Kissinger speculates whether at some stage in his career Colby had begun having moral qualms about his chosen profession. He was also bitter at Colby's triggering of the process that led to an unwarranted perjury indictment of his predecessor, Richard Helms, whom Kissinger regarded highly; Helms had sought to protect information about a covert operation in an open Senate hearing (having provided the same information to an appropriate committee in a closed hearing). Kissinger writes that Ford shared his disappointment with Colby's conduct but wanted to wait until the congressional ordeal was over before replacing him. Ford, in turn, treats Colby more gently in his own memoirs (especially in comparison to Schlesinger). Even in the process of dismissing him, as we have seen, Ford thanked him for the job he had done in "the most difficult of circumstances."

In truth, predictable as were the consequences of Colby's capitulations to Congress, Colby himself was not the problem. The core of the problem can be found in the passage in Colby's memoirs quoted above, in which he observed that the balance of power in Washington had shifted to Congress and he had to adapt. "I did not share the view that intelligence was solely a function of the Executive Branch and must be protected from Congressional prying," he also noted. This is an extraordinary statement. The CIA is not an independent regulatory agency, like the Securities and Exchange Commission, conventionally regarded as a creature of Congress; it was created by law in 1947 as an adviser to the National Security Council, which is an arm of the president. Congressional oversight has been strengthened considerably under new procedures that developed in this period, but strengthening congressional oversight is not the same as removing the CIA from its place in the Executive Branch. Yet the reality in the mid-1970s was as Colby described it—a major weakening of the executive power: Colby was simply more afraid of the wrath of Congress than of the wrath of the president.

Losing His Hat

Ford's transition team in 1974 had included among its recommendations that Kissinger relinquish his post as assistant to the president for national security affairs while remaining secretary of state. Ford agreed, believing that the conjoining of the two jobs was "totally contrary to the purpose and intent of the NSC." But he put off any action on that front, knowing that Kissinger wanted to keep both hats and not wanting to "make any changes that might be misunderstood overseas." But over time, Ford came to the conclusion that Kissinger's deputy Brent Scowcroft would win everyone's trust as his successor, and that this move would have its logical place as part of the elaborate reshuffle in October 1975.

Ford was right about Kissinger's preference to hold on to both positions, and reasonable in the concern about international reaction. It could only be seen as a diminution of Kissinger's authority, especially by foreigners who would not be so familiar with the logic of the claim that the ouster of Schlesinger was a great victory for him. In addition he was preoccupied by the gloomy expectation that he would become more and more the principal target of Ford's conservative opposition. After brooding on all this for some weeks he began composing a long letter of resignation; like many other Kissinger products (such as speeches) he circulated it to immediate staff and friends for editorial comments. This one, I recall, was a dozen pages or so and went through several drafts until it was a fairly polished and eloquent product. All of us familiar with the project were in a state of mourning for weeks. Then Kissinger went into the Oval Office to see Ford in early January carrying the letter still in "draft" (typed up double-spaced, without letterhead or signa-ture), explaining to Ford that he would sign such a letter if he was becoming a political liability. Ford rejected the whole idea out of hand. If by handing over the letter in draft Kissinger was hedging against the (slim) possibility that Ford might accept it, he needn't have worried; if Ford was amused by the tentativeness of this resignation, he never let on.

On reflection, Kissinger came to see Ford's decision to separate the two positions as the right one. Not only are they separate functions; there is an obvious conflict of interest between them. With Scowcroft reverting to the classical role of the honest broker—even to become the paradigm of that role—the system worked well and Kissinger's stature cannot be said to have seriously diminished. Ford in a news conference on November 3 still spoke of Kissinger's "dominant role in the formula-tion of and the carrying out of foreign policy." Ford later told David Rothkopf:

> I had good relationships with both Henry and Brent, and I used them as they should have been used under the law that was passed in 1947. I depended upon a good relationship with Henry as secretary of state, and he was a first-class one. But I, at the same time, used Brent and his new responsibilities as head of the NSC according to the law there as well.

Scowcroft describes his role modestly as supplementing or comple-menting Kissinger's role. He told Rothkopf that Ford wanted to be able to "step back and ask, 'What is this world about? What are my options?' And then Kissinger would present some options—A, B, C, D. Ford would then turn to me and ask, Are there any other options?"

In addition to this service to Ford—giving him the assurance that all bases had been covered—Scowcroft in his new role provided an impor-tant service to Kissinger, who relied on his counsel with respect to con-flicts with other departments or with the White House staff. Whether on the growing controversies over SALT and détente, or over inter-national economic issues on which Kissinger sought to launch a num-ber of new initiatives (see below), Scowcroft was now in a stronger position to affect the outcomes or mediate the disputes. This was espe-cially important when Kissinger was traveling (which was often) and waging the interagency battles at long distance. Knowing Ford's strategic backing of Kissinger's views, Scowcroft wielded his new clout most often in Kissinger's support. Rather than attempting to be competitive with Kissinger, which Ford did not desire, Scowcroft more often than not served as Kissinger's ally in interagency squabbles. Where Ford considered that his political straits constrained him to depart from Kissinger's recommendations, Scowcroft helped manage a soft landing.

International Economic Policy

When Kissinger was White House national security adviser in Nixon's first term, one criticism of his performance was that he played no significant role in international economic policy. A widely read analysis of Kissinger's NSC staff operation, by journalist John Leacacos, included this critical observation:

> During [the] first year about 70 percent of the bureaucracy's contributions to NSC economic studies came from the Treasury Department, and only 30 percent from State. No senior interdepartmental group for economics was organized. Receiving little attention from Kissinger, the NSC's own economic specialists carried no bureaucratic clout.

This was certainly the conventional wisdom of the time, though Kissinger's reputation for lack of interest in economics may have been exaggerated. George P. Shultz gives Kissinger credit, for example, for steering Nixon toward bilateral summit meetings with key European leaders in 1971 to repair relations after Nixon's abrupt devaluation of the dollar and other unilateral measures on August 15—a necessary and inevitable "accommodation," Shultz says, "between our economic and our political interests." Leaving aside the irony that Kissinger, who was criticized in 1971 for dominating foreign policy, was simultaneously being criticized for *not* dominating international economic policy, for our present purposes there is also the irony that as secretary of state he was criticized for, indeed, trying to dominate that, too.

Kissinger's role in international economic policy under Ford is worth dwelling upon for a variety of reasons. It was an important element of the Ford administration's foreign policy; it was an example of Kissinger in action as secretary of state and his relations with cabinet colleagues other than the usual NSC players, and of how Ford managed all this. The results, too, were rather more successful than those involving the

Pentagon and CIA. It also goes to the question of the State Department's capacity for taking the lead on policy matters that cut across departmental lines.

The NSC system, as we saw in both preceding chapters, has struggled over many decades to insure smooth coordination among State, Defense, CIA, and other departments and agencies involved in the traditional national security realm. While lip service has often been paid to the need to include economic issues, the fit has never been an easy one. The National Security Act of 1947 did not list the secretary of the treasury among the statutory members of the NSC. The economic concerns that seemed most relevant in those days had to do with wartime economic mobilization—this had been the economic preoccupation in World War II and it was the Cold War expectation of those who had come out of that experience. Thus, the office in charge of resource mobilization and civil defense, in its various incarnations over the decades, was a statutory member, until Nixon removed it by executive order. Every president beginning with Truman, however, has routinely included Treasury in the NSC process, by invitation, and recommendations to include the secretary in the NSC by statute are a staple of national security reform proposals.

The more serious question—and this is only half-facetious—is whether the secretary of the treasury really wants to be a member, or rather, whether he wants his department roped into the national security decision-making process. All the economic departments of the government—including Treasury, Commerce, Agriculture, Energy, Labor, and the Trade Representative—have powerful domestic constituencies and equally powerful congressional committees that take a proprietary interest in these agencies' activities; this is where the "iron triangle" of Congress, the bureaucracy, and interest groups is particularly strong. They are not the same committees that have oversight over foreign affairs or national defense, and the international dimension is not likely to be their main interest in life (except to promote exports).

Power has continued to gravitate to these economic agencies. There once was a time when the State Department had the predominant voice in international economic issues (with the NSC staff as its ally), with Treasury reigning supreme over the domestic economy. In recent decades, however, globalization has broken down whatever separation may once have existed between the two dimensions. As economist Fred Bergsten has put it:

Therefore, the external factors intrude across a whole range of interest groups, issues, etc., that never even heard of the world economy. Therefore, many more agencies, many more issues, many more domestic interests are involved, and it would be totally unrealistic to think State or the NSC could dominate the way it did before.

These domestic agencies strongly resist letting the "foreign policy boys and girls" play diplomatic games with their chips. That is how it often seems to them, especially in Republican administrations: The foreign policy crowd wants for political reasons to reach international arrangements that interfere with market forces, or else to impede for political reasons economic activities that the market would warrant. Therefore the economic agencies have traditionally resisted allowing major issues of concern to them to be presented to the president through the NSC process. If it goes through that process, the White House national security adviser gets to write the memorandum and the system may be skewed in the foreign policy crowd's favor. Since Nixon's time, therefore, presidents have created alternative interagency mechanisms, with varying success, to integrate all the various interests and points of view, separate from the NSC and from the exclusive control of the national security adviser. In 1971, Nixon created an interdepartmental Council on International Economic Policy (CIEP) in the White House, under first Peter G. Peterson and then Peter Flanigan as executive director; it established itself as a useful body even as a strong secretary of the treasury, John Connally, tried to stifle it.

Gerald Ford bowed to reality and established an Economic Policy Board chaired by his secretary of the treasury (William Simon)—again, separate from the NSC. This has proved a more durable model. Like George Shultz under Nixon, James Baker under Ronald Reagan, and Robert Rubin under Bill Clinton, Simon was a strong treasury secretary who took the lead in international financial policy. Ford kept a White House hand in by naming his assistant for economic affairs William Seidman as the EPB's executive director. And Seidman gave the NSC staff a behind-the-scenes role in the EPB's operations.

But what happens if a strong treasury secretary (e.g., Simon) runs up against a strong secretary of state (e.g., Kissinger)? Kissinger's initial reaction to Ford's Economic Policy Board was to ignore it. One of the preoccupations of his tenure as secretary of state—especially because of the global economic and political crisis triggered by the 1973 explosion in energy prices—was a series of international initiatives in the economic field. He was aided in these initiatives by an energetic career diplomat, Thomas Enders, whose bureaucratic sharp elbows seemed to assure freedom of action for the State Department until, alas, Kissinger was pulled into the EPB by the White House (in exchange for a seat on its executive committee).

The Kissinger initiatives were based on the idea that the United States should wield its economic power in accordance with a strategy, or in furtherance of strategic objectives. One example was grain sales to the Soviet Union. The Nixon administration had been embarrassed in 1972 when the Kremlin outsmarted the Agriculture Department and bought nearly a billion dollars' worth of U.S. grain at subsidized prices; the Soviets cleverly concealed their desperate need (after a bad harvest) and played our grain companies against each other. Having been burned once, Kissinger in the Ford administration did not want to repeat the experience; he wanted to use grain sales as leverage. As one inside observer recounts:

> On the issue of leverage, Secretary Kissinger argued that the U.S. grain crop was a tremendous asset, mainly because there was no substitute for it in the world. Merely pouring out the grain for "gold" was "very painful" when appropriately managed sales could buy a year or so of good Soviet behavior. He cited the skill with which the OPEC nations used their oil resources, urged that the administration maintain an "element of uncertainty," and cautioned against excessive eagerness in dealing with the Soviets.

It was linkage again. Kissinger—a convert to the EPB now that it gave him a say in these decisions—insisted that the Agriculture Department not authorize any new sales to the Soviet Union, formally or informally, without EPB review. The upshot was a five-year agreement with the Soviets that capped the amounts sold in each year. This was a compromise that all agencies accepted (though it led to vociferous protests from the farm lobby because of its constraints on sales).

The larger challenge of the period, as noted, was the energy shock of 1973, when the Organization of the Petroleum Exporting Countries (OPEC) quadrupled the price of oil and tipped much of the world into recession. Coming at the same time as the U.S. retreat in Indochina and the Watergate crisis at home, the economic crisis led to what

Kissinger feared was a creeping demoralization in the West; the Soviets crowed that the global "correlation of forces" was shifting in favor of "socialism" and Communist parties threatened to gain electoral ground even in Western Europe.

Kissinger's idea was to counter this trend on a number of fronts. He briefed Ford on August 17, 1974, barely a week into Ford's presidency: "We have to find a way to break the cartel. We can't do it without cooperation with the other consumers. It is intolerable that countries of 40 million can blackmail 800 million people in the industrial world." Where European countries were tempted to appease OPEC, Kissinger sought to mobilize solidarity among the consumer nations as a counterweight to OPEC. The French for a time resisted this cooperation (on the Gaullist thesis that any American-led enterprise has to be resisted on principle), but eventually the French (under their new president Valéry Giscard d'Estaing) agreed to the U.S.-proposed International Energy Agency—to be headquartered in Paris, of course—and to other measures of energy cooperation among the industrial democracies.

In August 1975, Giscard proposed a meeting on economic policy among the leaders of the major economic powers; such a summit was held at Rambouillet in November. It was Ford's proposal (on Alan Greenspan's advice) to make this an annual affair. This was the origin of what soon became the Group of Seven, or G-7—the grouping of the leading industrial democracies (the United States, United Kingdom, Japan, Germany, France, Canada, Italy, plus the European Union). While the ostensible subject matter was economic—and there were significant matters of global economic policy to discuss—political topics were also discussed. Ford and Kissinger saw the forum as invaluable as a political directorate of the Western democracies, sorely needed to reinforce political solidarity and head off the demoralization threatening to engulf the West.

The second element of U.S. strategy was to split the Third World. The vast majority of developing nations—poor, and without oil—were suffering the most severe economic blow themselves from the higher oil prices. Yet they were pulled toward appeasement of their OPEC brothers by a sense of helplessness, by OPEC promises of aid (rarely kept), and by radical notions of a "New International Economic Order" in which their commodities too might someday be cartelized. Kissinger wanted the United States, by a series of multilateral economic initiatives, to demonstrate to the non-oil-producing developing countries that their interest lay with the existing global economic system and not with Marxist ideological fantasies. In a series of major speeches to international bodies in 1974, 1975, and 1976, he let loose a steady stream of policy initiatives, including a United Nations World Food Program, a special lending facility at the International Monetary Fund to finance oil purchases for the poorest, mechanisms to improve developing countries' access to capital markets and new technology, structural improvements to the world trading system, and a special development initiative for Africa.

Pushing these economic proposals through the United States government was not easy. As noted, every single one of the proposals trod on the expertise and turf of some other department or agency with important domestic and congressional constituencies for whom Kissinger's grand strategy must have seemed a bizarre abstraction. Kissinger and his staff were also tempted occasionally by the idea of commodity agreements or other mechanisms that represented interference with market forces, on the ground that the poorer countries needed special help if they were not to be harmed by the volatility of the international economy as it was then working. These ideas ran into significant opposition among economic conservatives in the Ford administration.

Usually Kissinger simply took the bureaucratic initiative, charging his State Department experts (and NSC staff allies like Robert Hormats and me) to draft a speech for him to deliver to some important upcoming international meeting; the draft speech, laden with new proposals, would then be sent around to the other agencies for clearance—usually with not a lot of time to spare before the delivery date. His key aide Thomas Enders was sometimes accused of playing other agencies off against each other, approaching them bilaterally and sometimes misleading them about other agencies' positions. The aggressive approach was an early test of the EPB mechanism. Ford would often break the deadlocks himself if compromises could not be worked out, and as discussed earlier, the State Department was eventually domesticated into the EPB process.

Some other kinds of interagency conflicts were harder to resolve. At one point, Treasury Secretary Simon called the shah of Iran a "nut" because of the shah's aggressive promotion of OPEC price increases. The shah wanted to develop Iran rapidly and thought oil had been underpriced for too long. Despite the serious American disagreement with him over the price hikes and the global crisis they produced, Kissinger and Ford saw the shah also as a key strategic ally in a region threatened by Soviet-backed Arab radicalism that was entrenching itself in Syria, Yemen, the Palestine Liberation Organization (PLO), and Saddam Hussein's Iraq. At Kissinger's urging, Simon retreated and announced he had been quoted out of context. Kissinger accepted the concession, though he remained puzzled as to what context might make our ally find it palatable to be called a "nut."

Kissinger's tenure as secretary of state was thus a time not only of strong political leadership of the State Department but of leadership by the department in an important area of policy involving other powerful cabinet agencies. State's role was insured by Kissinger's bureaucratic tenacity but most of all by conceptual leadership—by his articulation of a broad strategy toward the intersection of political and economic interests that Ford enthusiastically embraced. While events conspired to deny them this coherence in broad policy toward the Soviet Union, this set of issues remains an instructive example for future secretaries of state who aspire to restore at least some of their department's historical preeminence.

Straddling an Earthquake

Ford was caught by surprise by the Reagan challenge, and thrown off-balance by it. He considered himself a conservative Republican and a conservative president: He pushed for a defense buildup after a long period of decline in defense spending; he pleaded with Congress in 1974–1975 to support our allies in Indochina; he struggled to defend U.S. intelligence agencies against congressional assault. At the end of 1975, he fought to continue a U.S. covert action program against Cuban-Soviet military intervention in Angola, which Congress blocked. He considered his policy toward the Soviet Union a firm one. The arms agreement he had reached with Brezhnev at Vladivostok in November 1974 would establish equal ceilings for the strategic missiles of the two sides, correcting the (misleading) impression of inequality left by Nixon's 1972 accord. The Helsinki Final Act, which he signed at a thirty-five-nation summit meeting in the summer of 1975, enshrined human rights for the first time as a core issue of East-West relations in Europe, and also enshrined principles that delegitimated military interventions like the Soviet invasions of Hungary and Czechoslovakia. Ford and

Kissinger attempted to rebuild Western morale and unity in the wake of the energy and economic crises of the period.

Yet the Ford administration was overwhelmed by events. Its policy toward the Soviet Union was essentially taken out of its hands: Conservatives took away the carrots in its policy—such as arms control and trade—while liberals took away the sticks—the defense programs and strong geopolitical actions (as in Angola) to counter Soviet expansionism. One bellwether was the decision of George H. W. Bush, Colby's successor at CIA, to respond to conservative pressures in 1976 by appointing an outside group (dubbed "Team B") to critique U.S. intelligence on Soviet military and other activities. Team B's conclusion was that the CIA had tended consistently to underestimate the Soviet threat—which, when it leaked, became another weapon against Ford's and Kissinger's policies.

Ford's political weakness had deeper causes. In large part it was the result of the deadly economic combination of inflation and recession, as well as the Watergate debacle whose legacy still burdened Ford (especially the unpopular pardon of Nixon). A Gallup Poll in early January 1976 showed 46 percent of respondents disapproving of Ford's performance in office, with only 39 percent approving. In the foreign policy dimension the American demoralization was magnified, I am convinced, by the humiliation of the outcome in Indochina, even if that was rarely mentioned by name. There were no bitter recriminations when the war ended, no "stab in the back" theory. With the bloodbath in Indochina in April 1975 came a kind of bipartisan amnesia: Liberals were embarrassed at the grisly outcome of an abandonment they had passionately argued for; conservatives were embarrassed at the failure of an intervention they had strongly supported. Other issues, therefore, became surrogates for a nationalistic reaction. That is what propelled Ronald Reagan's powerful challenge to Ford in 1976; it is what propelled Reagan into the presidency in 1980 after the Soviet invasion of Afghanistan and President Carter's Iran hostage crisis compounded the sense of national humiliation.

The foreign policy part of Reagan's campaign against Ford in 1976 was based on the theme that the United States was falling behind the Soviets in the military field and that U.S. policy, especially arms control, was only weakening us further. Reagan called for a military buildup; he denounced Kissinger and the firing of Schlesinger. He urged Ford not to go to the Helsinki summit, as that would only concede Soviet domination of Eastern Europe. He argued that the Panama Canal should remain U.S. property because we had built it (rather than be the subject of a negotiation with Panama to head off an explosion of Panamanian nationalism in the U.S. Canal Zone). The charismatic Reagan touched a chord in a party and a nation tired of humiliation and demoralization. Thus he launched a formidable challenge to a sitting president of his own party:

> Under Kissinger and Ford [Reagan declared], this nation has become Number Two in a world where it is dangerous—if not fatal—to be second best. All I can see is what other nations the world over see: collapse of the American will and the retreat of American power. There is little doubt in my mind that the Soviet Union will not stop taking advantage of détente until it sees that the American people have elected a new President and appointed a new Secretary of State.

The struggle lasted through a long season of hotly contested Republican primaries beginning in February with the outcome in doubt until the national convention in Kansas City in August. Ford won the early string of primaries, beginning with an ominously narrow win in New Hampshire on February 24, but moving on successfully through Florida, Massachusetts, Vermont, and Illinois, until a major upset by Reagan in North Carolina in March. Scholar Michael Barone describes what followed:

> The remainder of [the] war for the Republican nomination followed a course reminiscent of the prolonged trench warfare of World War I. Both sides fought hard and neither gained much ground. In May and June, Ford won primaries in West Virginia, Maryland, Michigan, Kentucky, Oregon, Tennessee, Rhode Island, New Jersey, and Ohio— states in which Republicans had established a presence by the time of the Civil War. Reagan won primaries in Georgia, Indiana, Nebraska, Arkansas, Idaho, Nevada, Montana, South Dakota, and California— states in which (with the exception of Indiana) Republican strength dated from some later time.

Ford made a courageous decision in April, shortly before the May 1 Texas primary, to authorize Kissinger to proceed with a major diplomatic initiative in Southern Africa, including a push to persuade Rhodesia's white minority to accept majority rule. Ford's political advisers warned him it would hurt in Texas—indeed, Ford lost badly in Texas and this undoubtedly contributed—but he supported Kissinger's strategy to strengthen moderate forces in Africa under pressure from Marxist radicals. Ford told his political advisers: "I cannot judge whether the political impact will be good or bad. But we must do this because it's the right thing to do."

This was not just the traditional battle between two strong candidates for their party's nomination. The fact that a sitting president was under challenge was unusual. But, more than that, Barone's roster of which states were old territory for the Republicans and which were new tells the story of the political earthquake that was under way in the GOP. As political analyst Jonathan Martin elaborates:

> Where "Regular Republicans" reigned or still held considerable sway . . . the more moderate Ford did better. But in states with little in the way of a Republican tradition, Reagan won the day. . . . Ford embodied the good-government northeastern and Midwestern party of Rockefeller, [Henry Cabot] Lodge, and [Arthur] Vandenberg. He was, in many ways, representative of the end of an era. . . . Those states that, as Barone explains, Reagan won in part due to their minimal Republican tradition have something else in common—all except California are what we now call red states and form the core of the modern GOP.

IF THE SAGA of Schlesinger versus Kissinger in the cabinet was part of the narrative of the revolution engulfing the Republican Party, the drama of William Colby was emblematic of the constitutional revolution that was occurring simultaneously. Colby saw the balance of power tilting so strongly toward Congress as to render the CIA less an institution of the Executive Branch than a virtual servant of Congress. While the focus of this book is not on executive-legislative relations, the Colby phenomenon requires some explanatory context. Vietnam and Watergate left a legacy of new restrictions on presidential power that are now embedded in legislation. A paradox of the period was that while the Republican Party and the country seemed to be shifting gradually to the right, the Congress elected in November 1974 (in the wake of Watergate and the Nixon pardon) had shifted sharply to the left.

Michael Barone calls the Democrats' victory in 1974 one "of stunning proportions": They gained forty-six House seats over their 1972 numbers and controlled the House by a margin of 290 to 145, while increasing their control of the Senate by three. The previous Congress had begun the process of imposing some important restrictions on a weakened Nixon, including in Indochina and over war powers. The new Congress took up with a vengeance where its predecessor left off.

The catalogue of new legislative restraints on executive power from that period is a long one. Reagan, when he was president, used to speak of "over 100 separate prohibitions and restrictions on Executive Branch authority to formulate and implement foreign policy" enacted since the 1970s. Some of these restrictions came from conservatives (such as the Jackson-Vanik linkage of U.S.-Soviet trade to freer emigration from the Soviet Union), but the overwhelming majority came from the left:

- The War Powers Resolution, passed over Nixon's veto in November 1973.
- Prohibitions on U.S. military action in support of allies in Indochina, and reductions in security assistance to them, from 1970 to 1975.
- An embargo on U.S. military aid to Turkey after the Cyprus crisis in 1974.
- Prohibition of a U.S. covert program of military assistance to forces opposing the Cuban-Soviet military intervention in Angola.
- Expanded oversight and control over intelligence activities, resulting from the investigations into alleged intelligence abuses.
- Freedom of Information Act amendments, enacted over Ford's veto in 1974, removing the Executive Branch's exclusive power to determine what information can be kept classified on national security grounds.
- Limitations on numbers of U.S. military personnel deployed abroad, such as the ceilings on the number of U.S. Marines in Lebanon in 1983–1984 and on U.S. military trainers in El Salvador in the 1980s.
- A variety of legislated restrictions based on human rights considerations, which limit or attach conditions on economic and security assistance to friendly countries (e.g., El Salvador and Indonesia).
- A regime of nonproliferation controls and sanctions restricting various forms of bilateral cooperation with countries that have failed to comply with international safeguards or have violated unilaterally set U.S.

criteria (e.g., at various times, India, Pakistan, Brazil, Argentina, China, and Egypt).

• Limits on the president's power to impose economic sanctions or controls for foreign policy purposes (or, in some cases, conversely, mandating such sanctions without allowing presidential discretion).

• Elaborate new procedures of congressional oversight over U.S. arms transfers to friendly countries.

• Much tightened requirements for reprogramming of funds, by which congressional committees can deny presidents the flexibility they used to have in the use of authorized or appropriated funds to respond to rapidly changing conditions.

• Growing use of earmarking of aid funds to compel the expenditure of designated amounts for countries favored by Congress, which usually has the effect of squeezing out funds for other friendly countries under the fixed ceiling of the assistance budget.

Officials in recent administrations have become accustomed to struggling with these legislative restrictions, which they treat as part of the landscape. Government lawyers and accountants consume weeks and months struggling to find legal ways to perform certain tasks or to provide aid to certain allies in the national interest, sometimes in emergency conditions. Denial of presidential flexibility was a deliberate goal of these legislative constraints, and they have achieved their purpose. A few restrictions have been repealed or relaxed (like the Turkish embargo in 1978, the Angola restrictions in 1985, and the Indonesia restrictions in 2005), but that kind of effort usually takes years. The broad categories listed above embrace hundreds of statutory provisions (many of which duplicate each other, or overlap), as well as reporting requirements and restrictions that presidents can waive in certain conditions; some restrictions are presidential commitments exacted by Congress as the price of support for other presidential initiatives. But the scope of this legislative micromanagement is now enormous. In 1964, the House and Senate foreign affairs committees began publishing a handy joint compilation called *Legislation on Foreign Relations*. The 1964 edition was a volume of about 650 pages. By 1985, it had grown into three volumes totaling more than 4,000 pages. The most recent complete set comprises five volumes, published over a number of years, totaling over 9,500 pages. This represented a revolution in the balance between the two branches of government.

A Lasting Legacy

An unelected president, Ford was on the defensive from the early days of his tenure, under pressure from the conservative challenge in his party and the Democratic congressional resurgence. In the end, his race against Democratic nominee Jimmy Carter was remarkably close—a 51–48 percent loss. So the question arises whether an elected Ford, with a popular mandate and removal of the cloud over his authority, would have been able to recover lost ground, either in the party or at the other end of Pennsylvania Avenue. This is impossible to answer. Perhaps his victory would have enabled the moderate wing of the Republican Party to regain its footing and its dominance for an additional period of years, while restoring the defense budget and rebuilding popular and congressional support for his concept of a strong foreign and defense policy. We will never know. In 1976 at least, the forces arrayed against him were powerful ones, in a period of unusual turmoil. The revolution in the party might have continued regardless, with the charismatic Reagan continuing his pursuit (as he did) for 1980. Meanwhile, the Democrats' domination of Congress was to last two more decades, pulling national policy to the left. The straddle may have been more than Ford—or any president—could manage.

Those times have left their mark. A later CIA director, Robert Gates, observed in a speech in 1987 that the CIA found itself "equidistant" between president and Congress. It was an echo of Colby. (When Gates published the speech as an article in *Foreign Affairs*, he inserted the word "involuntarily" with reference to the "equidistance," in a welcome bow to the National Security Act.) Thus, even if Reagan's strong performance in the Oval Office was to remind us that the institution of the presidency was far from dead, the centrifugal pull of Congress on our bureaucracy never reverted to the earlier status quo.

Most of the officials now struggling to formulate and implement policy in this environment do not remember a time when these legislative restrictions did not exist. The burdens have been absorbed in bureaucratic routine. But one who did remember was Dick Cheney. It was a thirty-five-year-old Dick Cheney who as White House chief of staff watched President Ford and his administration being overwhelmed by this tidal wave. "It wasn't personal and it wasn't directed at Ford in that sense," Cheney said a few years later. "It was institutional in the sense that it was directed at the presidency." Decades later, he called the Ford period "the nadir of the modern presidency in terms of authority and legitimacy."

There cannot be any doubt that this was one of the formative experiences of Dick Cheney's life. As a young member of Congress he became an outspoken champion of restoring executive authority, in both foreign and domestic policy, when other of his new colleagues (Newt Gingrich, for example) were calling for a further strengthening of Congress's role. During the congressional investigations of the Iran-Contra affair in the Reagan administration, as we shall see in Chapter 6, Cheney led the Republican minority side in an articulate defense of presidential actions and presidential prerogatives that was more impressive than anything emanating from a demoralized White House. The same conviction clearly infused his later actions as vice president—the conviction that it was not always this way, that it has done harm, and that (especially in a time of war) it was time to push back.

CHAPTER FIVE

Jimmy Carter

J IMMY CARTER, like virtually every other president discussed in this book, came into office determined to avoid what he saw as the errors of his predecessors. When he hired Zbigniew Brzezinski as his assistant for national security affairs—another high-energy foreign-born foreign policy intellectual—he made clear to Brzezinski that he did not want him to be another Kissinger. Carter in his memoirs says he welcomed the "natural competition" between the State Department and the White House national security adviser and did not want the latter to dominate as Kissinger had done. He agreed with Brzezinski "most of the time" on substance, Carter says, but he nonetheless "appreciated" the continuing differences between the two organizations because he believed these differences maximized his own ability to make the final decisions and thereby control the process.

By the same token, Carter did not want Cyrus Vance, the distinguished lawyer he chose as his secretary of state, to be another Kissinger and to dominate the process as Kissinger had done as secretary of state. In an appearance as president-elect before the Senate Foreign Relations Committee, Carter said:

> I intend to appoint a strong and competent Secretary of State, but I intend to remember . . . that the responsibility [for the conduct of foreign policy] lies in the White House with the President. I will be the President and I will represent the country in foreign affairs.

Toward the end of his term, Carter still had Kissinger on his mind: "There have been Presidents in the past, maybe not too distant past, that let their Secretaries of State make foreign policy. I don't." As time passed, Carter realized he had the opposite problem: Like so many other occupants of the Oval Office he came to lament the "inertia" and lack of strategic innovativeness at Foggy Bottom. While Vance, unlike William Rogers, had had prior experience in the national security field (including in the Defense Department), he proved a disappointment to Carter as Rogers did to Nixon.

Carter, in short, wanted Vance and Brzezinski to be counterweights to each other. He later told interviewers from the *Harvard Business Review*:

> I deliberately chose advisers with disparate points of view. I wanted the very conservative, stable, and cautionary reaction of the State Department on the one hand and the more dynamic, innovative advice from the National Security staff on the other hand. . . . I wanted a broad assortment of opinions before I made a judgment.

Brzezinski and Vance indeed had sharply opposing philosophies. Brzezinski, like Kissinger, came out of a European tradition that drew sober lessons from history; he was a thinker with a geopolitical world-view, realistic about the role of power in world affairs even as he shared the president's and the Democratic Party's commitment to human rights. He saw the challenge of Soviet power as a global one, and viewed other issues—especially the role of China—in the context of that competition. Like Kissinger, he was a hardened veteran of faculty politics.

Vance, like William Rogers, was a gentleman lawyer, moderate by instinct in philosophy and personality. He was comfortable reflecting the institutional views of his department. He thought it was wrong to make the competition with the Soviet Union the preoccupation of U.S. foreign policy:

> A flaw in our foreign policy during this period [Vance later wrote] was that it was too narrowly rooted in the concept of an overarching U.S.-Soviet "geopolitical" struggle. Obviously, such a conflict did exist and it was of major dimensions. But our national interests encompassed more than U.S.-Soviet relations. . . . Many developments did not fit neatly into an East-West context. . . . Global interdependence, once a fashionable buzzword, had become a reality.

Carter's memoirs bear out Brzezinski's contention that the president wanted a White House–centered rather than cabinet-centered system.

Thus, Carter leaned toward strengthening Brzezinski's hand in some respects as a way to strengthen his own. Brzezinski was given cabinet rank—which Kissinger as White House assistant never had; Brzezinski chaired a key interdepartmental group (the Special Coordination Committee), as Kissinger had done, but the other members around the table were cabinet secretaries, not deputy or under secretaries (unlike Kissinger's Review Group). Brzezinski early on, at Carter's urging, became a public spokesman for the administration, giving on-the-record interviews and appearing on television talk shows, which, again, Nixon never allowed Kissinger to do until almost the end of his first term. Brzezinski even hired his own press secretary on the NSC staff, which raised eyebrows in Washington. But there is no doubt that Carter wanted him to play this role, disappointed as he was in Vance's inability or unwillingness to be a forceful or articulate public educator concerning the administration's policies. Vance recognized in retrospect that he should have devoted more time and effort to being a spokesman, but he remained bitter at Carter for allowing Brzezinski such a prominent role.

Eventually Brzezinski was also given some important substantive assignments as Carter's special envoy in the Kissinger mode. He led the secret negotiations with China that led to normalization of relations. He negotiated a swap of Soviet spies for Soviet dissidents. He helped organize Middle East and Arab responses to the Soviet invasion of Afghanistan, and played a role in organizing West European allies' responses to Soviet missile deployments in Europe. Carter sent him to have a private conversation with Anwar Sadat about Carter's domestic political prospects and how they would affect U.S. Middle East diplomacy. He also came to take the lead, with Defense Secretary Harold Brown's support, in setting policy toward the SALT negotiations with the Soviet Union, which was managed through the Special Coordination Committee that Brzezinski chaired.

State Department officials were extremely bitter about Brzezinski's aggressiveness in excluding them from the sensitive negotiations with China. Brzezinski and Vance had different substantive approaches to the issue, with Brzezinski eager to normalize with China as leverage against the Soviet Union, and with State more cautious out of concern at disrupting the SALT talks with the Soviets. Brzezinski sent a key decision memorandum to Carter without consulting with Vance. State officials were convinced that press leaks from Brzezinski undermined

Vance's standing with the Chinese during a visit Vance paid to China; Brzezinski seems to have coaxed the Chinese into inviting *him* to visit China, where he supplanted Vance as the principal U.S. negotiator. When Brzezinski headed his own delegation to Beijing, he excluded assistant secretary of state Richard Holbrooke from a key meeting with Chinese leader Deng Xiaoping. He continued meeting secretly in Washington with Chinese envoys while taking elaborate precautions to insure that this took place without State's knowledge.

I leave it to historians to decide how this compares with how Nixon and Kissinger treated William Rogers on China policy, but there is a resemblance. In this case, too, the president sided with his national security adviser on both the substance and the procedure. In an extraordinary letter to *Foreign Affairs* in 1999, Carter put it bluntly:

> I was leery of channeling my proposals through the State Department because I did not feel I had full support there and it was and is an enormous bureaucracy that is unable and sometimes unwilling to keep a secret. . . . Secretary Vance was conversant with every dispatch we sent and had constant access to me, so I did not give much weight to his disgruntled subordinates in the State Department, some of whom had been a constant source of complaints to the news media regarding the national security advisor's having too much influence over foreign policy. If these assistants at the State Department felt excluded . . . it was because of my orders to hold information closely so that our efforts would not be subverted.

In a phenomenon we have seen before, Carter perceived the many leaks attacking Brzezinski as a "surrogate for attacks on himself," since he had made the decisions that were being attacked. In December 1978 Carter convened a meeting with Vance and Brzezinski to try to smooth out the deteriorating relations between them, and made that point explicitly. Recall that Gerald Ford made the same observation to Henry Kissinger with respect to attacks on Kissinger emanating from James Schlesinger's Pentagon. Presidents notice such things.

Despite these victories, however, Brzezinski remained continually frustrated. He encouraged Carter to do what President Kennedy had done after a year in office—clean house at the State Department to put more loyalists in key subordinate positions. But Carter did not do so. And Brzezinski chafed at his formal equality with Vance when he felt

Carter's interest lay in strengthening him further. He later told an interviewer:

> Carter, quite rightly in my judgment, wanted it to be understood as *his* system, and therefore he wasn't prepared to make the assistant's role as explicit as perhaps it should have been; moreover, he wasn't prepared to make the personnel decisions that I said earlier were necessary, namely to purge those who really were not fully loyal to his views. And as a consequence, there was always practical bifurcation, ambiguity intensified by the emphasis placed publicly on the primacy of the secretary of state.

In short, Carter was true to his word in not giving Brzezinski free rein. Reading between the lines of Carter's memoirs one can sense a certain distancing, even amid the personal compliments that seem genuine enough. Carter says he encouraged the NSC staff to be "unrestrained" in making innovative proposals—"and consequently [I] had to reject a lot of them." He and Brzezinski "had many arguments about history, politics, international events, and foreign policy—often disagreeing strongly and fundamentally." Brzezinski, in turn, lamented in his diary at the end of 1978 that "unlike Kissinger, who had in Nixon a clear ally in shaping a grand strategy for the country, I have to do it through indirection." While the president tended to be tough on specific issues of Soviet policy and sided with Brzezinski when there was a bureaucratic showdown, Brzezinski feared that Carter was "very much tempted by the vision of a grand accommodation with Brezhnev."

President Carter's "balanced" system thus made perfect sense on an organization chart, but it masked a fundamental flaw that Brzezinski's diary entry points to—the philosophical schizophrenia of the president, of his worldview, and of his resulting policies. Nixon and Kissinger were united in what might be called a conservative philosophy—a tragic view of history in which conflicts are not always reconcilable and enemies must often be resisted. It is a consistent view of how the world works and how human nature is designed; it reflects in international affairs some of the realism of the framers of our Constitution in opposing power to power and assuming the fallibility, not the perfectibility, of man. It sees the world whole, relating disparate events to each other, which is one of the meanings of taking a strategic view. Whether one agrees with this philosophy or not, having a philosophy insured consistency—both between the two men running the policy and in the kind of policy they conducted.

Jimmy Carter was an engineer by training, not a geopolitician. As such he can be said to be part of the American pragmatic tradition, which considers issues case by case, leaning sometimes toward one view and sometimes toward the other, "on their merits." Lawyers come out of a similar tradition. Brzezinski does not conceal his disappointment at the "absence of historical perspective" in Carter, nor his gentle reproach of the "occasionally surprising naïveté" of his president, despite his own earnest and intensive tutoring over four years. Thus, the system that Carter set up only enshrined the philosophical schizophrenia of its chief. Carter indeed dominated the process as he sought, but he gave no clear direction. The "balance" of two opposing philosophies was not the system's strength but its weakness—the root of its incoherence. A senior Carter aide has commented to me that Carter had no consistent philosophy in foreign policy except that what had gone on in his predecessors' administrations was bad.

The Carter System

Carter's determination to keep the reins of control in his hands was reflected in other aspects of his management style. He, too, started out with a more open and collegial "spokes of the wheel" arrangement in the White House, as did Gerald Ford, but eventually gravitated toward appointing a chief of staff. Carter also became known for his personal micromanagement of White House affairs, appointing a Georgia cousin (Hugh Carter, Jr., known as "Cousin Cheap") to oversee White House expenses and administration. Legend had it that the president was personally managing the scheduling of reservations on the White House tennis court; this was not true, but the story reflected the intense interest he took in details of administration—to insure frugality, assert his authority, and demonstrate his engineer's technical competence. On policy matters, he read voraciously—three hundred to four hundred pages daily, Richard Neustadt was told; on foreign policy, he was given 100 to 150 pages every night, Brzezinski told Brent Scowcroft. Scowcroft was astounded and thought it too much of a burden on any president, who should be focusing on the forest rather than the trees.

If micromanagement was one problem, his aversion to politics was another. Carter's "anti-political attitude used to drive me nuts," his vice president, Walter Mondale, later complained, "because you couldn't get him to grapple with a political problem. . . . Carter thought politics was sinful." To Professor Neustadt, this was "suggestive of a President more unpolitical in some respects than Eisenhower," which for Neustadt was not at all a compliment but a grim warning of the lack of the "power sense" that presidents need to dominate their administrations.

Carter's national security process was—in the Democratic tradition— more loosely structured than that of his Republican predecessors. The National Security Council met formally only ten times in Carter's term, compared with the 125 meetings during the eight years of Nixon and Ford. Carter much preferred a more intimate forum, his breakfast at 7:30 a.m. every Friday in the Cabinet Room with his national security team (principally his vice president, secretaries of state and defense, the national security adviser, and a few White House aides). This was, he has said, his "favorite meeting of the week." Carter resisted Brzezinski's suggestion that there be a formal agenda; instead, Brzezinski often simply suggested topics to the president shortly before they walked from the Oval Office into the breakfast. No formal records were kept, which often led to conflicting interpretations of what had been decided. Only very late in the administration, after an embarrassing foul-up that led to the public retraction of a U.S. vote on a U.N. Security Council resolution on Jerusalem in March 1980, did Carter authorize Brzezinski to circulate an authoritative summary of his decisions. Thus, the failings often laid at the door of Lyndon Johnson's Tuesday lunches—which Walt Rostow rebutted—seem to have been more true of Carter's Friday breakfasts.

This presidential event was supplemented by a weekly Vance-Brown-Brzezinski luncheon, its venue rotating among the three, without aides or notetakers. All sides seem to have found this a useful forum for ironing out some differences, and successor administrations have benefited from following the precedent. But Vance remained forever jealous of Brzezinski's direct access to the president and the leverage this gave him. Vance regrets that he did not fight harder to insist on a right to clearance on drafts of presidential directives; State Department historians also note glumly that the president often wrote marginal comments on Brzezinski's weekly foreign policy summaries and that the security adviser and his staff "used these Presidential notes (159 of them) as the basis for NSC actions."

Another important and positive innovation of the Carter administration was its elevation of the substantive role of the vice president. This had been a declared aspiration of many administrations since the April day in 1945 when Harry Truman was thrust into the Oval Office uninformed of major policies including the existence of the atomic bomb. But with Walter Mondale an experienced and substantial figure in his own right, Carter wisely brought him into the inner circle. Mondale was the first vice president to be given a West Wing office close to the president's (rescued from exile across the street in the Executive Office Building). Mondale had his own one-on-one weekly lunch with the president, and played an important role as adviser on matters of both politics (frustrated as we have seen he sometimes was) and policy. He undoubtedly added some maturity as well as Washington political savvy to a White House that needed both.

Contradictions

The contradictions in the Carter presidency were foreshadowed in the 1976 campaign, when candidate Carter strove to position himself both to Gerald Ford's right and to his left simultaneously. Carter borrowed extensively from the then current critique of U.S.-Soviet détente: He argued that détente as then practiced was one-sided, that the Soviets were exploiting it, that the United States was acquiescing in Soviet domination of Eastern Europe. A close observer has noted the parallels between some of Carter's campaign rhetoric in 1976 and some of Ronald Reagan's. Carter also put human rights front and center in U.S.-Soviet relations in a forceful way. At the same time, many other of Carter's themes were familiar liberal themes—cutting the defense budget, pursuing strategic arms control, emphasizing humanitarian rather than military assistance to friends, paying more attention to the Third World, and rejection of what he considered the amoral balance-of-power approach of his predecessors.

Some of the tensions among these different impulses quickly revealed themselves in the new administration when it formulated its approach to SALT. The framework that Ford had agreed upon with Leonid Brezhnev at Vladivostok in 1974 would put both sides at an equal level ("equal aggregates"), though at high numbers (a total of 2,400 ICBMs, with a sub-ceiling of 1,320 on ICBMs with multiple warheads). Carter had the option of completing a treaty on the basis of the Vladivostok deal, which he might have accomplished fairly quickly.

Vance favored this course, but he was overruled. Others on the new team, including Carter, rejected it for various reasons. William Hyland, an astute Sovietologist and former Kissinger aide whom Brzezinski retained on his staff, reports that many on the new team thought it beneath their dignity simply to continue and complete the approach of their predecessors. Vladivostok was dismissively branded the "If Ford Had Won the Election" option.

Carter and his team instead were attracted to the idea of a bold and more comprehensive initiative pressing the Soviets for deep reductions in ICBMs on both sides. This concept appealed to liberals because it seemed a more ambitious quest for nuclear disarmament (as opposed to mere strategic arms "limitation"). But the idea had also been advanced by many conservative critics of the Nixon-Ford policy including elder statesman Paul Nitze and Senator Henry Jackson. Conservatives liked it because it sought deep reductions particularly in the category of large, silo-based ICBMs, which posed the greatest risk to the U.S. retaliatory force and in which the Soviets had a significant advantage. The desirability of such an outcome from the U.S. point of view could not be doubted; what was less clear was whether the United States had the bargaining leverage to compel Soviet acceptance of such a result. Gerald Ford had barely begun the process of securing congressional approval of increases in the defense budget, reversing many years of decline; Carter would eventually pursue the same goal. But neither president was yet achieving anywhere near the leverage with the Soviets that Ronald Reagan would achieve by his rapid military buildup a few years later.

Carter decided to put forward a comprehensive new proposal emphasizing deep reductions (down to 1,800 to 2,000 total ICBMs, and to 1,100 to 1,200 ICBMs with multiple warheads). As a fallback, however, he decided also to present to the Soviets a more modest concept proposing some reductions in the Vladivostok numbers (to 2,000 ICBMs, to include 1,200 ICBMs with multiple warheads). These two options were hammered out at two NSC meetings on March 19 and 22.

Meanwhile, other events were taking place in the U.S.-Soviet relationship. Carter's commitment to human rights, including as a core element in U.S. policy toward the Soviet Union, was a fundamental principle of both his campaign and his presidency. But in the multifaceted relationship we had with the Soviet Union, it proved difficult to calibrate this new element. Soon after Carter's inauguration, the State

Department—on its own initiative—began issuing a flood of statements championing human rights. One such initiative was a declaration of sympathy for Charter 77, the monitoring group set up by Czechoslovak activists; another was in support of Soviet scientist and human rights champion Andrei Sakharov. Carter decided to endorse these State Department initiatives, while letting it be known that he would have appreciated their being cleared in the White House. Then the president decided that he should reply personally to a public letter addressed to him by Sakharov appealing for U.S. support for a number of Soviet dissidents. Not wanting to leave himself open to charges of moral laxity like those leveled at Gerald Ford for not receiving Aleksandr Solzhenitsyn in the White House in 1975, Carter sent Sakharov a strong letter, including a sentence of sympathy for "prisoners of conscience." In a widely circulated news photo, Sakharov proudly displayed the letter he received with Carter's signature. In addition, a White House meeting was arranged for recently released Soviet dissident Vladimir Bukovsky, who met with Mondale in the Roosevelt Room. The Soviet response to all these activities was a scathing letter from Brezhnev to Carter stressing that the Soviet leadership would not "allow interference in our internal affairs, whatever pseudo-humanitarian slogans are used to present it."

All this took place in the first few weeks of the new administration, as it was preparing its new SALT proposals to be delivered by Secretary of State Vance on a trip to Moscow at the end of March. A new administration has every right to make changes in policies; that is its mandate from the American people, and the Soviets should not have been surprised that Carter's critique of SALT and advocacy of human rights during his campaign presaged a significant change. But the Soviets were not prepared for what they were faced with. The entire history of strategic arms negotiations up to then had occurred in the Nixon-Ford-Kissinger period. The Soviets were not only unaccustomed to abrupt changes; they were also accustomed to a procedure in which Kissinger would give Ambassador Dobrynin a heads-up with respect to any new U.S. proposals so that Brezhnev would not be caught by surprise when Kissinger showed up in Moscow. This was not simple courtesy; it was a way to allow the Soviet bureaucracy time to chew on new proposals so that the Kissinger-Brezhnev discussions would be more productive. In this case, with more abrupt changes in store—and against the background of the more assertive U.S. posture on human rights—there was no such preparing of the ground.

William Hyland, the holdover on the NSC staff, was particularly amused by one aspect of the procedure. "To guard against leaks, both Carter and Brzezinski insisted that the SALT decisions be drafted without interagency clearances; thus the delegation's instructions [drafted in the White House] were a virtual secret from the other departments." Hyland was badgered during the trip by other delegation members wanting to see the president's instructions. With Vance's concurrence, Hyland had to refuse. "When I told Vance of my embarrassment, he laughed and said that while he had ordered me to protect the instructions, he had not expected me to get caught. So a Ford holdover was entrusted with the mission of keeping Carter's secrets safe from his own delegation." Hyland recognized it as a Nixonian moment.

The bigger problem, however, was that Brezhnev, presented with the deep cuts option and the modified Vladivostok option, rejected them both. This was a shock; the Carter team had assumed that the modified Vladivostok option would be a mutually acceptable fallback. The Soviets' motivation is not clear. Whether out of pique at the human rights campaign, or a rigid commitment by their military bureaucracy to the original Vladivostok numbers, the Soviets just said no. Vance, on returning home, had to admit an American miscalculation and the administration was roundly criticized in the media for incompetence. *The Washington Post* called it the most disorderly retreat from Moscow since Napoleon's.

HYLAND DOES NOT SPARE his new colleagues his own critique of their complacency, but he also believes the Soviets erred in such a peremptory response:

> Had the Soviets moved quickly to consolidate an agreement, even in vague terms, they probably could have created a better foundation for a relationship with Carter; they could have gained a tactical advantage over the Chinese and perhaps they could have avoided the problem of the new American ICBM, the MX, to say nothing of the emergence of [Reagan's] Strategic Defense Initiative. Some Soviets have since admitted to me that they missed a chance.

In any case, the abortive March 1977 trip to Moscow set the negotiations back a period of months. The experiment in getting to the right of their Republican predecessors was a failure; no Democratic administration could sustain such a hard-line posture. Soon enough, eager to achieve an agreement, the Carter administration drifted back closer to the Vladivostok framework. Its procedures, and the coherence of its positions, improved. Negotiations continued, and produced by mid-1979 a SALT II Treaty that, inter alia, capped both sides' strategic delivery systems at 2,250 (slightly below the Vladivostok ceiling of 2,400).

The problem by that point, however, was that the passage of time was very unkind to the Carter administration. By 1979, U.S.-Soviet relations were burdened with significant developments in another sphere—namely, a Soviet campaign of geopolitical opportunism in the Third World. In early 1977, there was a minor Soviet-Cuban military intervention in the Shaba region of Zaire (now Congo), from across the border in Angola. Later in 1977, Cuban troops commanded by a Soviet officer led Ethiopian forces against Somali troops that had tried to occupy the disputed Ogaden desert. The government in Afghanistan was overthrown by a Communist coup d'état in April 1978. In May 1978 came a second Shaba invasion. A coup in South Yemen pushed the Aden government further in a pro-Soviet direction. In the winter of 1978, Moscow signed a "friendship treaty" with Hanoi that encouraged Vietnam to invade Cambodia at the end of the year.

The Soviets and their allies seemed to be on a roll. Following the collapse of the American enterprise in Indochina in April 1975, and Congress's refusal to allow the Ford administration to respond to a Cuban-Soviet military intervention in Angola at the end of 1975, Leonid Brezhnev was to proclaim at the Twenty-fifth Soviet Party Congress in February 1976 that the global "correlation of forces" was tilting against "imperialism." He hailed the victories in Indochina and Angola. "No impartial person can deny that the socialist countries' influence on world affairs is becoming ever stronger and deeper," he boasted. A year and a half later, Soviet support for "national liberation movements" was even enshrined in the new constitution of the USSR. The West, as noted in the last chapter, was reeling from the energy shocks and was also worried about the growing political strength of Communist parties even in Western Europe.

All this raised an issue that became sorely divisive in the Carter administration, namely whether the United States should draw some conclusions from this and make some connection between arms control and Soviet behavior in the world. This was "linkage" again. Arms control advocates like Vance wanted to insulate SALT from these other events; they shrank from any kind of significant response or reaction to the Soviet moves out of fear of jeopardizing SALT. On this, Harold Brown at Defense and Cyrus Vance at State were united. At White House meetings in early 1978, for example, Brzezinski urged that the United States dispatch an aircraft carrier task force to the vicinity of Ethiopia to indicate the depth of U.S. concern. Vance and Brown argued against it, and Carter sided with them.

Brzezinski was convinced that the weak U.S. response to this Soviet offensive would jeopardize not only international stability, but ultimately SALT as well. In this he was borne out, as the Soviets' aggressive behavior undermined American congressional and public support for SALT when the treaty went before the Senate in June 1979. The treaty died there—the final nail in its coffin delivered by the Soviet invasion of Afghanistan in December 1979. But Brzezinski remained convinced that the turning point had come in Ethiopia, in early 1978 when the United States had failed to react to the Soviets' Ethiopian adventure. That emboldened them to go further, and the global environment deteriorated from there. SALT was "buried," Brzezinski often said, "in the sands of the Ogaden." His "greatest regret," he admitted a few years later, was:

> that I was unable to convince the president and others to deal with the Soviet relationship in a somewhat different fashion. I always felt that we shouldn't be engaging only in the legalistic, specific, technical, and complicated negotiations, but that we should engage them also in protracted, sustained discussions in depth and at length, in which we would try to make the Russians understand what was meant by reciprocity and restraint in a genuine détente relationship. And I felt that these discussions could only succeed if they were paralleled by actions that would give credibility to what we were saying.

The administration's conceptual problem with respect to Soviet policy was further revealed in mid-1978 when the president delivered a speech on the subject at the U.S. Naval Academy in Annapolis. Vance had submitted a speech draft emphasizing the complexity of the U.S.-Soviet relationship and the need for lowering political tensions on a reciprocal basis. Carter produced his own draft, however, borrowing some of Vance's language but adding some tougher passages, especially about the nature of the Soviet regime. Vance was frustrated by what he saw as a "stitched-together" product that only reflected the divisions in the administration. But Carter was pleased with the outcome, believing that the speech "spell[ed] out more clearly" how he saw the overall relationship with the Soviet Union.

Brzezinski continued to deplore what he saw as his State Department colleagues' tendency to "shy away from the unavoidable ingredient of force in dealing with contemporary realities, and to have an excessive faith that all issues can be resolved by compromise," and their inclination to "equate foreign policy with endless litigation and to confuse détente with acquiescence." But as we saw earlier, Brzezinski lamented that unlike Henry Kissinger he did not have consistent backing from his president. Carter was torn: "[B]ecause he was so intelligent," Brzezinski wrote delicately, "he did tend to see more sides to an issue than perhaps occasionally was necessary, and . . . he was pulled in opposite directions by conflicting advice from his immediate associates."

This was especially true on two issues. The debate over linkage in U.S.-Soviet relations was one. The other was the Iranian crisis—the revolution that toppled the shah in 1978–1979.

The Fall of the Shah

When the shah stood with Jimmy Carter on the South Lawn of the White House for the welcoming ceremony for his state visit on November 15, 1977, mounted police in the distance were trying to contain a group of anti-shah demonstrators outside the White House grounds. Wafts of tear gas reached the South Lawn and the shah, the president, their wives, and other dignitaries found themselves mopping or rubbing their eyes to contain the tears. Carter saw it as an augury of the hostage crisis to come: "The tear gas had created the semblance of grief. Almost two years later, and for fourteen months afterward, there would be real grief in our country because of Iran." But the visit was an augury for a deeper reason—because what the president said to the shah during the visit reflected the contradictions in U.S. policy that would help bring that crisis about. In the public greeting on the South Lawn, Carter repeated the strong statements of U.S. solidarity with the shah and his country that every U.S. president since Franklin Roosevelt had expressed. Once they repaired safely inside, after a larger meeting in the Cabinet Room, Carter took the shah aside to a small private room near the Oval Office and expressed his concerns about human rights in Iran; he urged the shah to consider reaching out to dissident groups and "easing off" on police actions against them. This kind of pressure from an American president on his internal policies was new to the shah; he responded politely but firmly that he would enforce his country's laws.

As the domestic unrest within Iran grew to engulf the shah, this was to be the pattern of U.S. policy over the next fourteen months—expressions of support, coupled with recommendations for political concessions to his opponents—a pattern that confused the shah and contributed to his hesitations; it had the same effect on the Iranian military, who we were expecting to be a stabilizing factor. In the context of the upheaval that was taking place, this U.S. posture was full of contradictions, reflecting divisions within the Carter administration and, in the end, a conflict within the president's own mind.

The upheaval in Iran was the product of many causes and disparate forces. The shah failed to accompany the country's rapid economic modernization with a political modernization that could have co-opted the middle classes into the system. He dealt harshly with his opposition. In 1953, when a leftist government that tried to topple him was itself toppled by the CIA, the shah enjoyed support from many key groups in the society, including the merchant class and the clergy. By 1978, his political rigidity had alienated them. Thus the revolution against him at first appeared to be a broad-based coalition embracing the merchants, students, and many moderate elements, in addition to the reactionary clerics; only gradually did it become clear that, as in Petrograd in 1917, vacuums are often filled by the most ruthless, the most disciplined, the most fanatical. And U.S. policy was helping create that vacuum.

There were two points of view in the U.S. government. One view, strongly held in the State Department, was, in essence, that the shah was a retrograde figure, that we should seize the opportunity to help effect a transition, and that moderate elements in the revolution represented a new order that we could get along with. The opposing view, represented especially by Brzezinski (and also James Schlesinger, whom Carter had appointed energy secretary), was that the shah was a strategic ally in a vital region and that if we undermined him, or the army, we were risking strategic disaster. Carter sided with Brzezinski for much of the period, determined to bolster the shah's morale and his resistance to the revolutionary tide.

These reassurances were all the more necessary because the shah was highly susceptible to conspiracy theories. His foreign policy through his whole career had been grounded in the solid support of the United States; now he was in unfamiliar territory. From the beginning of the Carter administration he found U.S. policy to be "confusing and contradictory" and he assumed the worst. Henry Kissinger, visiting Iran as a private citizen in June 1978, found the shah convinced that Washington and Moscow were colluding to divide up Iran. Kissinger told him it was impossible. In September, the shah expounded the same theory to visiting *Time* correspondents, confiding to them his conviction that the CIA was backing the revolution. Unfortunately the head of French intelligence was telling the shah around the same time that the rumors that Carter wanted to replace him were true. And to his dying day he believed it was the American intention all along.

Despite the general view of the shah as a brutal dictator, his problem during this period was a weakness of will, exacerbated not only by these fears of American abandonment but perhaps also by the cancer that he knew (but we did not know) was killing him. During the summer and fall of 1978 he made concessions to his opposition and did not crack down ruthlessly; his police handled some protests brutally but only enough to inflame passions, not suppress them. The shah flirted with different political alternatives—either a coalition government that would seek to co-opt moderate elements from the opposition, or a military government that would restore his authority and allow him to reach out politically from a position of strength. Carter sent him a message in early November assuring him of U.S. support "without any reservation whatsoever, completely and fully," whatever course of action he chose. Brzezinski conveyed the message to him personally by phone, because he and the president were concerned that the U.S. ambassador in Tehran, William Sullivan, and the State Department, were not conveying such clear-cut support in their own communications with the shah.

Other presidents, as we have seen, have had their frustrations with the State Department. What confronted and frustrated Jimmy Carter was a group of midlevel State officials intellectually and morally opposed to the shah on human rights grounds, optimistic about America's natural affinity with a revolution they continued to see as broad-based and reformist, and tenaciously bending the implementation of U.S. policy in their preferred direction whatever instructions they received from the president. Carter and Brzezinski were unable to impose their will on a determined Foreign Service, especially when the secretary of state acted as the spokesman and champion of the department's view.

The shah in fact established a military government in early November, but it strengthened his position only briefly. A general strike began later in the month, and the Ayatollah Ruhollah Khomeini, in exile, called for the shah's violent overthrow. Carter and Brzezinski were still seeking to buck up the shah's morale. Carter told Vance on November 10 "to be sure that the State Department officials below him supported my position—that the Shah should know that we are with him." Brzezinski later wrote:

> Sometimes the Shah expressed confidence that the military would get hold of the situation; on other occasions he would firmly state that he would not spill blood. Sullivan's cables did not give one the impression that the American Ambassador was exerting himself to reinforce the Shah's willpower.

At the turn of the year, the shah agreed to appoint the Western-educated moderate opposition figure Shapour Bakhtiar as prime minister of a coalition government. By this time the mounting pressures were so powerful that Bakhtiar felt compelled to ask, as a condition of taking office, that the shah leave Iran. This was a measure of how far and how rapidly the ground had shifted. The shah hesitated, looking to the U.S. government for advice. Whereas the president's view had been— and remained—that the purpose of any political concessions was to enable the shah to remain in power, the State Department was explicitly of the view that the possibility of a moderate pro-Western government, with army support, now depended on the shah's removal. Carter continued to reject this and was infuriated by continued leaks to the media suggesting U.S. doubts about the desirability of the shah's remaining in power.

The shah vacillated between departing, as Bakhtiar and the opposition were clamoring for him to do, and ordering the military to suppress the opposition by force. His will was clearly flagging. In early November, when *Newsweek* correspondent Arnaud de Borchgrave had told him that some of his foreign supporters would back his use of military force, the shah wept. "There had already been too much violence, he said; he would not be the cause of more bloodshed." In a meeting with Ambassador Sullivan on December 26, the shah asked Sullivan point-blank what the United States wanted him to do. Sullivan's reply embodied all the ambiguity that Brzezinski was struggling to avoid:

> Sullivan reported [that he had told the shah] that the United States supported his efforts to reestablish law and order. The Shah asked then whether he was being advised to use the iron fist even if it meant widespread bloodshed and even if it might fail to restore law and order. Sullivan reported that he responded by saying that if the Shah was trying to get the United States to take the responsibility for his actions, he doubted that he would ever get such instructions from Washington. He was the Shah and he had to take the decision as well as the responsibility.

Brzezinski, disturbed by this ambiguity, arranged a meeting of principals in the White House to agree on a tougher follow-up message. The upshot was a complicated cable that Brzezinski, in his memoirs, cites as a considerable toughening of support, while Vance, in his memoirs, hails it as a clear message to the shah that we would not support his use of the "iron fist" to maintain his throne. Within days, bowing to what he saw as inevitable, the shah agreed to leave the country, in effect embracing the theory that without him, the moderate Bakhtiar government and the Iranian military could better maintain a cohesive resistance to the revolution than they could with him.

Focus then shifted to the role of the military. Carter dispatched a senior U.S. military officer, General Robert Huyser, then deputy U.S. commander in Europe, to talk to the Iranian military. Huyser's declared mission was to help the military retain their cohesion to support the moderate government and the possibility of long-term collaboration with the United States. But this assignment masked its own ambiguity: Did we want the military to take over by force if that was the only way to stop the revolution, or not? Brzezinski's hope was that it would do so. But just as Sullivan never answered that question when the shah asked him point-blank, so Jimmy Carter never answered it when Brzezinski strove to move U.S. policy to this ultimate step.

ONCE THE SHAH departed his country on January 16, 1979, the U.S. government was left with only the illusion of a policy. The momentum of revolution was irreversible (and perhaps had been for some months).

Khomeini's triumphal return to Iran swept away the Bakhtiar government, and eventually also the moderate elements in the revolution. The military—like the shah, waiting for some signal from Washington that never came—were paralyzed by the Huyser mission, not galvanized. They had no experience of politics and, without the shah, the lifelong object of their loyalty, they were directionless; and so the army, too, disintegrated under the pressure of events.

For the purposes of this book, the lesson to draw is the price paid for the contradictions in U.S. policy, the ambivalences that were never resolved. Through most of the period, Carter supported Brzezinski's view of the strategic stakes involved and repeatedly complained of leaks from State that undermined decisions he had made. But in the Carter system, State controlled the implementation of policy. The White House never trusted the U.S. Embassy to deliver categorical messages of support as the president intended, but the president's efforts to enforce his wishes were sporadic—at one point in February 1979 he met with a group of midlevel State officials and castigated them for disloyalty and leaking—and Brzezinski did not have the bureaucratic clout to enforce them on the president's behalf. Nixon's option of simply excluding and bypassing State was not available.

A second problem was that Carter's agreement with Brzezinski's tough line went only so far. As we saw, the desire to nudge the shah toward political liberalization was built into the policy from the beginning. Toward the end, the painful question was whether to advise the shah, or the military, explicitly to use force. Brzezinski favored doing so but the president did not; it reached the point that Brzezinski thought he was annoying Carter by continuing to raise it or hint at it. In the end, Carter, who prided himself on his morality and had campaigned on the contrast he drew with his predecessors, could not stomach such a course. Certainly Ambassador Sullivan was right that the shah ought not to be shifting such a burden onto our shoulders, but he did. Normally it would be a truism that the shah's survival ought to be more important to him than to us; in this case, however—especially after the nightmare the world has lived through for a generation since then—the truth of that proposition is not so obvious. Carter, in any event, took refuge in repeated public statements that we had no desire to interfere in the internal affairs of Iran. This was an evasion.

To condone or endorse a military crackdown has to be one of the most agonizing questions any president could face, given the opprobrium that would be heaped on the United States for whatever role it played. For a Democratic president it was probably an impossibility. Of the chief executives we are considering in this book it is easiest to imagine Nixon making such a decision. Nixon was no stranger to opprobrium; indeed he tended fatalistically to consider it part of his lot whatever he did. He and Kissinger could understand clearly what the strategic stakes were. Brzezinski and Schlesinger did as well. But in advance of events, as opposed to hindsight, one is relying on intuition, and they found it impossible to convince their president of consequences that might be avoided if their advice were taken. Nor, in fairness, could anyone have imagined the strategic enormity of what did ensue.

Lessons

The Carter administration had a number of achievements to its credit, amidst a turbulent period in international and American politics. The Camp David accords between Egypt and Israel, building upon the Kissinger shuttles, were a historic milestone in the diplomacy of Arab-Israeli peace. The "Carter Doctrine" proclaimed the vital U.S. interest in the security of the Gulf. Relations with China reached a new stage, with full normalization, and provided new leverage against the Soviet Union. In the defense field, there were advances in strategic doctrine and defense modernization, including progress in stealth aircraft technology and deployment of the MX ICBM and Trident submarine. This improving defense posture helped shore up a U.S.-Soviet strategic balance at reasonably stable levels that Carter's successor, Ronald Reagan, continued as a matter of policy even though the SALT II treaty failed of ratification. The administration began a substantial program of aid to anti-Soviet insurgents in Afghanistan that ultimately inflicted a significant strategic defeat on the Soviet Union. The Panama Canal treaties enabled the United States to maintain the defense of the canal while shedding the intrusive presence on Panamanian soil that would have assured a generation of nationalistic upheaval.

But Carter's foreign policy difficulties, which contributed to his defeat for reelection in 1980, also teach some lessons about the factors that lead to success or failure in presidential leadership.

Brzezinski argued for a time, after leaving office, that the role of the assistant to the president for national security affairs should be strengthened. He made a strong case that amid all the turbulence of the modern era there is a premium on central direction and integration of the various elements of policy, which can come only from the White House, not the State Department. He cited the many examples of Carter's inability to impose his will on the career service. He proposed that the national security adviser's pivotal role be acknowledged, strengthened, and institutionalized by being given a statutory basis, including confirmation by the Senate.

The Senate Foreign Relations Committee held a hearing on this idea in April 1980. The committee had before it at that moment the example of two recent national security advisers, Kissinger and Brzezinski, who had to one degree or another eclipsed the secretary of state. This the committee (and many others) regretted, and from the committee's point of view the idea of making this elusive and increasingly powerful White House figure answerable to the Senate might be part of the solution. But the overwhelming majority of eminent figures whose opinion the committee canvassed—including Richard Neustadt, Andrew Goodpaster, McGeorge Bundy, Walt Rostow, and Brent Scowcroft—were adamantly opposed to the idea. Making the position subject to confirmation, they believed, would only enshrine the elevated role of the national security adviser as a rival to the secretary of state, compounding the problem more than solving it. Many of them also stressed that the president in any case has need of a confidential adviser accountable to no one but the president—which is "an inside, not an outside, job," as Bundy put it.

We have Jimmy Carter's own testimony as to the problem of the State Department in his administration, but Brzezinski, in his proposed solution, may have been looking through the telescope from the wrong end. It is striking, of course, that a liberal Democratic president like Carter perceived the problem of State in terms not dissimilar from Nixon—the poor intellectual quality of its work, its institutional biases and unresponsiveness to political authority. Indeed, Carter's problem with Vance was a variant of Nixon's problem with Rogers: It was the weakness of a secretary of state unable or unwilling to impose political direction on the career bureaucracy in the president's name. One hypothetical solution is Nixon's—simply to exclude State, as if it were possible to carve out its plot of land in Foggy Bottom and float it down the Potomac. We have seen the price paid for that—and in any case, State does have its hands on the levers of implementation of policy. If Nixon's extreme exclusionary approach is itself excluded, then the solution is not a stronger national security adviser but a stronger secretary of state. As I have suggested, "stronger" in this context has a particular meaning—a secretary of state who is loyal, both personally and philosophically, to the president and able and willing to impose the president's agenda on a recalcitrant bureaucracy. The job of the security adviser is then to arm the president so that a strong secretary of state receives firm guidance (and monitoring) from the White House.

An additional problem for Carter was the institutional weakness of the office when he inherited it after what were seen as a series of failed presidencies. In the last chapter we saw the extent of the congressional revolt against the so-called imperial presidency. Richard Neustadt asked himself in 1979, watching Jimmy Carter (after Carter then too seemed a failure): "Is the presidency possible?" Was the job simply too big and too hard for any human being in this modern era? He cited a number of causes of this institutional weakness, including the new power of Congress and complexity of dealing with it, the expansion and fragmentation of the Executive Branch, the growing power of interest groups, and the expansion of staffs all over Washington. Carter had entered office seeking to restore presidential authority by relegitimating it, which he aimed to do by displays of personal humility—walking up Pennsylvania Avenue during his inaugural parade, carrying his own luggage on and off *Air Force One*, wearing cardigans on television, insuring frugality in the White House, and so forth—all to rid the office of its "imperial" pretensions. The perverse irony of Carter's quest, however, is that his shedding of the trappings of presidential authority came at a time when that authority needed strengthening, not weakening. What Walter Bagehot called the "dignified" elements of a constitutional system have their place in inspiring people's loyalty, confidence, and deference.

A final lesson of the Carter experience is that the key is not the role of the national security adviser or the secretary of state but the role of the president. Carter built a system, as we saw, that did insure his pivotal role as the "decider." That turns out to be necessary, but not sufficient. Carter's intelligence and tenacity were often in evidence—most conspicuously, for example, in the extraordinary negotiation he mediated personally between Egypt's Anwar Sadat and Israel's Menachem Begin at Camp David. But in other, less successful, endeavors his philosophical schizophrenia tore away at the consistency that effective policy requires. Cyrus Vance wrote: "A question troubling Congress, the allies and the American public in the spring of 1980 was whether the Carter administration had a coherent view of the international situation, a sense of global strategy, and consistent policies and objectives."

The challenge of managing conflict within one's administration is a recurring one, and often difficult to avoid. In later chapters we will see Ronald Reagan and George W. Bush wrestling with similar problems. But the difficulty is exacerbated if the president doesn't know his own mind. While Reagan and Bush 43 struggled with divisions between cabinet officers, one has the sense that they both came into office expecting a more united government and thus ended up in that position involuntarily. Carter seems to have chosen a system that enshrined his own— divided—view of the world. In such circumstances, the task of running national security policy, difficult enough to start with, becomes even harder.

CHAPTER SIX

Ronald Reagan

T HE PARADOX OF RONALD REAGAN is that he was one of the most important presidents of the modern era, who left his bold imprint on his administration and on history, yet on issues on which he was less engaged, his management of his government has to be rated among the weakest. On the positive side of the ledger was, especially, the transformation of the generations-long conflict with the Soviet Union, as well as a major program of reform in domestic economic policy. In both these areas, he came with a clear sense of purpose. After leaving office Reagan told an aide: "I had an agenda I wanted to get done. I came with a script." On the negative side were lapses like the Iran-Contra affair as well as protracted conflicts among his senior subordinates that led to frustrations and failures (Lebanon being the most conspicuous). "He was better suited to leading the nation than commanding its government," his principal biographer, Lou Cannon, concluded.

But both sides of this paradox deserve their proper respect. There are studies of his administrative process (usually focusing on Iran-Contra) that tend toward the dismissive, but they thereby miss an important forest through the trees on the broad question of presidential leadership. "[T]he whole of Reagan's performance," says Cannon shrewdly, "was often greater than the sum of its parts." And those who admire Reagan (as I do) need to be clear about his weaknesses, if only to draw usable lessons for our inquiry in this book.

Reagan as president was a more enigmatic figure than most of his detractors or supporters realized. Whatever the management weaknesses, he had considerable strengths that lay elsewhere, and I do not mean just his Hollywood-nurtured ability to deliver a speech with feeling or to walk into a room with a tall, commanding stride. He did have a

remarkable physical presence in a room, which reflected an inner com-
posure as well as whatever Hollywood had taught him. But Reagan also
had an innate political shrewdness and knew his country's mood. He
could not have left such an imprint on his times without embodying
something of substance. Published compilations of his pre-presidential
speeches and broadcasts—written by him, not ghostwriters—testify to
his intellectual curiosity and grasp of issues. His presidential diaries,
published in 2007, also indicate a man attentive and thoughtful, as well
as "principled [and] confident," in the words of their editor. His critics
alternated between denouncing him for his ideological convictions, on
the one hand, and insisting (usually after one of his electoral victories)
that the American people had voted only for a genial man with a smile
They could not have it both ways.

He was an unabashed believer in American exceptionalism: America
was great and good and had a moral mission to be the "shining city on a
hill." Where Jimmy Carter had often contrasted American ideals with
American performance, Reagan cast never a doubt on his country's sin
cerity. Where Carter had sought, in the post-Vietnam era, to teach
America its limits (especially to dampen the frustrations of the Iran
hostage crisis), Reagan rejected the defeatism that this seemed to imply
and sought to restore the country's faith in its limitless possibilities. It
was America's Soviet adversaries, he forthrightly declared as early as
1982 and 1983, who were facing a systemic crisis. Jimmy Carter, in a
sense, was an interruption of the country's recovery from the Vietnam
trauma, and the foreign policy embarrassments of Carter's presidency
only insured that, after him, that recovery would burst forth with a
vengeance.

Similarly in domestic policy, Reagan's passion to reduce the burden
of government on the economy came at a time when, fifty years after the
New Deal, Western societies were discovering that an excess of bureaucracy, regulation, and taxation was burdening the entrepreneurship and
innovation that are the ultimate sources of growth. At the Bonn economic summit of May 1985, all the leading industrial democracies
endorsed this perception.

The intellectuals' mockery of Reagan was thus misplaced. His convictions coincided with the historical moment to powerful effect. A
famous essay on intellectual history by Isaiah Berlin is based on a line
from a fragment of Greek poetry: "The fox knows many things, but the
hedgehog knows one big thing." Jimmy Carter was perhaps a fox but

Ronald Reagan was surely a hedgehog. He was also totally impervious to what the editorial boards of *The New York Times* and *The Washington Post* thought—a truly liberating quality for a conservative president. Nixon had been constantly tortured by the liberal criticism, struggling either to defy it or win it over.

Management Problems

Like all his predecessors, Reagan came into office with his own philosophy of the job. In contrast with Jimmy Carter, he was not shy about embracing the symbolic grandeur of the office, partly as a matter of deliberately restoring its public authority but also out of personal reverence for it: He made a point of never taking his coat off when in the Oval Office. His management style was closer to that of a chairman of the board than chief executive officer. In another conscious contrast with Jimmy Carter, he was determined to focus on the "big picture," avoiding the micromanagement that was widely held to be one of Carter's weaknesses.

Indeed he was accused of the opposite deficiency. Reagan's work habits were much derided, and he joked about it himself: "It's true hard work never killed anybody, but I figure, why take a chance?" Two weeks short of his seventieth birthday when he took office, he followed a schedule that writer William Doyle calls "ruthlessly geared to preserving his energy." He needed his eight hours' sleep, and regular rest breaks (labeled "staff time") were written into his calendar. He came into the Oval Office around 9:00 a.m. and typically returned to the Residence by 5:30 p.m.; usually he took Wednesday afternoons off and often left midafternoon on Friday for a weekend at Camp David.

Critiques of Reagan's management style, even from loyalists, are replete with adjectives that suggest a contradictory mixture of strengths and weaknesses: bold, stubborn, passive, lazy, incurious, inattentive, detached from the policy-making process, remote, guileless, relentlessly optimistic, innocent, et cetera. Both sides in the administration's internal quarrels, "moderates" and "ideologues," each feared that the president was being manipulated by the other. His eyes sometimes glazed over in complex discussions. When he finished reading from his five-by-eight-inch cue cards in an official conversation, the conversation often drifted off. The jokes he cracked in important meetings in the Situation Room or with foreign visitors were sometimes apt, sometimes a device to hide his uncertainties. There are stories of his being sent a policy options memorandum with boxes for him to mark his choice and of the memo coming out of his office with all the boxes checked (though Richard Nixon did the same thing once in a distracted moment).

But the picture of a passive Reagan should not be exaggerated either. His reticence in large meetings was often simply due to a fear of leaks. He did not usually nap during his "staff time," but read mail or simply relaxed. Donald Regan, who served as chief of staff, reported:

> Every afternoon he went home complete with material—homework: briefing books, intelligence briefings, reports from State, DoD, materials submitted by Cabinet officers, legislative analysis on whether or not he should sign a particular bill. When he brought that stuff back at 8:50 or 8:55 in the morning, he not only had parts underlined, but pages annotated. You knew he had done his homework.

According to William Doyle:

> A random inspection of dozens of Reagan's diary files at the Reagan Library reveals not a somnambulant shirker but a seventy-something man who took a round of live ammunition in the chest in his second month on the job and went on to endure a tough daily schedule of frequent high-pressure private meetings and public events, plus a regular schedule of presidential functions at night, plus weekly radio addresses on Saturdays and sometimes more functions on the weekends, topped off with regular bursts of national and international travel. . . . [I]t seems the height of responsibility that he paced himself as he did.

By all accounts he was comfortable making decisions. Alexander Haig, who served both Nixon and Reagan, compared them: "[Nixon] would sit in anguish for hours over a decision before it was made. I never sensed that with Reagan. He was the most graceful and easy decision-maker I've ever seen." He demonstrated his mettle early in his first year by breaking an illegal strike by the air traffic controllers' union—a bold decision that did much to establish his political authority.

Reagan had an unusual degree of influence over events by virtue of his ideas and his communication of them. His speeches were powerful not only in their rhetoric and masterly delivery but in the message they conveyed. Over and over again, he propagated his belief in the illegitimacy and vulnerability of the Soviet system and his confidence in the fundamental goodness and resilience of the free nations. His strength as a "conviction politician" was an important element in his leadership. He almost single-handedly transformed the terms of the domestic and international debate.

REAGAN'S DECLARED MANAGEMENT model was cabinet government. As he had governed in California, he wanted his cabinet officers, not his staffers, to be both his principal advisers in their fields and the individuals responsible for executing his policies. But while espousing cabinet government, Reagan as president did not leave himself naked. He and his White House aides made the fullest use of the presidential appointment process to place loyalists in policy jobs around the cabinet departments, and his palace guard was alert to defend his prerogatives.

Reagan himself spent two hours a week on personnel matters, at least during the first two years. To Reagan, the selection of the three thousand political appointees was vital to insure that the cabinet departments were linked to his policy priorities. "We wanted our appointees to be the President's ambassadors to the agencies, not the other way around," as longtime aide Edwin Meese put it. Before inauguration, transition teams of loyalists studied each department and agency and came up with ideas for structural reforms as well as key personnel. A staff of one hundred in the White House screened candidates for philosophy as well as competence and integrity. The Reagan team is widely regarded as having had more success than most preceding administrations in shaping the leadership of the bureaucracy by these means.

This success naturally stirred opposition. Much of the literature on the Reagan administration is filled with criticism of the "ideologues" and "crazies" who came in with Reagan and who interfered with the more "experienced" and "moderate" folks as the latter sought to conduct policy as it should be conducted. The careful reader will take this with a grain of salt. The Reagan administration was challenged in its own way by the divisions in the Republican Party that had engulfed Gerald Ford. The party had united behind Reagan, but the large talent pool that he brought with him now included many veterans of the Nixon-Ford era as well as new people of generally more conservative bent. To deny the legitimacy of the new people, however, was to deny the results of the election as well as to deny the president the support in his own govern-ment of individuals who actually shared his beliefs. He *was* different from Richard Nixon and Gerald Ford, and this was bound to be reflected in his policies. Nor was Reagan the first to see the importance of personnel. Jimmy Carter in his time was accused of appointing scores of liberal activists to sub-cabinet positions to replace depart-ing Republicans. Very few of our presidents have followed the self-denying (and self-destructive) approach of John Quincy Adams. "Personnel *is* policy," is another Washington maxim of very long standing that every incoming president will learn the truth of soon enough if he or she is serious about giving political direction to the policies of the government.

The palace guard was the famous "troika," sometimes dubbed the "three-headed monster." It turned out to be a formidable animal. Edwin Meese, Reagan's chief political adviser in Sacramento, had expected to be White House chief of staff, but this was blocked by Michael Deaver, who thought Reagan would be better served by someone with Washing-ton experience. Thus, James A. Baker III—a longtime associate not of Reagan but of Vice President George H. W. Bush—became chief of staff, with Deaver as his deputy and Meese as "counselor" to the presi-dent. Reagan welcomed their presence as a buffer, and the three seem to have worked together smoothly to guard his interests. Alexander Haig, Reagan's first secretary of state, was surprised to see all three seated at the cabinet table during early cabinet meetings.

In the name of cabinet government, the position of the assistant for national security affairs was downgraded. It was to be, once again, a staff position with a coordinating function. This was a conscious decision to reempower cabinet secretaries, as well as to avoid the kind of embarrass-ing battles that had marked the Kissinger versus Rogers and Brzezinski versus Vance eras. Richard Allen, the first occupant of the job under Reagan, was stripped not only of the cabinet rank that Brzezinski had enjoyed but also of his direct line of access to the president; Allen was to report to the president through Meese. Allen was comfortable with all this, and indeed had proposed to Reagan during the 1980 campaign that he promise in a speech that he would restore the national security adviser to the role of staffer and honest broker. This Reagan did. And Allen is proud that he took his office physically back downstairs to the West Basement where Bundy and Rostow had labored (and Kissinger for his first year and a half). Meese took the upstairs corner office.

The flaws in this system soon appeared, as we shall see. There was considerable turmoil over eight years, including a succession of national security advisers (Richard Allen was the first of six). The Reagan presidency can usefully be divided into three periods. The first was the era of the troika, through the first term. The troika turned out to be as serious a problem for the secretary of state, at least during Haig's tenure, as any high-powered national security adviser would have been. Allen was replaced in early 1982 by William Clark, a close California friend and confidant of Reagan who by his stature upgraded the position—he reported directly to Reagan and was, effectively, on a par with the troika (which they resented). Clark's relationship with his president was one of the closest of the modern period. But Clark's relationship with two secretaries of state, Alexander Haig and George Shultz, was difficult, and for the nearly two years of Clark's tenure (until October 1983) there was indeed a replay of the State-NSC tensions that the new team had hoped to avoid.

At the beginning of the second term, the troika broke up—chief of staff James Baker switched places with Treasury Secretary Donald Regan, and Meese became attorney general. Regan dominated the White House staff, and the next two national security advisers, Robert (Bud) McFarlane and Vice Admiral John Poindexter, lacked Clark's clout. Though the office physically moved back upstairs when Meese left, functionally it reverted to a more modest honest broker role. This was the period of the Iran-Contra affair. The house-cleaning that followed led to Donald Regan's departure and to a calmer period under Frank Carlucci and then Lieutenant General Colin Powell as the national security adviser. I had returned to the NSC staff during this time, beginning under John Poindexter and remaining through the Carlucci-Powell period.

The Iran-Contra episode is usually described as the NSC staff run amok. In fact I would argue it was an aberration in a system whose dominant problem was something else—a protracted struggle between the secretaries of state and defense, which persisted through all three phases and which the White House was unable to resolve. "Nothing ever gets settled in this town," George Shultz once famously lamented. The national security adviser—deliberately weakened institutionally—was (except under Clark) unable to exert strong influence in the president's name.

Even in a system of cabinet government, the national security adviser has an essential role in managing the process, but his (or her) effectiveness depends on presidential engagement. Where Reagan's strong convictions were engaged, he made decisions, but often the system did not produce consistent policy or effective execution. Like Nixon, Reagan detested personal confrontations with his subordinates. The result, in James Baker's words, was often "a witches' brew of intrigue, elbows, egos, and separate agendas." The looseness of the structure, and the detachment of the president's management style, left the system vulnerable to end runs into the Oval Office or to prolonged stalemates, both of which left all sides continually frustrated. We will see this problem recur through the remainder of this chapter.

The Rise and Fall of Alexander Haig

The first management crisis was the tumultuous, and brief, tenure of Reagan's first secretary of state. Alexander Haig's aborted career at State is a mystery in many ways, most of all because of the contrast between his successful performance in the Nixon administration and his frustration in Reagan's.

Haig was a bright young colonel assigned by the Pentagon to be Henry Kissinger's military assistant beginning in the 1968–1969 presidential transition at the Pierre Hotel in New York. He had come highly recommended to Kissinger by many officials in the Johnson administration. Kissinger had been advised by his predecessor and old Harvard colleague McGeorge Bundy not to appoint a deputy: Bundy had hired Carl Kaysen, a high-powered Princeton professor whom Bundy had found hard to control. So Kissinger repelled the entreaties of those civilians on his staff who yearned to be his deputy, and instead relied for administrative support on his military assistant, who so capably performed the function over the first year and a half that he became de facto deputy and was rewarded with the title in mid-1970.

It was Al Haig who smoothed out Kissinger's rough edges, who managed the NSC staff's operations and looked after its morale. Kissinger had no experience as a manager, nor the temperament for the role. Unsure of his relationship with Nixon, and preoccupied with State's continuing efforts to undermine the president's policy and himself, Kissinger was no mother hen to his staff nor a smooth bureaucratic operator. Haig, a much more gregarious personality than either Nixon or Kissinger, deployed the necessary bureaucratic finesse. After some explosion or other in Kissinger's office, Haig would emerge and make a calm phone call to Secretary Rogers's executive assistant or Secretary Laird's military assistant and the problem would be resolved or eased or at least the message passed in some constructive fashion. Haig kept his cool. But I remember poking my head into Haig's tiny office at quiet moments and finding him seated at his desk, chain-smoking and grinning at me with a red-faced intensity that suggested his heroic self-discipline was not as effortless as it seemed.

Haig's role grew over time as Nixon got to know him, especially while Kissinger was traveling on some secret mission. As an active duty military officer, Haig owed loyalty to his commander in chief and also to his immediate boss; as differences developed between Nixon and Kissinger on some issues—for example, the tactics of the Vietnam endgame—this was a test of skill. Kissinger eased the problem by bringing Haig along with him to the Paris negotiations. Despite grumbling I heard from Kissinger at the time, I think Haig pulled off the balancing act with honor.

Haig's own starring role then came as Nixon's White House chief of staff in May 1973 after Haldeman's resignation over Watergate. Nixon, distraught, pulled Haig back from his brief stint as army vice chief of staff. Now the task was to manage Nixon, another larger-than-life personality, through a monumental political and personal trauma. Haig kept the whole U.S. government on an even keel. In the end, it meant greasing the skids for an unprecedented presidential resignation. Haig received praise from many quarters, including Watergate special prosecutor Leon Jaworski, for the integrity with which he performed this second historic mission.

All this makes the failure of Haig's third act—as Reagan's secretary of state—difficult to explain. A man of great talent, who under Nixon proved himself bureaucratically astute, under Reagan seems to have misjudged his bureaucratic situation and his president.

Perhaps there were other signs. The day after President Ford took the oath of office in August 1974, Haig came in to see him with a ten-page memorandum on White House operations that stressed the importance of his continuing role as chief of staff. Haig said that this included the power of hiring and firing, and inter alia he recommended the dismissal of Robert Hartmann, one of Ford's close aides. Ford was outwardly noncommittal, and privately shocked. It convinced him that, superb as Haig's performance had been during Nixon's final days, he was not the right man for the Ford White House.

Consciously or unconsciously, Haig in the Reagan era may have been trying to emulate what he had seen his mentor Kissinger do successfully, in two areas. During the 1968–1969 transition, he had worked with Kissinger and other colleagues on the famous Key Biscayne memorandum to the president-elect proposing significant changes in the NSC system including taking the chairmanship of a key committee away from State. On inauguration day 1981, still in his formal clothes, Haig appeared at the White House with a draft directive on the national security policy-making process, which would among other things bring the chairmanship of a similar group back into the State Department.

Contrary to some accounts, Haig did not just spring this on his colleagues. Reagan had assured him of his support for State's lead role, and Haig had promised the president such a memorandum. Haig had also negotiated the text of the directive with the new secretary of defense, Caspar Weinberger, the new CIA chief, William Casey, and national security adviser Richard Allen, who all supported it. But Haig had not included the troika in these deliberations and they reacted badly. Meese received the document from Haig on inauguration day, asked a number of pointed lawyerlike questions, stuffed it in his briefcase, and effectively left it there for a year.

Nixon had actively sought—indeed, insisted upon—the terms of Kissinger's memo in 1968, and chief of staff Haldeman had backed Kissinger up. The troika, unfamiliar with the issue and sensitive to Reagan's prerogative, saw Haig's assertiveness as a challenge. Their antennae had been up for weeks, perhaps since Senator Paul Tsongas (Democrat of Massachusetts) had told Haig at his confirmation hearing that, given his "raw talent," he was bound to "dominate" the new administration. The comment was widely repeated in the media and became part of the conventional wisdom. The troika suspected that Haig nursed presidential ambitions of his own. Haig had also dismissed the State Department transition team—the Reaganites who had been looking into State personnel and structure—as soon as he took office, in a manner that offended loyalists. The palace guard, on alert ever after, convinced themselves that Haig's draft directive was an effort not to carry out the president's will but to impose his own.

Haig's problem was not, at bottom, ideological; it was not that he was a moderate "Nixon-Ford retread" in an administration of Reaganites. To be sure, many of Haig's run-ins were with administration conservatives such as Weinberger, Casey, and U.N. ambassador Jeane Kirkpatrick. But in Reagan's first year it was Haig who pushed, for example, for a tougher U.S. policy against the Communists in Central America, even against Fidel Castro ("go to the source," Haig argued). But at that point the White House troika wanted Reagan's first-year priority to be his domestic economic reforms, and Mrs. Reagan weighed in with her concern that the president not do controversial things that reinforced his "belligerent cowboy" image. Haig was pushing too hard.

The second feature of Haig's approach was his frequent threats to resign. This, too, he had seen Kissinger do, indeed develop into an art form. But we know that both Nixon and Ford considered Kissinger indispensable and that his battles with others were on behalf of presidential wishes. Reagan and his minions tended to see Haig's restiveness as a bid for dominance or for presidential support on issues where the president's desires were not so clear-cut. Reagan's diaries show frequent irritation at Haig's squabbles with the White House staff as well as with Weinberger. Haig never had Reagan's consistent backing.

The fact that George Shultz, Haig's successor, endured similar struggles with conservatives in the administration shows that there was a structural problem, not only a personal one. Shultz, too, was bureaucratically tenacious and he, too, consumed a lot of his and the president's time threatening to resign over these struggles, just like his distinguished predecessors. But Shultz was better at finding allies in the White House (like Michael Deaver, and especially Nancy Reagan), and by his calm demeanor somehow managed to insure that Reagan never viewed these frequent threats of resignation as an assault on himself. If Haig had not pushed so hard he could well have ended up the "vicar" of foreign policy as he sought—and as Shultz achieved.

By January 1982, William Clark had replaced Richard Allen as national security adviser. Haig had shrewdly chosen this confidant of Reagan as his deputy secretary of state; Clark's shift to the White House seemed to bode well for Haig because it upgraded the status and clout of the security adviser and meant a potential ally among Reagan's senior team. But within months, his relationship with Clark deteriorated. In May and June 1982, for example, there were some interagency disagreements over the crisis in Lebanon. Haig was insisting that the president endorse his recommendations (such as a draft cable of instructions to the field); Clark insisted on airing the differences before the president at an NSC meeting. Haig thought events would not brook a delay and dispatched the instructions on his own initiative. On June 25, he came in to see Reagan one more time, threatening again to resign. Reagan's diary entry for that day reads: "Today was the day—I told Al H[aig] I had decided to accept his resignation. He didn't seem surprised but he said his differences were on policy. . . . Actually the only disagreement was over whether I made policy or the Sec[retary] of State did."

The Evil Empire

Policy toward the Soviet Union in what turned out to be the terminal phase of the Cold War is the area in which Ronald Reagan has left his strongest mark on history, and he did so even amidst a good deal of bureaucratic disarray. At one level, his administration was as divided as Jimmy Carter's, with more ideologically anti-Soviet senior officials like Caspar Weinberger, Jeane Kirkpatrick, and William Casey on the one side, and more moderate individuals like George Shultz (with the backing of Nancy Reagan) on the other. The battles among these strong personalities were continual; the key question for our purposes is whether these battles reflected a schizophrenic president, like Carter, or some different management disorder.

The Reagan administration put an unusual amount of effort into articulating its basic strategy toward the Soviet Union, not only in presidential speeches but more importantly in classified policy directives. In the Reagan era, these were called National Security Decision Directives (NSDDs). In the Nixon administration, directives of this kind usually transmitted tactical decisions or, on occasion, Nixon's decisions in response to the interagency studies conducted in the NSC system; they were usually not elaborate philosophical expositions. (Nixon's broad policies were more fully articulated in his four public reports to Congress on foreign policy, drafted by Kissinger and his staff.) For Reagan, however, these internal directives were a primary vehicle for articulating broad strategies. Usually their contents were laboriously negotiated among the departments and agencies. Nevertheless, the content—especially of these early documents on Soviet policy—reflected the strong influence of a group of ideological soul-mates of the president on the NSC staff.

On U.S.-Soviet relations, three such directives, signed by the president, stand out. In response to the Communist martial-law crackdown in Poland in December 1981, NSDD 32 (March 1982) called for tight-ened sanctions against the Soviet Union and a variety of means, overt and covert, of expanded aid to the Solidarity movement in Poland as part of a broader policy to "neutralize" Soviet control over Eastern Europe. Second was NSDD 66 (November 1982), on East-West eco-nomic relations, which sought to rally U.S. allies to a strategy of restrict-ing technology transfer to the Soviet Union or energy dependence on it. Third and broadest was NSDD 75 (January 1983), which declared the following to be the "tasks" of U.S. policy toward the Soviet Union:

> 1. To contain and over time reverse Soviet expansionism by competing effectively on a sustained basis with the Soviet Union in all inter-national arenas—particularly in the overall military balance and in geographical regions of priority concern to the United States. This will remain the primary focus of U.S. policy toward the USSR.
> 2. To promote, within the narrow limits available to us, the process of change in the Soviet Union toward a more pluralistic political and economic system in which the power of the privileged ruling elite is gradually reduced. The U.S. recognizes that Soviet aggressiveness has deep roots in the internal system, and that relations with the USSR should therefore take into account whether or not they help to strengthen this system and its capacity to engage in aggression.
> 3. To engage the Soviet Union in negotiations to attempt to reach agreements which protect and enhance U.S. interests and which are consistent with the principle of strict reciprocity and mutual interest.

NSDD 75, in its aspiration, was a significant break with decades of U.S. policy that had focused on containment of the Soviet Union's external aggression and generally eschewed "roll-back" of Soviet gains or attempts to exert direct pressure on the internal evolution of the Soviet system. Now the United States was pressing the Kremlin on several fronts. The boldness with which this new strategy was articulated owed much to the pen of Richard Pipes, a distinguished Harvard scholar of Russian and Soviet affairs and longtime critic of détente, now on the NSC staff. The "roll-back" activities would, in practice, owe much to the energy of CIA director William Casey. He would be in charge of the measures aimed at weakening the Soviet grip on Poland and Eastern Europe and expanding the covert program (inherited from the Carter administration) of aid to Afghans fighting to drive the Soviet army from their country. The directive also stated the U.S. goal "[t]o avoid subsidizing the Soviet economy or unduly easing the burden of Soviet resource allocation decisions, so as not to dilute pressures for structural change in the Soviet system." To advance this goal, Casey would collude with Crown Prince Fahd of Saudi Arabia to reduce oil prices in the early 1980s to depress Soviet revenues.

Over the next few years, the United States would also step up military or financial aid to anti-Communist insurgent movements opposing Soviet client states in Nicaragua, Angola, and Cambodia, in addition to Afghanistan. (Legislation that had barred Ford and Kissinger from aiding the Angolans fighting the Cuban-Soviet intervention in 1975 was repealed under Reagan in 1985.) The Soviets were overextended; the Reagan administration perceived a Soviet vulnerability and adopted a deliberate strategy of raising the costs to them of this Third World adventurism.

NSDD 75 showed the signs of interagency negotiation; it had something for everyone. For the Pentagon, it contained a ringing endorsement of U.S. military modernization and the effort to restrict Western military and dual-use technology transfers to the Soviets. The State Department opposed the more exuberant "roll-back" language, but was overruled. State was mollified by sections that stressed the importance of collaboration with allies, of diplomatic engagement with the Kremlin on arms control and other issues, and of educational and cultural exchanges. Some of the goals in the NSDD were to prove incompatible with each other (as when the European allies resisted the U.S. attempt to constrain energy and technological trade with the Soviets), and many of them were to become the subject of contention within the administration (such as when the State Department actually attempted to negotiate with Moscow on arms control and other issues).

The hard-line strategies outlined in the NSDDs were not the only guides to Reagan's thinking, however. When it came to practice, as we shall see, George Shultz more often than not had Reagan's backing for his diplomacy. As early as April 1981, while still recovering from his gunshot wound after an attempted assassination, Reagan sent two letters to Leonid Brezhnev—a formal letter shaped mainly by the State Department, but also a long, personal, handwritten appeal for a better world: "Is it possible," he wrote, "that we have permitted ideology, political and economic philosophies, and governmental policies to keep us from considering the very real everyday problems of peoples?" In April 1983, a few weeks after his "evil empire" and SDI speeches, he noted in his diary that, despite opposition from the NSC staff, he was supporting George Shultz in his "quiet diplomacy" with the Soviets. Reagan added:

> Some of the N.S.C. staff are too hard line & don't think any approach should be made to the Soviets. I think I'm hard-line & will never appease but I do want to try & let them see there is a better world if they'll show by deed they want to get along with the free world.

In a televised address from the White House on January 16, 1984, devoted to U.S.-Soviet relations, Reagan appealed to the common interests of the two superpowers in reducing nuclear weapons, defusing regional conflicts, and improving bilateral ties.

Some liberal critics saw Reagan's policy, especially in his first term, as a mass of contradictions. Moscow, they said, could not take such U.S. overtures seriously when they were accompanied by the relentless ideological campaign to delegitimate the Soviet system; arms control proposals from Washington were hard to accept when they were blatantly one-sided and also punctuated by a series of Pentagon reports documenting allegations of Soviet cheating on prior agreements. But beneath the apparent contradictions and the bureaucratic competition in Washington, there was a logic to what Reagan was doing. As the United States and the West recovered their economic and military strength and political self-confidence, Reagan began to see himself as in a position to do business.

ONE MAJOR OBSTACLE to a breakthrough was that through the whole of his first term there was no Soviet interlocutor. "They kept dying on me," he used to joke. Brezhnev died in November 1982, his successor, Yuri Andropov, in February 1984, and Konstantin Chernenko in March 1985. Reagan tried to strike up a correspondence with Brezhnev's successors as well. But the foreign policy of the Kremlin gerontocracy seemed to be on autopilot during this period—frightened by Reagan, deepening its involvement in the Afghan morass, and preoccupied with its internal paralysis. Only when Chernenko was succeeded by Mikhail Gorbachev did serious dialogue become possible.

Between 1975 and 1985 there occurred a great reversal of historical fortune—by 1985, a palpable political recovery and economic dynamism in the West and a Soviet system that began to see itself in crisis. That is what Reagan and Gorbachev, respectively, embodied, and Reagan sensed the opportunity. In his first term, he was laying the predicate. On September 24, 1984, at the United Nations General Assembly, he declared: "America has repaired its strength. We have invigorated our alliances and friendships. We are ready for constructive negotiations with the Soviet Union."

No one can doubt Gorbachev's pivotal role in the easing of tensions that followed. It is worth taking note, however, of Gorbachev's own analysis at the time. The essence of the "new thinking" that he and his reformist colleagues were celebrating when they came into power in March 1985 was a repudiation of the foreign policy of their predecessors—an arms race the Soviet Union now knew it could not win, quagmires in Afghanistan and other Third World conflicts from which they were struggling to extricate themselves. In a series of candid articles in authoritative journals, these Brezhnev policies were now criticized as "incompetence" and "miscalculations" that had produced "unprecedented new pressure from imperialism" and caused "enormous losses" to the Soviet Union. On October 15, 1985, seven months after he took power, Gorbachev explained to his party colleagues: "It has been necessary to work out a new understanding of the changes in the correlation of forces that are occurring." There was a "very dangerous shift" in the policies of the imperialists, he said, in seeking military superiority and suppressing liberation movements. It was "imperative to take a realistic view." The Kremlin would have to "take into account the changing situation in due time, face the reality without any bias, objectively appraise current events, and flexibly react to the demands of the moment."

"Realistic" was a compliment that Moscow had often bestowed on Western leaders who were conciliatory; they were praised for accommodating themselves to the objective trend of history that Soviet policy embodied. Reagan would be entitled to return the compliment. The new Soviet leaders repudiated the policies of their predecessors as costly miscalculations—but they were miscalculations in part because the West had reacted, and they were more costly because the United States had raised the costs. This is the evidence for those who think Gorbachev was as much the result as he was the cause of what transpired in the 1980s.

The Battle of Washington

This historical trend was partly obscured by the bureaucratic battle that raged in Washington, however. The now famous policy directives, eloquent as they were, reflected mainly aspiration and did not determine how the aspiration was to be pursued. George Shultz in his memoirs makes just one passing reference to one of them, when he cited to Reagan one of the elements of NSDD 75 that the State Department had a particular liking for (cultural exchanges). Shultz is dismissive of the ideologues on the NSC staff, and attaches more importance to memoranda of his own that he sent the president outlining a four-part agenda for a U.S-Soviet dialogue (arms control, human rights, regional conflicts, and bilateral relations).

Similarly with Reagan's speeches: The president's blunt assertion in March 1983 that the Soviet Union was an "evil empire" was generally viewed as an embarrassment at State. Usually the advance draft of a presidential speech on foreign policy was circulated to the key departments on a close-hold basis for comment, but during my years at the State Department I do not recall that most of these speeches, after the president delivered them, were widely invoked in the building as fundamental guidance. (The "evil empire" speech, made to the National Association of Evangelicals, was not thought of as a foreign policy pronouncement and State saw no advance draft.) The surprise unveiling of Reagan's Strategic Defense Initiative (SDI), tacked onto the end of a routine defense policy speech in the same month, was withheld from State until the last minute because of the likelihood of State's opposition. Speeches by the secretary of state (drafted principally by the Policy Planning Staff, which I headed for a time) received much more attention in Foggy Bottom, in part because they tended to be more detailed expositions of operational policy.

GEORGE SHULTZ HAD HIS OPENING—a mandate from Reagan to pursue negotiations. In June 1983, with Reagan's blessing, he outlined to the Senate Foreign Relations Committee a strategy to engage the Soviet leaders in a diplomatic process on concrete issues. But others in the administration had their own ideas of whether Shultz's efforts were faithful to the president's true wishes.

Strategic arms control was one such arena of bureaucratic infighting. Reagan (like Jimmy Carter before him) began his administration with proposals that were radical departures from previous U.S. policies. While Reagan turned out to be more successful than Carter, the road to success was a rocky one. In the field of strategic (intercontinental-range) offensive missiles, Reagan like Carter proposed deep reductions; as for intermediate-range missiles (INF), he proposed their abolition. To stress the reductions, the Strategic Arms Limitation Talks (SALT) of his three predecessors were given a new name—the Strategic Arms Reduction Talks (START). Reagan had a profound personal aversion to nuclear weapons; his desire to abolish all of them was genuine. (His commitment to SDI, indeed, sprang from his faith that defensive systems could ultimately render nuclear offensive weapons obsolete.) But he presided over a bureaucratic stalemate. At times, his insistence on SDI and on deep reductions of missiles strengthened the hand of conservatives in the administration who wanted to stand fast on his original proposals, resisting compromise with the Soviets. At other times, Reagan's nuclear abolitionism strengthened the hand of Shultz, who could argue that achieving a negotiable result was the best way to achieve at least a step toward the president's vision.

No serious arms control business was likely to be accomplished with the Soviets, in any case, until they saw the failure of the massive propaganda campaign they waged in Western Europe in 1983 to block NATO's deployment of "Euromissiles," which were a response to new, multi-warhead missiles deployed by the Soviets in the 1970s. The Soviets in fact walked out of the strategic arms negotiations when the allies deployed the missiles. By that time, in addition, Reagan's SDI had injected a new element into the picture; the Soviets (who had themselves pioneered the field of anti-ballistic missile defenses) were desperately eager to stop American progress in the same field. The thrust of Soviet diplomacy after 1983 was a proposed negotiation to block or slow down SDI. This the United States was bound to reject, but Reagan at the U.N. General Assembly in September 1984 answered it by proposing a comprehensive resumption of talks on "issues of concern to both sides," including not only offensive reductions but also "the relationship between offensive and defensive forces."

The U.S. strategy, in other words, was to try to leverage Soviet concern about SDI into a comprehensive negotiation that would reduce the offensive weapons which were the main American strategic concern. (It was an echo of Nixon's strategy leading to the 1972 accords—essentially trading limits on a U.S. ABM system for limits on Soviet offensive missiles.) Shultz and McFarlane saw SDI as an effective bargaining chip that would eventually bring the Soviets back to the table—as indeed it did in early 1985. However, Shultz and McFarlane had not entirely reckoned with their president, who saw SDI as a goal in itself and was not at all interested in trading it away. At the Reykjavik summit in October 1986, Gorbachev would make sweeping concessions on offensive missiles—conditioned on concessions from Reagan on SDI. Reagan refused. That summit broke up in disarray, but Reagan eventually won Gorbachev's agreement to the offensive reductions anyway.

In Washington, the bureaucratic battles were many. The SDI proposal had not originated in the Pentagon (it had come, rather, from Reagan and his own consultations with a variety of scientists and strategists), and indeed the Pentagon had opposed it for fear of upsetting allies. But defense secretary Weinberger quickly became SDI's most ardent bureaucratic champion—"more Catholic than the Pope" on the subject, according to his military aide, Colin Powell. The Pentagon rallied to the president's concept whenever it saw the State Department as too tempted to trade some limits on SDI in exchange for a comprehensive agreement. At one point in 1985, for example, the Pentagon began to argue that (contrary to the conventional wisdom) the 1972 ABM Treaty could be interpreted to permit development and testing of space-based ABM systems; Shultz strongly objected. The Pentagon was a fervent advocate of any interpretation that freed up U.S. programs or that made compromise with the Soviets more complicated.

On the eve of Reagan's Geneva summit with Gorbachev in November 1985, Weinberger sent the president a letter cautioning him against agreeing to limits on either offensive or defensive U.S. programs. The letter somehow found its way to *The Washington Post* and *The New York Times*. Just as we saw Presidents Ford and Carter in earlier chapters react sharply to such intramural leaks, Reagan was angered. McFarlane writes that Reagan "thought the leak unnecessary, a signal that someone didn't think he could handle the account and that he needed a public goading to keep him in line. It represented lack of confidence in him and a breach of teamplay."

The story of strategic arms control in the Reagan administration is a long and complicated one, but, from today's perspective, what is notable is the difference that Reagan's personal engagement made—when it occurred. He had given Shultz a mandate, but did not actively engage in maintaining discipline in the administration when Shultz found himself embattled. The efforts of successive national security advisers to keep peace in the cabinet did not avail. "He really disliked personal confrontation," McFarlane later told an interviewer. "It wasn't a matter of his not seeing value in the competition between Cabinet officers. But he was always quite upset about the shrillness between Cap [Weinberger] and George [Shultz]." In another interview McFarlane recounted that he had complained once to the president about the backbiting, only to be told:

Bud, I know what you're describing, and I don't disagree with the description. These are my friends. I'm not going to fire either one. And I know that if Cap were secretary of state, I would get very bad policy advice. But he's my friend, and I'm not going to change that. I'm going to look to you to manage the relationship, and to bring the disagreements to me, with your own advice on how it ought to be resolved in each case.

Richard Nixon and Henry Kissinger had striven to insure that U.S. arms control negotiating positions with the Soviet Union reflected a coherent strategy, integrating defense and foreign policy interests, and not merely the resultant of contending bureaucratic forces. The Reagan administration set its sights lower—it considered itself successful when it managed to agree on a bureaucratic compromise at all. Reagan's personal involvement made a difference, especially his adamant refusal to sacrifice SDI. But the weaknesses of the process were exposed at the Reykjavik summit, when Gorbachev caught the U.S. side by surprise with his sweeping new proposals and the Americans hastily improvised their responses.

Another dimension of Reagan's relationship with Gorbachev—and the paradoxes of Reagan's management of his own government—are illustrated by the president's famous speech at the Berlin Wall on June 12, 1987, in which he appealed to Gorbachev to tear it down. When the White House speechwriters began to circulate the advance draft for comment, State's institutional reaction was fierce. The NSC staff had also taken on a different coloration by that time; attrition and the wake of Iran-Contra had swept away the original ideological Reaganites, many of whom had been replaced by career experts. Colin Powell, then deputy national security adviser, decided that the NSC staff would support the State Department position, which was forcefully advocated by Secretary Shultz. By that time, I had moved back to the NSC staff, where—to my eternal shame—I was one of those seeking extensive changes to the draft, including deletion of the famous line: "Mr. Gorbachev, tear down this wall!"

The changes that we bureaucrats proposed, at least the significant ones, were of two kinds. One had to do with policy content—to be specific, we wanted more of it. The speech as finally delivered included some proposals for improving exchanges between West and East Berlin, but they were thin gruel; we hoped the president would use the bully pulpit to advance U.S. positions on a host of larger issues of interest to Europeans, particularly arms control. We thought it a missed opportunity when the White House speechwriters shrank these ideas down to brief references. It is not the worst impulse of the bureaucracy to want to engage the president as the chief spokesman for his administration's policies; on the contrary, this should be encouraged. But, it is up to the president to decide these things.

The more infamous battle was over the appeal to Gorbachev to tear down the wall. The State Department argument was essentially that such rabble-rousing would embarrass the West Germans present, especially Chancellor Helmut Kohl. Kohl was a staunch NATO ally, having proved his courage in the German deployment of Euromissiles. But West Germans of all political parties had made their peace with the ugly status quo including full diplomatic recognition of the East German regime. German-Soviet relations were also poor at the time. No doubt this was not the sort of speech a West German leader would have given. It is not an accident that almost all the experts who weighed in, at State and on the NSC staff, were experts on Germany, and their preoccupation was how it would resonate in the German context.

Reagan, we can see now, had something totally different in mind. His audience was Mikhail Gorbachev. He had spent time with Gorbachev at two summits by then, at Geneva and Reykjavik, and had sensed something about the young Soviet leader who presented himself so proudly as an agent of change. Some at State, in desperation, even tried to use this against the offending sentence: After meeting Gorbachev, the president had let it be known that he did not want to "personalize" the U.S-Soviet conflict—so that was another reason to cut the line. George Shultz argued vehemently up to the last minute that the line would offend the Soviet leader. Reagan dismissed the argument.

After repeated drafts came out of the Oval Office with the sentence intact, we should have gotten the message. In his limousine on the way to the Brandenburg Gate to deliver the speech, Reagan smiled to his deputy chief of staff Kenneth Duberstein: "The boys at State are going to kill me," he said, "but it's the right thing to do."

There is no way to demonstrate that the speech changed the direction of history. In light of what later happened, certainly, watching a replay today of Reagan declaiming that line with his full rhetorical power sends chills down one's spine—though perhaps more so now than it did at the time. Nevertheless, the whole affair is a vivid example of a president's possessing a strategic and moral insight that escaped his experts. Reagan's intuition about Gorbachev was undoubtedly right. A few days before Reagan delivered the speech, thousands of young East Germans clashed with police on the other side of the wall shouting "The wall must go!" Then, in front of the Soviet Embassy in East Berlin, they chanted "Gorbachev! Gorbachev!"—appealing over the heads of their own leaders to the great reformer of the Soviet system. A year and a half later, on a visit to Germany in early 1989, one of Gorbachev's closest aides distanced the Kremlin from the wall that its puppets had built: "We didn't build this wall—this isn't our wall," declared Aleksandr Yakovlev. Later that year, when East Germany's final crisis came, Gorbachev interposed no resistance to the wall's collapse.

Central America

U.S. policy-making on Central America was a "swamp," George Shultz once wrote. Shultz blamed it on the weaknesses of an NSC process that could not resolve the bureaucratic battles and produce consistent policy. There is no doubt that Reagan saw the Central American Communists (the Sandinista regime in Nicaragua, the guerrillas in El Salvador) as a geopolitical and ideological threat, and he was wary of making political concessions to them. He fought hard for military and economic assistance to those resisting the Communists—including the anti-Sandinista insurgents dubbed the "counterrevolutionaries," or "Contras." At the same time Reagan was strongly averse to any idea of embroiling the United States militarily in Central American wars; his memoirs reveal a genuine sensitivity to Latin fears of the "Great Colossus of the North," and also a clear perception that the U.S. public would not support such involvement. It would be "lunacy" to invade Nicaragua, the president told Shultz in January 1986. A few years later, Reagan complained to aide Duberstein about the conservatives: "Those sonsof-bitches won't be happy until we have 25,000 troops in Managua, and I'm not going to do it." At times he sided with Shultz's diplomacy; at other times he sided with the hard-liners (Clark, Casey, Kirkpatrick, Wein-berger) who opposed it as too accommodating to the Sandinistas.

This duality in Reagan's mind was not by itself unreasonable. With more consistent leadership, it might have been turned into a coherent, balanced policy that combined power and diplomacy, strength and flex-ibility. Instead, as with the strategic arms negotiations, operational pol-icy on Central America was made by a tug-of-war between the two forces, a continuing and erratic struggle for Reagan's soul. More often than not, U.S. policy actions derived not from presidential direction but from alternating assertions of bureaucratic self-will by the various sides.

Indeed the program of U.S. covert support for the Contras itself began as a bureaucratic compromise. At the beginning of the adminis-tration, when Alexander Haig was arguing for a blockade of Cuba in order to choke off supplies to the Central American Communists, he found no takers. Weinberger wanted no part of it, believing Central America a diversion from his main task of rearming the United States against the Soviet Union; as noted earlier, the White House troika and Mrs. Reagan wanted no part of it either. Thus, when CIA director William Casey came up with a covert program of pressures on Nicaragua, it became everyone's fallback option. Reagan had no trouble approving this. It was this CIA program of pressures that later grew into a significant insurgent army.

Initially the domestic controversy focused on El Salvador, where the administration sought congressional support for military and economic assistance for a Salvadoran government resisting a Communist insur-gency. This was broadly supported in the administration, but in Con-gress and in the country it triggered fears of "another Vietnam." In opposing Central American Communism the United States was stand-ing against "the tide of history," Senator Chris Dodd (Democrat of Con-necticut) proclaimed portentously (and very wrongly) in 1983. The administration was also accused of propping up rightist dictators and condoning death squads. The policy in El Salvador was rescued from much of its torment in May 1984 when, under U.S. pressure, a free election was held that brought to power José Napoleón Duarte, a respected Christian Democrat whose hatred of the extreme right dated back to the early 1970s when an earlier election victory was stolen from him by the military and he was imprisoned and tortured. With this success, controversy over El Salvador ebbed, and the focus shifted to Nicaragua. Congressional pressures mounted against the increasingly visible Contra program.

Throughout this evolution, the State Department was eagerly pursuing diplomatic solutions. This began in late 1981 under Haig, when Thomas Enders—the same energetic foreign service officer who had helped Henry Kissinger make international economic policy (see Chapter 4)—pursued with the same energy a dialogue with the Sandinistas. Enders visited Managua in August 1981 and proposed a deal: Essentially the United States would accept the legitimacy and finality of the Nicaraguan revolution and normalize relations with it, provided it ended its military supply of Communist insurgencies in neighboring countries. This overture got nowhere. In fact, it was based on a serious misunderstanding of the nature of the Sandinistas, for whom support for regional revolution was the heart of their "internationalist" duty. "This revolution goes beyond our borders," Tomás Borge, one of the most militant of the *comandantes*, proclaimed in July 1981.

Enders's activities became the subject of bitter disputes between Shultz and national security adviser William Clark. Shultz in his memoirs repeatedly accuses Clark of a "grab for power" or "usurpation of power" as Clark tried to block diplomatic moves that Shultz believed he had Reagan's mandate to pursue; by the same token, Clark and his conservative staffer Constantine Menges (usually backed by William Casey) kept coming up with schemes that Shultz thought absurd. Clark and his staff, in turn, accused Shultz of bypassing an orderly interagency process by end runs into the Oval Office, denying the president the benefit of dissenting views. Menges even kept count, later claiming that over a five-year period Shultz was guilty of at least seven attempts to short-circuit interagency scrutiny, in the pursuit of diplomatic accommodations that Clark and others thought unwise. Casey once wisecracked to Shultz: "George, don't be a pilgrim." "What's that?" Shultz asked. "An early settler," Casey replied.

In early 1983, Enders came up with a new proposal—to engage Mexico and other outside countries in promoting a regional settlement. Conservatives in the administration were skeptical, believing Mexico an unlikely ally given its tilt toward the Sandinistas. Clark tried to kill it. He persuaded Reagan instead to dispatch U.N. ambassador Jeane Kirkpatrick (a Latin America scholar) on a trip to several Central and South American countries in February to deliver a personal letter from Reagan to heads of state expressing U.S. solidarity. On her trip, one sympathetic U.S. ambassador showed her an EYES ONLY FOR THE AMBASSADOR cable that Enders had sent around to all the capitals she was to visit, saying, in effect: There is a new Central America strategy coming, which will be decided once Secretary Shultz returns from a trip to China. In other words, just ignore Kirkpatrick and the letter she is carrying. When Kirkpatrick showed the cable to Reagan upon her return, he was furious, and the episode led to Enders's transfer a few months later.

Shultz in turn was caught by surprise in July 1983 when the media reported on Big Pine II, a six-month-long U.S. military exercise off both the Atlantic and the Pacific coasts of Nicaragua in which three thousand U.S. combat troops along with Honduran troops would conduct war games on Honduran territory. Clark had persuaded the president to approve the exercise, and Shultz had not been consulted. The leak of the exercise produced an uproar in Congress and contributed to the defeat in the House a few weeks later of the administration's request for aid to the Contras.

Shultz then obtained Reagan's approval to pay a quick visit to Managua on June 1, 1984, for a dramatic airport meeting with Nicaragua's president Daniel Ortega. Weinberger, Casey, and Kirkpatrick were informed only after the president had given his approval; they were not pleased. Kirkpatrick later remarked: "[S]ince he didn't keep anybody informed, Casey or Cap or anybody, everybody felt free to develop their own fantasies, as in a Rorschach test" of what the secretary of state was up to. Enders's successor, Langhorne (Tony) Motley, a political appointee and ex-ambassador to Brazil, was a more genial fellow than Enders, but the problems continued. Though the Ortega meeting had led nowhere, State was eager to follow it up with a new diplomatic plan. When others got word of a new State plan, they managed this time to force an NSC meeting at which the pros and cons could be argued out in front of the president. At the end of the lengthy and stormy meeting, held on June 25, the president made a Delphic pronouncement that no reliable deal with the Sandinistas was likely, but continuing the diplomatic effort might help shore up congressional support for the Contras.

McFarlane and the NSC staff interpreted the discussion and the president's remarks as a rejection of State's specific plan but a general mandate to continue diplomacy; a directive was issued in this vein, signed by the president. Shultz disagreed vehemently. Having already dispatched his negotiators to Mexico the day before to meet with the Sandinista representatives, he telephoned McFarlane to say he thought the president had given him a green light. With McFarlane's grudging acquiescence, Shultz instructed his negotiators to present the plan as it had been prepared. But this initiative, too, led nowhere.

In sum, while Shultz often complained of Pentagon obtuseness and NSC obstruction, we can see that he was no slouch himself at making his way into the White House and winning permission to pursue his diplomacy. From his point of view he was seeking (and obtaining) reauthorization from Reagan to overcome bureaucratic obstruction of what the president had already authorized. Not every State Department scheme was well thought out, however. In the absence of leverage, many of the U.S. diplomatic initiatives seemed to risk an outcome that could be a disguised formula for the consolidation of Sandinista power, with no corresponding diminution of Sandinista subversion in the region. As head of the State Department's Policy Planning Staff at the time, I told Shultz I thought we had a weak hand.

GRADUALLY U.S. POLICY acquired leverage, and coalesced around a more coherent strategy, but it took a while. The electoral success of Duarte in El Salvador, and the growth of the Nicaraguan Contras into a significant peasant army, shifted the spotlight of U.S. and regional attention onto Nicaragua's internal dictatorship. In earlier years, the State Department had been dismissive of the idea of democratization. Thomas Enders had barked to NSC staffer Constantine Menges in 1981: "Constantine, this is the real world. Get serious. There is no chance for democracy in Nicaragua." But by 1985, Nicaragua was the only dictatorship left in a region of democracies. The regime's heavy-handedness in suppressing its opposition in a 1984 election had disillusioned many of its U.S. defenders—and Reagan's own overwhelming reelection in 1984 led a group of moderate Democrats to seek to collaborate with the administration on a bipartisan policy, one of whose main consensus elements was insistence on democracy in Nicaragua.

A key figure in this evolution was Elliott Abrams, a young neoconservative intellectual who became Shultz's assistant secretary for Western Hemisphere affairs in the summer of 1985. In an earlier incarnation as assistant secretary of state for human rights, Abrams had championed a human rights policy that evenhandedly challenged dictatorships of both left and right. (He was to have a major hand, for example, in the U.S. pressures on Augusto Pinochet in Chile that led to his stepping down from office.) When Abrams succeeded Motley in the Western Hemisphere post, he steered Shultz toward an approach that intensified diplomatic pressure on the Sandinistas' internal repression, and Shultz also became an increasingly vocal champion of U.S. aid to the Contras.

The bureaucratic tensions in the administration over Central America eased considerably, as the different factions coalesced around this approach. Conservatives championed the Contras and welcomed the ideological combat with the Sandinista regime; moderates appreciated that the leverage was being put in the service of diplomacy. Abrams thus helped put Shultz in a much better bureaucratic position vis-à-vis the administration's conservatives; the new policy put Reagan and his administration in a much better position vis-à-vis Congress; and the resulting national policy even more importantly positioned the United States in the right place strategically in Central America. Eventually the leverage of the Contras, and the focus on democracy that had been so disparaged originally by the career diplomats, produced an international agreement in 1987 that required the Sandinistas to hold a free election in 1990. Relying too much, apparently, on Chris Dodd's assessment of the tide of history, the Sandinistas were quite shocked when they lost.

The Iran-Contra Scandal

In late November 1986, the Reagan administration was shaken by the revelation that its White House/NSC personnel had been secretly selling arms to Iran and diverting some of the funds to support the Nicaraguan Contras. To many observers, this affair is emblematic of the administration's bureaucratic indiscipline in the national security field. The scandal led to joint Senate-House hearings and also to the president's appointment of a Special Review Board headed by Senator John Tower (Republican of Texas). The Tower Board, which also included former Secretary of State Edmund Muskie and former national security adviser Brent Scowcroft, published a thoughtful report in February 1987, drawing a number of lessons about the proper role of the NSC staff and national security adviser. Sound as these lessons are, however, my own view of the affair puts the emphasis somewhat differently.

It is important to separate the two dimensions of the affair—the overtures to Iran, and the diversion of funds for the Contras—since they illustrate two different dimensions of the administration's bureaucratic problems. The overtures to Iran were most emphatically a presidential decision, reflecting a policy to which the president was strongly committed. It was not a case of presidential inattention or of subordinates acting without his authorization. On the contrary, Reagan agreed with aides who were convinced there was potential for a strategic opening to Iran. Shultz and Weinberger knew of it, and strongly opposed it. I heard them joke to each other that, with all the many issues on which they were at loggerheads, here was a case where they agreed and presented a common opinion to the president—and were overruled.

I moved from State back to the NSC in March 1986 and knew about the Iran policy. I also told my new NSC colleagues, including national security adviser John Poindexter and Lieutenant Colonel Oliver North, that I thought it was strategically crazy. With the Iran-Iraq War still raging, a victory by Iran's new revolutionary regime would have been a strategic disaster; all America's Arab friends were backing Iraq, and U.S. policy tilted in that direction as well. The United States was waging a major diplomatic campaign, in fact, to stanch other nations' transfer of arms to Iran. Nonetheless, Bud McFarlane was called out of retirement to travel secretly to Tehran in May 1986 for what was hoped to be a political discussion. He brought with him, as tokens of goodwill, an (Israeli-baked) chocolate cake with a skeleton key design in the frosting, and a pallet of Hawk antiaircraft missile spare parts.

Reagan sincerely believed in the potential for a breakthrough with Iran, and this explains his stubborn public insistence that his policy was not a trade of arms for hostages. While he cared deeply about the hostages in Lebanon, the overarching purpose of his actions was not limited to retrieving them; it was the broader strategic opening with Iran. The various weapons that the U.S. side provided to Iran (not only Hawk parts but TOW antitank missiles) were meant as a token of the U.S. commitment to this larger goal, just as Iran's help with release of hostages was to be their token of the same. In the end, since the strategic relationship never materialized, operationally all that was taking place was the movement of a few arms and a few hostages; that was all that was left of the policy.

Most of the postmortems on the Iran-Contra affair focus on process—on the inappropriateness of the role of the NSC staff. In my view, however, the blunder in this case was substantive more than it was procedural. The strategy was doomed for substantive reasons no matter how or by whom it was carried out; it seriously undercut the core U.S. policy at the time, which was to oppose Iran. That was, and remains, the basis of my own disagreement with what was done. Despite that objection, however, it is also my view that presidents deserve the benefit of the doubt on the procedural point. It was Reagan's prerogative to overrule his cabinet secretaries, and it was also his prerogative to turn to his staff for execution rather than delegate it to a bureaucracy that had made its rebellion against his decision quite clear.

The diversion of some of the proceeds to the Contras was a different matter. Poindexter and North kept this secret from the president as from everyone else. It was the revelation of the Contra dimension that turned the affair from a policy embarrassment into a political crisis, given the emotionalism that Central America was already engendering. With the Democrats' recapture of the Senate in November 1986, a maximum congressional assault was guaranteed. Democrats also charged that the diversion violated legislative restrictions on direct or indirect U.S. aid to the Contras. The fact that Poindexter went out of his way to protect the president's "plausible deniability" indicates how close to the edge he knew he was skating; thus he took on a huge political risk on his own initiative, without a safety net of any kind.

A very demoralized White House, which saw the departure of chief of staff Donald Regan as well as of Poindexter and North in the wake of the revelations, was content to blame everything on the departed employees. It was left to congressional Republicans to defend the president's prerogative and make the argument that the NSC staff's actions, however unwise, were not illegal. This they did. The most vigorous and articulate defense of the administration was made by the Republican minority report resulting from the congressional investigation—a brief shaped by Representative Dick Cheney of Wyoming. Cheney's vigorous defense of Reagan helped propel him to national recognition and toward a leadership role in the Republican Party. But it also reflected a conviction formed in the Ford years when he had witnessed firsthand the congressional assault on executive authority. Cheney's instructions to Michael Malbin, his staffer and principal draftsman on the Republican Iran-Contra report, were: "Wherever the facts of this investigation lead, let them lead. Your job is to preserve the institution of the presidency."

The Tower Board enumerated the many "mistakes of omission, commission, judgment, and perspective" committed by Reagan's NSC staff, and marked them as a warning to future officials of "potential pitfalls they face even when they are operating with what they consider the best of motives." The board then made a number of recommendations relating to transparency, collegial deliberations, and responsible behavior on the part of the NSC staff. It recommended, for example, that the NSC staff stay out of the covert action business, and hire a senior legal adviser. It also urged that the national security adviser report directly to the president, not through the chief of staff—a correct acknowledgment that the *weakness* of the position had been its problem for much of the Reagan administration. All these recommendations were adopted. But these procedural fixes seem, in retrospect, rather small in light of the magnitude of the political crisis that had erupted.

The Tower Board is often cited for its conclusion that "[a]s a general matter, the NSC Staff should not engage in the implementation of policy or the conduct of operations." George Shultz took advantage of the opening provided by the scandal to approach the new national security adviser, Frank Carlucci, and tell him, in effect: "You shouldn't meet with foreign ambassadors; you shouldn't travel; you can't chair meetings. And State has to know everything you are doing." Carlucci politely declined. (He did promise that Shultz personally, if not State as an institution, would know everything he did.) Cyrus Vance, a decade earlier, had made similar demands on Zbigniew Brzezinski, who also politely refused. The bottom line is that there is no way to tell a president how he may or may not use his own staff.

Carlucci had it right: Transparency is a better principle to emphasize. Especially in the post-Kissinger era, no national security adviser can be expected to remain a hermit in the basement, avoiding contact with foreigners or Congress or the media. (Ironically, the one who tried hardest to do that was John Poindexter.) In professional and social Washington, the security adviser will come in contact with foreigners, legislators, and media; likewise most security advisers have been sent on missions abroad. Good governance requires not that this be stopped, but that it be in the service of policies that are transparent to other senior officials and openly deliberated upon. Which person is the best one to carry a message is a tactical question, and there will be times when a president may legitimately give the assignment to an immediate adviser who can travel less conspicuously and speak with the special authority of the White House—often to counterparts in the immediate offices of other heads of government.

These matters are for a president to decide. In the end, the Tower

Board had no choice but to recognize—as Senator Henry Jackson had recognized a quarter-century earlier—that every president needs the flexibility to choose the most congenial system of policy-making. Thus the board, after all its investigation and deliberation, recommended no legislative changes in the role, structure, or authority of the NSC or its staff.

Lebanon and the Use of Force

In relations with the Soviet Union and policy in Central America, the Reagan administration, for all its stumbles and disarray, worked its way toward successful outcomes. Ultimately it could be said that the president's policy instincts served him well even if his manner of policy-making did not. In Lebanon, however, the results were more deadly. Reagan sent U.S. military forces to Lebanon in 1982 and withdrew them in bloody and humiliating circumstances in 1984. The debacle occurred because of a policy failure in two dimensions: a miscalculation of the changing political circumstances on the ground in Lebanon, and a bureaucratic stalemate in Washington that Reagan was unwilling to break.

U.S. troops arrived in Lebanon in benign circumstances as neutral peacekeepers. Israel had invaded Lebanon in June 1982 to crush the Palestine Liberation Organization (PLO). In August a multinational force (MNF) was created, with U.S. participation, to shield the orderly withdrawal of PLO leaders and guerrillas from Lebanon. The United States contributed about eight hundred Marines, who accompanied British, French, and Italian forces. Israel, Syria, and all factions in Lebanon endorsed the exercise, and Reagan could emphasize, with justification, that there was "no intention or expectation that U.S. Armed Forces will become involved in hostilities." As the MNF was completing its mission in mid-September, seven hundred to eight hundred Palestinian civilians were killed in refugee camps at Sabra and Shatila near Beirut by Lebanese Christian militias aligned with Israel. A second MNF deployment was thereupon organized, this time with the goal of bolstering Lebanese government authority in the Beirut area. The United States contributed 1,200 Marines to this effort, with the same—legitimate—expectation that this was a neutral humanitarian mission with broad support and low risk of involvement in hostilities.

Subsequently the political ground in Lebanon shifted dramatically under the Americans' feet, yet the U.S. government did not draw new conclusions about the mission and the vulnerability of its forces. The major new development was a peace agreement between Lebanon and Israel, mediated by Secretary of State George Shultz and signed on May 17, 1983: All Israeli forces were to withdraw from Lebanon in exchange for peace. The agreement was immediately denounced by Syria as a betrayal of the Arab cause, and Syria egged on its radical allies in Lebanon to overthrow the Lebanese government by force. Syria, though bloodied by the Israelis in their original invasion of 1982, had been rearmed by the Soviet Union and was recovering its self-confidence. Meanwhile the Israeli public was tiring of the Lebanese adventure, demoralized in part by political hand-wringing in the wake of the Sabra-Shatila disaster; Israeli forces started pulling back unilaterally.

The balance of forces in Lebanon was thus tilting badly, and the peace agreement did not reflect the new geopolitical reality. The U.S. Marines and their MNF allies found themselves in the middle of an escalating war around Beirut. Terrorists had blown up the American embassy in April; they struck the U.S. and French barracks in October, killing 241 Marines and 59 French troops.

The United States faced a choice. If the peace agreement was strategically important to us, then there was a case for using U.S. military leverage to insure the survival of the Lebanese government that had signed it. Shultz made this case, arguing that to allow Syria and its radical allies to topple a U.S.-brokered peace agreement would set an ominous precedent for Arab-Israeli diplomacy and embolden radical forces throughout the Middle East. He urged greater use of the Marines or of U.S. naval firepower offshore to assist the Lebanese government in its ongoing battle with the Syrian-backed radicals. Secretary of Defense Weinberger and the Joint Chiefs of Staff, in contrast, wanted U.S. forces in no such role; they wanted the Marines out of Lebanon, or at the very most confined to peacekeeping duties rather than taking sides in the battle.

Either Shultz's policy or Weinberger's policy would have been a coherent choice. What Reagan did, however, was evade the choice and split the difference. In August 1983 he authorized the MNF to stay, but only in a purely peacekeeping role. In December, he agreed to step up artillery fire against Syria's Druze allies lobbing shells at the Marines, but only if precise Druze targets could be identified and not against Syrian forces in the area. Every time a specific decision was presented to him to respond to the deteriorating situation, the president would agree to an incremental increase in military pressure but never a decisive one. The mighty battleship *New Jersey*, for example, joined the naval task force off the coast but used its 16-inch guns only sporadically—never in a sustained, systematic way to affect the battle. The Pentagon interpreted Reagan's orders in minimalist fashion, concerned that greater involvement would only magnify risks. In December, it unilaterally ended reconnaissance flights over Lebanon without consultation with State.

"We're a divided group," Reagan lamented to his diary. But the upshot of his incrementalism was that the United States was engaged enough to be taking sides and staking its prestige, but not enough to win. As the Marines on the ground took casualties, congressional support eroded. An agreement with the Democratic congressional leadership in September 1983 to continue the Marine deployment another eighteen months simply collapsed after the barracks bombing. In the final phase, Donald Rumsfeld was named presidential envoy for Lebanon and the Middle East. (I accompanied him on some of his missions.) He figured out immediately that the bigger problem was not in Beirut but in Washington. He and his team came up with an alternative approach—to pull all the Marines out (since they were a political liability and performed no military mission) while stepping up training of the Lebanese armed forces and more aggressively applying U.S. naval and air power to help them win. Reagan adopted this approach in January 1984—but the situation had deteriorated so far that, while the Marines came home, the second half of the new policy was never implemented. The Lebanese government collapsed.

Just as President Bill Clinton discovered in Somalia in 1993, what started out as a relatively risk-free humanitarian involvement turned into something else as the political context changed on the ground. The policy requirement then is to draw the proper conclusions: Do we still want to be there? If not, we should get out. If yes, we need to insure that our military exertion is adequate to the goal we have decided is important. Reagan was usually reluctant to order the U.S. military to fight a war that its leaders did not want to fight. Yet he was also persuaded by Shultz's argument that the United States had a strategic stake in the outcome; thus he was always reluctant to "cut and run" until the very end when defeat was imposed. Reagan had to choose between two conflicting strategies, but he never did. Splitting the difference meant only incoherence.

CONTRAST LEBANON with Reagan's decisiveness over Grenada. By the fall of 1983 a radical Marxist regime was coming apart and plunging the tiny Caribbean island into anarchy, putting into apparent jeopardy not only neighboring island states but a group of American students at a local medical school. In this case, too, Cap Weinberger's Pentagon was reluctant to get involved, but Reagan overruled them. Reagan went ahead with his decision even when the Marine barracks bombing happened in Beirut a few days before execution, which took some political courage. The Normandy landing it was not, but the liberation of Grenada had its deeper importance: Its success—and popular support—marked the breaking of the post-Vietnam taboo in America against the use of military force.

An important bureaucratic factor, especially in the Lebanon case, was the Defense Department's view of its own foreign policy interests. The United States has extensive military partnerships in the Arab world; many go back to the Carter administration when moderate Arabs drew closer to us in the wake of the Iranian revolution. These relationships are a significant achievement of U.S. policy. But for Secretary Weinberger, and to some extent to the Defense Department as an institution, they meant a reluctance to fight a war against Arabs. Weinberger had no problem with the initial small Marine deployment to Lebanon which was to protect Palestinians (though he was more nervous about the second MNF mission). But when the Lebanese engagement turned into a struggle against Syria to defend an Israeli peace agreement, this Weinberger wanted no part of. By the same token, when Libyan-backed terrorists attacked the Rome and Vienna airports in December 1985, Reagan wanted to retaliate against Libya but Weinberger and the chiefs dug in their heels. A frustrated Reagan ordered Poindexter to start preparing for the next time: "I don't want any excuses." After a Libyan terrorist attack killed U.S. servicemen at a disco club in West Berlin in April 1986, Reagan, this time, ordered it.

After the Lebanon debacle, Weinberger ordered a Pentagon study of what had gone wrong, headed by a retired admiral. One of the study's conclusions was that the United States had not worked hard enough to develop "diplomatic alternatives" to resolve the political conflict, as opposed to "military options." Shultz was outraged. He believed the diplomacy to preserve Lebanon had faltered precisely because U.S. military leverage was undercut by the Pentagon. Hearing him rail privately on this theme several times, I suggested to him that he say it publicly. He invited me to draft a speech on the subject. "It was precisely our military role in Lebanon that was problematical, not our diplomatic exertion," he declared in a speech to the Trilateral Commission in April 1984. Shultz went on in this speech to explain that power and diplomacy are not distinct alternatives but mutually dependent; in an age of complex challenges like terrorism, the United States needs to confront its enemies with an array of discriminate tools including military force.

It was this Shultz speech that prompted Caspar Weinberger to respond with his own famous pronouncement, sometimes known as the "Weinberger Doctrine," on the principles that should guide the use of force. Addressing the National Press Club in November 1984, the secretary of defense laid out six criteria that should be met whenever a president decides on the use of American military power:

- The issue should be "vital to our national interest or that of our allies."
- Once committed, we should have the "clear intention of winning."
- We should have "clearly defined" objectives and "send the forces needed" to accomplish those objectives.
- The relationship between the objectives and the size of the forces should be "continually reassessed and adjusted if necessary."
- Before we commit, "there must be some reasonable assurance" of congressional and public support.
- Committing U.S. forces to combat "should be a last resort."

The "Weinberger Doctrine" is sometimes known as the "Powell Doctrine," since a version of it was also espoused by Colin Powell, who after serving as Weinberger's military assistant went on to a brilliant career as chairman of the Joint Chiefs under Bush 41 and then secretary of state under Bush 43. In shorthand, it became known as a doctrine of avoiding incrementalism in the use of force. This is not the place for an extended discussion of the Shultz-Weinberger debate on the use of force, except to note the irony that the next significant military activity by the Reagan administration violated a number of Weinberger's criteria but had his enthusiastic support nonetheless.

This was the decision in March 1987 to provide U.S. naval convoys to protect Kuwaiti oil tankers in the Gulf against Iranian attack during the Iran-Iraq War. Despite the Weinberger emphasis on applying overwhelming force to minimize risks, this was a very limited application of military power, open-ended in its commitment, with risks that were hard to calculate, and it became the target of increasing congressional agitation. Yet the Pentagon was even more enthusiastic about this mission than State, and a colleague of mine on the NSC staff had to remind the Pentagon of the need for a plan for protecting the convoys should they come under Iranian attack. The convoying continued, without incident, until the Iran-Iraq War ended, and represented a policy success. That there was consensus in the U.S. government despite the risks was a bureaucratic success as well. Secretary Weinberger saw it—correctly—as a positive policy for the United States in the Arab world, and somehow this convinced him that it was perfectly consistent with the six criteria of his 1984 speech.

Panama and the Rogue Elephant Justice Department

A war that did *not* occur in the Reagan administration was the war to topple dictator Manuel Noriega in Panama. This, too, is a story of bureaucratic confusion—this time involving not only a recalcitrant Pentagon but a Justice Department that did not consider itself obligated to coordinate with others. Throughout this book we have seen how, over the many decades since 1947, procedures have fitfully evolved in the NSC system for coordinating or integrating the activities of the State Department, Defense Department, CIA, and the White House. In Chapter 4 we noted that successive administrations have wrestled with how to integrate international economic policy into overall national security policy-making; this is still a work in progress. By the end of the twentieth century, however, yet another problem had appeared—how to include in a coherent national security framework the growing international activities of U.S. law enforcement agencies: the FBI (which now has offices overseas), the Drug Enforcement Administration, and other Department of Justice activities.

In February 1988, federal grand juries in Tampa and Miami handed down indictments of Manuel Noriega on drug-trafficking and racketeering. These indictments launched the United States into a political crisis with Panama for which there was no coordinated U.S. government strategy to follow up because the Justice Department had made no effort to coordinate its actions with other agencies, and the U.S. government was deadlocked for the remainder of the Reagan administration over what to do next. The crisis festered until Reagan's successor, President George H. W. Bush, ended it by war: U.S. forces invaded Panama in December 1989 and captured Noriega.

The Department of Justice, insisting on its legal responsibilities and on the sanctity of grand jury proceedings, jealously guards its prosecutorial decisions against interference from outsiders. Although indictments of foreign leaders can raise obvious issues of foreign policy, Justice's willingness to share information with other concerned agencies has been ad hoc and sporadic. Even though the president is constitutionally the chief law enforcement officer of the land, Justice has been known to resist sharing too much information even with the president or White House staff lest it tempt their assertion of a contrary opinion. Before the indictments of February 1988, Justice officials had reported occasionally to an interagency group dealing with Panama on the status of its investigations of Noriega, but not with a view to being dissuaded. The State Department's Elliott Abrams, in charge of Latin American affairs, was especially reticent for personal reasons, having run into legal trouble over his (minor) role in the Iran-Contra affair. The line between "obstructing Justice" and "obstructing justice" is a fuzzy one, and the referee who will decide whether you have crossed the line will be a very annoyed Justice Department official.

Thus there was no U.S. strategy to apprehend Noriega or to follow up in any other way. Noriega was a well-entrenched dictator. Conceivably, if there had been a concerted U.S. strategy aimed at bringing him down, indictments might have been a part of such a strategy. But that is not how events unfolded. Two U.S. attorneys launched the United States into a political crisis with Panama for which the U.S. government was unprepared.

The Reagan administration immediately deadlocked over what to do. The State Department (Shultz and Abrams) urged an aggressive policy to bring the dictator down. At Situation Room meetings, they argued, for example, for the creative use of the U.S. military presence in the Canal Zone to shake the Noriega regime (shows of force including sonic booms over the capital, exploiting dissension within the Panamanian armed forces, helping the political opposition, even a commando raid to snatch him). Aside from sending some additional troops, however, Defense was opposed to military action. Frank Carlucci had replaced Weinberger as secretary of defense, but the Pentagon remained cautious about intervention. Thus, the pattern of Lebanon reasserted itself: Reagan wanted Noriega out but was unwilling to order his military to do something they were unwilling to do. He remained sensitive about the United States' appearing the gringo bully in Latin America.

A second bureaucratic dispute broke out over whether to offer a plea bargain to Noriega—quashing the indictments in exchange for his stepping down. State wanted to pursue this avenue, too (backed up by the shows of force). Justice was extremely reluctant, but this time Reagan stepped up to the decision and overruled it. The discussion leaked, however, and led to a storm of bipartisan protest against letting Noriega off the hook. Vice President Bush, running for president, argued passionately against the deal. The negotiation fell through, in large part because of reluctance on Noriega's side.

The bureaucratic lessons here are many. The Justice Department's coordination with other agencies has improved somewhat since then. On June 30, 1988, Attorney General Meese sent a memorandum to White House chief of staff Howard Baker promising timely notification to the White House in the future if prosecution of a foreign leader was contemplated. Today, Justice participates more regularly in interagency deliberations in the NSC system, permitting greater transparency and coordination. After the al-Qaida attack on the USS *Cole* in the port of Aden in October 2000, however, the American ambassador to Yemen and the FBI forensic team dispatched to investigate the attack clashed repeatedly over who was in charge. These relationships, too, are still a work in progress.

The most important overall lesson, of course, is the central role of the president. Sometimes there are issues on which it makes sense to split the difference between opposing views, or to navigate a jagged course among the conflicting positions of one's advisers. In arms control and on Central America, that is how Reagan proceeded. Bureaucratically it was the line of least resistance; he did not want to make a stark choice among his closest associates. Given that lengthy and complex negotiations were involved, it is arguable that no lasting price was paid; the world adjusted. Clumsy as the process was, it inched U.S. policy forward toward practical results.

Managing a crisis, however, brings other imperatives into play.

Events move rapidly, putting a premium on coherence and speed in both decision and execution. The goal must be to seize the initiative and sustain it—to make the opponent react to *our* moves and to dominate events. In such a situation, splitting the difference between conflicting strategies can only produce incoherence. Jimmy Carter in the crisis over the shah of Iran, or Ronald Reagan in the crisis in Lebanon, discovered the hard way the price that can be paid for a policy that embodies such contradictions within it. With Carter, it was a contradiction in his ultimate purposes; with Reagan, it was an impulse to evade a stark choice. In both cases the result was indiscipline in the government, with grievous consequences. Richard Nixon wanted to know what his real choices were, even if his advisers all agreed; he was prepared to step up to a stark decision. Presidents who avoid hard choices in the name of bureaucratic harmony may think they are minimizing political risks; on the contrary, they may be magnifying risks if the result is a conflicted policy that sacrifices effectiveness. They will be judged, in the end, not by the smoothness of their bureaucratic procedure but by whether they shaped events according to their purposes.

Lebanon and Panama were two important failures in what was in other respects a highly successful presidency. Some found it easy to belittle Reagan's intellectual capacities. But our analysis points to the key conclusion that the more engaged he was personally, the more successful his administration's policies were. Where he held back, or was uncertain, the system did not work. Where he did impose his will—whatever his weaknesses as a manager—he provided the decisive leadership.

CHAPTER SEVEN

George H.W. Bush

G EORGE HERBERT WALKER BUSH inherited from Ronald Reagan, among other things, the festering crisis in Panama, and the way he handled it was an early indicator that the new administration operated in a very different manner from its predecessor. Under Bush, the bureaucratic stalemate between State and Defense over this issue quickly ended. Dictator Manuel Noriega helped matters along, to be sure, with a stream of provocations, including hundreds of incidents of harassment of U.S. servicemen and their families by Panamanian troops and then, in May 1989, with the blatant rigging of an election to install a puppet of his as president of the country.

One of Bush's first acts in the Oval Office was to approve a covert action program aimed at bolstering Noriega's opposition. After the stolen election, U.S. Southern Command (SOUTHCOM), based in those days in the Canal Zone, expanded its patrols, training flights, and other military exercises in and around Panama. The U.S. ambassador, and military dependents, were called home. Two thousand additional U.S. troops were sent to Panama. These were measures of political and psychological pressure of the sort that George Shultz had advocated during the Reagan administration but that had been resisted by Frank Carlucci's Pentagon. The new secretary of defense, Dick Cheney, supported all these measures without hesitation. When the commander of SOUTHCOM was identified as part of the bureaucratic resistance to strong action, Cheney secured his replacement by an officer regarded as more aggressive.

The final provocations came in December 1989, when Panamanian troops opened fire on four U.S. officers in a car and killed a Marine lieutenant; the same night, a Navy lieutenant and his wife were stopped at the same roadblock and detained, the wife threatened with rape before they were released after four hours. After a last briefing on the military plan on a Sunday afternoon in the residential quarters of the White House, Bush decided: "Okay, let's do it. The hell with it." An invasion force of ten thousand U.S. airborne troops, joining the forces already in Panama, overwhelmed the Panamanian military, seized the country, and captured Noriega. The U.S. attorneys in Tampa and Miami finally had their man.

The New Cast of Characters

There is a risk that a chapter on George H. W. Bush in a book such as this will be boring. Tolstoy famously observed in *Anna Karenina* that all happy families are alike, while every unhappy family is unhappy in its own way. He then wrote about an unhappy one. From the management point of view, the administration of our forty-first president was the most collegial and smoothest-run of the presidencies we are considering. It had its share of policy quarrels and bursts of ego, but nothing resembling the high drama or low melodrama of its predecessors. This is because it was led by a president who was consistently the master of his brief, and whose personal engagement preempted bureaucratic warfare. He was blessed with cabinet secretaries at State and Defense who saw themselves and acted as the president's men, imposing his agenda on their sometimes recalcitrant bureaucracies instead of becoming the spokesmen for that recalcitrance. The assistant to the president for national security affairs served effectively as honest broker and coordinator, his effectiveness insured not only by his own skill but by the palpable reality that the president, personally, was in charge.

Bush lacked the charismatic qualities of Ronald Reagan, as well as Reagan's political dominance in the Republican Party and in the country. What Bush had was an unusual accumulation of experience in foreign affairs, having been vice president for eight years, and before that the U.S. permanent representative to the United Nations, chief of the U.S. diplomatic mission in China, and director of central intelligence. Except for the brief stint at CIA, what he was accumulating was knowledge, more than executive experience. Of the presidents we are examining in this book, only Nixon had comparable background in the subject matter and comparable confidence in his own understanding of policy. Bush, like Nixon, came into office knowing most world issues and many leaders better than his cabinet secretaries did. On an issue like China, for example, Bush himself sometimes acted as if he were the "China desk officer," to the amusement or irritation of his staff.

Bush carried with him a personal self-assurance, moreover, that Nixon's introversion denied him. Awkward as he was in some circumstances, Bush had the natural gregariousness of the politician—even more so than the aloof Reagan. Coupled with his substantive knowledge, this gregariousness guaranteed that he would engage enthusiastically in personal diplomacy, picking up the telephone and taking charge of policy implementation himself to an unusual degree. By the end of 1989, for example, Bush had found time to chat by telephone with every head of government in Latin America. This served him in good stead when he ordered the invasion of Panama that December; the goodwill he had accumulated contributed to the muted reaction from Latin leaders usually hypersensitive to the very thought of Yankee military intervention. The "mad dialer" was the name he acquired among State Department officials who had to scramble to find out what he was up to. He wanted to be a hands-on president, and he was.

His management style was open and informal. His key subordinates' access to him was easy. Regular meetings of the National Security Council gave way to smaller Oval Office meetings of the "Core Group" or "Gang of Eight"—usually including Secretary of State James A. Baker III, Secretary of Defense Cheney, national security adviser Brent Scowcroft, JCS chairman Colin Powell, White House chief of staff John Sununu, Baker's deputy Lawrence Eagleburger, Scowcroft's deputy Robert Gates, and Vice President Dan Quayle. Transparency was the cardinal rule, and most flare-ups of temper over four years had to do with cases of one principal or another being blindsided (most often inadvertently) by something that another was doing. The informality worked, first of all, because the transparency principle was generally observed; there were no end runs or attempts to bypass or exclude. Second, the president was always engaged, and deferred to. Scowcroft was the impresario and enforcer of this process, and a basic condition of trust prevailed. There were differences of view on many issues, but they were argued out and the president decided. It was a tight group, and its deliberations were remarkably free of leaks. "[W]e made the national security apparatus work the way it is supposed to," Baker wrote later.

Robert Gates, who revered Bush, has a somewhat sharper assessment:

His weaknesses in foreign policy were reflections of his strengths: he was at times too patient and too forgiving of the ambitions and game-playing of both foreign leaders and some of his own people. He was at times loyal to some who did not deserve it or return it.

And we will see below some hints of whom Gates was referring to. Jealousies and suspicions of motives and other human frailties are the norm in Washington; what is striking is that under Bush 41 they were never as debilitating as they were in some previous (or later) administrations.

BRENT SCOWCROFT was described by a journalist in 1990 as "the short, balding figure at Bush's side—at the golf course, on the speedboat, in the Oval Office, the ever-present adviser, the confidant." Trained as a fighter pilot, then earning a doctorate in international relations at Columbia, he went through his Washington trial by fire in the Nixon White House, first as Nixon's military aide, then as Kissinger's deputy through the ordeal of Watergate and the bureaucratic wars of that era. He was one of the few to survive unscathed. In 1975, Gerald Ford elevated Scowcroft to be Kissinger's successor.

Taking on the same job under George Bush, Scowcroft became the only person thus far to serve in the position twice. But it was a different job the second time around. Ford, he knew, reposed total confidence in Kissinger, and therefore his role then was to facilitate that relationship—protecting Ford's options but also Kissinger's flanks. By the time of Bush 41, Scowcroft had emerged as a significant and respected Washington figure in his own right. He had been asked by Reagan to chair a presidential commission looking into U.S. strategic forces; he had been a member of the Tower Board examining the Iran-Contra affair. By then his exemplary conduct of his office under Ford had already become the paradigm of the honest broker model of the security adviser's position—it was the "Scowcroft model." For Bush, Scowcroft would provide two key things—first, an intellectual contribution to the shaping of strategy, particularly on arms control, given his preeminent expertise in the field, and second, a strong hand for a crucial management task. Bush, the hands-on president, had appointed heavyweights James Baker and Dick Cheney to the cabinet, and would want Scowcroft's active help in maintaining presidential control. "It is probably accurate to say that the NSC staff and Brent were . . . concerned about what State might be up to," Bush observed in a dry understatement in his memoir.

Scowcroft was also responsible for a bureaucratic innovation in the NSC system that has been retained by successor administrations. It was his idea to create what is known as the Principals Committee—an interagency committee of the key cabinet secretaries, chaired by himself, in effect a National Security Council meeting without the president. This would be the forum of last resort for ironing out interagency disagreements or framing those disagreements for presidential decision. The cabinet secretaries obviously speak more authoritatively for their departments' views than their deputies can, and at such a meeting they can modify their own views as they choose (which subordinates usually may not). Thus, the forum can move issues closer to resolution in a way that can be very useful for a president. Bush appreciated Scowcroft's ability to "knock heads" and resolve some disagreements "before he let them in my door."

Zbigniew Brzezinski had chaired such a cabinet-level committee for some issues, but the idea of the national security adviser chairing a meeting of cabinet secretaries who outrank him in protocol terms—is, on the face of it, an anomaly. In the 1940s, in the first years of the NSC, it was thought that the secretary of state or vice president would preside in the president's absence. Henry Kissinger, as noted, never chaired cabinet-level meetings when he held only the White House position; the fact that several of his successors have done so is in part a tribute to the transformation in the nature of the position that he bequeathed to them. It was also, under Bush 41, a tribute to Scowcroft's stature and reputation.

DICK CHENEY was not Bush's original choice to be secretary of defense. Senator John Tower of Texas was the first nominee, but failed of confirmation because of allegations of alcoholism and womanizing. The choice of Cheney was inspired. In light of the unusual camaraderie that the Bush team enjoyed, David Rothkopf is right to speculate that, had Tower been confirmed, "he might not have fit in as well, nor been as easy for the president to manage" given his years as an independent power in the Senate. Cheney was a team player. In Robert Gates's estimation, while Cheney "presented his views forcefully and consistently, when he lost he didn't leak or try to play games behind people's backs." By all accounts, Cheney was more hard-line in his convictions on some issues than the rest of the Bush team, especially with respect to the Soviet Union, but the disagreements never reached a level of personal animosity, certainly not anything approaching the bitterness of the Shultz-Weinberger rivalry. They seemed, rather, to be intellectual disagreements over the substance of policy more than they were contests over the protection of bureaucratic turf. In Washington, it is the latter that give the rivalries most of their force.

Cheney's attitude to the use of American military power was not inhibited by a "Vietnam syndrome." Indeed, it was a desire to overcome the "Vietnam syndrome." When the Pentagon gave the Panama operation the name Operation Just Cause, Cheney, joking with reporters, called it "Operation Just Because"—as if to say, we did it just because we could, and we want the world to see that we can.

Cheney was also the unreconstructed Cold Warrior on the Bush team. Early in the administration, Scowcroft came up with a proposal that the United States and the Soviet Union both withdraw substantial ground troops from Central Europe, down to lower equal levels; it was meant as a test of Gorbachev and (if implemented) a significant reduction of the "smothering presence" of Soviet forces in the region. Cheney opposed it, skeptical of Gorbachev and uncomfortable with such a radical move. (Bush, contrary to his public image of caution, was eager for new initiatives and adopted the proposal.) Similarly in the Strategic Arms Reduction Talks (START), Cheney was doubtful of Gorbachev's good faith and wary of risky moves. In late 1991, as the Soviet Union headed toward breakup, it was Cheney who most openly welcomed the disintegration of our geopolitical rival, while Baker and others clung longer to Gorbachev as the benign moderate leader holding the USSR together against less benign centrifugal forces.

Cheney established his firm control at the Pentagon early on. In his first news conference as secretary of defense, he publicly rebuked the Air Force chief of staff for negotiating with members of Congress, without his authorization, on a controversial plan for missile defense. A few months later, as noted, he relieved the SOUTHCOM commander for foot-dragging over military action in Panama. Later, in the run-up to the Gulf War, he dismissed another Air Force chief of staff for loose talk to the press about plans for a bombing campaign. But he treated the chairman of the Joint Chiefs, General Colin Powell, with respect and generally gave him free rein to speak his mind to the president wherever Powell and he disagreed. There were several occasions, whether over Panama or the Gulf War, when the president and Scowcroft were suspicious that senior military planners were reluctant to provide timely or adequate plans for war. Scowcroft reports his unhappiness with a military briefing on Iraq and Kuwait at one point in October 1990: "It sounded unenthusiastic, delivered by people who didn't want to do the job." When military planners came to the president with high estimates of the numbers of men and arms that would be needed—perhaps thinking these would discourage the president from acting—it was Cheney's strategy to advise the president that he should simply accede to the requests. "Dick led the way for the military," Bush recalled, "which I think is the model our Constitution envisioned: armed forces headed by civilians who were leading, not pushing, the military to understanding and fulfilling the missions set for them by the President."

Cheney's performance, in short, especially with respect to the use of force, was a contrast with the performance of the secretaries of defense who had preceded him in the Reagan administration. He was a classic example of a cabinet secretary acting as the president's man at the head of his department, imposing the president's agenda, not as the spokesman to the president of his department's institutional perspective. For Cheney, civilian control of the military meant responsiveness to presidential direction.

Both of these, moreover, were of a piece with his long interest in restoring presidential authority vis-à-vis Congress. Early in his term, Cheney took on the perhaps quixotic mission of challenging the accumulated congressional micromanagement of DoD's affairs. In July 1989, he appeared before the House Armed Services Committee with an array of charts demonstrating the high cost, in dollars and work-hours, of legislatively mandated reporting requirements:

> *Every working day*, for example, entails on average almost 3 new General Accounting Office (GAO) audits of DoD; an estimated 450 written inquiries and over 2,500 telephone inquiries from Capitol Hill; and nearly 3 separate reports to Congress *each* averaging over 1,000 man-hours in preparation and approximately $50,000 in cost. In addition, senior DoD officials spend upwards of 40 hours preparing for the 6 appearances as witnesses and the 14 hours of testimony that they provide on average for *each* day Congress is in session.

In January 1990, his office published a more comprehensive White Paper elaborating on the burden that congressional micromanagement imposed on national defense policy. It catalogued a great expansion of congressional involvement in defense budget line items (including the growth of earmarks), Congress's expanded intervention in management of defense programs, a growing duplication of effort as a result of multiple and overlapping committee jurisdictions in Congress, and other problems.

The common thread in all these endeavors—whether civilian control of the military, presidential direction of defense policy, or resistance to congressional encroachments—was, for Cheney, the defense of presidential prerogative. This is the same Dick Cheney who had served in Gerald Ford's White House in a time of congressional ascendancy, and who in Congress defended Ronald Reagan over Iran-Contra. From this perspective, Cheney's later preoccupations as vice president under George W. Bush (Bush 43) do not suggest such a discontinuity as often alleged.

JAMES A. BAKER III was perhaps the most colorful character in the administration, the only larger-than-life personality in the cabinet. A close personal friend of the president from their younger days together in Houston, Baker characterized it as a "big brother–little brother" relationship. Baker had already gained substantial policy experience as White House chief of staff and secretary of the treasury under Reagan, but he considered that his strong suit was his mastery of the intersection of policy and politics. The title of his memoir of his time at State— *The Politics of Diplomacy*—tells much. "[M]ore comfortable with action than with reflection," he admits, he considered his understanding of American domestic politics a great asset since so much of recent history had underscored the importance of American public support if any policy were to be sustained. A lawyer by training, he exemplified the practical, lawyerlike, case-by-case approach to problems that we have seen in other secretaries of state from the same profession. Pragmatism was his watchword; he considered international politics as a complex negotiation—actually "a series of discrete problems that required solutions." Thus, not surprisingly, even his successes gained him a reputation as more a tactician than a strategist.

He had many successes to his credit. Formation of the broad international coalition in support of the Gulf War, the passage of key U.N. Security Council resolutions that helped mobilize the coalition, the Madrid Arab-Israeli peace conference that followed the war, the diplomacy that united Germany within the Atlantic Alliance, the agreement by which the former Soviet republics that had nuclear weapons on their soil yielded them up to Russia—these achievements would stand out in any administration. His personal closeness to George Bush guaranteed that he would be seen in the world as embodying the will and authority of the president; this was a considerable asset, even if internally the relationship was more complex.

Baker came to the State Department with a determination to be the president's man. There could be no doubt of his personal or political loyalty. He continually reminded his staff that the wishes of "the guy who got elected" were his and their marching orders. "I headed to State assuming that the President made foreign policy, not the Foreign Service," he wrote. This is exactly the conviction that I have been praising in cabinet officers who act on it and criticizing in those who lack it. But there was an edge to Baker's attitude that deserves comment. He was convinced, for example, that his immediate predecessor, George Shultz, had been too reliant on the Foreign Service and too much a prisoner of the institution; this he was determined not to be. This may account for his snubbing of Shultz during the 1988–1989 transition. Only toward the end of the transition period did Baker pay a call on the incumbent and outgoing secretary of state. Shultz found this rankling as well as puzzling since the Reagan administration considered that it had had a rather successful foreign policy.

Baker's memoirs contain the all-too-familiar criticism of the Foreign Service for its institutional rigidity and lack of imagination and initiative. Alas, little had changed since the days of John Kennedy. Baker's response, as he explains, was "to centralize policy authority in a small team of talented, loyal aides, and build outward from them." Unlike, say, Henry Kissinger, who brought only a few aides with him from his NSC staff and who ran the department through able career officers whom he selected, Baker brought his own team of half a dozen close aides to the seventh floor—the top floor of the building and the exalted level of the secretary and his immediate staff. It was this team that was to provide the bold ideas, discretion, and political and personal loyalty that he required to impose his (and the president's) agenda. The department's assistant secretaries, traditionally the workhorses of an administration, found themselves subordinated to this elite on the seventh floor. Baker's inner circle was an unusually talented group of individuals, and the administration's successes owe a great deal to their ideas—such as the "Two Plus Four" diplomatic formula by which the two Germanys and the four World War II Allies (United States, United Kingdom, USSR, and France) resolved the thorny issue of German unification. This team provided much of the intellectual content of the administration's foreign policy. A strong case can be made that, as in the case of Nixon and Kissinger's groundbreaking diplomacy, a more ponderous procedure might not have produced as good results.

Yet there was a defensiveness in all this that remains puzzling in a man as self-assured as Baker surely was. Some of Baker's team made vigorous efforts to reach out to the career diplomats as time went on, and Deputy Secretary of State Lawrence Eagleburger, a Foreign Service veteran, became an important member of the team. Yet many foreign service officers never overcame their initial impression that they were distrusted and excluded from the inner workings of policy-making. On April 1, 1989, what purported to be a special edition of the State Department *Newsletter* was circulated in the building. One article, entitled, "FSO's Capture Baker Staff Member," read as follows:

> Mr. Robert B. Zoellick, the Counselor of the Department, inadvertently disembarked from a malfunctioning elevator on the Fourth Floor of the Main State building yesterday afternoon. He was promptly captured by a gang of about a half dozen toughs from the EUR [European affairs] bureau and held briefly. Zoellick managed to escape after about an hour in captivity and flee to the safety of the Seventh Floor.
>
> It is not known whether Mr. Baker will retain Zoellick in his present position since the Secretary is known to be very suspicious of any of his five trusted staff members who might have been captured by the FSOs.

A companion article reported that the secretary himself had expanded his security guard detail after the incident, lest even the boss be captured by the Foreign Service.

Earlier, I quoted a dry comment by Bush as to the need for Scowcroft and his staff to keep an eye on "what State may be up to." Even the politely worded memoirs can barely conceal the concern in the White House about the State Department's enthusiasm for diplomatic initiatives that seemed not well thought out. State's eagerness for diplomatic activism in this case was probably due less to Baker's being captured by the Foreign Service than to his own instinct to minimize the president's domestic political risks. The Bush-Scowcroft memoir notes, more than once, Baker's reluctance to contemplate the use of force to liberate Kuwait and his eagerness to hold a high-level meeting with the Iraqi leadership before the war, despite Scowcroft's nervousness about the wisdom of such a move. Just before the ground war began (and on the same evening as the president's State of the Union address), Baker and Soviet foreign minister Aleksandr Bessmertnykh issued a joint statement that implied a relaxation of U.S. terms for a cease-fire. Not only was the content of the statement a misstep, but the president was blindsided (and his speech upstaged) and was—by Bush's own account—"furious" at Baker.

In early November 1990, during the U.S. troop buildup in the Gulf that preceded the Gulf War, Thomas L. Friedman of *The New York Times* wrote a column quoting "senior Administration officials" saying with approval that Baker had been acting as a "brake on any immediate impulse to use military force." Baker was said to look at events "less emotionally" than Bush and to be "motivated by an acute awareness of the risks, international and domestic," of going to war; therefore Baker was said to be somewhat more willing to give diplomacy and economic sanctions a chance to work. Friedman observed, moreover, that Baker had seemed to be "avoid[ing] a high profile" during the first two months of the Kuwait crisis. There is no way to determine what sources Friedman relied upon for this analysis of Baker's thinking (though it might just be worth noting that Baker devotes a long passage in his memoirs to how much he valued his off-the-record contacts with Friedman). How the president must have reacted to the Friedman column can be guessed: Other journalists reported the complaints of some of the president's closest advisers about Baker's tendency to distance himself when these controversial decisions were being made. Robert Gates, then Scowcroft's deputy, is on record with a similar observation. Gates summed up his assessment:

> Baker was a real piece of work. . . . Watching him work his counter-parts abroad, members of Congress and the press, and even Scowcroft and Cheney, was to see a master craftsman of the persuasive and backroom arts at the peak of his powers. I respected Baker and came to like him. I also was always glad he was on our side.

The Transformation of Europe

It was on George H. W. Bush's watch that Mikhail Gorbachev finally lost control over events and presided over the dissolution of Moscow's Central European empire and then of the Soviet Union itself. This is not the place for a detailed discussion of this extraordinary turn of history. Suffice it to say that the peaceful evolution that took place was not foreordained. Such tumultuous events could have led in a different direction, and at times threatened to. That the outcome was one fully consistent with U.S. interests and with the long-term peace and freedom of Europe owed much to an intelligent American diplomacy in which George Bush led his government.

The pivotal issue that had to be resolved was procuring Soviet acceptance of, first, the unification of Germany and, second, of unified Germany's remaining in the Atlantic Alliance and in NATO's integrated military structures. These Soviet concessions were essential to Europe's future stability. Eventually the Soviet leaders would be brought around to understand this. Yet, four and a half decades of Soviet foreign policy since Stalin had been devoted, above all else, to suppressing such a possibility. It seemed not only a self-evident geopolitical imperative for Soviet policy but one animated by a still powerful emotion owing to the 27 million Soviet dead of World War II. In 1991, there were twenty-four Soviet divisions stationed in East Germany, totaling 338,000 troops, plus 208,000 related civilians. No satisfactory outcome was imaginable without the Kremlin's consent to remove them.

There is some irony in the fact that the Bush administration came into office with a policy toward the Soviet Union that was more hard-line than Ronald Reagan's. Scowcroft, for example, believed that Reagan, having started out with his "evil empire" rhetoric, had then shifted too far to the other extreme—of believing that the Cold War's underlying confrontation had already gone away because of the new style and rhetoric of Mikhail Gorbachev. Scowcroft saw in Gorbachev a man determined to preserve and revitalize the Soviet system, not to end it, and likewise saw no willingness yet by the Soviet leadership to relinquish its military and political dominance in Central Europe. Dick Cheney and Robert Gates shared this skepticism, though in Scowcroft's case, as we have noted, it led him to come up with proposals for conventional arms reductions in Europe that might weaken that Soviet grip.

But Gorbachev had already taken a fateful step in the same direction before George Bush had even taken the oath of office. In a major speech to the United Nations General Assembly in December 1988—the first U.N. appearance by a Soviet leader since Nikita Khrushchev's boorish performance in 1960—Gorbachev had announced an overall reduction of the Soviet military establishment by 500,000 men, including a withdrawal of 50,000 men and 5,000 tanks from Central Europe. Hard-line colleagues in the Kremlin reportedly opposed such a move as radical and risky—and they were proved right. In retrospect this troop reduction announcement is what first took the lid off—suggesting to the people of Central Europe a weakening of the Soviet commitment to maintain satellite regimes by force. As opposition to Communist rule began to bubble up during 1989 in Central Europe and in the Baltic republics of the USSR, aside from a few incidents of bloodshed the predominant signal emanating from the Kremlin was to confirm that impression. On November 9, 1989, climactically, East German border guards offered no resistance when East and West Berliners overwhelmed the wall.

Even after the wall fell, however, the prevailing assumption in Europe was that East and West Germany would respond to this new development by expanding the political and economic interchange between them, and the two German states would continue to coexist happily ever after. Anything more than that was assumed to be out of the question due to adamant Soviet opposition. West German chancellor Helmut Kohl started out with that assumption, too, but as he watched the populations of both Germanys sweep away the barriers and saw the illusion of the East German authorities' legitimacy evaporating before his eyes, he seized the initiative and, in a speech to the Bundestag on November 28, committed himself to a process leading to unification. Not only in Moscow but in Margaret Thatcher's London and François Mitterrand's Paris was this greeted by consternation. Fearing the power of a united Germany, they all wanted to slow events down.

Inside accounts of the Bush administration make clear that Bush himself was the first to see the inevitability of German unity and the first Western leader to declare unequivocal support for Kohl's initiative. The State Department was skeptical at first, comfortable in the status quo, and even Scowcroft's view was close to State's. Baker visited the East German capital in December and reported optimistically to Bush about the East German leaders' commitment to "reform and peaceful change" in their regime—missing the point that the regime was by then a discredited shell. The president's view prevailed. As events accelerated, the administration set for itself the task of persuading its recalcitrant allies and, most important, the Soviet Union, to accede gracefully to the absorption into West Germany of the East German regime.

When Bush met with Gorbachev on shipboard off the coast of Malta in early December 1989, the Soviet leader was conflicted. He said he was prepared to "let history decide the outcome" but he was angry that "Mr. Kohl is in too much of a hurry." He called for "prudence." As if on cue from Dana Carvey on *Saturday Night Live*, Bush readily agreed, reassuring Gorbachev that he would continue to avoid grandstanding. Gorbachev said he appreciated that. Bush, often criticized for his understated management of these events, made it a cardinal point of his strategy not to rub Gorbachev's nose in a Soviet defeat that Bush saw as inevitable. "We're going to win the game," Bush told Helmut Kohl the following February, "but we must be clever while we are doing it."

One could see Gorbachev's thought process gradually moving toward where he would end up. He told Bush at Malta, for example, that he accepted the U.S. role in Europe. This was not an empty grace note or a favor to the United States; rather, it was a recognition that if one had any reason to fear a united Germany in the heart of Europe, part of the cure was a continued U.S. military presence on the Continent. But it was not until the following May that Gorbachev would follow this logic to its proper conclusion—that is, allowing united Germany to stay in NATO's integrated military structure (and thus its forces under U.S. command). In the meantime the Soviets were still tempted to try to block unification or else to insist on some form of German neutrality as the price for it.

It was Baker's team at the State Department that came up with the Two plus Four formula for a diplomatic process by which this all would be negotiated. This allowed the two German states to work out the terms of their merger, backstopped by the four victors of World War II, which had up to that moment been exercising certain occupation rights in Berlin deriving from the 1945 Potsdam agreement. The Two Plus Four procedure gave the reluctant Europeans and Soviets a formal role but left the ball in German hands where it belonged. It gave the United States a role, too, and provided a framework for the Soviets to save face. Intense legwork by the indefatigable Baker helped produce the result. While unification was probably unstoppable, the Soviets' acceptance of the terms that we deemed essential was not inevitable. This acceptance undoubtedly resulted in part from the Bush administration's avoidance of triumphalism over the fall of the Berlin Wall; as its officials have insisted, this reticence was not a lack of "vision" but an intelligent strategy.

The future of the Soviet Union itself was the source of more significant intellectual hesitations within the Bush administration. As early as April 1989, while Baker was preparing for his first visit to Moscow as secretary of state, Dick Cheney blurted out in a CNN interview his pessimistic assessment that Gorbachev would "ultimately fail" in his efforts to reform the Soviet system. Baker phoned the president to complain, and Cheney himself called Baker to apologize for speaking out of turn. Baker said he did not necessarily disagree with the analysis, but the administration should not be saying this out loud (and in any case, it shouldn't be the secretary of defense saying it). Six months later, the State Department was shown for clearance the draft of a speech that Scowcroft's deputy Robert Gates planned to deliver at Georgetown University. Gates, an expert Sovietologist from his CIA days, planned to give a sober assessment of the prospects for Gorbachev's reform program. I was on the NSC staff at the time and was helping Gates with his speech. This time Baker called Scowcroft to complain; Gates's gloomy tone was too much in contrast with the positive thrust of what Baker had been saying about U.S.-Soviet relations in the wake of his own meetings with Soviet leaders. Gates revised the draft to include several upbeat quotes from Baker, but to no avail; Baker insisted the text be killed.

Baker was certainly right that the administration had to speak with one voice, and that voice should be that of the president and secretary of state. These incidents, however, small as they were, were emblematic of an important tension within the administration—between a Reaganite truth-telling and a desire to smooth Gorbachev's way forward. Generally the latter instinct won out. The prevailing view was that the United States had a strategic stake in Gorbachev and wanted him to succeed against his hard-line adversaries in the Politburo and in the country. But this approach left the administration looking flat-footed and caught by surprise when events unfolded as they did.

The test came later, in 1991, after a failed coup attempt by Soviet party and military hard-liners who held Gorbachev under house arrest for three days in August. Gorbachev was "saved" by the bold response of Boris Yeltsin—popularly elected as leader of the Russian republic—who stood atop a tank in Moscow and faced down the coup plotters. (Strong public condemnation of the coup by the Bush administration also helped to undermine it.) But I put the word "saved" in quotation marks above because the collapse of the coup paradoxically undermined Gorbachev as well. He was surviving by a balancing act between a hard-line opposition and a democratic reformist opposition; the collapse of the hard-liners tilted the balance irreversibly toward Yeltsin. The structure of the Soviet system suddenly began to look very rickety.

Soon enough, unrest in Ukraine and the Baltic republics raised the prospect of the dissolution of the USSR. Should the United States welcome this and recognize the independence of these entities? Or side with Gorbachev in trying to hold the Soviet structure together? At two crucial Oval Office meetings of the Gang of Eight on September 5 and October 11, the senior players argued it out in front of the president. Cheney argued for an "aggressive" approach: "The break-up of the Soviet Union is in our interest." He endorsed an idea of Gates's, namely to move quickly to establish American consulates in all the republics of the USSR so as to nudge events in that direction. Baker argued, on the contrary, for "strengthening the center"; our hopes for a peaceful transition to a reformed Soviet system continued to rest on Gorbachev, who was struggling against centrifugal forces that were hard-line and more troublesome for us. Baker proposed that we announce a number of principles we cared about—self-determination for the republics by democratic means; respect for existing borders; human rights; adherence to the Soviet Union's treaty obligations; central control over nuclear weapons, et cetera—and declare our principles rather than any preference as to the continuation or breakup of the USSR.

As Scowcroft later admitted, these unexceptionable principles notwithstanding, the Bush team never came around to a "tight" administration policy toward the breakup of the Soviet Union. This was partly because of the disagreements among the key people, partly because of the rush of events, and partly because of a concern about the diffusion of control over nuclear weapons. But the Baker view, in essence, became the prevailing view. The president earned criticism for a speech to the Ukrainian parliament on August 1, 1991, that cautioned: "Americans will not support those who seek independence in order to replace a far-off tyranny with a local despotism." This warning was aimed not at Ukraine but at other places where a more rabid nationalism threatened an upsurge of violence—Yugoslavia, Georgia, and Moldavia, for example. But it nevertheless confirmed the public impression of an administration clinging to the status quo of the USSR amidst rapid—and fundamentally positive—change. In the same vein, Bush, having invested so much in the personality of Soviet leader Gorbachev, was accused—including by none other than Richard Nixon—of giving inadequate support to the Russian democratic revolution represented by Boris Yeltsin.

The Gulf War

The Gulf crisis unfolded over a period of several months—from Saddam Hussein's invasion of Kuwait on August 1, 1990, to the launching of coalition air operations on January 16, 1991, to the initiation of the ground war on February 23, to its end four days later. Through this period, American public opinion was brought around to support a war to liberate a faraway country that few Americans had ever heard of and to which we had no pre-existing defense commitment. By early December, opinion polls showed 50–60 percent support of the president's policy; by early January public support had grown to 65–80 percent. This represented a notable feat of presidential leadership; it was also an exercise in effective bureaucratic management.

At the president's first meeting of the NSC after Saddam's invasion, on the morning of August 2 in the Cabinet Room, a consensus emerged that the United States had to defend Saudi Arabia, but the conversation was inconclusive beyond that. Scowcroft reports that he was "appalled" by the undertone of resignation at that first meeting, which suggested acquiescence in the Iraqi occupation of Kuwait. The president, too, wanted better than that; after the meeting was over he and Scowcroft agreed to convene a second NSC meeting twenty-four hours later, at which they hoped to elicit more concrete proposals for action.

In the meantime, Bush flew off for a day trip to Aspen, Colorado, to deliver a speech and for a conversation with British prime minister Margaret Thatcher. Scowcroft, on the flight with Bush to Colorado, sensed the president was leaning toward the use of force to evict Saddam from Kuwait. Mrs. Thatcher, too, found Bush resolute, and she reinforced this. (Her famous admonition to Bush—that it was "no time to go wobbly"—came a few weeks later, urging that the United States and Britain vigorously enforce the economic sanctions that the U.N. Security Council had just imposed on Iraq.) On the aircraft, as well,

Bush worked the phones. He called Egyptian president Hosni Mubarak and Jordanian King Hussein, who were still hoping for some kind of peaceful path to Iraqi withdrawal; Bush warned that the continued occupation of Kuwait was "unacceptable" and urged them to convey that message to Saddam.

Meanwhile, at the Pentagon, Secretary of Defense Cheney was leaning in the same direction as the president. But his new chairman of the Joint Chiefs of Staff, General Colin Powell, was a major figure in his own right. Powell, who had become chairman on October 1, 1989, was the first man to exercise throughout his term the full powers of the chairmanship as they had been transformed by a significant Defense Reorganization Act (called the Goldwater-Nichols Act) in 1986. That legislation elevated the status of the chairman as the principal military adviser to the president and the secretary of defense. While the service chiefs remained important advisers, the chairman was no longer merely the first among equals, obligated to present the consensus recommendations of a corporate body. Likewise the 1,600-person Joint Staff now reported directly to the chairman, instead of to the Joint Chiefs as a whole. The legislation also elevated the importance of the regional commanders—in this case, General Norman Schwarzkopf, head of U.S. Central Command. In fact, the chain of command now ran from the president through the secretary of defense directly to the regional commander, bypassing the chairman of the Joint Chiefs. But there was no doubt that Powell, given his charisma and unique experience (including as President Reagan's assistant for national security affairs), was bound to use the new powers of the chairman to the full. Throughout the Gulf crisis it was Powell, not Schwarzkopf, who had most of the interaction with the president and the secretary of defense. This was partly because Schwarzkopf had moved his headquarters to Saudi Arabia, but also partly because of concern about his voluble temperament. "Norm Schwarzkopf, under pressure, was an active volcano," Powell has said. As the planning progressed, Powell was briefing the president almost daily.

But Bush, Scowcroft, and Cheney could also see early on that Powell was personally reluctant to contemplate offensive military operations. A defensive deployment of U.S. troops to deter an Iraqi attack on Saudi Arabia was one thing; offensive action to drive Iraqi forces out of Kuwait, as Powell pointed out correctly, was a much bigger task. The president, who was heading in that direction, relied on Cheney to bring the military along. "Dick was probably ahead of his military on this," Bush noted.

On August 2, in the afternoon following Saddam's invasion of Kuwait, Cheney and Powell and their top aides convened in the secretary's conference room at the Pentagon to consider what to advise the president when he returned from Aspen. Powell candidly expressed his concerns, which were political. Having been a military aide to Weinberger, Powell adhered to Weinberger's 1984 six criteria for the use of American military power—the most important of which was an assurance of public support before doing so. Powell stressed to Cheney his conviction that American public opinion would support a defense of Saudi Arabia but not a war to liberate Kuwait: "I don't see the senior leadership taking us into armed conflict for the events of the last twenty-four hours," Powell argued. Cheney's response was that the Department of Defense owed the president a recommendation: "He will look to us. The others can't do it. So what do we do?" Powell recommended the United States start with diplomatic efforts. "I am opposed to dramatic action without the President having popular support."

The next morning, August 3, with the president's approval, Scowcroft led off the second NSC meeting forcefully expressing his own view that Iraq's occupation of Kuwait should not be allowed to stand. Accommodation to the Iraqi aggression, he said, "should not be a policy option." Cheney spoke up firmly in agreement—and so did the State Department representative. Secretary Baker had not yet returned from a trip to the Soviet Union, and was represented by Deputy Secretary Lawrence Eagleburger. Scowcroft and Eagleburger were old friends, sharing the battle scars of having served as assistants to Henry Kissinger. Ironists and foreign service officers will enjoy the picture of Eagleburger the FSO being so stalwart a supporter of the military options that the president wanted aired, while his boss the secretary of state, who expressed such mistrust of the Foreign Service's loyalty to the president, was later to be chided for distancing himself from the president at various moments during the crisis.

At this NSC meeting, Powell ventured a question in front of the president along the lines of what he had said to Cheney: Was it worth going to war to liberate Kuwait? Cheney later upbraided him for overstepping his authority: "Colin, you're Chairman of the Joint Chiefs. You're not Secretary of State. You're not the National Security Advisor anymore. And you're not Secretary of Defense. So stick to military matters." Powell understood that he had been out of bounds. Cheney thenceforth insisted on absorbing the fullest information on the military planning, and from multiple sources inside the Pentagon, not just funneled through the chairman. He spent hours peppering Powell and his staff with questions about the plans, to refine them and screen them before they were briefed to the president.

Bush soon ordered 250,000 U.S. troops to the region to bolster Saudi Arabia and bided his time. As the initial buildup neared completion, at a meeting on October 30, this time in the Situation Room, the president asked for a discussion of what his choices were—standing pat, or driving Iraqi forces out of Kuwait? Powell outlined a military plan for accomplishing the latter. As Powell recounts:

> When I finished, Scowcroft asked, "What size force are we talking about?"
>
> "We're approaching two hundred and fifty thousand for the defensive phase," I said. "But if the President opts for this offensive, we'll need a hell of a lot more."
>
> "How much more?" Scowcroft asked.
>
> "Nearly double," I said. "About another two hundred thousand troops."
>
> "Whew," Scowcroft said, his gasp echoed by others around the room. I glanced at the President. He had not blinked.

After some additional conversation, the president said simply, "Okay, do it."

Baker had returned from the Soviet Union in early August with an important trophy—Moscow's agreement to a joint declaration condemning the Iraqi invasion of Kuwait. Soviet cooperation in the Gulf crisis was arguably a significant payoff from the administration's continuing relationship with Gorbachev. Meanwhile, James Baker's State Department applied itself to mobilizing a thirty-four-nation political and military coalition, securing a series of U.N. Security Council resolutions in support of the effort, and eventually collecting on allied pledges of $53 billion to finance U.S. war costs.

Thus, the ingredients for a coherent U.S. policy were in place—a president who gave direction to his government, a secretary of defense who gave direction to his department, and an energetic diplomacy led by the president and his secretary of state in tandem. There were debates, of course. Margaret Thatcher, for one, argued strenuously, especially with Baker, against putting too much stock in U.N. Security

Council resolutions. She believed (correctly) that Kuwait and the coalition were entitled to exercise the inherent right of collective self-defense as acknowledged in Article 51 of the U.N. Charter; she did not want to set a precedent for the view that Security Council resolutions were required to authorize every use of force. The American side argued, in reply, that such Security Council resolutions would be diplomatically useful in helping to mobilize broad international support, and that—especially important to Baker—they were necessary to bring along the U.S. Congress. The Democratic-controlled Congress, voting its authorization on January 12, 1991, was indeed persuaded in part by the international legitimacy that the U.N. resolutions were seen to convey. (Twelve years later saw an interesting reversal of the process. In the run-up to the 2003 Iraq War, it was a British prime minister who insisted on the pursuit of a U.N. Security Council resolution to authorize the use of force. The administration of Bush 43, moreover, obtained congressional resolutions of support first, in the hope of using them as leverage to generate support in the Security Council.)

Baker, as we have noted, was eager for a high-level meeting with the Iraqis to demonstrate that the United States had gone the extra mile. The proposal was to invite Iraqi foreign minister Tariq Aziz to Washington for a meeting with Bush, and to send Baker to Baghdad to meet with Saddam. Scowcroft was nervous about this proposal, fearing that a clever Iraqi diplomacy could turn this into the illusion of a negotiation, confuse the issue, and weaken the coalition's resolve. But Bush approved the idea. In the end, the Iraqis accepted only a meeting between Baker and Aziz in Geneva, which took place on January 9, 1991. The Iraqi minister's performance was so stubborn and defiant that it vindicated Baker, helping strengthen the administration's case—in Congress and internationally—that it had exhausted all the options short of war. Bush later defended Baker—perhaps with another sly dig—expressing admiration for his overall performance: "I don't like the criticism of him, because his diplomacy has been absolutely superb."

The most controversial decision of the Gulf War was Bush's decision to end the ground combat after one hundred hours, leaving important units of Saddam's Republican Guard to escape and forswearing any military action to overthrow Saddam Hussein's regime in Baghdad. This is not the place to reopen the debate. The important point for our purposes is that this decision reflected unanimity in the Bush administration. Different elements in the U.S. government had different reasons for coming to the same conclusion, and there was no internal controversy. Having achieved the liberation of Kuwait, Powell and his military colleagues strenuously opposed prolonging the killing of helpless Iraqi troops along what the media were calling the "highway of death"; they saw this as a matter of military honor. Baker and his State colleagues worried that the coalition would shatter at the unilateral American pursuit of a goal—regime change—that other countries had not signed up to, and warned that improvising an assault on Baghdad was an invitation to trouble. Dick Cheney agreed with this analysis. Bush and Scowcroft in their joint memoir concede that they acted on some mistaken assumptions: When the ground war was ended, the administration was convinced that Saddam's Republican Guard had been utterly destroyed. As it turned out, because of the swiftness of the Marines' sweep into Kuwait, many Guard reserve divisions were not drawn south into the coalition trap, and therefore survived. There was also a comfortable assumption that Saddam's regime would fall on its own, discredited by defeat, like a rotten fruit. And there was a concern about Iran, looming over the horizon—that is, a desire to calibrate the degree of defeat of Iraq so as not to leave too much of a vacuum there and unbalance the regional balance of power.

Such a fine calibration is difficult to achieve in war, in the best of circumstances, and the incomplete results of the 1991 Gulf War can legitimately be said to have left behind a strategic problem. Saddam Hussein survived, restored his tyranny, and steadily eroded the system of external restraints and sanctions that a series of postwar U.N. Security Council resolutions sought to impose on him. The difficulties that Bush 43 ran into when he imposed regime change in 2003 might be seen as proof of the unwisdom of regime change and a ringing vindication of Bush 41's restraint in 1991: Leaving a political vacuum in a major Arab country is no small problem, since diverse and powerful forces will inevitably attempt to fill it. Alternatively, it could be argued that the task might have been easier in 1991, before the ascendancy of radical Islamism that later in the decade threatened to envelop the whole Middle East. This debate will not be settled here.

Assessment

Bush's foreign policy accomplishments were substantial. Not only the liberation of Panama and Kuwait are to his credit, but his calm management of the collapse of the Soviet empire in Europe avoided a variety of dangers that were much more real at the time than they are bound to seem in retrospect. At home, politically, he fell victim to the Churchill effect: With the world's major dangers having gone away, the American people in 1992 denied him reelection because his skills seemed no longer needed in an era when domestic policy issues seemed to dominate.

Contrary to the cliché that he lacked vision—"the vision thing," as he called it himself—Bush did articulate, repeatedly, the concept of a "new world order" that would follow the Cold War. It was the optimistic picture of a world in which relations among the major powers would remain as harmonious and cooperative as they had been during the 1990–1991 Gulf crisis, reflected in the unanimous resolutions of the U.N. Security Council that framed it. Bill Clinton would borrow the same concept and elaborate upon it. Unfortunately the great-power harmony would not survive the decade, and a violent challenge would come at us from a very different and unexpected direction early in the new century.

But Bush was always more comfortable as a pragmatist than as a conceptualizer. And this had its costs. When he announced in October 1987 his campaign to succeed Reagan as president, he declared, obliquely but deliberately, his differences from Reagan: "I am a practical man. I like what's real. I'm not much for the airy and abstract; I like what works. I am not a mystic and I do not yearn to lead a crusade." This was a true statement of fact and self-description, but it was also a position. He came into office determined to be his own man, not an appendage to Reagan. He made sweeping personnel changes among the three thousand political appointees in his administration, which came as a bit of a shock to many Republican loyalists who were expecting to stay on in a third Republican term.

But this posture of independence left Bush politically vulnerable. James Baker, his chief political strategist, was of the same mold as Bush—proudly pragmatic, problem-solving, unideological. Yet Bush owed his election in large part to Reagan's success. In drifting away from Reagan, Bush and Baker also drifted away from the base of the Republican Party as Reagan had transformed it. Bush thus left himself open to a conservative challenge to his reelection in 1992 (in the form of both Patrick Buchanan and Ross Perot). This is every incumbent's nightmare; in a reelection year one wants to tack to the center, not be pulled toward one's base. But when such a challenge occurs within one's own party, it is a sure sign that a political miscalculation has already been made somewhere along the line.

There were also other costs. Bush's readiness to distance himself from Reagan in style and philosophy is also part of the reason why, when most Americans think of the end of the Cold War, they tend to associate it not with Bush, on whose watch it occurred, but rather with his predecessor. What Bush skillfully managed, Reagan's vision had shaped.

CHAPTER EIGHT

Bill Clinton

BILL CLINTON WAS ELECTED at a golden moment when national security challenges seemed no longer to rank high on our national agenda. The Cold War had ended; it was a time of American ascendancy globally, even in crisis spots like the Middle East where moderates seemed stronger than ever in the aftermath of the Gulf War. The main issues facing the country in 1992 seemed to be economic, whose handling would come naturally to a Democratic administration. Clinton promised if elected to "focus like a laser beam" on these problems, and one of the mantras of his campaign was: "It's the economy, stupid." This meant a focus first on the domestic economy, and on international economic issues as an adjunct to that. During the transition after his election, in a meeting with House Democratic leaders, he interrupted veteran Foreign Affairs Committee chairman Lee Hamilton of Indiana who was giving a brief survey of the international scene: "Lee, I just went through the whole campaign and no one talked about foreign policy at all, except for a few members of the press."

Conventional wisdom has it that Clinton as president had no sustained interest in foreign affairs. The truth is more complicated than that. For the first two years or so, it was probably correct that his priority interests lay elsewhere. David Gergen, who served as an adviser to Clinton during that initial period, as well as to Republican presidents, assessed Clinton thusly:

> In the Cold War, presidents typically spent at least 60 percent of their time on foreign affairs; with Bush |41|, the figure could rise to 75 percent. Clinton early on reversed the tables: domestic affairs probably consumed 75 percent of his time, foreign affairs less than a quarter.

This was a source of a number of serious problems, including stumbles involving the use of military force and other problems that festered due to neglect. But Clinton learned lessons from this experience, and his policy-making process regained its balance in later years. More generally, the problem was not that Clinton was intellectually uninterested in foreign policy but that he was unfocused. Highly intelligent, he was subject to what his onetime political aide Dick Morris called "a tendency toward intellectual clutter," which caused him to lose focus on priorities. Nor did he want to spend a lot of political capital on foreign policy issues.

He came into office with a broad vision of a post–Cold War international order. Essentially he took George Bush's concept of a harmonious relationship among the major powers and carried it further—to a full-blooded Wilsonian vision of a world of human rights and democracy, the flourishing of the United Nations and other multilateral institutions, and cooperative responses to transnational challenges such as nonproliferation, economic globalization, and environmental protection. In his 1992 campaign he repeatedly criticized President Bush for "coddling tyrants from Baghdad to Beijing." Events would confront Bill Clinton in office with uncomfortable contradictions among these different impulses.

In Bill Clinton's eight years there were successes—economic initiatives like congressional assent to the North American Free Trade Agreement and World Trade Organization; the weathering of financial crises in Mexico and Southeast Asia; admission of three new Central European democracies to NATO; support for Russian reformers; a peace accord in Northern Ireland; agreements that brought a respite to violence in Bosnia and Kosovo; and near-success in Israeli-Palestinian diplomacy. Where he did focus himself, or delegated to capable people, there was coherence. In other cases, the loose informality of his style of decision-making often permitted bureaucratic stalemate and indiscipline.

People and Institutions

Many, if not most, administrations contain philosophical divisions—bureaucratic rivalries sharpened by ideological or policy differences. Such divisions tore at Gerald Ford's and Jimmy Carter's administrations, as well as Ronald Reagan's; as we shall see in the next chapter, they plagued George W. Bush as well. Democratic and Republican administrations alike are often tested in this way, reflecting the big-tent nature of our political parties and the broad party coalitions that presidents usually attempt to reflect in staffing their governments. But managing such a government then puts a premium on a president's leadership skills. Presidents need to be prepared for it—to have this in mind when they select their key subordinates, and ideally to have some clarity about their own convictions and to understand that they will need to resolve the differences.

In Clinton's case, part of the problem was a set of contradictions within the liberal camp—an allergy to military intervention deriving from Vietnam, challenged by a more activist humanitarian interventionism driven by a commitment to human rights; a tension between human rights and the much vaunted economic interests; battles over free trade and protectionism; and a tension between economic goals and traditional security concerns. His decision making was made more complicated by public and congressional attitudes that were, for much of his term, averse to his military interventions and other dimensions of his liberal internationalism.

FOR SECRETARY OF STATE, Clinton chose Warren Christopher, a California lawyer who had been deputy secretary in the Carter administration. Hardworking, self-effacing, and supremely cautious, Christopher, like so many other lawyers who have held the job, proudly considered himself a pragmatist, not a strategist. On issues of military intervention he was a dove, but otherwise critics saw him as having no consistent beliefs or guiding philosophy. By the criteria of this book, he was not one to impose his will forcefully on the bureaucracy. Indeed, his memoirs record his pride in his reliance on the Foreign Service. Clinton himself acknowledged the doubts about Christopher's effectiveness. But there are those who believe that the last thing Clinton wanted was a forceful, independent personality with strong ideas of his own in charge of the State Department. In this case the motive was not (as with Kennedy or Nixon) to avoid having a competitor so that the president could run foreign policy himself; it was, as David Halberstam suggests, to avoid a strong figure who would only raise the prominence of issues that Clinton wanted on the back burner. As several presidents we have discussed in this book discovered, however, weakness in a secretary of state—whatever the reason—has a tendency to compound rather than to solve a president's problems.

The new national security adviser was Anthony Lake, a thoughtful ex–foreign service officer who had served in the American embassy in South Vietnam, then briefly on Henry Kissinger's NSC staff, then as director of the Policy Planning Staff at State in the Carter administration. Vietnam was the formative experience of Lake's career; he had resigned from Kissinger's staff because of discomfort with Nixon and his policy. Lake took a prominent role in articulating the new administration's philosophy, which he called a strategy of "engagement" (diplomatic and humanitarian engagement in the world) and "enlargement" (of the zone of democracy). Military intervention was something Lake cannot have been viscerally comfortable with, but as the Balkan crises unfolded he found himself in the interventionist camp because of outrage at the atrocities being committed. He admitted to being "emotional" about Bosnia, and agonized at times over his inability to formulate a stronger policy that could command support from his president.

Two committed hawks were Vice President Al Gore and Madeleine Albright, U.N. ambassador in Clinton's first term and then Warren Christopher's successor. Gore had won a claim to national security expertise by voting in the Senate in favor of Bush 41's Gulf War resolution (after agonizing over the decision until the night before). With his tenure, according to the experienced David Gergen, the vice presidency reached another new level of power and influence at the center of policy-making. Gore was a key adviser, and was given important substantive portfolios including managing cooperation with Russia. Albright came from a family that had fled Hitler; her worldview was accordingly more colored by the Munich experience than by Vietnam, and she became an advocate of muscular intervention in an administration populated by a number of more cautious souls.

A pivotal figure throughout was Samuel (Sandy) Berger, Lake's deputy national security adviser in the first term and successor in the second. A trade lawyer by background, he seemed at first glance to embody the new administration's emphasis on economics. But Berger's true talent and focus were political. He was strongly liberal by conviction—he had met Clinton when they both worked for George McGovern's 1972 campaign—but Vietnam was not for him the same traumatic experience as for Lake and others. He had been active in Democratic foreign policy salons during the long years out of office. As Lake's deputy, he served as NSC liaison to the political side of the

White House and sat in on reelection strategy meetings. As security adviser he was known most of all for his acute sense of Clinton's political needs and for policy advice that was attuned to them. Clinton's memoirs speak about Berger with a particular warmth.

Bill Clinton's relations with his military were never good. His avoidance of military service as a young man, and his announced intentions to permit gays in the military and cut the defense budget preceded him into office. The anti-military attitudes of some of his left-leaning staff also became known—including an incident reported by Elizabeth Drew in which a young woman on the White House staff, greeted by a senior military officer, responded contemptuously, "I don't talk to the military." Word of this quickly spread in the Pentagon.

These problems aside, the Defense Department under Bill Clinton was permitted to revert to the cautious, anti-interventionist mode seen in the Reagan administration. General Colin Powell, chairman of the Joint Chiefs, his prestige enhanced by the Gulf War success, was a powerful presence in the room in any deliberation; he remained a voice of caution with respect to the use of force. In his memoir he tells the story of a 1993 debate over Bosnia in which he had urged military restraint, only to be rebuked by Albright: "What's the point of having this superb military that you're always talking about if we can't use it?" Powell says he thought he would "have an aneurysm"; he was shocked by what he saw as the cavalier way this new team of civilian colleagues was ready to move U.S. troops around like toy soldiers on a board game. When Powell retired in the fall of 1993, part of his legacy was an apparent determination by Clinton not to appoint so charismatic a figure as Powell's successor. Clinton's two subsequent chairmen, Army Generals John Shalikashvili and Henry (Hugh) Shelton, were less likely to carry the political weight that Powell did either within or outside the administration. But they shared Powell's resistance to the use of force in the Balkan or other crises.

Clinton's three secretaries of defense were not activists either. Les Aspin, who had been a brilliant defense expert when a committee chairman in Congress, proved ineffectual as an executive; Powell, indeed, had warned Clinton that Aspin was not a good choice for the job. Aspin presided over a series of failed interventions in the first year, and paid the political price. His successor, William Perry, a brilliant scientist and respected defense and arms control expert, did not play a pivotal role in foreign policy discussions; he sided with the cautious military during the Bosnia crisis until the Serb massacre of Muslims at Srebrenica in 1995 forced the administration's hand. Perry was succeeded in January 1997 by William Cohen, a former Republican senator, who in the Senate had voted with many fellow Republicans against Clinton's Bosnia intervention. Thus, unlike the tenure of Dick Cheney under Bush 41, the civilian leadership of Clinton's Pentagon was not inclined to override the caution of the military. On the contrary, in the Kosovo crisis Cohen would only reinforce it.

THE CLINTON ADMINISTRATION sought to emulate its predecessor in an important respect, by adopting its formal policy-making structure without change. Just below the level of the National Security Council, Bush and Scowcroft had come up with the innovation of the Principals Committee—the NSC without the president, chaired by the national security adviser. A level below that was the Deputies Committee, chaired by the deputy national security adviser. The Clinton team seems to have adopted this system for a variety of reasons. It made sense to be seen emulating the practices of a predecessor who had been widely regarded as a model of competence in this field. Lake, in addition, had co-authored a book that made the cogent argument that incoming administrations should shake the habit of politicizing these matters to the point of reflexively changing the arrangements they inherit just to demonstrate some kind of superiority.

The Principals and Deputies committees met frequently, under Clinton as under Bush, but the unstructured quality of the new president's engagement marked a subtle difference. Bush 41 had been more in command. Under Clinton the system seemed to rely more on the interaction of his subordinates, with presidential involvement more sporadic. "[U]nlike Bush's team, Clinton's lacked a captain," in the words of scholars Ivo Daalder and I. M. Destler. Sandy Berger has commented that formal or structured NSC meetings were reserved for times of crisis:

> Clinton did not attend NSC meetings per se. The president came to NSC meetings during crises, the Haiti meeting or Kosovo or Iraq, and he and the vice president would come down for an hour to the Situation Room and meet together. But he preferred either to let Tony [Lake] or me run the meetings and then bring him either a memo,

which laid it out so that he could decide, or we would call a meeting in
the Cabinet Room or in the Oval Office.

The Clinton administration, like Reagan's, sought bureaucratic consensus among the principals. "There is a comfort you get in hearing that all
your advisers agree," Lake told an interviewer. The Principals Committee was the natural place to pursue this—presumably in the hope of
sparing the president the need to engage. But often there was no consensus, and there are many reports of Clinton's irritation when foreign
policy disagreements were presented to him to resolve.

Even when the president was deeply engaged, discipline was not his
strong suit. Meetings lasted hours; for the first several years he was
notoriously behind schedule through much of the day. Colin Powell,
having seen firsthand how things worked in both the Reagan and Bush
administrations, was offended by the lack of discipline:

> [T]he discussions continued to meander like graduate-student bull
> sessions or the think-tank seminars in which many of my new colleagues had spent the last twelve years while their party was out of
> power. Backbenchers sounded off with the authority of cabinet officers. I was shocked one day to hear one of Tony Lake's subordinates,
> who was there to take notes, argue with him in front of the rest of us.

Clinton hated to be confined by formal structures: "A strict, formal
structure just won't cut it," he told *Time* magazine shortly after his election. "There's too much you miss if you don't forage around yourself." As
William Doyle has commented:

> This sounded much like the romantic management disorder of his
> hero John Kennedy, but the bitter experiences of Ford and Carter
> should have taught Clinton that the presidency had now grown far too
> enormous to be run through a "spokes of the wheel" structure without
> a strong chief of staff.

While the president met with Lake almost daily, regularly scheduled
contact with his senior national security team was not a feature of the
early years of the administration. James Woolsey, Clinton's first CIA
director, had his own stories to tell. In the summer of 1993 he got

together for breakfast with Secretary of Defense Aspin, his old friend, and compared notes on their access to the president. As Woolsey later recounted:

> Aspin asked [me], "Did you think when we got these jobs that we'd get together with the president sometimes and talk to him about what we were going to do?" And I said, yeah, I thought that. He said, Well, I'm not doing that, are you? And I said, No, I'm not. I thought you were. He said, No, I'm not. And I don't think Chris [Warren Christopher] is. And he looked up at the ceiling and he said, I wonder who is.

The Economists, Stupid

The answer to Aspin's question was: the economists. On December 10, 1992, about five weeks after his election, Clinton announced his new economic team—including Texas senator Lloyd Bentsen as treasury secretary and investment banker Robert Rubin as assistant to the president for economic policy. On December 14–15, Clinton convened an "economic summit" in Little Rock of three hundred business and labor leaders and economic thinkers to brainstorm publicly about economic policy. Only on December 22, a week later, did he announce his new national security team. Soon after inauguration he issued an executive order creating a new institution called the National Economic Council (or NEC)—an "NSC for economics"—parallel to the National Security Council.

As we have seen, many recent presidents have wrestled with the question of how to integrate domestic and international economic policy with the classical issues of national security policy. Presidents beginning with Nixon have experimented with parallel structures, one of the more successful being Gerald Ford's Economic Policy Board. Clinton's NEC—its own structure consciously modeled after the NSC—was in formal terms a cabinet-level body chaired by the president, with the mandate to coordinate the process of advising the president and monitoring implementation of his decisions. The assistant to the president for economic policy (Rubin), comparable to the national security adviser, was to manage the NEC's operation and lead a staff; an interagency NEC Principals Committee would meet at cabinet level, chaired by Rubin, and an NEC Deputies Committee would be chaired by Rubin's deputy. A clever innovation to foster collaboration between the NEC and NSC was the designation of common staffers—dual-hatted individuals serving as both the international economics experts on the NSC staff and as the national security experts on the NEC staff. By all accounts the two staffs worked smoothly together at all levels. The utility of the new institution was confirmed when Clinton's Republican successor, George W. Bush, continued the NEC system as he inherited it—returning the compliment paid to his father's NSC arrangements.

CONTENTIOUS POLICY PROBLEMS soon arose, however, which were not all amenable to smooth staff relations. They posed serious philosophical dilemmas to this Democratic administration, and many of them arose out of contradictions among the president's 1992 campaign promises. One difficult issue was relations with China.

Clinton had been particularly harsh in his campaign criticism of George H. W. Bush's policy toward China. The Tiananmen massacre of June 1989 was still a fresh memory, as was Bush's effort to maintain political relations with China on an even keel after those events. "The administration continues to coddle China," Clinton proclaimed in a December 1991 speech, "despite its continuing crackdown on democratic reforms, its brutal subjugation of Tibet, its irresponsible exports of nuclear and missiles technology, its support of the homicidal Khmer Rouge in Cambodia and its abusive trade practices." Sandy Berger later announced Clinton's view that "[t]his is going to be an arm's-length relationship at best between Washington and Beijing." But China's phenomenal economic boom was already a palpable reality, and the prospects for expansion of U.S.-China trade were powerfully attractive to many in this country—in both parties, and in Congress and the administration—interested in "the economy, stupid."

The immediate issue facing President Clinton was the annual renewal of nondiscriminatory trade status for Chinese goods (then called Most Favored Nation status, or MFN; now called Normal Trade Relations). A bitter battle immediately broke out between the champions of human rights (in the State Department, Congress, and the activist community) and the champions of economics (Commerce, the U.S. Trade Representative, and the business community). The State Department itself was divided between the human rights and East Asia bureaus, on the one hand, and bureaus dealing with economics and nonproliferation, which were interested in doing business with the Chinese.

At first, Clinton sided with the foreign policy side of the house, which in this case meant those who wanted to link the continuation of MFN to human rights. His executive order of May 1993 renewed MFN for China for one year but conditioned it on Chinese improvements in the status of human rights. The Chinese reacted badly to this overt pressure. When Secretary of State Christopher set off on a visit to China in March 1994, the Chinese defiantly launched another crackdown against dissidents; in Beijing, Christopher was sternly lectured by Premier Li Peng that China's internal practices were none of our business, and a meeting with President Jiang Zemin was abruptly canceled. "Rough, somber, sometimes bordering on the insolent" was how Christopher described Chinese behavior in his trip report to Clinton. After these humiliations, U.S.-Chinese relations only deteriorated further. As China policy became the subject of an intense domestic political debate, the White House stepped in to take charge of the policy. The NEC staff (which had not been significantly involved in the original decision) now teamed up with the NSC staff to steer the president toward a change of direction. While Clinton was able to point to a few improvements in Chinese human rights practices over the course of the year, he essentially abandoned the linkage in his May 1994 executive order renewing MFN.

Another kind of tension within the administration came over relations with Japan. During the Cold War, Japan's importance as a treaty ally and linchpin of U.S. security policy in Asia provided an incentive to both sides to mute the tensions over the large trade imbalance and Japanese barriers to imports from the United States. Those days were over. Clinton chose as U.S. trade negotiator Mickey Kantor, a Los Angeles lawyer who had been chairman of the 1992 campaign. Kantor told the Senate in March 1993:

> Past Administrations have often neglected U.S. economic and trading interests because of foreign policy and defense concerns. The days when we could afford to do so are long past. In the post–Cold War world, our national security depends on our economic strength. . . . When all is said and done, opening foreign markets is our main objective.

As Jeffrey Garten, under secretary of commerce, put it a few years later: "Commercial diplomacy must become more central to overall foreign policy, more expansive, and more aggressive."

"Aggressive" was the appropriate word for the way the new administration approached its first trade negotiations with Japan, aiming at setting strict numerical targets for a boost in U.S. exports to Japan. Clinton visited Japan in July 1993 and claimed victory when the Japanese accepted, not numerical targets, but the principle of "objective criteria" for improvements in the trade balance. Under these pressures—and partly because of the early signs of the great Japanese economic slowdown that was coming—the Japanese government of Kiichi Miyazawa fell. His successor, Morihiro Hosokawa, refused to make significant concessions when he met with Clinton in February 1994. Administration economists began planning retaliatory sanctions, and then Hosokawa's government fell in April. The State Department—through leaks to the press—began a counteroffensive within the U.S. government, emphasizing the damage being done to the U.S.-Japan alliance and to the U.S. security position in Asia. Again, the NEC staff joined with the NSC staff to play a moderating role. A trade deal was struck with Japan by July 1995, heading off U.S. sanctions, and it was Washington that had backed away from confrontation. Said one senior official to *The New York Times*: "We all looked over the precipice and discovered we couldn't see the bottom. The sanctions were a big risk. So we took what we had in hand." By the time of a Clinton visit to Tokyo in early 1996, he was expressing a newly acquired appreciation of the importance of the security alliance.

On both China and Japan, domestic political pressures pulled Clinton in different directions until ultimately the international reality imposed itself. MFN was not going to be the weapon that would transform China's Communist system; with Japan, security trumped economics in the end as it usually does. On other issues, the NEC/NSC team managed to produce more effective results with less public embarrassment. The administration won congressional assent to the North American Free Trade Agreement in the fall of 1993, and the NEC Principals devised much of the strategy. The joint NEC/NSC staff ably performed the role of "sherpas" for the annual G-7 Economic Summits, a role that had been traditionally fought over between State and NSC.

A year later, at the end of 1994, Mexico was on the verge of financial crisis and Robert Rubin took the lead in U.S. policy, putting together a $40 billion U.S. and international financial package to restore confidence in the Mexican market and stave off a collapse. But it was Rubin—not the NEC as such—that played the lead role in the U.S.

government. Rubin had become treasury secretary, and just as when Henry Kissinger became secretary of state in 1973 the center of gravity of policy-making moved with him. Rubin's tenure at the NEC had gained him wide respect, and his performance at Treasury only added to it. The NEC remained a valuable coordinating mechanism, but power always gravitates to those in whom others (especially the president) repose the most confidence. The model of a strong and loyal cabinet officer proved itself once again. A testimony to Rubin's personal stature in the administration is that he asked to be able to continue to attend White House senior staff meetings, and was invited to do so—a faint echo, perhaps, of Kissinger's two-year retention of his NSC hat after moving to State. But it was also not an accident that the biggest international star to emerge from the Clinton administration was from the economic team, not the national security team.

Russia Policy

One of the most significant events taking place in the world in that decade was the evolution of post-Soviet Russia. It was also a subject that needed, and received, presidential attention. Clinton had eighteen meetings with Boris Yeltsin and three meetings with his successor, Vladimir Putin, and made five trips to Russia, during his term of office, in the crucial formative period of the new Russian state and its policies. The formulation and execution of U.S. policy also benefited from a clear chain of command: The man in charge was Strobe Talbott, one of Bill Clinton's oldest friends and closest foreign policy confidants. For the first year, Talbott had a complicated title as "ambassador at large and special adviser to the secretary of state on the new independent states of the former Soviet Union"; thereafter he was deputy secretary of state. As Clinton has commented: "I don't think five people could repeat Strobe's [original] title, but everybody knew what he did: he was our 'go to' man on Russia." He was in effect the U.S. secretary of state for Russia policy.

The trajectory of Russia's evolution, and of U.S.-Russia relations, was not a success story in this period. The early hopes for Russian democracy and economic reform were not fulfilled. Yeltsin's clumsy rule by decree, violent clashes with the parliament, and later alliance with the oligarchs, gave way in 2000 to the unmistakably authoritarian Putin. The early years of Russia's foreign policy were years of an extraordinary collaboration with the United States under Yeltsin's reformist and pro-Western foreign minister Andrei Kozyrev. But by the beginning of 1996, the firing of Kozyrev and his replacement by Yevgeni Primakov symbolized the nationalist turn in Russian policy. Primakov, a shrewd and elusive veteran of the Soviet era, embodied what could be called a "Gaullist" foreign policy—a reassertion of Russia's pride and independence, especially independence from the United States, and its alignment with others (China, France) whose priority was to promote "multipolarity" in the world as an obstacle to American dominance. By the end of Clinton's term, the hopes for natural consensus in the Security Council had faded away, demonstrated particularly in the Balkan crises.

It would be unfair to lay the blame for this at Clinton's door. In the early 1990s there were debates about the alleged mistake of "personalizing" U.S. policy—that is, of investing too much in a Kremlin leader who was thought congenial to U.S. interests. International relations over the long term depend on more durable factors than personalities. Bush 41 and his team, as we have seen, came into office accusing Reagan of investing too much in Gorbachev; Bush, in turn, was accused of sticking too long with Gorbachev; and Republicans were to accuse Clinton of investing too much in Yeltsin. In a tumultuous period of Russia's evolution, however, it was hard to avoid perceiving a significant American stake in the outcome of Russia's internal struggles; Yeltsin was battling against an unappealing coalition of Communists and ultranationalists. And the formative period of the new Russian state's posture in the world was bound to be affected to some degree by what kind of international environment it was that the Russians, in turn, perceived. Even Richard Nixon, the hardheaded geopolitician, was giving private advice to Clinton that the United States had to throw its weight behind Yeltsin. "He may be a drunk," Nixon told Talbott, "but he's also the best we're likely to get in that screwed up country over there." Nixon had given the same advice to Bush.

The Clinton administration declared that its policy was a "strategic alliance with Russian reform." It devoted considerable effort with Congress and the allies to come up with significant economic assistance—on the order of $2.5 billion in U.S. aid as part of a total of $28.4 billion in international assistance. It set up a bilateral commission led by Vice President Gore and Russian prime minister Viktor Chernomyrdin to foster other cooperation. In 1994, Russia was admitted formally to the

G-7 group of industrial democracies, the annual economic summits begun in the Ford administration—no longer as a guest but as a full member of what thereafter became known as the G-8. Russia was also given formal status as a partner of NATO, through a NATO-Russia Council. The United States and its allies sought in other ways to acknowledge Russia as an equal, and to make clear their political backing of Yeltsin and the reformists.

The efforts made were considerable, but the problem was something else: The conciliatory steps were consciously intended to make it easier for Russia to acquiesce in what seemed to be the unavoidable continuing consequences of the breakup of the Communist empire. These consequences included Central and Eastern Europe's eager alignment with the West (through both the European Union and NATO); crises in the former Yugoslavia in which the West intervened to halt the Serb brutalization of Muslim populations; Western protest at Russia's military suppression of rebellion in Chechnya; and the strict conditions imposed by the International Monetary Fund in return for international aid. Other issues accumulated on which Russia and the West had different perspectives—especially our frustration with Russian nuclear cooperation with Iran, and the growing U.S. interest in deploying defenses against rogue state ballistic missiles.

To the Russians, this looked like a combination of mounting pressure, condescension, and taking advantage of Russian weakness. An impartial analyst, looking over this long list of contentious issues, might well conclude that not all were truly vital to the West and on some of them we might have cut the Russians some slack. (Unfortunately, different analysts would have different opinions about which ones to drop.) Overall, however, we were dealing with two probably inevitable historical phenomena—first, the cleanup of the unfinished business of the collapse of empire, and then, Russia's recovery (political, economic, and psychological) and quest to regain as much as possible of its lost position. As William Hyland and others have noted, the initial high hopes for both Russian democracy and "strategic partnership" were unrealistic.

In terms of process, nonetheless, Talbott's memoir is a chronicle of active engagement in Russia policy by a president conventionally perceived as disengaged from foreign policy. Talbott had bureaucratic clout, derived from his position as Clinton's intimate friend and adviser. Whatever his formal title and rank, he was credible as the agent of an engaged president. With a small staff, he chaired the relevant inter-agency committee and ran Russia policy in State. He kept in regular and close contact with Sandy Berger, when he was not communing directly with the president. All this gave Talbott a strong hand in relations with other departments. At Treasury, he had an ally in Lawrence Summers, who as under secretary and then deputy secretary collaborated with him in putting together the U.S. and international packages of economic assistance.

The Pentagon was at first opposed to bringing the Central and East Europeans into NATO. The U.S. military was wary of expanding the formal defense commitments of the United States; it was unenthusiastic about taking on new allies whose military capabilities were thought to require vast U.S. effort and resources to bring up to NATO standards. But consultation with the Pentagon produced a creative compromise—the so-called Partnership for Peace (PfP)—put forward by General John Shalikashvili, a NATO program of defense cooperation with the new democracies. PfP was an intermediate status, a way station on the path to full NATO membership though without any definite commitment to go further. It served a number of the administration's purposes: It was the beginning of necessary defense cooperation with the Central and East Europeans. But it also enabled Clinton to fend off Republican pressure for immediate NATO enlargement—to stretch out the process in the hope of easing Russian pain.

Military Interventions

The shadow of Russian opposition lay over the Clinton administration's most significant military undertakings, in the crises in Bosnia and Kosovo. But the Russia factor only added to the inhibitions that came from other sources—especially from the series of stumbles in Clinton's first year. Clinton and his team were clearly not comfortable with military intervention. They had philosophical qualms, and the style of decision making did not easily lend itself to the sustained rigor required for such endeavors.

Bosnia came up fast on the agenda. Clinton had harshly criticized George H. W. Bush in the 1992 campaign for insufficient activism in opposing Serb predations against Muslim and Croat minorities in Bosnia. One of the new administration's first acts was to reject a compromise proposed by the international mediating team of Cyrus Vance and David Owen, which was thought to be not tough enough on the Serbs. When it came to formulating its own policy, however, the Clinton team was divided. A stronger option, pushed by the more activist members of the administration, was called "lift and strike"—it proposed lifting the U.N. arms embargo against Bosnia so that the Bosnians could arm themselves against the Serbs (who were getting arms from neighboring Serbia), and it posed the threat of U.S. or NATO air strikes if Serb aggression did not stop. Secretary of State Christopher was dispatched at the beginning of May 1993 to visit Europe and sound out the allies. The fact that Christopher was personally opposed to the "lift and strike" idea, and was not a very forceful personality to start with, doomed the exercise. The American ambassador in London watched as Christopher made the pitch to British leaders with "all the verve of a solicitor going over a conveyance deed."

A coalition of the unwilling quickly formed—a secretary of state who had no stomach for it; a secretary of defense (Aspin) who was also against it; the U.S. military (led by Colin Powell), who invoked the Weinberger principle that limited military steps were unlikely to be decisive; Europeans who had sent peacekeepers to Bosnia but didn't want actually to fight anyone; and the more cynical French, who were pro-Serb. Most important of all was the president's own hesitation, which was visible to all. After a disconcerting conversation with Clinton at the White House, Aspin sent word to Christopher while Christopher was in Europe: "[The president] is going south on this policy. His heart isn't in it." Two more years would go by before the administration would summon the will, and the leverage, to force a satisfactory outcome.

In the summer of 1993 came a brief clash with Saddam Hussein. Kuwaiti intelligence broke up an Iraqi plot to kill former President Bush on a visit to Kuwait in April. In retaliation, Clinton in June ordered a strike by twenty Tomahawk cruise missiles against Iraqi intelligence headquarters in Baghdad, carefully staged in the middle of the night to minimize Iraqi casualties. The action was widely criticized as ineffectual. In his memoirs, Clinton attributes the modest targeting plan to Colin Powell and suggests he would have been willing to do more. Yet at the time, Clinton's discomfort at the use of military force was such that he was reported to be "tense and wobbly" after ordering it and kept asking his aides if they were sure it was the right thing to do.

In October came the debacle in Mogadishu, Somalia, immortalized in the book and film *Black Hawk Down*. As Ronald Reagan experienced in Lebanon, U.S. forces entered Somalia on a benign peacekeeping mission, only to feel the political ground shift under their feet. Somalia was in the midst of a civil war. President Bush 41, at the very end of his term, under political pressure, had sent 25,000 U.S. troops to Somalia with the narrowly defined mission of providing security for humanitarian relief supplies. The Clinton team reduced the U.S. contingent to about 4,000 troops and expanded the mission. U.N. ambassador Albright was the most fervent advocate of a new objective—tipping the balance in the Somali civil war by defeating the warlord Mohammed Aidid. As the peacekeeping forces found themselves deeply embroiled, Aspin and Powell wanted out. They repeatedly sought guidance from the White House but received none.

When the disaster happened—two helicopters downed, eighteen American troops killed, seventy-four wounded, and the corpse of one American dragged through the street by Aidid's cheering mobs broadcast over international television—Clinton was shocked. At his hotel on a visit to San Francisco, he railed at his aides in conference calls to Washington: "How could this happen?" He had never been given a "realistic assessment" of "what we were up against." "No one told me about the downside." "We've been jerked around for months" by the United Nations, which had taken over command of the peacekeeping operation. Later he ruminated to others about firing his advisers.

Then came Haiti. This problem, too, he had inherited from Bush. Elected President Jean-Bertrand Aristide, an ex-priest who had been defrocked by the Catholic Church for his leftist "liberation theology," was overthrown by a military coup in 1991 by Lieutenant General Raoul Cédras. The Bush administration committed the United States to restore Aristide to power, but its failure to do so was another of Clinton's campaign accusations in 1992; political pressures then grew on Clinton to deliver on the promise. In July 1993, U.S. mediation produced an agreement for a peaceful turnover.

In October, a small contingent of more than two hundred lightly armed military trainers and engineers, American and Canadian, was scheduled to go to Haiti for six months for a training mission. A debate took place in the administration about whether they should go in, with Les Aspin arguing strongly that—given Cédras's unreliability—they should not. After an interagency discussion (in which the president did not participate) Aspin was overruled; Lake and Berger thought it was important to look strong. The trainers were aboard the USS *Harlan*

County off Port-au-Prince when an unruly crowd of Haitians, some of them armed with handguns, appeared on the dock shouting anti-American slogans including the menacing taunt: "Somalia! Somalia!" Another debate broke out in the administration, but no one had the stomach for a fight. The *Harlan County* pulled away, as the Haitian mob cheered. Again, Clinton's reaction was anger at his staff.

The administration would recoup in Haiti a year later. Despite the Defense Department's opposition to intervention, Clinton ordered a military plan drawn up and—having learned a lesson from Somalia—he personally reviewed the plan at the Pentagon. In September 1994, the imminence of a U.S. invasion provided the leverage for a diplomacy that restored Aristide to power without bloodshed.

The stumbles of the first year left their residue, however, in the form of both increased inhibitions and diminished credibility. When Rwanda was torn apart by genocidal warfare in 1994, the administration was gun-shy. After the al-Qaida attacks on American embassies in Kenya and Tanzania in August 1998, the White House asked the Defense Department to propose options for special operations to kill or capture Osama bin Laden in Afghanistan. A similar request was made in 2000 after the al-Qaida attack on the USS *Cole* in Yemen. In neither case did the Pentagon come up with a serious plan. Military planners argued that the intelligence was insufficient and large numbers of U.S. personnel would be needed. At the White House it was suspected that the military was not inclined to undertake risky operations on behalf of a president it did not trust.

Bosnia and Kosovo

American involvement in Bosnia and Kosovo in Bill Clinton's second term is the story of a recovery of lost ground—of a president gradually leading his government to overcome its inhibitions and internal divisions and marshal the leverage to give effect to its diplomatic aspirations. While Clinton had campaigned in 1992 against Bush's alleged passivity in Bosnia, he came into office with no interest in military intervention there—a conviction only reinforced by the stumbles of 1993. "They keep trying to force me to get America into a war," he complained about the incessant television coverage of Bosnia atrocities. As the Bosnia crisis festered for the next two years, different parts of the government leaked their versions of events to the media to deflect blame or influence the president; memos by Madeleine Albright leaked from New York, for example, with the apparent purpose of building support for her advocacy of air strikes against the Serbs. The Europeans rejected stronger options unless the United States sent troops alongside theirs— which Clinton knew that Congress would oppose. Meanwhile at Defense, the military remained strongly allergic to U.S. intervention; Secretary of Defense Perry was willing to support use of NATO air power for clearly defined purposes, but drew the line at ground troops. Perry reportedly did not consider Bosnia important enough to do battle over within the Pentagon or with the allies. In these circumstances, Clinton was content to leave Bosnia to the Europeans, and to the Principals or Deputies committees, and concentrate on other issues.

When a Bosnian Serb military offensive became the focus of international attention and protest, however, Bosnia grew into a major political problem. By 1995, Clinton was politically on the defensive. Jacques Chirac, newly elected president of France, reversed France's pro-Serb policy and began calling for allied action. In June, Clinton responded to allied pleas with the major step of promising that U.S. ground troops would indeed be available in certain conditions—if U.N. forces needed help in withdrawing, if a U.N. unit required emergency extrication, or to help police a peace agreement. But in July, Serb militiamen retook the town of Srebrenica, humiliating a Dutch peacekeeping battalion; they gathered some eight thousand Muslim men and boys in a soccer stadium and summarily executed them. Adding to the anguish in Washington was Chirac's public comment around this time that France was alone in wanting real action and that "the position of leader of the free world is vacant."

Clinton exploded. One July evening around 7:00 p.m., while he poked away at golf balls in an area near the Oval Office known as the Eisenhower Putting Green, members of his press staff and NSC staff came to talk to him about Bosnia. "This can't continue," he fumed. "I'm getting creamed!" The session went on for more than three-quarters of an hour: "This has got to stop. We've got to find some kind of policy and move ahead. Why aren't my people doing more for me?"

This presidential reengagement was an opening for Anthony Lake, who had been quietly working with his NSC staff to prepare a new, more activist strategy. The president now supported Lake. At an Oval Office meeting a few days later, Vice President Gore spoke passionately about halting the genocide. The president agreed: "The United States can't be a punching bag in the world anymore." At the Pentagon, as well, Perry and Shalikashvili both understood that Srebrenica had changed things, and they could see the president's new commitment. Perry, Shalikashvili, and Warren Christopher made an important visit to London to a NATO conference later in July and—after more vigorous presentations than Christopher's two years earlier—won a NATO consensus on a more forceful use of air power. The allies recognized that NATO's credibility was now on the line, just as Clinton had reached a similar conclusion about his own.

Richard Holbrooke was put in charge of a new diplomatic effort. Holbrooke, a dynamic if volatile star in the Democratic foreign policy firmament, had been ambassador to Germany in the first term but was eager to play in the Washington game; he was named assistant secretary of state for European affairs. He understood better than some of his colleagues that diplomacy had no chance without leverage. In August, the army of neighboring Croatia retook control of the Krajina, a region of Croatia that local Serbs had proclaimed their own territory. The prospect of a Croatian offensive had prompted nail-biting in Washington: Warren Christopher and the Pentagon feared anything that could widen the war, while Albright, Holbrooke, and others in State saw advantage in the opening of a second front against the Serbs and inflicting a defeat on them. The Croatians repeatedly asked the U.S. government whether Washington would approve, but Washington was deadlocked. American diplomats sympathetic to Croatia managed, with a wink and a nod, to convey that while there was no green light from Washington, there was no red light either. One official called it an "amber light tinted green." Clinton later said that he, too, was "rooting for the Croatians," but this does not seem to have been communicated as a presidential decision.

The Defense Department continued to betray its nervousness, however, in ways occasionally disconcerting to the diplomats. Holbrooke recounts a Principals meeting on September 11 at which Perry unexpectedly proposed a "bombing pause." Christopher, Lake, Albright, and Holbrooke all correctly opposed this, recalling the fecklessness of such moves during the Vietnam War and knowing that it would weaken U.S. diplomatic leverage. Then Admiral William Owens, vice chairman of the Joint Chiefs, spoke up and suggested that NATO was running out of bombing targets to attack and the United States would therefore either have to return to the NATO Council and the U.N. Security Council for a broader set of targets (a nonstarter in both cases) or else wind down the bombing campaign in two or three days. Holbrooke (dubious as he was about what Owens claimed) reacted by speeding up the negotiations; he managed in three days to win Bosnian Serb agreement to halt the siege of Sarajevo, which allowed us to halt the bombing as a matter of policy.

The reversal of French policy under Chirac, the Croatian offensive in the Krajina, and the more forceful posture in Washington provided for Holbrooke the leverage for a successful diplomacy. The United States convened a peace conference in November at Wright-Patterson Air Force Base in Dayton, Ohio. Holbrooke conducted the negotiation without micromanagement from Washington. Warren Christopher attended many of the sessions, and reported to the president, but Holbrooke had no direct contact with Clinton after Dayton started. By the end of November 1995, the presidents of Bosnia, Serbia, and Croatia agreed on a complex arrangement for a federal Bosnia, enforced by a NATO-led peacekeeping force including U.S. troops. While Defense had relented on the U.S. troop contribution, it successfully blocked a significant U.S. role in training and equipping the Bosnian Muslims, which Holbrooke (and the president) had seen as an important contribution to the long-term balance of forces.

THREE YEARS LATER, however, Serbian dictator Slobodan Milosevic's belligerence had found another outlet—this time, a brutal crackdown in Kosovo, an autonomous province of Serbia populated by ethnic Albanian Muslims. Muslim refugees poured into neighboring Albania and Macedonia, threatening to destabilize the region. By the summer of 1998, NATO was planning military options to block the Serbian government's continuing military offensive. After diplomatic efforts failed, Clinton in the spring of 1999 agreed to U.S. and allied air strikes. While his national security team told him optimistically that Milosevic would fold in seventy-two hours, the NATO bombing campaign in fact went on for seventy-eight days before Milosevic desisted.

The success in Kosovo had to survive its own share of bureaucratic problems. As the crisis built in 1998, Madeleine Albright—now secretary of state—was again the hawk. Convinced that negotiations with Milosevic would fail, she repeatedly urged stronger action, including the threat of NATO air strikes. But Berger blocked her phone calls to the president and the Principals deadlocked. "We're just gerbils running on a wheel," she complained to colleagues. The new team at Defense, Secretary William Cohen and General Hugh Shelton, were reluctant warriors, dubious that air strikes would work.

The pivotal figure this time was General Wesley Clark. Dual-hatted as the U.S. commander in Europe and as supreme allied commander in NATO, he was the field commander in charge of the war. A former Rhodes Scholar from Arkansas like Bill Clinton, Clark had been the Joint Staff representative on Holbrooke's negotiating team at Dayton and had strong convictions about the menace of Milosevic. In this activism he was the right man to run the war; unfortunately he found himself seriously out of step with his civilian and military superiors in the Department of Defense. Shalikashvili had been effective at bridging the bureaucratic gaps, working well with State and more supple in his relations with the White House. Shelton, a grayer figure, simply reinforced Cohen's resistance to intervention. Clark was in constant friction with Cohen; once the president ordered the bombing Clark developed his own regular contact with Sandy Berger in the White House. This only increased Cohen's resentment.

As the air campaign dragged on without result, Clark had three frustrations. One was the need for political consensus within NATO with respect to selecting targets. To hasten Serbian capitulation, Clark wanted to attack "strategic" targets, including infrastructure and command-and-control facilities in Serbia whose destruction would gain leverage over Milosevic to break his will; our European allies' sensibility would accept only "tactical" targets more directly related to the Serbian army's actions in Kosovo. Clark's second frustration was what he saw as the need to prepare for a possible ground war; this would be a fallback option if the bombing proved insufficient, and public knowledge of its preparation would add significantly to the credibility and persuasive force of the whole enterprise. He received U.S. and NATO authorization to begin planning. But Clinton feared a ground war involving U.S. troops, knowing there was no support for it in the Republican Congress. Secretary Cohen consistently opposed any serious consideration of it, determined that the air campaign succeed. Public hints of planning for a ground war probably, in the end, contributed significantly to Milosevic's cave-in, but Clinton in his memoir is adamant that he was opposed to a ground war all along.

Clark's third frustration was the way he was being treated by Washington throughout the military campaign he was leading in Washington's behalf. As we have seen, the Goldwater-Nichols defense reform of 1986 had elevated the status of the chairman of the Joint Chiefs as military adviser to the president, established an operational chain of command from the president to the secretary of defense directly to the field commander, and reduced the status of the chiefs as a collective body. This should have made Clark a key figure in the policy deliberations in Washington—not only because he was U.S. commander in the theater of war but because he was also managing the complex political task of holding a NATO coalition together. Bush 41 included General Norman Schwarzkopf in his Gulf War deliberations; though Powell overshadowed him and Schwarzkopf spent much of his time in Riyadh, he had many opportunities to communicate with the president. Bush 43, as we shall see in the next chapter, kept in continuous contact with his field commanders in Afghanistan and Iraq during both planning and operations.

But in Kosovo, the chain of command almost became unlinked. Cohen and Shelton, disliking Clark's activism, seemed determined to reduce his public visibility and his influence over presidential decisions. Clark considered that he was leading a mission that the president had ordered. When he sought guidance from Cohen as to the secretary's wishes on Balkan policy, Cohen was often uncommunicative. Yet Cohen reprimanded Clark when his news conferences seemed too exuberant for Cohen's taste. Cohen tried to exclude Clark from attending a NATO summit meeting in Washington in April (Clark attended anyway, in his capacity as allied commander); he succeeded in blocking Clark's attendance at a meeting the president held with the Joint Chiefs at the White House in early June. Clark did not believe his Pentagon superiors were conveying his views accurately to the president in his absence. Cohen seemed to use the Joint Chiefs as a buffer against Clark, frequently invoking objections that individual service chiefs put forward against requests that Clark submitted for equipment or other support. Clark wondered if this was consistent with the intent of the Goldwater-Nichols reform.

The conflicting pressures on Clark reflected the conflicting pressures on the administration. Albright and Berger, the activists, had suffered through the vacillations and humiliations of the early years, including in the Balkans, and did not want to go through the same again. In fairness to Cohen, his reluctance stemmed not only from the reluctance of his military but from his knowledge of his former colleagues in Congress; that knowledge was, after all, one reason why he had been chosen secretary of defense. "I voted against your Bosnia policy," he once coldly reminded the president. Cohen vividly remembered the pummeling that Les Aspin had received over Somalia, and believed that that episode had done lasting damage to Clinton's credibility as commander in chief. He knew from his own conversations the aversion on the Hill to anything smacking of U.S. ground intervention in Kosovo. And the adamancy with which Clinton in his memoirs emphasizes his own opposition to the same is testimony to the objective constraints that Clark was operating under, even if he chafed at those constraints.

It was fortunate in the Kosovo case that—contrary to many experts' predictions—American air power alone proved sufficient to produce a successful result. Clinton showed political courage in persevering in the face of growing criticism as the weeks passed. But there were political casualties. One was Wesley Clark's military career. The Pentagon forced his early retirement from his command and from his career, on complicated legal grounds relating to the alleged need to put his successor on the job earlier than usual. The president, who appreciated the job that Clark had done, approved what he was told was a normal rotation; he seems not to have known, until after the fact, that he had forced Clark's early retirement.

There was also a paradoxical effect on alliance relations. Given the collective success that the Kosovo outcome represented, it should have heralded a positive era in U.S.-European relations. But in the 1990s the European allies were building their own institutions in the European Union, and the huge imbalance between American and European military capability—displayed dramatically in the Balkan crises—was painful for them to watch. Thus, Kosovo only spurred the construction of new EU political and military structures, to create a counterweight to what the French were calling the American "hyperpower." Europeans were thus pleased that the key negotiator in the Kosovo settlement was Finnish president Martti Ahtisaari—acting on behalf of the EU—and not Richard Holbrooke.

As discussed earlier, U.S.-Russian relations also suffered. While Russia was given a role in partnership with NATO in the Kosovo peacekeeping force, Russia looked on with great pain as NATO demonstrated its military superiority against Slavic cousin Serbs—and as NATO did so without any kind of endorsement by the U.N. Security Council (since Russia had blocked any such endorsement). Russia was at the beginning of a phase that was soon to become familiar—lining up, reflexively, against assertions of American power.

The Jimmy Carter Problem

A peculiar feature of Bill Clinton's foreign policy was its susceptibility on two occasions to the unsolicited diplomatic intervention of former President Jimmy Carter. One of Carter's principal activities after leaving office in 1977 was his continuing effort to engage in international diplomacy as a freelance elder statesman and peacemaker. In 1994 he offered his services to the Clinton administration to break impasses with respect to both North Korea and Haiti. That the administration assented to this intervention was another symptom of a lack of rigor, a lack of conviction with respect to its own policies, its own capability, and its own personnel. In 1995, the administration more successfully fended off an attempt by Carter to inject himself into the Bosnia negotiation.

The personal relationship between Carter and Clinton was never warm. On the face of it, they had much in common. Two Southern governors, the only Democrats to break the Republicans' near monopoly on the White House during the entire forty-year span of this book, they both won election by positioning themselves successfully on the moderate wing of their party, closer to the center of the national debate. Most of Clinton's senior national security team had served in midlevel positions under Carter. Nonetheless, the Clinton team saw Carter's legacy as a reputation for incompetence with which they did not wish to be associated. During the 1992–1993 transition, Carter flooded the president-elect with phone calls offering his services and advice. Clinton refused to take the calls, passing them instead to Warren Christopher; Christopher, in turn, tried to pass them on to one of *his* aides. Carter was reportedly deeply wounded by how the Clinton people were treating him.

In mid-1994 the Clinton administration was engaged in a diplomatic effort to mobilize international pressure on North Korea to head off its pursuit of nuclear weapons. Pyongyang was blocking inspections by the International Atomic Energy Agency (a U.N. body), and the administration was attempting to forge a consensus in the U.N. Security Council for economic sanctions. North Korea was protesting that U.N. sanctions would be a hostile act. A sense of crisis was building; the administration was even sounding the familiar refrain that military options were not ruled out. Jimmy Carter panicked at all this. On June 1, he phoned Clinton and said he wanted to go to Pyongyang to resolve the crisis.

Clinton was extremely annoyed at Carter's intervention (and vented his anger to, among others, former President Gerald Ford). After consulting with his advisers, he authorized Carter to go—but stressed that the United States would not agree to suspend the sanctions effort unless North Korea froze its nuclear program, let the inspectors complete their work, and committed to new talks with the United States. Off Carter went to Pyongyang, where he publicly declared his opposition to sanctions and praised the regime of Kim Il-sung. He then appeared live on CNN and announced that Kim had agreed to allow the inspectors to continue, and in return for this "very positive step" the administration should back off from sanctions and agree to talks. This was not what Clinton had insisted on, but he was stuck. The effort to organize sanctions in the U.N. Security Council collapsed. By October, the talks had produced the so-called U.S.-North Korea Agreed Framework, which the Clinton administration believed halted North Korea's nuclear weapons development. Republican critics considered it an unreliable agreement, whose weaknesses were produced in part by Jimmy Carter's aborting of the international pressures that were mobilizing. In any case, Clinton came around to forgive Carter his interference.

In September 1994, Carter propelled himself into the Haiti crisis. As noted earlier, the administration was putting severe pressure, including the threat of military action, to force General Cédras's departure and President Aristide's restoration. On September 15, Carter telephoned Colin Powell (retired a year from his position of JCS chairman) and asked if Powell would join Carter and former Senator Sam Nunn (Georgia Democrat) on a peace mission to stave off an invasion. Powell said he would join if President Clinton wanted this mission to take place. That afternoon, Powell received a phone call from Clinton, who complained of Carter as a "wild card" and worried that "the next thing you know, I'm expected to call off the invasion because he's negotiating a deal." But Clinton told Powell he thought the North Korea adventure "didn't turn out too badly," and concluded that the Haiti mission could be helpful if it confronted Cédras with the unambiguous necessity to back down.

Clinton was determined that U.S. forces would go ashore; the only question was whether it would be a forced entry or a peacekeeping mission in the context of a peaceful handover of power. While in Haiti, Carter repeatedly phoned Clinton to ask for delays in the scheduled invasion, which he "desperately wanted to avoid." Cédras finally relented, less than an hour before U.S. paratroopers were scheduled to begin arriving. The 15,000-member multinational force went into Haiti without violence.

The Haiti mission accomplished what the administration sought; in the North Korea case it is arguable either way. But in both cases it does not speak well of the administration's diplomatic team that an unwanted outsider could so easily insert himself. When a White House press release was being drafted to announce the Carter-Nunn-Powell mission, the president approved a draft that read: "With President Clinton's approval, Jimmy Carter . . ." Press secretary George Stephanopoulos intercepted it, pointing out to Clinton that "presidents don't *approve* missions like this, they *order* them." The draft was changed and the dignity of the Clinton presidency preserved.

As in other areas, Clinton learned from his mistakes. In September 1995, at a tense moment during the Bosnia crisis, Carter contacted the administration on behalf of the Bosnian Serb leadership to try to head off a resumption of the NATO bombing. Carter had a CNN camera crew standing by outside his office ready to announce a cease-fire agreement. The administration (in the person of Strobe Talbott) politely but firmly told him: No, thanks.

Assessment

William Hyland sums up Bill Clinton as "a transitional figure wedged between the end of the Cold War and the beginning of a new century." After his reelection in 1996, a poll was taken of a group of American historians supervised by Arthur Schlesinger, Jr. Schlesinger saw in Bill Clinton "a rare combination of talents and infirmities." On the one hand, he was a man of "penetrating intelligence," a skilled political leader with intellectual curiosity. On the other side of the ledger were his lack of self-discipline, his "erratic" judgment of people, and a resilience that some saw as opportunism. There is no doubt that Clinton gradually became more comfortable in foreign policy—witness his personal leadership of the Camp David Israeli-Palestinian negotiation in the fall of 2000.

It was a transitional period, moreover, that postponed a number of problems. With respect to Saddam Hussein's Iraq, the goals of American policy escalated during the Clinton presidency without a corresponding commitment to means. In October 1998 Clinton signed the Iraq Liberation Act, which made it U.S. policy to remove Saddam's regime, and on several occasions he forcefully articulated the danger that was thought to be posed by Iraq's weapons of mass destruction. Saddam's constant defiance of U.N. Security Council resolutions was met by occasional U.S. air strikes without decisive effect. By 1997, however, when the administration sought new sanctions from the U.N. Security Council, France had joined Russia in opposition. By the end of Clinton's term, the cumulative effect of Saddam's repeated challenges to the United Nations was the erosion of the Gulf War coalition against him; the lineup in the Security Council became: the United States and United Kingdom on one side, Russia, France, and China on the other. A new coalition—of those interested in restraining American power as an end in itself—was forming.

The principal lesson of Bill Clinton's presidency, for our purposes, is the importance of focus, sustained engagement, and willingness to spend political capital. Success in domestic policy has an episodic quality; usually one can select an issue on which to focus and make legislative proposals. Foreign policy crises usually impose themselves, and a successful policy in response to them requires sustained, coherent, and consistent policy-making that resolves internal differences and integrates the various elements of national power. Clinton clearly gained self-confidence in his second term, and the process also worked well when he delegated to a strong individual. This was true, for example, with respect to Robert Rubin in international economic policy, Strobe Talbott in Russia policy, Richard Holbrooke in Bosnia, and former Senator George Mitchell in Northern Ireland. These individuals had credible leverage as representing the president's will and they used it. Needless to say, the same principle applies to Clinton's own engagement at Camp David II. In other administrations, we have seen this bureaucratic focus residing in a strong secretary of state.

As in previous chapters, the conclusion is that when there is a sustained commitment by the president, either in person or by delegation to a strong and trusted subordinate, coherence is possible. Where there are policy or philosophical disagreements among the principals, they will not be reconciled without presidential engagement. Similarly, when a cabinet department is unresponsive to presidential wishes, only the president can impose discipline. No system—whether collegial or hierarchical, formal or informal—will work otherwise.

CHAPTER NINE

George W. Bush

O N AUGUST 23, 2001, after seven months in office, President George W. Bush paid a visit to an elementary school in his home-town of Crawford, Texas. A student asked him if it was "hard to make the decisions" as president. He replied:

> Not really. If you know what you believe, decisions come pretty easy. If you're one of those types of people that are always trying to figure out which way the wind is blowing, decision making can be difficult. But . . . I know who I am. I know what I believe in, and I know where I want to lead the country.

The controversies that engulfed him are still fresh at this writing, but it is not too soon to attempt a dispassionate analysis of his manner of leading his government. As he suggested to the students in Crawford, Bush liked to see himself as "the decider," in the Trumanesque image of a gutsy chief executive taking on tough decisions and not looking back. Indeed, the boldness of many of his policies and doctrinal pronounce-ments made him a consequential president, whether one liked him or hated him. Concepts such as preemption in the war against terrorism, or the promotion of democracy, are big ideas with a respectable pedi-gree and lasting importance whether one agrees with Bush's approach to them or not. Many of the controversies over his decisions, however, were also controversies over how these decisions were made.

The Washington Post once mischievously published a list of fourteen quotations from different sources, inside and outside the administra-tion, calling his policy-making process "dysfunctional." The accusers included champions of both the State and the Defense departments, the two main antagonists in the interagency struggles (who seemed to agree on at least this one thing). Like Ronald Reagan, George W. Bush presents the paradox of a leader capable of great decisiveness but who set up or tolerated a system that impeded his exercise of it. On the most momentous issues of his presidency, his own judgment was often better than that of some of his senior advisers. Yet the system floundered when it did not have his decisive intervention, and it sometimes fostered bitter bureaucratic resentments even when it did.

For a serious student of policy-making, however, the definition of "dysfunctional" has to be more than just having one's own policy preference overruled in a presidential decision. The careful reader will need to discount for that factor in many accounts that have appeared up to now. That one loses out in an interagency debate does not automatically mean the process is not working right. Those who compiled the multiple occurrences of the term "dysfunctional" usually failed to note that many of the critics quoted were making contradictory accusations: Some were criticizing a reputed "cabal" of Vice President Dick Cheney and Defense Secretary Donald Rumsfeld who were said to tip the scales of policy-making unfairly in their direction and whom national security adviser Condoleezza Rice failed to control. Others were referring to what they saw as insubordination and rebellion by the Department of State and Central Intelligence Agency against decisions the president made, which, likewise, the national security adviser was said to be unable to control. Others, more neutrally, were referring to bureaucratic stalemates that were allowed to fester.

In truth, the facts varied from issue to issue; the bureaucratic balance of forces fluctuated over time. The most important question to ask is: Where was the president during these various debates? Did he decide the matter, siding with one group of advisers over the other, as was his right? Or did he fail to decide, allowing deadlocks to persist? What was the nature of the problem or problems he faced in his cabinet subordinates and how did he cope with them?

Team Bush

White House speechwriter David Frum, who spent many hours observing Bush, painted a complex portrait of contradictory qualities. He described Bush as "relentlessly disciplined," a man able to inspire great loyalty, and bold in his ideas—yet also a man "sometimes glib, even dogmatic; often incurious and as a result ill informed; more conventional in his thinking than a leader probably should be." But Frum also listed Bush's virtues—decency, honesty, rectitude, courage, and tenacity.

Bush, like Reagan, was probably surprised by the intensity of divisions in his administration. He won his party's nomination in 2000 by positioning himself successfully in the party's center; he was seen as more conservative and "tougher" than his father, yet he benefited from the reflected glow of his father's moderate image, not to mention the political organization he inherited, and he espoused what he called a "compassionate conservatism." When he formed his government after the 2000 election, he seems to have intended a collegial policy-making process like his father's. He put together what was regarded as an impressive national security team of seasoned veterans.

Bush had absorbed some principles of management from his Harvard Business School education and from his experience as owner of the Texas Rangers baseball team. Published accounts of this business experience, and of what it taught him, present a rounded impression of an executive who aimed at decisiveness and collegiality, boldness and patience, loyalty and accountability. As with Reagan, again, there was a heavy emphasis on trust in subordinates and delegation to them, and a desire for consensus among them. When that consensus was not to be had, as we shall see, the system often broke down.

First, like most of his Republican predecessors, Bush 43 saw his job as focusing on the big picture and delegating the details. Just as Reagan and his colleagues saw this approach as a positive contrast with Jimmy Carter, so George W. Bush saw it as a needed change from Bill Clinton, who like Carter was criticized for immersion in details at the expense of vision. The president's job was to make the big decisions confidently, as Bush told the Crawford students.

Second, one of the lessons taught at Harvard Business School is that executives must often make decisions under conditions of uncertainty. There is never perfect information, yet managers must act before all the desired information is available. How to cope with this? Students are taught to analyze facts, make reasonable inferences, weigh probabilities, and assess as best they can the costs and benefits of acting or not acting. This is not only a business school principle; it is a stark necessity of presidential leadership. Henry Kissinger wrote many years ago of the dilemma of the statesman—that to shape events he must act before all the facts are clear; if he waits for perfect certainty the moment when events could be shaped will have passed. This puts a premium on a leader's vision, intuition, and courage. It is a dilemma inherent in the responsibility of any leader who wants to impose purpose on events and not become their prisoner.

Bush told Bob Woodward that he trusted his intuition: "I'm not a textbook player. I'm a gut player." Intuition, we all know, has its limits. Bush famously said after he met Vladimir Putin in June 2001 that he had gotten a "sense of his soul," discovering spiritual qualities that had not hitherto been widely observed in the ex-KGB operative. Conservative writer Richard Brookhiser, in another perceptive portrait of Bush, pointed out that the tendency of the president and his aides to exalt the virtues of instinct could "seem like a rationalization, a cover for his lack of more obvious qualifications, such as intellect conventionally measured." But Brookhiser also quoted White House aide Karl Rove's comparison of Bush to Eisenhower, on the ground that both men had a "wiliness about being underestimated."

Third, Bush startled Bob Woodward with a comment contrasting himself with his father: "[T]he vision thing matters. That's another lesson I learned." According to many accounts, Bush's model of leadership was not his father, but Ronald Reagan. No one can claim that Bush 43 shied away from ambitious actions and large ideas, whether in foreign policy or in domestic policy. Despite the controversy surrounding his election victory in 2000, Bush considered that he had a mandate to be a purposeful leader and to spend whatever political capital he had for his agenda.

Bush as baseball executive revealed another feature of his concept of leadership. As managing general partner of the Texas Rangers he was not the master of baseball strategy or financial details but by all accounts he acted skillfully and energetically as the leader of an executive team. "He very much believes that the chief executive's responsibility is to manage the other executives," a former associate said. He made strategic decisions, and did so easily; he hired good people and held them accountable; he had "an uncanny ability," according to another account, "to create consensus and contentment among prickly peers and subordinates." He organized the effort to fund and build a new ballpark. He had a gift for public relations that disarmed the skeptics with a "beguiling charm" and "vastly improved the brand." He sat in the stands with the fans, even during team slumps, absorbing their complaints and promoting the team.

This psychological dimension of leadership has its significance. During tense moments in the war to liberate Afghanistan in 2001, for example, Bush saw it as his duty to demonstrate resolve, both to the public and to his subordinates. In an important and revealing passage, he told Bob Woodward:

> [A] president has got to be the calcium in the backbone. If I weaken, the whole team weakens. If I'm doubtful, I can assure you there will be a lot of doubt. If my confidence level in our ability declines, it will send ripples throughout the whole organization.

Woodward tells the story of a moment in late October 2001 when the U.S. military effort in Afghanistan seemed to have bogged down and critics were clamoring that it was a "quagmire." National security adviser Condoleezza Rice informed Bush that there was hand-wringing among some in his government, which annoyed him much more than the criticism in the media. He summoned his senior people to an NSC meeting on October 26 and asked them stern questions: Is this the military plan we all agreed on? (Yes.) Does anyone have any new or different ideas to propose? (No.) Well, then, we need to be steady and see it through: "Resist the second-guessing. Be confident but patient. It's all going to work." His cabinet officers came away braced and encouraged. Two weeks later the war broke decisively in favor of the United States and its Afghan allies.

One man's courage can be another man's stubbornness, of course. Whether a display of presidential resolve is the one or the other may not be obvious right away, and some of these assessments may be better left to the historians. Bob Woodward entitled a later book on Bush *State of Denial*, which captures the writer's harsher judgment of Bush's refusal to shift course in Iraq. But Bush was on to something. Military experts know this resolve to be a principle of command.

Holding subordinates accountable is another basic management tenet. Bush came to the White House asserting that "a good executive is one that understands . . . how to hold people accountable for results." In Texas, he had shown he meant it. When the club president, manager, and general manager could not deliver a successful baseball team, Bush dismissed them. In the presidency of his father, when White House chief of staff John Sununu was judged to be an obstacle to the smooth running of the White House team, President Bush 41 assigned to his son the task of approaching Sununu to seek his resignation. As we shall see, Bush 43 found this principle of accountability harder to implement in his own administration.

The upshot of all this was that, whether or not he realized it, George W. Bush by his style of leadership was raising the stakes for his administration. For one thing, to pursue a bold agenda with a weak political mandate was to magnify political risks. But his concept of leadership as purposeful and resolute also put a premium on coherence of policy-making and discipline in execution. His reliance on a "team" made their collegiality and their performance all the more important.

Colin Powell at State

Colin Powell is one of the outstanding public figures of the last generation. I served under him on the NSC staff when he was the deputy national security adviser and then the national security adviser in the last two years of the Reagan administration. As an active duty lieutenant general, dependent on the U.S. Army for his career, he could have been pulled by conflicting institutional loyalties or suspected of the same, while occupying a White House position in which being an honest broker remains the model. Yet Powell carried it off with integrity and came away with universal respect, demonstrating a fine political skill in the best sense of the word. A few years later, as chairman of the Joint Chiefs under Bush 41, despite his professional unease about the Gulf War he carried out the president's orders loyally and was one of the architects of a brilliant military victory. Charismatic as well as capable, as a private citizen a few years later he passed over a serious opportunity for the 1996 Republican presidential nomination, and perhaps even for the presidency itself. Politically, he called himself a "Rockefeller Republican," though in his 1995 memoir he admitted that "[n]either of the two major parties fits me comfortably in its present state."

When George W. Bush named him secretary of state, Powell entered the office in January 2001 with a clear concept of how he intended to lead the department. During a telephone conversation I had with him then about a possible job at State, Powell described his desire to give the main role to career professionals and to run the organization in a traditional way. By this he meant two things. One was a determination to streamline the structure of the department in order to clarify the chain of command. When he arrived, for example, he found that there were fifty-five "special envoys" or ambassadors-at-large reporting to the secretary; he abolished as many of them as he could (some had a statutory origin), ultimately eliminating twenty-two. The point of this streamlining was to restore responsibility to the regular regional and functional offices in the building—to "empower the desks at the State Department," as White House press secretary Ari Fleischer put it at the time.

There were other indicators of the same intention. Richard Haass, an experienced policy expert who had served on Bush 41's NSC staff, took the job of director of State's Policy Planning Staff. This is a job I had held under George Shultz. The office can be of value to a secretary of state as a gadfly to the bureaucracy by providing strategic perspectives different from what the secretary receives from the bureaus and desks. But Powell did not want gadflies, and Haass never had the impact that he might have had. By the same token, the seventh-floor position of "counselor" of the department, which James Baker had filled with a key member of his inner circle, went unfilled throughout Powell's tenure. He had little use for offices that did not exercise operational responsibility. Undoubtedly, much of this reflected Powell's experience with the military principle of "not jumping the chain of command"—that is, respecting the hierarchical structure and deferring to the operational responsibility of the officials in the chain.

Even more important, Powell's desire to "empower the desks" meant reliance on the Foreign Service. Most key assistant secretary positions went to career officers, and in the principal policy-making jobs there were only a few political appointees. White House aide Karl Rove clashed with Powell over this early in the administration, but gave way. As Powell said in his confirmation hearing, "part of my plan with the State Department is to put our Foreign Service officers in charge of the work of the Department, to motivate them, to give them a sense of responsibility and let them know we trust them, we have confidence in them."

The most eminent of the political appointees who made it through was John Bolton, who became under secretary of state for arms control and international security affairs and a pivotal figure on issues such as the nuclear weapons programs of Iran and North Korea. Bolton believes that Powell saw the value of having a true-blue conservative in his entourage. "You do cover my right flank," he told Bolton once, "and it needs covering." Bolton's memoir records that Powell stood by him loyally during all the congressional political assaults that he (Bolton) came under. But the memoir also reflects Bolton's constant frustration and isolation in a department in which most of the important officials reflected a policy mind-set he considered out of step with the president's.

Bolton tells of instances in which Powell took on the bureaucrats. One issue was the new International Criminal Court (ICC), which Bill Clinton's administration had agreed to but which the Bush administration decided to disengage from. The Bush team was convinced that this new court, unaccountable to any government, its prosecutions not subject to U.N. Security Council veto—imagine Kenneth Starr on an international scale—was likely to become a politicized weapon against American officials and military personnel. The Bush administration not only withdrew its signature from the ICC treaty but launched a campaign to reach bilateral agreements with as many countries as possible not to surrender each other's citizens to the ICC. Such agreements were eventually reached with more than one hundred countries—a remarkable achievement by the State Department, which some of the senior career diplomats virtually refused to assist in until they were bluntly ordered to do so by Powell. Another instance was Bush's condemnation of Iraq, Iran, and North Korea as the "axis of evil" in his January 2002 State of the Union address. This was followed by leaks to the media by State Department officials denying that these characterizations would have any relevance to U.S. policy toward those countries. Powell surprised a meeting of his senior staff by declaring sternly that the president believed strongly in what he said and no one in the State Department "should try to take the edge off what the president said, or try to spin it."

Powell was later criticized by liberals for excessive loyalty to the president, especially over the Iraq War. These examples cited by Bolton show him, indeed, striving to be loyal and to impose this loyalty on his department. But Powell had helped create, or magnify, his own problem. The philosophy of "empowering the desks" reflected a view of stewardship of the department at odds with much of the philosophy we have seen earlier in this book. Where Henry Kissinger and James Baker had come into the building with a determination to impose political direction on the career service, Powell chose to embrace the organization. He seems to have done this as a matter of orderly management as he saw it; his own moderate instincts on policy only reinforced it. Whatever the intention, the result was to increase the probability that when controversial issues presented themselves, whether Iraq or Iran or North Korea, Powell's State Department would find itself out of step with the more conservative members of the administration—which very often included the president.

Thus, one of the key building blocks was in place for a divided government. It was inevitable that the moderate views of the State Department, led as it was by a moderate who generally shared its institutional philosophy, would leave the institution out of sync with a conservative secretary of defense and vice president. What was not inevitable was that the feuds would be so persistent—and that the president would have such difficulty in managing them.

EARLY IN THE ADMINISTRATION, Powell made a public misstep on the subject of North Korea. He declared at a news conference on March 6, 2001, that the Bush team would "engage with North Korea to pick up where President Clinton and his administration left off." The Clinton administration had reached an Agreed Framework with North Korea in 1994 intended to halt its nuclear weapons program, and was moving toward normalizing relations with Pyongyang. Powell, in speaking this way, was reflecting the preference of the career diplomats of his East Asian and Pacific affairs bureau, many of whom had helped shape the Clinton policy. In December 2000, during the transition, Powell had been briefed at his home in McLean, Virginia, by Clinton's State Department North Korea team, and he seemed impressed by what he heard. At the time Powell spoke in March, however, the Bush administration had made no decisions on the matter, and conservatives such as the vice president, secretary of defense, and the Republican congressional leadership viewed the Clinton diplomacy as seriously flawed. The president himself called Rice at 5:00 the next morning, furious when he read Powell's remarks in *The Washington Post*. Rice called Powell to tell him of the president's displeasure, and Powell later publicly confessed he "got a little too far forward on my skis." The incident was a harbinger of the bureaucratic brawl that would begin in earnest a year and a half later when North Korea was caught cheating on the 1994 agreement.

It took Powell a long time to develop a personal camaraderie with the president. "There existed a distance between these two affable men," Bob Woodward wrote, "a wariness—as if they were stalking each other from afar, never sitting down and having it out, whatever the 'it' was."

Only in the late spring of 2002—after some sixteen months in office—did Powell ask the president for periodic private meetings with him in the Oval Office, a common—and obviously crucial—opportunity for harmonizing views and building confidence (recall Kissinger's regular meetings with Ford). Apparently Powell thought to ask for this only after he got wind of the fact that Rumsfeld was requesting and having such meetings. Powell, recalling from his own experience as Reagan's national security adviser that everyone in the world wants face time with the president, had not wanted to intrude on the president's time. His deputy, Richard Armitage, an experienced bureaucratic operator, convinced him that he needed the same access as Rumsfeld. So he began having such meetings, and later declared himself satisfied that he was having the access he wanted.

But the mutual unease between Bush and Powell seems never to have gone away, and much of the problem had to do with the substance of policy, not simply personality. By all accounts, Powell was uncomfortable with what he saw as an impetuosity in the White House and inadequate attention to the benefits of international consensus-building. He and his State Department colleagues blamed Cheney and Rumsfeld for skewing U.S. policies in this direction. Those who sympathized with Powell complained that a "cabal" of the vice president and secretary of defense had undue influence over the president, putting a "thumb on the scales" of the policy-making process. But another revealing moment in Woodward's *Bush at War* is the weak response that Bush gave when asked about Powell's contributions. "Powell is a diplomat," Bush responded. "And you've got to have a diplomat." This was less than a passionate presidential embrace of what Powell was engaged in.

Associates and friends of Powell have said that often when he thought he had persuaded the president of some moderate diplomatic course to pursue, the president reversed direction after a short period, apparently due to the influence of Cheney and Rumsfeld. "Somebody got to the President after I did," he used to lament. The premise of that characterization is that the president's natural inclination lay with Powell, and the influence of others was a distortion. An alternative hypothesis would be that this president's natural instincts lay on the conservative side, and that when Powell thought he had fully persuaded the president in a private conversation without the presence of those with contrary views, he was often mistaken. George Shultz had had a similar experience with Reagan: Reagan most often sided with Shultz in their private sessions, but there were occasions (especially on Central America) when the issue was forced into an NSC meeting in which all the players could argue it out in front of the president, with the result that the president tilted back to the conservative side. Victories won by bureaucratic end runs are often short-lived. The disorderliness of this procedure—of competitive end runs into the Oval Office—is a serious management deficiency in itself. (Colin Powell, when he was Reagan's national security adviser, had seen it as part of his job to head off this sort of thing.) In any case, the president's wishes are the ultimate and legitimate arbiter. If the "cabal" consistently includes the president, it's not a cabal but a presidential preference.

Rumsfeld at the Pentagon

Where Colin Powell took charge of the State Department with the intention of empowering the existing organization, Donald Rumsfeld took over at the Department of Defense with the opposite intention. It was widely believed in Republican circles that civilian control of the military had weakened in Bill Clinton's presidency and political authority needed to be reasserted. (Some of this impression, ironically, was due to the charismatic Colin Powell's tenure as a strong chairman of the Joint Chiefs.) Having served once before as secretary of defense (under Gerald Ford) and having run two major corporations successfully, Rumsfeld had experience as a hands-on executive not shy about imposing his will. His friend Newt Gingrich linked some of Rumsfeld's style to his experience as a college wrestler at Princeton: "The sport," Gingrich said, "tends to produce very confident people who don't mind being visible, because everybody can watch them, and ain't nothing between them and winning and losing." Rumsfeld, he said, was smart, "stunningly competitive," with a "disciplined, focused ability to think about things."

Rumsfeld quickly asserted his control. He returned for his second tour in the E-ring office of the secretary of defense with an agenda, which he called "transformation." He had the president's explicit mandate to "challenge the status quo inside the Pentagon," and he went about it with gusto. There is no doubt this is what animated Rumsfeld the most and what he most wanted to leave as his legacy. He was convinced that the U.S. military had not yet shaken off the doctrines, structures, and systems of war-fighting left over from the Cold War; in the twenty-first century the United States would face threats from unpredictable directions, including from possible new rivals, rogue states, terrorists, and others with weapons of mass destruction and missiles to deliver them. Therefore he wanted the U.S. military to restructure itself rapidly to emphasize flexibility, agility, better intelligence, innovative use of information technology and outer space, defenses against missiles, and new ways of war-fighting. He expanded the scope and missions of special operations forces, and he introduced a new process for more frequently updating war plans. Overseas, he launched a realignment of U.S. bases and forces, questioning Cold War deployments and forcing commanders to rethink what the requirements were in a new era.

Much of this was met with bureaucratic resistance from a military establishment—one of the most conservative of institutions—that had not experienced so assertive a reformist civilian leadership since Robert McNamara in the 1960s. Rumsfeld's abrupt personal style also rankled. There were those who found him intimidating. (My own impression was that he respected those who stood their ground—such as General Tommy Franks, the commander who planned the Afghan and Iraq campaigns.) After a while, management procedures in the department became more regular. Relations with the Army, however—the service that had the hardest time adjusting to new missions and concepts following the demise of its Soviet land-army rival—remained difficult the longest; the struggle over its modernization was quickly followed by the stresses of the prolonged Afghanistan and Iraq deployments. The liberation of Afghanistan in 2001 seemed to vindicate Rumsfeld's emphasis on innovation and flexibility. He was delighted by photos of U.S. Army Special Forces in Afghanistan—on horseback—with laser designators calling in precision air strikes from their handheld radios. The Iraq War, however, not only put considerable stress on U.S. ground forces but required a rapid relearning of counterinsurgency skills that the Army had forgotten since Vietnam.

RUMSFELD'S ROLE in the interagency battles over policy became controversial; he and his old friend the vice president were the "cabal." As a statutory member of the NSC, the secretary of defense has a voice in foreign policy discussions just as the secretary of state has a voice on any other topic. On diplomatic issues, generally, agencies tend to defer to State, but most of the big national security issues facing the Bush administration—withdrawal from the ABM Treaty; negotiations over North Korean and Iranian nuclear programs; Afghanistan and Iraq—

involved interests of many departments. Indeed, the need to integrate the diplomatic, military, and other dimensions of policy is why the National Security Council was created.

The vehicle by which Rumsfeld prepared himself for these inter-agency deliberations was the office of the under secretary of defense for policy, headed by Douglas Feith. My office—assistant secretary for international security affairs—was responsible for advising Rumsfeld on policies in most regions of the world, under Feith. (A parallel assistant secretary dealt with Europe; I had the rest.) We were the foreign policy arm of the Pentagon. The Policy office, as it was known, and especially my staff of regional experts, was quite small compared with the large organizations in each of the regional bureaus at State, but we churned out papers for Rumsfeld and briefed him before his attendance at meetings of the NSC or Principals Committee. Feith or I often accompanied Rumsfeld (or his deputy, Paul Wolfowitz) to these meetings, as well as attending meetings of the Deputies Committee ourselves.

On any issue on the NSC table, the Defense Department is entitled to submit its own paper outlining a proposed policy or strategy, or to propose amendments to papers drafted by others. The frequency with which we took the initiative to do this has turned, in some quarters, into another example of the Pentagon's undue influence over U.S. policy. This is puzzling. Marc Grossman, who was State's capable under secretary for political affairs and Feith's counterpart, is on record stating his admiration for the speed and quality of the papers that the Policy office produced. The White House, for its part, found our efforts helpful as well. I recall a moment when my Latin America experts mentioned to Feith that the interagency drafting of a new presidential strategy for the Western Hemisphere (a National Security Presidential Directive, or NSPD) was expected to take six months. Feith, incredulous, asked why such a noncontroversial document would take so long. He proposed that our office do its own draft in the next few days and submit it to the White House to jump-start the process. We did, and it did. But as policy controversies developed on many other issues, Feith's office became a bureaucratic and journalistic target.

The Unprecedented Vice President

Lynne Cheney, wife of the vice president, turned up on Comedy Central's *The Daily Show* in October 2007 to promote a memoir she had written. To the surprise of host Jon Stewart and amusement of her audience, she presented Stewart with a gift—an eighteen-inch statue of Darth Vader—the dark villain who, for some, had become the image of her husband. She called it a "family heirloom."

There is no dispute that Dick Cheney had an unusual influence in national security policy as George W. Bush's vice president, and, as with all recent president–vice president relationships, its mystery is only deepened by the fact that only the two men know the real content of their private conversations. As a former White House chief of staff, congressional leader, and secretary of defense, Cheney was bound to carry substantive weight. His close personal and philosophical bond with Donald Rumsfeld—for whom he had once worked as a young aide in his first job in Washington—was also a bureaucratic factor of undeniable importance. But, even more important, he seems to have established an intimate relationship with the president.

The modern vice presidency can be said to have begun with Walter Mondale in the administration of Jimmy Carter. As we have seen, Carter treated Mondale as a valued political ally and granted him a West Wing office, where most of his predecessors had been confined to the old Executive Office Building next door. Mondale was an important source of political advice in a White House that had few senior people of Washington experience. Carter's attorney general, Griffin Bell, complained at length in his memoir that Mondale and his strategically placed former staffers had undue influence over Carter's policy-making on a range of domestic, legal, and foreign policy issues. Al Gore was believed to have unprecedented influence, as we have seen, in Bill Clinton's administration. Gore's national security adviser, Leon Fuerth, was "a very major player" in the NSC staff's work. While comparisons are difficult—the size of the vice presidential staff and office budget have not recently been disclosed—some experts believe Cheney's staff was about the same size as Gore's in total, though Cheney's national security staff may have been somewhat beefed up. Some have said that Cheney enjoyed "considerably more time with the president" than his predecessors—not only a weekly private lunch and the formal meetings (cabinet and NSC) but also hours of additional time together—but I have not seen documentation of this comparison.

The accusation often made was that Cheney's close relationship with the president, his statutory role on the NSC, his participation in Principals Committee meetings, his affinity of views with Rumsfeld, the beefing up of his national security team, and his staff's participation in NSC staff and interagency meetings, all added up to a decisive tilting of the policy-making process. This is the origin of the "cabal" thesis and it seems to have been the perception at the State Department. Wherever Cheney and Rumsfeld were was said to be the "center of gravity" of U.S. policy.

My perception from the Pentagon was different. There were undoubtedly issues on which the vice president's private views communicated to the president had a particular impact, but they were not as many as generally claimed. The attempt to assert broad presidential powers over detention and surveillance of alleged foreign terrorists is clearly one such category. Given Cheney's historical passion to preserve what he saw as the constitutional powers of the executive, especially in wartime, reports of his strong convictions on this score are credible. The secrecy of most of the relevant internal debates leaves it difficult for outsiders to know, but the testimony of former Justice Department and Pentagon lawyer Jack Goldsmith is also credible with respect to the influence of the vice president and his staff. In any event, I am told authoritatively that the vice president's passion to preserve presidential powers was also shared by other senior White House officials, and it is easy to believe it was the president's natural conviction as well.

On other issues, we in the Pentagon perceived a more level playing field than did those from other agencies whose accounts have generated most of the public commentary. We considered that our views were rejected by the president on many issues—including on important points over Iraq—and our frustrations with the slow deliberative process were similar to the frustrations expressed by others. I was present at Principals meetings at which Secretary Powell's recommendations on diplomatic courses of action were approved by national security adviser Condoleezza Rice despite the vice president's disagreement. Cheney strongly opposed Powell's U.N. diplomacy before the Iraq War, but the president sided with Powell. There were times when we were convinced that Powell had a special relationship with Rice, bypassing the formal interagency procedures that would allow us to interject our view. There was no evidence for any such "special relationship" between Powell and Rice; indeed, subsequent accounts suggest the relationship between them was strained. The State Department even considered at times that she was in collusion with Cheney and Rumsfeld, or an "enabler" to their nefarious influence, or attempting too much to "position" herself to personal advantage. As I read these accounts, I am struck most of all by the mirror-image quality of the suspicions on both sides. Below, when we consider particular issues, we will see a more complex picture than what either side imagined. The pivotal factor was always the president. Sometimes he sided with one side, sometimes with the other; sometimes he deferred judgment.

ON AUGUST 26, 2002, during the run-up to the Iraq War, Cheney gave a speech to the Veterans of Foreign Wars warning of the menace of Saddam Hussein's weapons of mass destruction, and he cautioned that the return of U.N. inspectors to Iraq would bring "false comfort." This time it was Powell's turn to be furious, since the president had decided at an NSC meeting ten days earlier that he would go before the U.N. General Assembly in early September to challenge the U.N. to confront Saddam. While the president had made no decision on a role for U.N. inspectors, Cheney's remark seemed to commit the United States to oppose it. Rice took her and Powell's concerns to the president, who agreed. He told her: "Well, why don't you call Dick and tell him what you want him to do?" She did, delicately chiding him for foreclosing the president's options. Cheney steered clear of the issue in subsequent speeches.

As for the vice president's allegedly decisive influence, White House insiders scoffed at the notion. They saw Cheney as a heavyweight counselor, given his deep knowledge of both policy and process, but they recalled many occasions when the president did not follow his advice. Speechwriter David Frum concluded: "Cheney was certainly a powerful figure within the administration. But those who identified him as a shadowy shogun who secretly controlled Bush, the weak mikado, could not have been more wrong."

Rice, Hadley, and the Interagency Process

The device of the Principals Committee was invented by President Bush 41. As we have seen, it was a forum of cabinet secretaries chaired by the assistant to the president for national security affairs (then Brent Scowcroft). Bill Clinton's administration made use of it, somewhat differently. In its own way it was emblematic of some of the problems under Bush 43.

Control of the Principals Committee was the subject of an early test of strength between Rice and Cheney. In the early years of the NSC, particularly the Eisenhower administration, the vice president presided at NSC meetings in the president's absence. Since the Principals were, in effect, the NSC minus the president, Cheney took a run at asking Bush to appoint him chairman of the Principals. "She threw a fit," according to a colleague, invoking the more recent precedent and pleading with Bush: "[T]his is what national security advisers do." He agreed. Thus it came about that the supposedly all-powerful vice president sat at the table with cabinet secretaries at Principals meetings chaired by an assistant to the president.

The job of assistant to the president for national security affairs contains within it a number of functions—staffing and advising the president, managing the interagency process, monitoring implementation of presidential decisions. Condoleezza Rice saw the first role as the most important. She spent extraordinary amounts of time with him, not only as confidante and counselor but virtually as a member of the family. David Rothkopf recounts:

> On a typical day as national security advisor, she saw him seven or eight times, and many days she was by his side between four and six hours. She worked out in the gym with him. She spent so much time with him at Camp David that she had her own cabin there. She joined the Bush family for Sunday dinner on a regular basis.

Rice's closeness to the president and her chairing of the Principals Committee gave her, on the face of it, an enormous advantage. In the Pentagon we sometimes feared that she was interpreting agencies' views to the president, at the expense of our ability to present our views directly to him, as Rumsfeld could do at an NSC meeting. (Principals meetings were more frequent than NSC meetings.) This was a source of suspicions. But apparently the State Department's fears were similar to ours. More generically, Rice came to be accused of being weak and of neglecting her responsibility to manage the growing conflicts among the cabinet heavyweights. Armitage once cracked that she was an "acceleratron," meaning that she reinforced Bush's wrong impulses when she should have been putting a brake on them.

With respect to Iraq, for example, she has been criticized harshly for not challenging assumptions or pressing alternative points of view on the president before he made his decisions. Perhaps she might have done more of this. But (as we will see below in our discussion of Iraq) I am not convinced that the main mistakes in Iraq policy were mistakes of process.

My own view of Rice is more sympathetic. First of all, it is no small task to provide psychological support to the person on whose shoulders rests the heaviest burden of decision in the world. Helping the president achieve a level of substantive and psychological comfort with this burden is indeed part of the job; Henry Kissinger considered it one of his most important tasks with Richard Nixon. As for managing the bureaucratic conflicts, it is clear she tried. Her inability to resolve serious deadlocks was not a matter of personal deficiency: No one elected *her* to decide major controversies of national security policy. Just as Zbigniew Brzezinski attempted (and often failed) to wield presidential influence as Kissinger had done, it was not credible to the bureaucracy if the president was not visibly backing it up. Just as Ronald Reagan's national security advisers were perceived as weak, the problem was not their personal qualities but the president's unwillingness to break the deadlocks himself. Bush 43, like Reagan, was often not prepared to break decisively with one side or the other in a policy dispute; he preferred his subordinates to reconcile their conflicts for him if they could. Sometimes Rice would ask him to call a cabinet officer to make his wishes clear, and he would say no, it was for her to do. He did not want to referee every dispute. (Note that in the August 2002 incident involving Cheney's speech, Bush asked Rice to make the call.) To break major deadlocks she would need more presidential backing than that.

Bush's preferred method of resolving disputes was to encourage a consensus of his advisers. At Principals or Deputies meetings, Rice and her deputy Stephen Hadley repeatedly conveyed the president's injunction to reconcile disagreements, to "merge" or "blend" or "bridge" competing proposals, to split the differences, to come up with compromises. Even where it was known where the president's substantive preference lay, we had the picture of a president reluctant to impose his own will; he wanted his preferred outcome to emerge from the process and to reflect the consensus of his government. This approach was reflected also in the work of the NSC staff. When I served in the Nixon administration, the NSC staff's most important product was memoranda to Nixon laying out options for his decision; Bush 43's NSC staff crafted laborious statements of broad policy attempting to capture the state of the interagency consensus, which the Deputies Committee laboriously argued over. Hadley told the NSC staff that good governance required this pursuit of consensus—apparently in the hope that it would minimize controversy and gain legitimacy for the outcomes.

As for Armitage's complaint that Rice "accelerated" Bush's wrong instincts, this was a misreading if not disingenuous; it more likely reflects State's disgruntlement at being overruled in cases where the president did choose sides. From the Pentagon's vantage point, State wasn't doing so badly. Colin Powell, given his national and international stature, had considerable leverage in the interagency struggles, whatever the president's preferences. Hadley was heard saying more than once during tense moments over Iraq in 2002–2003 that "we can't let the NSC fly apart"—meaning that State had to be mollified in some way (or, perhaps, that they could not afford to have Powell resign). This insured that State—despite its frequent public complaints—won many battles for the president's ear (if not his soul) or at least held its own sufficiently to cause unhappiness in the Pentagon when our preferences were not adopted. Indeed, it is part of the explanation for the deadlocks that frustrated everyone. Many times I heard Rumsfeld echo George Shultz's famous complaint: "Nothing ever gets settled in this town."

Cases and Controversies

A variety of problems arose in the Bush administration from this management system. In some cases, the pursuit of consensus led to frustrating delays. To take an example, Bill Clinton had begun an improvement of U.S. relations with India and Bush was eager to take it further. The Cold War had distorted the relationship of the two largest democracies—because of India's assertive neutralism in the early years, then the U.S. success in bringing China (India's rival) into the game against the Soviet Union (India's ally). The Cold War's end banished these distortions, and the new strategic reality of China's rise was pushing India and the United States together. The obstacle that remained was India's nuclear weapons program. Its nuclear weapons test in 1998 had forced the Clinton administration to apply legislatively mandated economic sanctions. A logical and promising avenue of U.S.-Indian rapprochement in the new century was to expand cooperation in high technology between the two mature economies in such areas as civilian space programs, civilian nuclear energy, missile defense, and other high-tech trade. The two countries needed to work out a plan for steps by India that would enable the United States to remove the legislative and regulatory obstacles to make such cooperation possible.

At a Deputies meeting in March 2003, Hadley announced that the president considered it was time to transform the relationship with India. But before any proposition could be put before the Indians, a divided U.S. government had to thrash out what it would be. Both State and Defense were internally split. In both departments, people who were focused on India policy favored trade liberalization for strategic reasons, while those responsible for U.S. nonproliferation policy considered India a conspicuous miscreant because it had never signed the Nuclear Non-Proliferation Treaty and they saw any significant concession to India as a weakening of the international nonproliferation regime.

In the Pentagon we worked out our differences fairly quickly. My office, responsible for regional relations, favored rapid improvement of ties with India. My colleague J. D. Crouch, responsible for nonproliferation policy, shared the concerns of his counterparts at State. Both of us worked for Douglas Feith, who supported the president's desire to move forward with India and asked Crouch and me to work out some compromises on the technical issues, which we did. In State, however, the impasse took much longer to resolve. The obstacle was John Bolton, who as State's nonproliferation "tsar" was adamantly against concessions to India that would legitimate its nuclear programs. It was ironic that the issue on which the usually frustrated Bolton seemed to have the most influence at State was an issue on which he was at odds with his conservative allies in the rest of the government. Lunching once with Bolton in the elegant eighth-floor dining room at State, I asked him half-jokingly if he planned to add democratic India to the president's "axis of evil" list. John just smiled.

As a result it took six months for the U.S. government to work out its position. The Defense and Commerce departments pushed for liberalization; State leaned in that direction but was hobbled by its internal divisions. I remember asking NSC staff friends why the president could not be presented with, say, two or three options, so he could just decide the matter. I was told that the president—despite his clear desire to change U.S. policy—wanted the departments and agencies to negotiate it.

While the India deliberation produced an agreement in the end,* on other issues the deadlocks were never resolved. One example was Iran. In the spring of 2003, the president asked his departments and agencies to develop an NSPD for him to sign setting forth a U.S. policy toward the Islamic republic. As our contribution to the deliberation, we in the Policy office in the Pentagon turned out "action plans" for increasing pressures on Iran; as drafts of the NSPD were circulated, we added our points. State disagreed with many of our points, leaning more toward diplomatic engagement. Repeated Deputies meetings chaired by Hadley failed to iron out the philosophical disagreements. The president reportedly sided with those skeptical of diplomatic engagement, but with the Iraq War heating up he also shied away from escalation of a conflict with Iran. The draft NSPD went nowhere—except to generate a few press leaks from State about the bellicosity of the Pentagon.

North Korea policy was another example of the president's attempting to split the difference between conflicting positions. Within the State Department, the Bureau of East Asian and Pacific Affairs (EAP), headed in the first Bush term by James A. Kelly and in the second by Christopher Hill, was the ardent champion of bilateral negotiations with North Korea. It was EAP that encouraged Colin Powell in his admiration for the Agreed Framework of 1994, which the Clinton administration believed had halted the North Korean nuclear weapons program. It had long been an article of faith among congressional and conservative Republicans, on the other hand, that the 1994 agreement was a mistake: While it placed international controls on North Korea's Yongbyon nuclear reactor complex, it provided no visibility into whatever else North Korea might be doing, in a country known to have the most extensive network of secret underground facilities on the planet. In return for this, the Clinton administration had eagerly pursued normalization of relations, with a high-profile visit by Secretary of State Madeleine Albright to Pyongyang and a near-agreement on a visit by President Clinton himself just before the end of his term.

In the new administration, the president let it be known through Rice that he wanted a North Korea policy "180 degrees" different from Clinton's, that he found the regime of Kim Jong-il "abhorrent," and that

---

*Eventually a game plan was agreed in the U.S. government in the fall of 2003 and with the Indians in January 2004. Its culmination was an accord on peaceful nuclear cooperation, reached in July 2005. As of late 2008 the fate of this accord was in the hands of the legislatures of the two countries.

we could have no more "business as usual" with North Korea. Bush told Bob Woodward of his visceral "loath[ing]" of Kim Jong-il, who starved his people and ran a massive system of prison camps. Any new agreement would have to include strict verification of all North Korean nuclear programs. Under pressure from Powell and from the liberal South Korean government of Kim Dae-jung, Bush in June 2001 authorized continued bilateral contacts with North Korea (through its U.N. mission in New York) and continued adherence to the 1994 Agreed Framework. But Bush toughened the U.S. position in other ways: He insisted on improved implementation of the Agreed Framework, on verifiable constraints on North Korean missiles, and on changes in North Korea's conventional military posture that would be less threatening to South Korea.

This would become the pattern of North Korea policy in Bush's first term—acceding to the need for diplomacy, but reassuring administration conservatives by toughening the content of the U.S. positions. This approach frustrated both sides. The firmer substantive positions were much less likely to appeal to the North Koreans, which was frustrating to State, yet the president's go-ahead for continued diplomacy gave State many opportunities to pursue its own quiet overtures toward North Korea, which continually aroused the conservatives' suspicions. One example was Powell's "accidental" meeting with the North Korean foreign minister at a Southeast Asian nations' conference in Brunei in July 2002—a meeting that Powell's aides acknowledge they had choreographed for days and on which he had not consulted beforehand with the White House. On at least two other occasions, Powell ignored opposition from elsewhere in the administration to authorize his diplomats to engage with the North Koreans, without consulting the White House.

In the summer of 2002, the administration was preparing a new diplomatic initiative toward North Korea when U.S. intelligence discovered that North Korea had a secret program to build a nuclear weapon via highly enriched uranium (HEU). This program, circumventing the restraints on the Yongbyon reactor, meant that North Korea was violating not only the 1994 Agreed Framework but also three other agreements it had signed—the Nuclear Non-Proliferation Treaty, the North-South Joint Declaration on Denuclearization of the Korean Peninsula (1992), and an International Atomic Energy Safeguards Agreement (1992). The HEU program had apparently been under way for a number of years, since the Clinton administration. A visit to

Pyongyang in October 2002 by a delegation headed by assistant secretary of state James Kelly, originally conceived as an occasion to offer a new U.S. initiative, instead became the occasion of a dramatic encounter in which Kelly confronted the North Koreans with the U.S. knowledge of their HEU program, and the North Koreans, to everyone's amazement, admitted it. State's diplomats were unhappy, however, that Kelly's instructions and talking points—vetted by an interagency process in Washington—did not permit him to engage in any give-and-take with the North Koreans. "A trained monkey who can speak English could do this job," Kelly griped. Thus, again, State was given the form but the conservatives were given the content.

The next major diplomatic step was China's agreement in early 2003 to host a six-party negotiation on the North Korean nuclear problem (United States, China, Japan, South Korea, North Korea, and Russia). While this initiative came as a surprise to most of us in the Pentagon— it was apparently worked out in White House backchannels, with State participation but not the Pentagon's—we understood that it reflected the president's desire for closer cooperation with China; thus it had a wider strategic purpose in his mind, whatever results it produced on North Korea. The six-party forum had the additional benefit that it included five countries all committed to the denuclearization of North Korea; this was expected to be a vehicle of diplomatic pressure. The North Koreans always preferred direct bilateral talks with the United States, so as to head off such a coalition, to go over the heads of the South Koreans, and to place their own agenda of demands on an equal footing to that of the United States. To avoid this and to maintain the multilateral pressure on their illicit nuclear activities, the White House instructed negotiator Kelly that he was not to have private bilateral conversations with the North Koreans in these multilateral meetings.

The State Department felt passionately, however, that direct bilateral talks with the North Koreans were the only possible avenue to success. Likewise, State was convinced that the administration would have to abandon its harsh rhetoric against the regime and be willing, in the end, to come to terms with it. In Senate testimony in February 2003, Richard Armitage suggested that the United States would have to talk to North Korea. Soon after, a Democratic senator called Armitage to tell him, "I saw the president after that, but the president said to us, 'That wasn't my policy.'" To which Armitage answered, "You watch. It will be the policy." The president was reportedly not amused when he heard of this.

Within two years, however, U.S. diplomats were congratulating themselves that they had turned the six-party talks into a façade behind
which all the serious business was conducted bilaterally with the North
Koreans.

In Bush's second term, shifts in personnel shifted the balance of
forces within the administration. Rice replaced Powell as secretary of
state; her deputy Stephen Hadley replaced her as national security
adviser. John Bolton, who had fought a rearguard action within State on
the North Korean issue, left to become U.S. permanent representative
to the United Nations. Robert Joseph, who had done his best, as umpire
on the NSC staff, to split the differences, left the NSC to replace
Bolton at State, but at State he discovered that Rice most often sided
with Christopher Hill of the East Asian and Pacific bureau. Rumsfeld,
preoccupied with Iraq and politically weakened, fought less hard on
these issues; briefing him before NSC and Principals meetings, I
detected an air of resignation on this. (Robert Gates, who replaced
Rumsfeld, played even less of a role.) Bolton, who became involved in
the subject again in 2006 when the issues of North Korean missile and
nuclear tests came before the U.N. Security Council, noticed that U.S.
policy in New York toughened whenever the president got personally
involved. But Rice, given her special relationship with the president,
now had the upper hand in the government, and she pushed the agenda
of State's East Asian and Pacific bureau. A spate of press articles
appeared hailing the new dominance of Foreign Service professionals in
Rice's State Department.

In February 2007, after several rounds of bilateral talks, Christopher
Hill reached an agreement with the North Koreans in Berlin. To its critics, the new accord strongly resembled Bill Clinton's 1994 Agreed
Framework in that, while it shut down the Yongbyon reactor again, it
provided no credible verification of whatever else North Korea might be
doing clandestinely elsewhere in the country—or in other countries.
Possible obstacles to the conclusion of this agreement, in the form of
critical views elsewhere in the administration, were bypassed. State
Department officials let it be known to the media, with some apparent
pride: "Rice telephoned Bush from Germany, and national security
adviser Stephen J. Hadley walked the president through its terms line
by line. The layers of interagency discussion that had previously
thwarted policy toward North Korea were simply eliminated." Days
passed after the public announcement of the Berlin accord before the

secretary of defense and chairman of the Joint Chiefs were informed of its content.

Usually, leaks about the bypassing of regular procedures come from the bureaucratic party that is aggrieved by the practice. Leaks like these, boasting of the maneuver, are more unusual. But the State Department was pleased with its success. It is reported that U.S. diplomats considered the Berlin setting for the final stage of the negotiation to be particularly symbolic because Berlin had been the venue for many Clinton-era bilateral negotiations with North Korea. Similarly, the U.S.-North Korean working group set up by the Berlin agreement to explore normalization of relations found a particular satisfaction in being able to meet, in the Waldorf Towers in New York, in what had been the official residence of John Bolton, who had left his U.N. post after failing of confirmation by the Senate.

Bush had second thoughts about the Berlin accord, according to three former colleagues of mine in his administration. "Buyer's remorse" is a phrase I heard. But the president had left himself no recourse but to accept it. In the first term, the evidence is ample that he was among the skeptics, and his skepticism was a restraint on the exuberance of a diplomacy that he seems to have tolerated more than enthused over—a diplomacy that was heading in a direction he had said he did not want to go. But essentially he was only splitting the difference. Like Reagan on START or Central America, the result was a messy process that frustrated both sides in the interagency debate—those who wanted to do more and those who wanted to do less. Bush managed the disagreements, instead of choosing a clear-cut position. In the second term, weakened politically by Iraq, Bush was not in a position to take on the foreign policy establishment in another battle; he seemed to acquiesce in the new balance of forces in his administration instead of shaping it. If he had a view contrary to what the State Department professionals were pursuing, he did not assert it.

The War in Iraq

This is not the place for a full-length treatment of the Iraq War and its controversies. Nor can I claim to be a neutral observer, having been involved in policy-making in the Department of Defense with respect to it. Nevertheless I will attempt to assess, in as balanced a way as I can manage, a few of the issues that relate to the topic of this book, that is, how Bush ran his government. At this writing (2008), the goal Bush set out to achieve in overthrowing Saddam Hussein—a stable, moderate Iraq in the place of a tyrant with hegemonic ambitions—may be within reach. But no one can deny that it has been a more costly and painful enterprise than its supporters expected.

Not everything that goes wrong in foreign policy is the result of a failure of process, however. In the Iraq War, the most fundamental problems in my view were substantive—some important assumptions with respect to its difficulty that proved to be mistaken. It is not clear that a different procedure would have led the president to decide the big questions differently.

The most important mistaken assumption related to the extent of the political vacuum that would be left by the removal of Saddam's regime. The U.S. government expected to find Iraqi *institutions*— civilian and military—to which it could give direction and then assist the Iraqis in finding new leadership for. But these disintegrated; no department or agency predicted the depth of the institutional implosion that occurred. Many of the problems encountered flowed from this. An important prewar debate that is relevant to this had to do with whether the United States should have an occupation at all, or whether an Iraqi political structure should be put in place as soon as possible after liberation. We will discuss this below, but it is an issue deserving of serious consideration by historians because it was at the heart of how postwar events unfolded.

A second fundamental problem in Iraq was the failure to adapt quickly to the difficulties once they arose. There is a military maxim that no war plan ever survives the first contact with the enemy. The requirement then is to respond with timely decisions that address the unexpected challenges, and do not compound them. Some of the problems of this kind were indeed management failures, and we will discuss them. But other of these problems, too, were the result of policy judgments and unanticipated developments more than they were failures of process. The security vacuum that opened the door for an insurgency, for example, was the product of a number of separate factors: a war plan that emphasized speed over mass (and thus limited the numbers of U.S. troops); the decision to build a new Iraqi army from scratch instead of trying to reconstitute the remnants of the old; collapse of the Iraqi police; lower numbers of international forces than had been expected; Turkey's last-minute denial of access for the 4th Infantry Division; and so on. Then came a delay in recognizing the seriousness of the insurgency and in designing a strategy to defeat it. For all this, Donald Rumsfeld was ultimately held accountable, though the factors had a variety of origins.

THE PRESIDENT'S DECISION to go to war, made finally in January 2003, came after more than a year of deliberation within the administration. The adequacy of planning—if it were to be measured by the volume of effort alone—would be difficult to fault. All agencies were involved. There were dozens of meetings of the NSC, the Principals, and the Deputies on all aspects of the war and on a variety of postwar contingencies. A working-level Executive Steering Group was set up in August 2002 under NSC staff chairmanship to develop interagency plans. Subgroups were devoted to political-military issues, humanitarian and reconstruction needs, energy infrastructure, coalition affairs, and public affairs. Serious potential problems such as Saddam's destruction of the oilfields were anticipated and avoided in the major combat phase.

Rumsfeld brought in General Tommy Franks of Central Command and JCS chairman General Richard Myers to brief the president on a regular basis on the war plan. There was an unprecedented degree of transparency and communication among the president, the secretary of defense, and the military leadership, marking a significant improvement over Bill Clinton in Kosovo or Richard Nixon in Indochina. Colin Powell, who had serious reservations about the drift toward war, spent more than two hours with the president over a private dinner on August 5, 2002, laying out all the risks as he saw them and the need for the maximum international support. Powell was confident afterward that he had had the chance to make his case in full, and indeed the president accepted his recommendation to seek international support via the U.N. Security Council. Powell also had private conversations, soldier to soldier, with General Franks, expressing misgivings about the small size of the invasion force but receiving Franks's assurances that he (Franks) was comfortable with it.

In October 2002, Rumsfeld sent Bush his own memo listing things that could go wrong, and the CIA sent forward its assessments of the risks of a possible conflict. The president had to weigh those risks against the risks of inaction as they were seen at the time, including Saddam's hegemonic ambitions, his links to terrorism, his (near universally assumed) possession of stocks of WMD, and the erosion of the policy of containing him through sanctions.

George Tenet, then CIA director, has complained that there was no single meeting in which the president asked his senior subordinates their view on the "central questions" of whether the United States should go to war or not. Bush admitted this to Bob Woodward, saying he did not need to canvass his cabinet in such a formal way because he knew their views. Was this a serious mistake, or not? The value of hearing multiple views at the same time was once stated concisely and persuasively by that master of organization, Dwight Eisenhower:

> I know of one way in which you can be sure you have done your best to make a wise decision. That is to get the responsible policy makers with their different viewpoints in front of you, and listen to them debate. I do not believe in bringing them in one at a time, and therefore being more impressed by the most recent one you hear than the earlier ones.

This is undoubtedly a good model, and it may go a long way to answering the question raised in Chapter 1 about procedural legitimacy—that is, what kind of process increases the likelihood that those overruled in a presidential decision will accept its fairness. Future presidents would be wise to follow this practice where they can.

Two qualifications come to mind, however. One is that there is no such thing as a guarantee that those overruled will not feel aggrieved anyway, or will not avail themselves of the opportunity to distance themselves afterward—especially if the policy runs into difficulties. Cynical as it may sound, the quietude of the overruled may depend more on how a presidential decision fares after it was made than on how it was made in the first place. The second point is that in the case of an intense deliberative process lasting over a year, Bush had a point. He knew everyone's views, he had heard every argument, and all sides had had ample opportunity to speak their minds. It is not clear that a grand debate in the Situation Room would have added significantly to the president's understanding of what wisdom there was in the U.S. government as to the risks of action or inaction. My impression is that insistence on a formal Eisenhower-like interactive process would have made more difference to the administration's North Korea policy than to the decision to go to war in Iraq.

· · ·

Some of the familiar bureaucratic problems of the Bush administration did assert themselves, however, and the president and his policy-making process did not deal with them decisively. Even Bush's decision to endorse Powell's U.N. diplomacy had about it the air of splitting the difference. Cheney argued strongly that the pursuit of a U.N. Security Council resolution might well fail and leave us worse off diplomatically: If Saddam were clever, he could tie up the U.N. inspectors in endless evasions; nor did the United States have any assurance that it could achieve U.N. blessing for the use of force in any foreseeable circumstances, given French, Russian, and Chinese opposition. Bush sided with Powell on this issue, despite reservations, presumably hoping at the very least to demonstrate a degree of deference to his increasingly restless secretary of state. As it turned out, Powell was initially vindicated by the U.N. Security Council's unanimous passage of Resolution 1441 in November 2002, which declared Iraq to be in "material breach" of its obligations to renounce WMD and warned of "serious consequences." It was the quest for a second resolution—more explicitly endorsing the use of force—that ran aground, however. British prime minister Tony Blair desperately wanted explicit U.N. authorization to satisfy his Labour Party. Meanwhile, the French government was quietly telling the Bush White House to "just do it"—to go to war on the basis of Resolution 1441 and not put Paris on the spot a second time. On this, Bush sided with his ally Blair—and was humiliated by French sabotage of the second resolution. Such are the joys of multilateralism.

Planning for postwar reconstruction was hampered by a number of bureaucratic problems. Given the importance of the principle of unity of command, Rumsfeld fought hard for this to be put under Defense Department control. This was done. State inevitably chafed as many of its personnel came under military command. The Executive Steering Group chaired by the NSC staff chafed at Rumsfeld's unwillingness to let activities that the president had assigned to the Pentagon be vetted by a working-level interagency committee. In October 2002, the White House asked Rumsfeld to delay setting up an office for postwar Iraqi reconstruction because of fear that it would undercut the president's diplomacy. At a time when Bush was trying to reassure the world of his desire for peaceful solutions, how could he explain why the Pentagon was already staffing an organization to run Iraq after the overthrow of Saddam? Eventually, an Organization of Reconstruction and Humanitarian

Assistance (ORHA) was created, under retired Army Lieutenant General Jay Garner, in January 2003, just two months before the war began.

At this point, Rumsfeld made a misstep that seriously embittered relations with the State Department. In February, Garner reported to Rumsfeld on his progress in identifying skilled people to serve as senior advisers to the various Iraqi ministries. When Garner showed him a chart listing several men and women from the State Department and the U.S. Agency for International Development, Rumsfeld bristled. For the most important ministries he instructed Garner to develop a different kind of process; he wanted to know the criteria for selection, the skills needed, and then multiple candidates for each job, including experienced private sector people and others outside the U.S. government. He then started crossing names out on the chart next to the key ministries. This created havoc for Garner, who had been trying to put a team together on an urgent basis, and at State, where these individuals presumably had volunteered for this hazardous duty and begun making personal plans. The bitterness at State was deep and lasting. There was also irony in view of Rumsfeld's later campaign to mobilize greater participation from State and other agencies in postwar duties in Iraq and Afghanistan.

A bigger problem for ORHA was that it became a political football within the Pentagon. U.S. military doctrine treated postwar reconstruction (sometimes called "stability operations") as "Phase IV" of any military plan.* The "planning order" sent by the chairman of the Joint Chiefs to General Franks in July 2002 included this requirement. For a considerable period, however, General Franks seemed to believe that others would be taking this burden off his shoulders—either Feith, the under secretary for policy (an office that is not in the military chain of command); or ORHA, which he treated as Rumsfeld's baby, not his; or the State Department. On December 19, an updated "planning order" was sent to Franks, calling attention again to Phase IV. As the Joint Staff grew nervous about Phase IV, an "execute order" was issued on January 10, 2003, which enlisted a separate command (U.S. Joint Forces Command) to assist Central Command with the work involved. These orders made clear that ORHA reported to Central Command (that is, to General Franks).

There is no doubt that the delays hindered preparation. What also

---

*Phase I, typically, is planning and preparation; Phase II is "shaping the battlespace," often by air operations; Phase III is major combat operations.

stands out in retrospect, however, is how badly the Defense Department and the entire U.S. government were organized for the nature and scale of the postwar reconstruction activities that turned out to be urgently required. The Joint Staff, in a post-Iraq "lessons learned" assessment, correctly concluded that stability operations should not be viewed as sequential to but as an integral part of combat planning. In November 2005, Rumsfeld signed a directive establishing that the Department of Defense should henceforth treat stability operations as a core mission in war-planning. A month later, the president signed an NSPD establishing the coordinator for reconstruction and stabilization in the Department of State, to coordinate government-wide economic assistance efforts. To the regret of many, however, including in the Pentagon, the new office in State was given little funding.

On another crucial issue, Bush reversed an important decision he had made, in part out of deference to the man in the field. One of the central prewar debates in the administration, as I have noted, was whether there should be a U.S. occupation at all, or for how long, or whether an interim Iraqi political structure should be put in place as soon as possible after liberation. Long before the war, we in the Pentagon were strongly urging that a lengthy occupation would be a mistake, only delaying the Iraqis' ability (and necessity) to fill the vacuum with their own new institutions. A memorandum I wrote to Rumsfeld on this subject in the summer of 2002 is featured prominently in a book written by Feith. Our fear was that the U.S. political authority would end up sitting in Baghdad imagining that it was running Iraq, while all sorts of hostile forces would run loose in the country. While no agency of the government, as noted earlier, predicted the extent of the vacuum that occurred, the situation that we encountered arguably strengthened the case for helping the moderate Iraqis fill it as soon as possible.

The opposing view, held strongly in State and CIA, was that to prepare such an Iraqi political structure in advance would mean undue reliance on the half-dozen exile groups with which we had been working; their legitimacy and ability were questioned, and one of them, Ahmed Chalabi's Iraqi National Congress, was a particular object of State and CIA suspicion. The hope was that new, locally based Iraqi leaders would emerge after liberation, and that with time a more representative leadership group would develop. (Five years later, almost all the leading Iraqi politicians came from the external groups.) I raise this issue not simply to complain that the Pentagon was overruled, but because of its importance and because of the way it was handled.

Before the war, after interagency debate, Bush decided at an NSC meeting on March 10 that we would establish an Iraqi Interim Authority "as soon as possible after liberation." This was not to be a provisional government but a vehicle for enabling Iraqis, both "internals" and "externals," to begin sharing responsibility for running the country. The president's decision was spelled out in unusual detail in the official "summary of conclusions" of the NSC meeting circulated a day later. After Baghdad fell, however, the difficulties encountered in Iraq gave Washington cold feet. When Ambassador L. Paul Bremer was chosen in May 2003 to be head of the Coalition Provisional Authority, the president suggested to him that the process of Iraqi self-government would "take a long time." On arrival in Baghdad, Bremer concluded that a multi-year U.S. occupation would be necessary before the Iraqis could run their own affairs, and he halted the efforts begun by Jay Garner to help Iraqi moderates organize. He shared State's view that the external groups could not be relied upon and that moderate forces and institutions needed to be built from scratch. Everyone in Washington (including the president, vice president, and Rumsfeld) deferred to Bremer. After a few months, Washington had second thoughts again. By October, Bremer was persuaded to agree to turn over sovereign authority to Iraqis by the end of June 2004—earlier than he had originally wanted. Nonetheless, the formal occupation lasted fourteen months. As to its effects, historians can debate whose arguments proved correct.

The chain of command with respect to the occupation was an anomaly in itself. Bremer's charter stated that he was subject to the "authority, direction and control of the Secretary of Defense." But he also had the title of "presidential envoy," and he concluded reasonably enough that his most important tie was to the White House. He developed a close personal connection with the president, and telephoned national security adviser Rice virtually every day. Meanwhile, many of his senior colleagues in Baghdad were from State. A tireless and forceful executive, with courage as large as the burden on his shoulders, Bremer skillfully made use of the bureaucratic complexity to carve out considerable freedom of action.

As PROBLEMS MOUNTED in postwar Iraq, the State Department, feeling itself the aggrieved party in these many bureaucratic battles, found ways of distancing itself. It let its views be known through friendly media, and shone special light on its rivals in the Defense Department. Beginning in 2003, there was a flood of tendentious leaks attributing all the difficulties in Iraq to alleged failings of the Defense Department— failure to do any postwar planning, suppression of State Department planning efforts, intent to install Ahmed Chalabi as leader of Iraq, and so on. Not all these leaks came from State Department sources, but many of them clearly did. It was a natural reflex of State to try to distance itself from the problems in Iraq, but it was equally natural of the White House to perceive that this was harming the president. Many of the accusations against the Pentagon essentially called into question presidential decisions. Senior White House officials made calls to Powell's office rapping knuckles over the leaks.

What the White House did not do in this case, however, was to launch a vigorous defense of the president's original decisions. Whether the issue was postwar planning or the failure to find WMD, the president and his aides shied away from defending his decisions or the rationale for going to war. They attempted to focus on the future—on Iraq's democratic hopes and the stakes in the Middle East. Thereby, they not only conceded much of the ground to the critics but underestimated how much the leaks were delegitimating and undermining the president's whole Iraq policy. Perhaps only when Democratic candidate John Kerry threw these same accusations at Bush during the 2004 presidential campaign did the White House realize the full extent of the damage these leaks had done to him.

The CIA was also heard from. The fall of 2004—just before the U.S. presidential election—saw an unusual proliferation of leaks from intelligence sources embarrassing to the administration. On September 16, *The New York Times* reported on a secret National Intelligence Estimate (NIE) with a grim prognosis for Iraq, including civil war as a "worst-case" outcome. Two weeks later, the *Times* cited prewar intelligence reports that had allegedly predicted serious internal problems in Iraq. Also in September, a senior CIA Middle East analyst was reported to assert that CIA warnings before the war had gone unheeded. A second senior intelligence officer, an expert on counterterrorism, was permitted by the agency to publish a book highly critical of its performance against al-Qaida; he commented to *The Washington Post* that "[a]s long as the book was being used to bash the president, they [his superiors] gave me carte blanche to talk to the media." In October, the Knight Ridder/Tribune chain reported that a secret CIA assessment contradicted what the administration was saying about Saddam's ties with al-Qaida. Patrick Lang, a retired Defense intelligence analyst with friends at the CIA, later commented: "Of course they were leaking. They told me about it at the time. They thought it was funny. They'd say things like, 'This last thing that came out, surely people will pay attention to that. They won't re-elect this man.'"

The CIA has not succeeded in overthrowing a hostile foreign government in a few generations; alas, its effort to overthrow the American government fared no better. Joking aside, what we saw was a breakdown in professionalism. The phenomenon is not unheard of; during the Indochina conflict the Johnson and Nixon administrations were targets of similar intelligence leaks. But in general we expect more discipline in these matters from the CIA than from, say, the State Department, and it is healthier for the republic if this expectation is lived up to. Many of the press reports over Iraq were misleading. The CIA's supposed prediction of a postwar insurgency, for example, was a speculation at the tail end of a long report and not even mentioned in the "key judgments" at the front of the paper. Overall, some of the CIA's prewar analysis turned out to be right, but much of it turned out to be wrong (including on the stocks of WMD and the reliability of the Iraqi police). Their judgments in this regard were not strikingly better than others'.

The main issue for us here is that politicization of our intelligence professionals is a serious matter for the longer term. Politicization can come from either of two directions—from the leadership of an administration, or from an impulse to oppose the leadership of an administration. The latter is no more desirable than the former. Future presidents of whatever party will come to regret the bureaucratic indiscipline, even if it has been indulged lately in some quarters because partisan temptations were too hard to resist. When it happens, it is not only the political leadership of an administration that suffers. It is decidedly unhealthy for the intelligence professionals to expose themselves to such political pressures; they risk losing credibility if they let themselves be drawn into positions of policy advocacy. In December 2007, for example, the unclassified summary was published of an NIE that asserted that Iran had halted its nuclear weapons program—a conclusion that undercut the administration's policy of mobilizing international pressure on Iran. The published summary was clumsily drafted and misleading. The resulting furor engulfed not only the Bush administration's policy-makers; the CIA was bombarded by accusations that it had crossed the line between intelligence analysis and attempts to change policies it didn't like.

The "Surge"

A final example of Bush policy-making in Iraq is the process that led to the president's announcement on January 10, 2007, that he was temporarily increasing the U.S. commitment in Iraq by five brigades (more than twenty thousand troops), in what was dubbed a "surge" of forces. I was part of the interagency team that was called together in the fall of 2006 to review Iraq strategy. It was a successful process, which produced a clear-cut course of action that led in turn to a strategic improvement on the ground in Iraq. Yet the process reflected all the paradoxes of George W. Bush's leadership. His own instinct was decidedly better than that of his principal advisers. He understood that his existing strategy was not succeeding; he opted for a show of additional American strength in Iraq rather than for an elegant retreat as many in our national debate were urging upon him. In these judgments he was both correct and courageous—he was the "calcium in the backbone," as he aspired to be. Yet he did not want to impose such a decision on his subordinates; he wanted it to emerge as the recommendation of his senior advisers, especially the military. The reluctance of the U.S. military to make such a recommendation forced Bush into what was for him an unusual assertiveness that extracted, if not imposed, what he wanted. The complex process took four months.

Bush and his closest colleagues in the White House came to the conclusion in the late summer of 2006 that the Iraq strategy was not working. The political progress evidenced by the series of successful Iraqi elections in 2005 had not translated into a stable and unified government, and the terrorist bombing of the Shi'a Golden Mosque in Samarra in February 2006 had let loose a vicious spiral of sectarian killing, especially in Baghdad. Despite the growing clamor to begin withdrawals, Bush sensed, on the contrary, that security in Iraq needed bolstering. Some outside critics had long been calling for troop increases. In September, Bush asked national security adviser Stephen

Hadley to begin rethinking the strategy, and at the beginning of October Hadley asked his senior NSC defense staffer, William Luti (a former colleague of Feith and me in Rumsfeld's Pentagon), to prepare a briefing on the military direction the United States should take. A week later, Luti produced a paper outlining the concept and mission for a surge of forces. In mid-November, Hadley's deputy J. D. Crouch (another former colleague from the Pentagon) called together a Deputies-level group from key agencies, announcing that the president wanted a new approach in Iraq and that he hoped for a unified recommendation from all his advisers. Only after a few weeks of inconclusive discussion did Crouch ask agencies to offer up concrete proposals reflecting their individual preferences. State's paper suggested the beginning of a military disengagement from major cities, leaving it to the Iraqis to suppress the sectarian violence. (Even the Joint Staff considered that unrealistic.) With more wisdom, the State paper also foresaw that more political progress might be made among the feuding Iraqi communities at the local or provincial level than at the national level, where political accommodation was deadlocked.

The Department of Defense, however, was suffering its own internal deadlock. General George Casey, commander on the ground, firmly resisted any suggestion of additional troops; he argued that they would only prolong Iraqi dependency and the image of the United States as an "occupier." Chairman of the Joint Chiefs General Peter Pace and General John Abizaid (Franks's successor at Central Command) supported Casey. I told Rumsfeld that based on my conversations with NSC staffers I believed the president wanted the Defense Department to put the surge on the table as an option. Rumsfeld was torn. Given the worldwide strains on the U.S. Army and Marines, the military's preference was to limit itself to the existing strategy of training and equipping the Iraqi forces so that U.S. forces could "transition out." That approach, however, had made strategic sense only before Samarra, when the Iraqi political process had seemed to be succeeding. The Samarra bombing, and the unprecedented blow it struck to Iraqi political cohesion, had created a new strategic situation that called for a reimposition of U.S. military power to suppress the sectarian violence—which was the precondition for any hope of recovery of the political process.

The interagency negotiation gradually produced the outline of a potential bargain: State and other agencies made a maximum commitment to deploy their civilian personnel in greater numbers—a "civilian surge" to match the military one—and all sides acknowledged that an improvement in security could not be sustained unless the Iraqis made political progress. These were the Pentagon's desiderata. But even then, the military made no commitments. An outside political figure who supported a troop surge asked Hadley in mid-November if the president would support it; Hadley's answer was: yes, but only if the military recommended it. As the Pentagon continued to drag its feet, the president encouraged Hadley to step up his quiet lobbying. Hadley called in General Pace and handed him Luti's paper; Crouch and Luti lobbied the Joint Staff representatives on the interagency group. The president stepped up his own lobbying, but still by indirection. In a December 13 meeting with his generals at the Pentagon, he told them: "What I want to hear from you is how we're going to win, not how we're going to leave."

The new secretary of defense–designate, Robert Gates, told the president he supported a surge. But the problem remained of how to bring along the military. On this, Rumsfeld did the president one last service. He continued to work with General Pace on a paper setting forth a unified Defense Department position; the memo was painstakingly massaged over seventeen drafts by Rumsfeld, Pace, the Joint Staff, and my office. Before departing the Pentagon, Rumsfeld approved it and sent it to the White House. Buried in the four-and-a-half-page paper was the suggestion that a surge of military resources might be useful if in support of clearly defined objectives and if accompanied by a surge in political, economic, and other efforts by the civilian side of the U.S. government.

PERHAPS PROFESSOR NEUSTADT would see Bush's indirect approach as a good example of a president exercising his "power to persuade." Bush told a journalist that he wanted to be "thoughtful and sensitive" in his handling of the military. Probably he had absorbed the conventional conservative wisdom about Lyndon Johnson and the Vietnam War, namely that presidents should not micromanage military operations. But on matters of strategy the commander in chief need not be so shy. As scholar Eliot Cohen has shown in his classic study, *Supreme Command*, strategic judgment and direction often come only from the political leadership, and successful war leaders have provided it—such as Lincoln, or Churchill. In this book, for example, we have taken note of Roosevelt's assertion of command over the North African campaign and of Nixon's in Cambodia.

In fairness to Bush in this instance, he had boxed himself in polit-

ically. Amidst all the deterioration in Iraq during 2006 he had taken public refuge in his reliance on what his generals were advising him; it was
bound to be difficult to shift course so explicitly and be seen suddenly
overruling them. If the generals he relied upon wanted to come home,
why was he sending more troops? But the complex process also
reflected his natural management style as we have seen in many other
areas. As Hadley told an NSC staffer after the president's decision, "It
had to come from the military."

In the summer and fall of 2006, as Bush gave the first indications of a
shift of course, he seems also to have made his decision to relieve Donald Rumsfeld. After three years, Rumsfeld was held accountable for the
failures of strategy—for the failure of the generals to respond effectively
to the growing insurgency, for their persistence in a strategy that wasn't
working. Rumsfeld—so much criticized for imperiously imposing his
will on the uniformed military in the Pentagon—ironically paid the
price for being excessively deferential to the commanders in the field.
As he did with respect to many of Bremer's decisions, Rumsfeld repeatedly told aides he was reluctant to second-guess his field commanders.
Quite possibly he shared the military's not-so-hidden desire to extricate
itself from Iraq, to leave "nation-building" behind, and yearned to get on
with "transformation" for the long term. In any case, for the president,
who was focused on the strategic necessity of succeeding in Iraq, it
must have been acutely painful to dismiss the cabinet officer in whom
he had seemed to repose the greatest trust. When Bush announced, on
November 8, 2006, that Rumsfeld was being replaced, the phrase "loyal
to his president" featured conspicuously in his words of praise.

"Decider" or "Dissident"?

In 2007, Bush made the surprising comment to an Egyptian pro-
democracy activist that he, too, often felt like a "dissident" in Washington. His bureaucracy, he said, was not responsive to his policy of
promoting democracy. "Bureaucracy in the United States does not help
change." As we have seen in this book, Bush was not the only president in
the modern era who believed his government to be unresponsive to his
wishes. Like Jimmy Carter during the Iran crisis, Bush came face-to-face
with the reality that execution of policy is in the hands of the permanent
government. A president needs not only the "power to persuade" but also
a variety of political tools to reinforce his powers of persuasion—political

appointees in the departments who are attuned to his wishes, and cabinet officers for whom the presidential agenda is the top priority.

Bush had problems with both the State Department and the Defense Department, but the problems were of different natures. In a conservative administration, State under Colin Powell often seemed the outlier. When Condoleezza Rice took over the State Department in the second term, this was thought to solve the problem; she had been more attuned than anyone else to Bush's thinking. On the strategic initiative toward India, for example, State suddenly moved decisively in the direction the president had presumably always wanted to go; the agreement with India on nuclear cooperation was reached early in her tenure in 2005. On Iran as well, State's policy under Rice seemed to some observers tougher than it had been under Powell, as she unveiled increasing support for democratic opposition groups in Iran.

Over time, however, the role of the career service reasserted itself in the department, and State's policy drifted in that direction. Especially with the departure of Rumsfeld, the balance of forces in the administration as a whole shifted in the State Department's direction. Hadley often acted as Rice's partner—perhaps analogous to Scowcroft's role in covering Kissinger's flanks in the Ford administration. Yet, unlike Gerald Ford, Bush 43 (if the North Korea case is an example) seemed ambivalent about the policy results.

The problem at the Pentagon was different. Here the issue was not a philosophical disconnect but a failure to deliver results. I will leave the specific debates on troop levels, strategy, and so on to the historians, but the president ultimately reached his own conclusions and held Rumsfeld accountable. The 2007 surge represented an assertion of Bush's personal leadership.

Bush followed it up in 2008, as another debate occurred in the administration over how fast to reduce U.S. troops in the wake of the apparent success of the surge. Rumsfeld's successor, Robert Gates, won plaudits for his more congenial style with Congress as well as the military. Initially Gates sided with those in the Pentagon who wanted U.S. troop reductions to continue in the second half of 2008—withdrawing not only the increment associated with the surge but as many as five additional brigades. This was responsive to those in the Pentagon concerned about the stress on the overall force and those in Congress eager to withdraw. The president, however, sided with General David Petraeus, Casey's successor as commander on the ground in Iraq, who wanted to stabilize force levels in the second half of 2008 to consolidate the gains that had been made. Unlike Melvin Laird during the Vietnam War, Gates deftly shifted to support the president once the president (again) made his wishes clearly known.

FROM MY VANTAGE POINT, the iconic figure in the Bush administration was not Dick Cheney, the Darth Vader caricature, but Stephen Hadley, the pursuer of bureaucratic consensus. That consensus was Rice's goal, as well, as chair of many Principals meetings, but Hadley—the calm, careful lawyer, the judicious and always even-tempered referee— epitomized it to me in the many Deputies meetings that I saw him chair in the first term, and then as Rice's successor. The model of good gover nance that they both sought to follow—clearly at the president's instruction—was noble in intent. But as Ronald Reagan discovered, the pursuit of bureaucratic compromise can be a fool's errand. Bush, like Reagan, was often surprisingly diffident about imposing his will. It was puzzling above all because Bush, in meetings where I saw him, was focused, determined, and well versed in the issues—more so than my recollection of Reagan in a number of such meetings.

Bush I believe was attempting to follow a management model from the business world, delegating to senior subordinates and relying on their judgment. But there are large differences between a president's situation and a CEO's. In a typical corporation, a CEO's senior subordinates have a more acute sense of whom they answer to; certainly there are nothing like the centrifugal forces that pull on a cabinet secretary— the congressional and media pressures, the institutional cultures and biases, the career professionals' knowledge that they will be there for the long term while their political masters are only temporary. Any president, of course, has to delegate to subordinates. But yet again we see that without the sustained strategic leadership of the president, a collegial system of management is subject to breakdown. Two kinds of problems can result, and Bush suffered from both of them. One major problem arises when there are deep disagreements among strong cabinet secretaries; these only the president can resolve. And second, even when there is consensus, it can be a lowest common denominator—a papered-over compromise that conceals the president's real choices. This was Richard Nixon's insight. It was not an accident that Bush's surge of forces in Iraq—the decision that may prove to save his legacy— did not originate in any bureaucratic consensus.

CHAPTER TEN

Lessons Learned

L IMITS ON THE POWER OF THE PRESIDENT, it is worth reminding ourselves, are built into our constitutional structure. While the framers, I believe, intended the president to have a significant degree of flexibility in the conduct of foreign affairs and as commander in chief, I doubt they would be surprised to learn of the centrifugal forces at work on the presidency in the contemporary period. Justice Louis Brandeis famously said of the doctrine of separation of powers that it was adopted "not to promote efficiency, but to preclude the exercise of arbitrary power." Richard Neustadt, reaffirming in 1990 his conviction that the modern president was a weak (rather than an "imperial") office, hastened to add that "most of the time, he is supposed to be weak. And in the normal course, getting what he wants is supposed to be hard. Those actually are attributes of constitutional government in the United States."

If the issue before us is limitation of the power of government, however, there is another perspective that should concern us today. The growth of the modern bureaucratic state has posed a particular problem—namely, how to insure the political legitimacy and political control of its actions. Governance is impossible without the modern state, but who is in charge of it? How does a president insure that decisions he makes are implemented? Democratic societies are not the only ones wrestling with this question. Indeed, it has been one of the most fundamental challenges to the philosophy of government in the modern era. The Communists thought they had the solution: They had a parallel institution—the party—to impose political direction on the state institutions. What they discovered, however, was that the party became a bureaucracy of its own, losing its revolutionary purity, weighed down by inertia and corruption. The Communists then thought they had the answer to that problem, too—the permanent purge, cracking the dictator's whip on the party itself. Mao Zedong's murderous "Cultural Revolution" in the late 1960s and early 1970s can be understood as a desperate and horrific lashing out to prevent what he saw as the descent of the party he founded into bourgeois mediocrity, led by bureaucrats seduced by the temptations of "the capitalist road."

Free societies are in the fortunate position that they have methods available to them that are not only less repugnant but also more effective. Americans may be the most fortunate in that our constitutional structure may be better equipped than some other democracies for insuring political direction of the administrative machinery. The system of presidential appointments and congressional oversight may be better able to exert such control than parliamentary systems, with their "fusion" of the executive and legislative branches and the greater power of the civil service. But all the democracies benefit from the most important feature of all: Political legitimacy in our societies is not bestowed in perpetuity by history or anyone else on a privileged group or institution. Legitimacy is instead a renewable resource, a source of authority bestowed—or withdrawn—by the people at regular intervals.

Our professional diplomats, uniformed military, and intelligence officers are the backbone of our national security institutions. They are the executors of policy, the institutional memory, the repository of experience, and the fount of expertise. As these words are being written, many of them are putting their lives on the line in distant theaters on behalf of national policies. To say that they deserve our admiration and gratitude is an understatement. Duty and professionalism are the standards of their performance. In the back of our minds, perhaps, there is a technocratic model of government in which these professionals should be left to go about their business uncorrupted by politics or even by policy influence from elected or appointed officials who may have their own philosophy or objectives in the matter. But in truth, this is the wrong model. The political process that is the ultimate determinant of national policy is not a corruption; it is the source of legitimacy. The abolition of politics is a mirage, and a dangerous one. There are differences of view about national policies; that's the point. How the choices get made is the essence of the matter. "The truth," British scholar Bernard Crick has written, "is that there is nothing, in this world at least, above politics. Politics is freedom."

The technocratic model is the source of some of the controversies that bedeviled George W. Bush's administration. One major controversy, for example, concerned alleged White House politicization of the role of U.S. attorneys, the appointment of U.S. attorneys having always been a matter of presidential discretion. Whatever the merits of White House conduct in that affair, the awkward and sensitive position of the Justice Department has been the subject of many debates since Watergate, with a perceived tension between the president's role as chief law enforcement officer and the department's role as guardian of the integrity of the law. (We saw this tension in the Panama case.) Jimmy Carter even proposed during his 1976 campaign that the independence of the Justice Department be insured by giving the attorney general a term of office not coterminous with the president's—virtually removing him from the president's cabinet. After his inauguration, Carter's attorney general Griffin Bell (who had suggested the idea) regretfully reported to Carter that Justice Department lawyers had concluded the idea was unconstitutional: Since it is the president's duty to "take care that the laws be faithfully executed" (Article II, section 3), the attorney general has to be answerable to the president.

In an earlier chapter we saw CIA director William Colby come to the conclusion that the CIA—even though its founding statute places it firmly under the president—was more than ever beholden to Congress, particularly in a political climate in which a weakened presidency was being attacked for past abuses. A later director, Robert Gates, wrote of the CIA as "involuntarily equidistant" between the two branches. It should not be surprising that the controversies surrounding George W. Bush—who was accused of politicizing intelligence analysis in connection with the 2003 Iraq War—have stimulated more of the same. Retired intelligence officer Paul Pillar, writing in 2006, took this idea to its logical conclusion, proposing that the CIA become an independent agency, separated from presidential control—modeled after the Federal Reserve, a "quasi-autonomous body overseen by a board of governors with long fixed terms."

There are many practical problems with such a proposal. Even if intelligence analysis were made independent to avoid risk of politicization, what about covert action? The trend of all intelligence reforms since the 1960s and 1970s has been to strengthen presidential accountability for intelligence operations, not to dilute it. Would we have to separate operations and analysis in order to achieve more autonomy for the latter—when another trend of recent decades has been to try to integrate them more closely?

But the problems with such proposals are not merely practical; they go to the heart of our notion of government. Again, the concept is wrong. I know of no political system in which intelligence is not part of the executive function, with respect to collection, analysis, and covert action. Precisely because of its sensitivity, it should remain part of the accountable structure of government—reporting to an accountable, elected president, subject to reasonable procedures of congressional (and judicial) oversight. The controversies over intelligence in the Iraq War were thoroughly investigated by the Senate Intelligence Committee and by an independent bipartisan commission. But separating these functions from policy supervision would only diffuse responsibility, as well as rendering them less responsive to the policy-makers who *ought* to be the ones giving them guidance as to their priorities, weighing the risks of their activities, and taking responsibility for the results.

Accountability is what presidents provide. Their ability to give effective policy direction to their government is the other side of the coin of that accountability. This book has explored how they can most effectively provide that policy direction.

Broad Lessons

I do not hide my unapologetic support for presidential authority in the Executive Branch. One of the main reasons is the principle just stated—of democratic legitimacy and accountability. But on the practical level, where the requirement is coherence of policy, the preceding chapters of this book should have provided more than enough examples of the price that is paid for its absence. In a turbulent world, the U.S. government—and therefore the president—needs to get ahead of events and shape them; this puts a premium on bold, timely, purposeful, and consistent policy-making. This includes the faithful implementation of policies as the president has decided them. These qualities are not the natural product of bureaucracies operating without strong political direction. The policy machinery will simply not work without effective presidential control over it.

The differences among the presidents we have discussed are striking, yet there are threads running through their experiences, and broad lessons to be drawn from each.

Richard Nixon represents one paradigm. His White House–centered system produced what was probably the most centralized, consistent, and strategically coherent policy-making of any modern presidency (China, Soviet Union, Vietnam)—but it came at the price of demoralization and alienation of the rest of the government. The exclusionary style of his management is not a model to be emulated. Yet his White House–centered NSC structure has essentially been followed by most of his successors. Nixon was also a president who jealously guarded his right to decide, because he insisted on knowing what his real choices were and he abhorred being presented with bureaucratic compromises. Nixon, more than Truman or Bush 43, deserves the title of the "decider."

Gerald Ford tried hard to avoid what were seen as the flaws of Nixon—he sought to restore cabinet responsibility and a collegial style of deliberation. But his collegial system failed because he never gained political control over the forces tearing his administration apart (particularly over policy toward the Soviet Union). The authority of the presidency was under assault, and his party was undergoing a revolution. Ford's aspiration to collegiality did not avail when his personal political strength and the strength of the presidency as an institution were in question.

Jimmy Carter set up a system to insure that he heard different points of view—from his conservative national security adviser Zbigniew Brzezinski and his liberal secretary of state Cyrus Vance. Carter (like Nixon) wanted to be able to decide, and thereby to be in control. This made sense in the abstract, on an organization chart, but Carter's system also reflected a philosophical confusion at the very top: What kind of a president is it who is so unsure from one day to the next whether his foreign policy should be conservative or liberal? The lack of intellectual consistency impaired Carter's ability to impose consistent political direction on a recalcitrant bureaucracy, which (as in the crisis over the shah) remained in control of the levers of policy execution.

Ronald Reagan's has to be regarded as one of the most significant presidencies of recent history. But it is also an object lesson in the need for consistent hands-on policy management. On many crucial issues—especially Soviet policy—Reagan imposed his will. On issues on which he was less engaged (Central America, Lebanon), however, his government was often rudderless; in such cases he hoped for a consensus of his advisers. Where consensus was unattainable, conflicts persisted.

Thus Reagan's attempt at collegiality, too, turned out at times to be a formula for policy incoherence.

George Bush 41 was, from a management point of view, more successful. His cabinet was a cabinet of heavyweights; its collegial operation was a function of strong direction from a president who was deeply engaged, thoroughly knowledgeable in the substance of policy, and comfortable imposing his will. Nor was he shy about commanding his generals (as in Panama and the Gulf War). If there were limits to his historical legacy, they were not the product of faulty procedures.

Bill Clinton was elected at a moment in history when domestic and economic issues seemed to dominate and to supplant traditional security challenges. Yet he was confronted by such challenges regardless— as will all future presidents. Conflicts festered not only in his bureaucracy but in the world, until crises forced themselves upon him. Through trial and error Clinton learned the importance of presidential focus, more disciplined procedures, and a willingness to spend political capital.

The travails of George Bush 43 present a number of paradoxes. The problem was not to be found in conspiratorial "cabals" run by the vice president's office but in a systemic failure to manage conflicts among his advisers. A president capable of great decisiveness adhered paradoxically to a management model that elevated the principle of deference to top subordinates. As with Reagan, Bush and his White House team strove hard for interdepartmental consensus, and where consensus was not to be had, the result was often protracted bureaucratic deadlock. Bush's chosen system of management impeded his exertion of presidential will and his ability to control dissension in his government.

Specific Lessons

There are a number of more specific lessons that can be learned from this historical experience. The first group relates to issues of procedure. A second group involves issues of structure. A third group deals with issues of personality.

Presidential Engagement. The most obvious thread running through the accounts of several of the recent presidencies is the lesson that where presidents did not engage personally, consistently, and forcefully, they often lost control. We saw this especially in the cases of Ronald

Reagan, Bill Clinton, and George W. Bush. These three men could not have been more different from one another, and yet, for different reasons, they sought to delegate to subordinates and rely on them in circumstances that, on occasion, rendered this a disability. With Reagan, the reasons probably had to do with age and a laid-back temperament. Bill Clinton could never be accused of an allergy to detail—he was hailed (or mocked) as an arch "policy wonk"—but in foreign affairs his problem was a lack of focus. With George W. Bush it seems to have been a CEO management model. All three had their successes when they did impose their will—Reagan on broad policy toward the Soviet Union; Clinton on Russia; Bush on the surge in Iraq. But when they hung back, for whatever reason, their administrations fell prey to feuding among senior subordinates and/or the problem of departments and agencies unresponsive to presidential wishes (Reagan in Lebanon; Clinton's early policy in Japan, China, and Bosnia; Bush in North Korea and Iraq).

There is no structure or policy-making procedure that can fix these problems. The National Security Council mechanism—the council, the subcommittees, the NSC staff—remains a flexible instrument that successive presidents have used in different ways. Bush 43 used the formal NSC procedures extensively for consultation; Bill Clinton much less so. But both leaders suffered from the similar problem that no structure can substitute for a president's sustained and credible engagement. The word "credible" is important here because it is the key to empowering a subordinate to act in the president's name. If the boss is thought not to care all that much about an issue, even an energetic subordinate will find his or her ability to act in the president's name undercut. This applies to a cabinet secretary as much as it does to a White House adviser: Nobody elected *them*. Thus, a vicious circle arises—feuds will not be resolved; delegation will not be effective. Credible presidential backing of a subordinate—as Nixon and Ford provided for Henry Kissinger, or Reagan (for the most part) for George Shultz, or Bush 41 for James Baker—makes delegation possible. Bill Clinton did this ad hoc (and not usually for his secretary of state).

Much, of course, depends on the quality of a president's team (more about that later). But whether the subordinates are weak or strong, presidential authority needs to be asserted. Weak subordinates will only shift the onus of making and enforcing hard decisions back onto the president; strong subordinates need even more to be under presidential control.

The Mirage of Bureaucratic Consensus. Chairman Mao used to write long essays on the issue of how to handle "contradictions." But it is not only Marxist-Leninists who are forced to confront the dialectics of policy conflict. Contradictions will always exist in an administration, given the big-tent diversity of American political parties, the exuberance of campaign promises, the institutional interests of different parts of the government, congressional and media pressures, interest groups, and so on. Another dimension of the imperative of presidential engagement is to face up to this. Yet many of our recent presidents seem to have yearned for their subordinates to resolve as many conflicts as possible before presenting the remaining differences to the president to resolve. To a certain degree, this is inevitable and desirable. A president cannot possibly be immersed in every issue without risking total exhaustion, and subordinates owe it to the boss to save him for the toughest and most important decisions. That is what any decision-making process should aim to do. But if there is no consensus on an important issue, pushing the departments and agencies to negotiate a compromise outcome can be an abdication.

For Richard Nixon, being presented with the real choices was the key to his authority and the raison d'être of his policy-making procedures. Shaping the national strategy was, in his view, his job. Other chief executives of the recent past, however, seem to have identified good governance with the fostering of bureaucratic consensus, as a matter of principle. This, too, is the wrong model. On key issues of policy, the president ought to be made aware of the options and the arguments, pro and con. Then it is up to him (or her) to decide; there is no compelling reason for a president to shun this duty within the limits of time and physical capacity. Bureaucratic consensus is often purchased at a high cost in terms of policy sharpness or coherence; bold ideas usually won't survive, and the results may well be anemic compromises. On the other hand, when the president has settled the basic issues—strategy, objectives, and policy direction—it makes sense to delegate to subordinates (say, the Principals Committee) to work out by consensus the program of steps to implement what the president has decided. This the president can be informed of, and bless, but that can be where the line is drawn between what needs to be decided at the very top and what can be delegated to others.

More serious risks can come from a president's trying to split the difference between sharply opposing positions. On many issues of domestic policy, and even in formulating U.S. positions in a prolonged negotiation, seeking compromise by splitting the difference can be a convenient method of buying bureaucratic peace. This is far from ideal, but probably the foreign government we are negotiating with is formulating policy in the same clumsy way. This can work sometimes, but as Reagan found in Lebanon, there will be cases—most importantly in the management of a crisis—where the price paid in policy incoherence is too high. These are times when splitting the difference is a false option and a president may have to choose between positions that are not reconcilable.

Often a president just has to overrule somebody (or everybody), even if it is unpleasant. A president will be judged by the efficacy of his policies, not by the smoothness of his bureaucratic procedures—by whether American policies have shaped world events according to American purposes, not by whether there is perfect morale inside the government. Boldness and coherence tend not to emerge from bureaucratic compromises; they are what a president is required to supply.

End Runs. When there is no bureaucratic consensus, and the process is deadlocked, the process becomes especially susceptible to end runs. Our judicial system is allergic to what lawyers call ex parte communications—roughly translated as contacts with a judge on behalf of one party, either without the knowledge of the opposing party or without giving the opposing party the opportunity to answer. The bureaucratic equivalent is an end run by one cabinet secretary into the Oval Office to try to get the president's approval of something behind the back of a cabinet rival who disagrees. Most White House national security advisers see it as their job to head off such maneuvers. As we have seen, victories won by end runs can be notoriously short-lived—in part because their legitimacy is usually not accepted by others.

The principle against ex parte communication is a valid one. The Eisenhower precept cited in the last chapter—the value of hearing one's advisers debate together in person—has considerable merit. Problems arise, however, if one attempts to apply the edict against ex parte communication too literally. Private time with the president is, in fact, essential for a cabinet secretary as a means of getting authoritative guidance and insuring harmony with the president's views. Secretaries of state and defense, even intelligence chiefs, should have such opportunities. Whether it's Henry Kissinger with Gerald Ford, or Colin Powell with George W. Bush, it's a good thing. Meanwhile the national security adviser and NSC staffers, for their part, are having conversations with individual colleagues in the bureaucracy every hour of the day. If the principle were taken to an extreme, every meeting would have to be a mass meeting and every phone call a conference call. The proper standard, rather, is to achieve a reasonable transparency in these separate dealings so that departments know the state of play in any deliberation and always have a fair chance to make their case. But this standard exists, it is worth pointing out, not merely for the edification of the cabinet departments but for the benefit of the president. As Eisenhower's precept implies, it is a way to insure that the president knows every argument, and its counterargument, before making a decision.

Leaks and How to Read Them. Unauthorized and/or tendentious disclosures to the media, as we have seen, are a favorite instrument of bureaucratic warfare. In a country with a First Amendment and no Official Secrets Act, they are here to stay. But all presidents deplore them. Walt Rostow, Lyndon Johnson's national security adviser, delicately described the sense of betrayal that a president can feel, which in LBJ's case often led to volcanic eruptions of temper:

> Presidents assume that their task is not easy and that a good deal of frustration is to be expected from the American political process and an intractable and volatile world. But leaks to the press from their own subordinates, usually inaccurate but complicating inherently difficult business, appear one more burden than their oath of office really required.

There is an art to reading leaks in the press. Even those inside the government—perhaps especially those inside the government—read these leaks avidly, not so much to learn new substantive information as to monitor the course of the bureaucratic wars being waged by extra-bureaucratic means. For the outsider, it is usually more difficult to tell who is winning, or even to understand what kind of blow is being struck. Often the most interesting part of the story—the leaker's real motive—is not being told. The careful reader will need to ask: If one part of the government is criticizing another, is there a larger bureau-cratic battle of which this story is a part? What seems to be the leaker's purpose? What seems to be the other side of the story, which so frus-trates the leaker, and which the journalist may not always give a voice to? There is always more than one side to the debate. The reader should also be wary of leaks complaining about improper procedures—more often than not, the story is really that the leaking side got overruled and is now trying to mobilize pressures to get a decision reversed, or slowed down in implementation. The aggrieved party would probably have had no problem with irregular procedures if the decision had gone the other way (as in the North Korea example in the previous chapter).

This brings us back to our topic, which is the Oval Office perspec-tive. A leak in the morning papers can be a source of important intelli-gence for a president about his own government: Who is playing by the rules and who is not? Who is stirring up pressure against the White House? If the leak is from one department against another, what are its implications for the president? Aside from the embarrassment of having dirty interagency linen aired in public, it could also be an instance of what Gerald Ford spoke about to Kissinger—a rebellion against the president for a decision he has made, or is about to make, and an attempt to mobilize public or congressional pressures against him. Even if the president's name is not mentioned, the leak could be—or quickly become—part of a bigger controversy. The president and his White House advisers are thus likely to draw their own conclusions from leaks, which are not always those intended by those doing the leaking. Bureaucrats need to be reminded that the president is watching.

Secretary of State and National Security Adviser. On this issue of policy-making structure, I have stated my conclusions in the early chap-ters. Richard Nixon in his first term, and Jimmy Carter, were frustrated by the State Department's lack of responsiveness to presidential direc-tion in important areas of policy. Both presidents therefore relied on their national security advisers not only for advice but to attempt to wrest control over policy execution. Zbigniew Brzezinski in his memoir recommended expanding the role and power of the national security adviser for this purpose. Henry Kissinger, having become secretary of state and thereby having seen it from both perspectives, put forward a different proposition: If the president has no confidence in his secretary of state, he should replace the secretary of state with someone he has confidence in, rather than attempt to bypass the State Department by creating an alternative machinery in the White House.

The Kissinger-Brzezinski phenomenon in the 1970s began a long period of fascination with the national security adviser and the role of the NSC staff. Based on recent decades of experience, however, the best model in my view is one in which the pivotal figure in the system is a strong and loyal secretary of state. But "strong" and "loyal" have a particular meaning. They mean a secretary of state who is trusted by the president to carry out policies in harmony with the president's wishes, and who sees himself or herself as the president's agent in the department, not the spokesman of the department in the president's cabinet. It is likely to mean resisting, rather than absorbing, the views and inclinations of the career service.

John Kennedy, Richard Nixon, and Jimmy Carter paid a price for choosing a weak figure as secretary of state in the expectation that this would enhance their own dominance of the system. On the contrary, it only added to the centrifugal tendencies of the department and compounded the president's problem of a department that was unresponsive to his preferences. As presidential scholar Stephen Hess has pointed out, no president need fear being overshadowed by a cabinet officer: "Cabinet members cannot successfully compete with a President, regardless of their past standing." Bill Clinton may have chosen a weak secretary of state for another reason—to keep foreign policy on the back burner—but this, too, backfired, in that it contributed to policy weaknesses that eventually led to crises.

A crucial and difficult question arises about presidential appointments in cabinet departments below the level of secretary. McGeorge Bundy, who as we saw was fervently of the view that cabinet secretaries must be loyal agents of the president, also believed that those secretaries ought to be allowed to choose their own subordinates. Since they are accountable to the president, they should be left to choose the staffs that they feel best enable them to do their jobs. Bundy saw little value in what he ridiculed as the "oh-so-skillful insertion of a President's man into the second or third level of a department" (as Kennedy had done at State at the end of 1961).

My own view is different, for two reasons. One is that the appointments power is a major tool of presidential control that I do not believe a president can or should trade away. The dictum "personnel is policy" has too much truth in it, in my experience. Using this tool was one of

Reagan's strengths. If there are individuals whom the president values for sharing his policy philosophy, then there should be a place for some of them in the departments that are in charge of implementation of his decisions. Second, the institutional strength of the career service normally requires more than one individual at the top, no matter how forceful a personage, to provide direction to it. Kissingers are rare. A cabinet nominee ought to welcome the prospect of bringing in other outsiders to help him assert control over the operations of the department. Indeed it has been suggested that this ought to be part of the definition of presidential control. If a cabinet nominee, conversely, views presidential appointees as potential adversaries rather than allies, then a problem lurks not far beneath the surface that will erupt sooner or later between the department and the White House.

While I am arguing here for a model that rests on the foundation of a strong secretary of state, an effective national security adviser remains indispensable—to arm the president for the policy engagement that is required; to insure that the bureaucratic process provides what the president needs; to help protect presidential interests. The security adviser is the guardian of the president's independence of judgment, and is also in a position to provide a strategic overview over the whole of national security policy. The Brent Scowcroft model (especially in his second incarnation, with Bush 41) was a model not only because of Scowcroft's reputation for fairness but for his being a strong right arm for a president who had no intention of being dominated by anybody. Scowcroft had important influence under Bush—not as a substitute for a weak secretary of state but as an instrument for presidential control of a strong secretary of state.

The role of the NSC staff, similarly, is to arm the president—to monitor what is going on in the government; to generate ideas for presidential initiatives; to provide the president with the wherewithal to make decisions and conduct diplomacy. In the previous chapter I noted the peculiar practice of George W. Bush's NSC staff of crafting long papers trying to capture the state of the bureaucratic consensus; these papers were offered up at interagency meetings, presumably to be blessed as a reflection of the consensus and then forwarded to the president for his endorsement. In the Nixon administration, by contrast, the more important role of the NSC staff was to craft memoranda to the president setting forth issues, options, and pros and cons to enable the president to decide things.

Should the NSC staff never have an "operational" role? I would answer as follows. The Nixon-Kissinger model of executing all the most important policies (China, Vietnam, Soviet Union) from the White House, bypassing State, is a nonstarter in any normal conditions. Resort to it in that period was the product of exceptional circumstances; while it achieved important results, a price was paid for it. One is reminded of the television ads for high-performance automobiles, which show hair-pin turns and other death-defying maneuvers, followed by a message on the screen: "Drivers are professionals. Do not attempt yourself." In normal times the most efficient system is to treat the implementation of policy as the province of the departments and agencies that, in fact, have their hands on the instruments of execution. Policy direction then needs to be insured by other means.

But no one is in a position to dictate to a president that he or she may not use a trusted adviser for a confidential or other mission. The precedent for that is ample, stretching back over a century. Normally the principle of transparency ought to govern at the top levels of the administration, so that the use of NSC personnel becomes merely a tactical question in the framework of a well-understood policy. So long as presidents are frustrated by the performance of their departments, however—which seems to be a recurring phenomenon—the temptation will be there to rely on the trusted adviser whose office is just down the hall. Not only Nixon but Carter felt that temptation. Dean Acheson conceded this point many years ago.

A word here about the Principals Committee. This innovation has lasted through three administrations, at this writing (Bush 41, Bill Clinton, and Bush 43). We have seen that it operated differently in each case, and future presidents will want to look at it carefully and at how it would fit their needs. It should (as in Bush 41) be a way of enhancing the president's role, not substituting for it or reducing it (which is one interpretation of how it worked under Clinton). And it needs to be managed in so transparent a manner by the national security adviser that cabinet secretaries do not worry that it is a screen behind which the national security adviser is exerting influence in unpredictable ways (a problem in Bush 43). The best cure for this, again, is the confidence that the main issues will be argued out in front of the president or that the president will, in other ways, have complete knowledge of everyone's views before deciding.

Institutional Reform. The concern expressed above about the performance of cabinet departments brings us to a larger structural issue that future presidents should take hold of—the project of reforming the interagency system. Sometimes it goes by the name of "a Goldwater-Nichols Act for the interagency process." Concretely, this involves building up the capacity of, particularly, the civilian departments of the government to carry out functions—postwar stabilization and reconstruction, for example—that have in recent years been left to the Department of Defense. More broadly it would mean that departments would cede some of their turf in the name of presidential flexibility, just as our individual armed services have given up much of their parochialism in the name of joint planning and operations. The result would be that in some instances the president could give State the lead; in other instances, Defense. From a presidential perspective, the benefit is to widen the range of tools and options available, as well as improve overall performance. Reforms of this kind will require reforms in executive-legislative relations as well, since much of the inflexibility built into today's system is the result of thirty-five years of legislation rigidly controlling Executive Branch programs and limiting presidential discretion.

Reform of the State Department is a related subject. A more capable State Department would affect the equation of our discussion—strengthening the department's traditional claim to interagency leadership, clarifying the answers to many of the questions raised earlier about the proper balance of forces in the government. Various reform proposals have been put forward by bipartisan commissions and think tanks. Some would involve a radical restructuring of the department's organization; others are more modest. The hope is not only to improve State's operational performance, but also to lay claim to greater support from a Congress whose chronic underfunding of State has created a vicious circle: The deprivation of funds only weakens the department further. One of the other lessons of recent history is that strong secretaries of state who enjoy the confidence of the president have managed to restore the department to a position of leadership in the government. This does not diminish, however, the desirability of improving the department's effectiveness by internal reforms.

A broader reform agenda could also be undertaken. Most of our national security institutions in the U.S. government—as well as international organizations—are the legacy of the Cold War era and might well stand in need of revision for a new era. This applies to U.S. institutions relating to public diplomacy, for example; they have not yet responded effectively to the urgent needs of the ideological struggle against violent Islamist extremism (in part because current law is weighted toward insulating them from U.S. policy objectives instead of helping advance them). Likewise international institutions like the United Nations, World Bank, and International Monetary Fund—all created in the mid-1940s—may need significant revisions to respond adequately to the very different political and economic conditions of a new century.

Civil-Military Relations. The U.S. military, we have seen, is also a career service whose bureaucratic role can be expected to reflect institutional interests like any other. But recent years have put unusual stresses on civil-military relations. First, as writers like Thomas Ricks have pointed out, there may be a worrisome and growing cultural divide between a more liberal, permissive society and a military community that still predominantly adheres to traditional values of self-discipline and patriotism; an all-volunteer military caste could drift further toward a regrettable isolation from the society as a whole. Second, the stresses of the Afghanistan and Iraq campaigns have reopened sensitive questions about the propriety (or duty, as some believe) of military personnel speaking out against national policies. A small number of retired generals, for example, called out publicly for the firing of Donald Rumsfeld in the spring of 2006—some with the implication of prompting their colleagues still on active duty to stand up more boldly against policy decisions they considered unwise. Both these problems raise profound issues that may loom larger in the years ahead, whichever party is in office.

Personalities. A final word about personalities. A president, staffing an administration, needs to look at more than paper qualifications. It is remarkable that John Kennedy picked Dean Rusk as secretary of state without knowing him. So much depends on personalities—the energy level of the cabinet officer; the compatibility of cabinet officer and president; the degree to which presidents have confidence in their subordinates' personal and policy loyalty. The tension between James Schlesinger and Gerald Ford was considerably exacerbated by personal styles. The president's dilemma is that so little can be predicted. On the face of it, from congressional experience and intellectual mastery of the subject matter, Les Aspin should have been a great secretary of defense.

A president always has the option of firing someone who turns out to be ineffective or disloyal. Richard Nixon and Ronald Reagan, however, were personally reluctant to fire people. Gerald Ford was less so, but he found out how risky it can be. Interestingly, prime ministers seem to have more flexibility to reshuffle their cabinets; it is accepted as a regular practice, and it gives prime ministers a mechanism both to weed out poor performers and to strengthen their own political dominance. (Of course, the civil service is there as a cushion when reshuffles take place at the top of departments.) But presidents, who put a whole new administration in place when they arrive, are not expected to be doing too much of this; it looks like sloppiness if they do. Ford thought he was straightening things out in his administration by a grand reshuffle; it went badly. As a result, most presidents endure silently for long periods before pulling the plug, if they do so at all. But a price is paid.

Presidents who enter office with a background in foreign policy will have the most options in selecting their cabinet. They need not be afraid of choosing strong personalities, either as White House adviser or cabinet secretary. As we have seen, they only benefit from it. Nixon (with Kissinger) and Bush 41 (with Baker and Scowcroft) are in this category; their own unusual experience and extensive exposure to the subject matter insured their self-confidence and their leadership, and their key subordinates were attuned to their desires. Ford, too, was unafraid to be surrounded by strong figures in his cabinet; he was undone by larger political forces beyond his control.

But a president who is less a master of foreign policy when coming into office, or who chooses not to engage systematically, can count on having difficulties. The system will then be inherently vulnerable to many of the problems we have traced in this book. Choosing weak cabinet secretaries, or secretaries who become spokesmen for their institutions, is in this circumstance likely to foster inertia and unresponsiveness. This was Jimmy Carter's and Bill Clinton's problem. Ronald Reagan had a stronger cabinet, and he imposed his will on matters he cared about, such as the competition with the Soviet Union. But on issues like Lebanon he remained aloof and tolerated debilitating conflicts in the government. A president who chooses—for whatever reason—not to sustain a dominant role in policy formulation would, on balance, as I have argued, be better off with strong cabinet officers. But such a president would also need to exercise special care in choosing cabinet officers who can be counted on to hew faithfully to presidential desires. (National security advisers in that environment would have their work cut out for them.)

Thus, the decisive factor in how national security policy-making works is not what kind of procedure, or what kind of structure, but what kind of people. And the American system depends to a breathtaking degree on the qualities of the one person in charge. The growth of a national security bureaucracy, and of coordinating mechanisms like the NSC system, was meant to help the president. That they have done, but they have also created a new dimension of challenges; the large modern machinery of government may be harder than ever to control. For those who care about national security policy, therefore, the key question turns out to be: not what we should look for in a policy-making process, but what we should look for in a president.

ACKNOWLEDGMENTS

For the opportunity to write this book I owe a special debt to Strobe Talbott and the Trustees of the Brookings Institution, who invited me to join them on my departure from government service in 2007. Strobe and I disagree often on issues of public policy, but his loyal friendship over three and a half decades has reflected a graciousness and warmth of spirit that are tragically rare in Washington and therefore particularly precious. My new colleagues at Brookings have reflected a similar spirit.

For financial support at Brookings I am very much indebted, first, to the Stephen and Barbara Friedman Endowed Fellowship. The Smith Richardson Foundation stepped in with a specific grant in support of this project: My special thanks go to Dr. Marin Strmecki, Senior Vice President and Director of Programs, whose advice and support have meant so much in the past. Significant additional support for my other work at Brookings is coming from the Starr Foundation, under the able chairmanship of Maurice R. (Hank) Greenberg, for which I am deeply grateful.

A number of individuals took upon themselves the burden of reading the entire manuscript and offering advice. These include Strobe Talbott, Henry Kissinger, Stephen Hess, and Aaron Friedberg. They also include William G. Hyland, a dear friend and former colleague who tragically passed away in 2008 but left me his characteristic legacy of pungent as well as wise comments on the text, which took on a special poignancy (and persuasiveness) after his loss. A number of other colleagues read portions of the text, including James Cannon, Robert Hormats, Nicholas Rostow, John O'Sullivan, Douglas Feith, and William Luti. I benefited also from numerous conversations with a variety of individuals in sensitive positions in several administrations whose candor to me in private should not have to come at the risk of any personal embarrassment to them. Therefore I have chosen not to list them by name. And much of the content of this book comes, of course, from my own observation.

Heather Messera was an exceptionally talented senior research assistant. Intrepid in exploring, discovering, and organizing material, as well as offering good editorial judgment, Heather also—being young—was able to assure that my labors did not evaporate into the computer ether when I pushed a wrong button. A truly indispensable service.

My editor at Alfred A. Knopf, the brilliant Andrew Miller, was a constant source of astute and fair-minded advice on substantive content as well as presentation. It was a pleasure to talk over the issues with him and to work with him. To my agent, Andrew Wylie, the best in the business, I owe a special debt for the birth of this project. Having seen many negotiators at work, I was duly awed by the opportunity to see him in action.

The special friendship of Henry and Nancy Kissinger, which stretches back over four decades, now goes far deeper than what I can adequately describe here or anywhere else. I touch briefly upon some of my debt to Henry in the Author's Note, but I cannot omit to repeat it here.

My wife, Véronique, to whom this book is dedicated, also read portions of the manuscript. Never shy in her thoughts, she was an incisive and unfailing source of good advice. I am grateful to her for that, and needless to say, much, much more.

The usual disclaimer must be repeated here. The opinions and conclusions in this book are not the responsibility of any of the aforementioned (or anonymous) individuals or institutions but are solely mine.

NOTES

Presidential speeches, news conferences, and other documents are readily available in several official compilations. The same is true of most statements by secretaries of state. I have done my best to identify such source documents by date and title to aid the reader.

AUTHOR'S NOTE

xi Others have written excellent accounts: See especially David J. Rothkopf, *Running the World: The Inside Story of the National Security Council and the Architects of American Power* (New York: Public Affairs, 2005); the many products of Ivo H. Daalder and I. M. Destler's National Security Council Project, sponsored by the Center for International and Security Studies at Maryland and the Brookings Institution, including a forthcoming book entitled *In the Shadow of the Oval Office* (New York: Simon & Schuster, 2009); Amy B. Zegart, *Flawed by Design: The Evolution of the CIA, JCS, and NSC* (Stanford: Stanford University Press, 1999); and Karl F. Inderfurth and Loch K. Johnson, *Fateful Decisions: Inside the National Security Council* (New York: Oxford University Press, 2004).

CHAPTER ONE: BUREAUCRACY, DEMOCRACY, AND LEGITIMACY

3 The story is apocryphal, but it well captures: See the number of episodes that approximate it in Doris Kearns Goodwin, *Team of Rivals: The Political Genius of Abraham Lincoln* (New York: Simon & Schuster, 2005), e.g., pp. 288–89, 464, 482, 669.

4 "Rather, it created": Richard E. Neustadt, *Presidential Power: The Politics of Leadership* (New York: John Wiley & Sons, 1960), p. 33.

5 "'He'll sit here'": Ibid., pp. 9–10 (emphasis in original).

5 felt compelled to go out of his way to debunk the notion of the "imperial presidency": Richard E. Neustadt, *Presidential Power: The Politics of Leadership from FDR to Carter*, rev. ed. (New York: John Wiley & Sons, 1980), pp. 279–80n.46.

5 As late as 1990 . . . Neustadt was still preoccupied: Richard E. Neustadt, *Presidential Power and the Modern Presidents: The Politics of Leadership from Roosevelt to Reagan*, rev. ed. (New York: Free Press, 1990), p. ix.

6 The president's authority over the civilian establishment: Harvey C. Mansfield, "Reorganizing the Federal Executive Branch: The Limits of Institutionalization," *Law and Contemporary Problems*, vol. 35, no. 3 (Summer 1970), p. 462.

6 The renowned constitutional scholar: Edward S. Corwin, *The President: Office and Powers, 1787–1957*, 4th rev. ed. (New York: New York University Press, 1957), p. 3ff.

6 "nearly complete fusion": Walter Bagehot, *The English Constitution* (Introduction by R. H. S. Crossman) (London: Collins/Fontana Library, 1963), p. 65.

6 the theory of the cabinet's collective responsibility: Ibid., pp. 21–22 (Crossman), 67–69 (Bagehot).

6 many would argue that prime ministerial government: Ibid., pp. 51–53 (Crossman).

6 When Winston Churchill assumed office: John Lukacs, *Five Days in London: May 1940* (New Haven: Yale University Press, 1999).

6 John Quincy Adams: Sen. William Pitt Fessenden (Republican of Maine) told Gideon Welles, Lincoln's secretary of the navy, in 1862, that he had heard Adams discuss the episode on the floor of the House. Gideon Welles, *Diary*, Vol. 1 (Boston: Houghton Mifflin, 1911), p. 197. See also Goodwin, *Team of Rivals*, p. 491.

7 he adamantly refused to consider: Robert V. Remini, *John Quincy Adams* (New York: Times Books, 2002), pp. 76–77, 101, 110.

7 Reagan and Ford permitted: Ronald Reagan, *An American Life* (New York: Pocket, 1990), pp. 215–16; Michael K. Deaver with Mickey Herskowitz, *Behind the Scenes* (New York: William Morrow, 1987), pp. 92–96; Walter Isaacson, *Kissinger: A Biography* (New York: Simon & Schuster, 1992), pp. 717–20.

8 three thousand so-called political appointments: This is the current number used by Paul C. Light of New York University, the foremost expert on the federal bureaucracy. It includes about seven hundred to nine hundred Senate-confirmed senior officials, six hundred to eight hundred members of the Senior Executive Service subject to noncompetitive appointment, and 1,600–1,800 "Schedule C" or "political" appointments exempted from the competitive service because of confidential or policy-determining duties. It excludes ambassadors, U.S. marshals and U.S. attorneys, advisory boards and commissions, and a variety of less central positions that, if included, would double or triple the total number. Communications to the author from Paul C. Light, May 9 and October 5, 2007.

9 two television series produced by the BBC: See, in book form, Jonathan Lynn and Antony Jay, *The Complete Yes Minister: Diaries of a Cabinet Minister, by the Right Hon. James Hacker MP* (London: BBC Books, 1989); and Jonathan Lynn and Antony Jay, *The Complete Yes Prime Minister: The Diaries of the Right Hon. James Hacker* (London: BBC Books, 1989).

9 "He'll be house-trained": Lynn and Jay, *Yes Minister*, p. 21.

9 "The PM must realize": Lynn and Jay, *Yes Prime Minister*, p. 165.

10 the "generalist" tradition of rotating civil servants: Eugene B. McGregor, Jr., "Politics and the Career Mobility of Bureaucrats," *American Political Science Review*, vol. 68 (March 1974), pp. 18–26.

10 "We only see them": Ehrlichman quoted in Richard P. Nathan, *The Plot That Failed: Nixon and the Administrative Presidency* (New York: John Wiley & Sons, 1975), p. 40.

10 "bubble up" from lower levels: Zbigniew Brzezinski and Samuel P. Huntington, *Political Power: USA/USSR* (New York: Penguin, 1977), pp. 207–8. They quote

Dean Acheson, "Thoughts About Thought in High Places," *New York Times Magazine,* October 11, 1959, p. 20ff.

10 Henry Kissinger in his memoirs: Henry Kissinger, *White House Years* (Boston: Little, Brown, 1979), p. 39.

11 a cabinet secretary has a strategic choice to make: Ibid., pp. 24–25. Kissinger cites Michel Crozier, *The Bureaucratic Phenomenon* (Chicago: University of Chicago Press, 1964), pp. 44–55, 187–98.

11 Theodore Sorensen, in a public lecture: Theodore C. Sorensen, *Decision-Making in the White House: The Olive Branch or the Arrows* (New York: Columbia University Press, 1963), p. 68.

11 Bundy . . . was more scathing: McGeorge Bundy, *The Strength of Government* (Cambridge: Harvard University Press, 1968), pp. 37–39.

12 "The members of the Cabinet": Neustadt, *Presidential Power,* 1960 ed., p. 39.

12 "A foreign policy achievement": Henry Kissinger, *Years of Upheaval* (Boston: Little, Brown, 1982), p. 434. See also Kissinger, *White House Years,* p. 30.

13 "energy in the Executive": Alexander Hamilton, "The Federalist No. 70," in *The Federalist* (Introduction by Edward Mead Earle) (New York: Modern Library, n.d.), p. 454.

13 "A President is not bound to conform": Alexander Hamilton, "The Public Conduct and Character of John Adams, Esq., President of the United States" (1800), in Henry Cabot Lodge, ed., *The Works of Alexander Hamilton,* Federal Edition, Vol. 7 (New York: G. P. Putnam's Sons, 1904).

14 Hamilton contrasted Adams: Ibid.

CHAPTER TWO: THE MODERN SETTING

15 "to advise the President": National Security Act of 1947, Public Law 253, 80th Congress (61 Stat. 495), section 101 (a).

16 a bipartisan insight shared by the Truman administration and Congress: Amy B. Zegart, *Flawed by Design: The Evolution of the CIA, JCS, and NSC* (Stanford: Stanford University Press, 1999), pp. 54–57.

16 "administrative chaos" of the Roosevelt era: Alfred D. Sander, "Truman and the National Security Council: 1945–1947," *Journal of American History,* vol. 59 (September 1972), p. 369.

16 "obtaining and collating for the use of the Cabinet": Arthur J. Marder, *From the Dreadnought to Scapa Flow: The Royal Navy in the Fisher Era, 1904–1919,* Vol. I: *The Road to War, 1904–1914* (London: Oxford University Press, 1961), pp. 341–44. On the American view of the CID, see Sen. Henry M. Jackson, ed., *The National Security Council: Jackson Subcommittee Papers on Policy-Making at the Presidential Level* (New York: Frederick A. Praeger, 1965), pp. 102–3 (testimony of Adm. Sidney Souers, May 10, 1960) and p. 247 (testimony of Don K. Price, August 17, 1961).

16 The United States, in contrast: Ernest R. May, "The Development of Political-Military Consultation in the United States," *Political Science Quarterly,* vol. 70 (June 1955), in Karl F. Inderfurth and Loch K. Johnson, *Fateful Decisions: Inside the National Security Council* (New York: Oxford University Press, 2004), pp. 8–9, 11–12; Mark M. Lowenthal, *The National Security Council: Organizational History,* Report No. 78-104 F (Library of Congress/Congressional Research Service, June 27, 1978), pp. 4–7.

16 FDR's improvisational management style: Arthur M. Schlesinger, Jr., *The Age of Roosevelt*, vol. 2: *The Coming of the New Deal* (Boston: Houghton Mifflin, 1958), pp. 520–22.

16 "You know I am a juggler": Henry M. Morgenthau, Jr., Presidential Diary, May 15, 1942, Morgenthau Papers, Franklin D. Roosevelt Library, quoted in William Doyle, *Inside the Oval Office: The White House Tapes from FDR to Clinton* (New York: Kodansha International, 1999), p. 19.

16 Secretary of State Hull was virtually excluded: Dean Acheson, *Present at the Creation: My Years in the State Department* (New York: W. W. Norton, 1969), pp. 87–88.

16 The 1942 landing in North Africa: Brig. Gen. Charles F. Brower, "The Commander-in-Chief and TORCH," lecture at the Franklin D. Roosevelt Presidential Library on the 60th anniversary of Operation Torch, November 12, 2002, at http://www.fdrlibrary.marist.edu/cbtorch.html.

17 The State-War-Navy Coordinating Committee: May, "The Development of Political-Military Consultation," p. 13.

17 had begun holding weekly meetings: Office of the Historian, Department of State, *History of the National Security Council, 1947–1997* (August 1997), p. 2 (at http://www.whitehouse.gov/nsc/text/history.html).

17 Truman . . . praised the work of the SWNCC: Harry S. Truman, *Memoirs*, vol. 2: *Years of Trial and Hope* (Garden City, N.Y.: Doubleday, 1956), p. 58.

17 Some of them became advocates of the new council: Inderfurth and Johnson, *Fateful Decisions*, pp. 17–20; Paul Y. Hammond, *Organizing for Defense: The American Military Establishment in the Twentieth Century* (Princeton: Princeton University Press, 1961), pp. 210–13; and Zegart, *Flawed by Design*, pp. 64–66.

18 Some of Truman's staff are on record as strongly suspecting: Anna Kasten Nelson, "President Truman and the Evolution of the National Security Council," *Journal of American History*, vol. 72 (September 1985), pp. 361 (citing interview with Elmer Staats) and 366 (citing interview with James B. Webb); Sander, "Truman and the National Security Council," pp. 378–79.

18 Key bureau officials alerted: Sander, "Truman and the National Security Council," pp. 378–79.

18 Truman understood fully: Truman, *Years of Trial and Hope*, p. 60.

19 At least one historian has wondered: Sander, "Truman and the National Security Council," p. 380.

19 Marshall . . . did see many of these implications: Michael J. Hogan, *A Cross of Iron: Harry S. Truman and the Origins of the National Security State, 1945–1954* (Cambridge, UK: Cambridge University Press, 1998), pp. 56–57; Nelson, "President Truman and the Evolution of the National Security Council," p. 363; Hammond, *Organizing for Defense*, p. 222; Rothkopf, *Running the World*, pp. 55–56.

19 the State Department's Policy Planning Staff: Nelson, "President Truman and the Evolution of the National Security Council," pp. 369–70.

20 "The situation we got into": Jackson, *The National Security Council*, pp. 250–51 (testimony of Don K. Price, August 17, 1961).

20 "abdicated its primacy": Ibid., p. 251.

21 At the NSC's very first meeting: Walter Millis, ed., *The Forrestal Diaries* (New York: Viking, 1951), p. 320; Nelson, "President Truman and the Evolution of the National Security Council," p. 366.

21 "I used the National Security Council": Truman, *Years of Trial and Hope*, p. 59.

21 he tended to deal with them directly: Office of the Historian, Department of State, *History of the National Security Council*, pp. 3–4.

21 When the Korean War began: James S. Lay, Jr. and Robert H. Johnson, *Organizational History of the National Security Council During the Truman and Eisenhower Administrations*, August 1960, Study Submitted to the Committee on Government Operations, United States Senate, by Its Subcommittee on National Policy Machinery, Committee Print, 86th Cong., 2nd Sess., 1960, pp. 17–18.

22 "Every President in our history": Truman, *Years of Trial and Hope*, p. 165.

22 THE BUCK STOPS HERE: Doyle, *Inside the Oval Office*, pp. 55, 351n.

22 Truman "loved to make decisions": Neustadt, *Presidential Power*, 1960 ed., pp. 172, 178.

22 "He likes things to run smoothly": "Mr. Truman After Five Years: Sizing Up His Faults and Merits," *U.S. News & World Report*, April 14, 1950, pp. 13, 14, 17; see sources collected in Doyle, *Inside the Oval Office*, pp. 60–62.

23 "I have an unhappy conviction": Acheson, *Present at the Creation*, pp. 466–68, other sources in Doyle, *Inside the Oval Office*, pp. 62–65.

23 "groupthink," or an object lesson in Peter Drucker's maxim: Irving L. Janis, *Victims of Groupthink: A Psychological Study of Foreign Policy Decisions and Fiascoes* (Boston: Houghton Mifflin, 1972), p. 60; Peter F. Drucker, *Management: Tasks, Responsibilities, Practices* (New York: Harper & Row, 1974), p. 472, quoted in Doyle, *Inside the Oval Office*, pp. 64–65.

23 Acheson had the same view: Acheson, *Present at the Creation*, p. 733.

23 In the Vietnam case fifteen years later: E.g., Leslie H. Gelb with Richard K. Betts, *The Irony of Vietnam: The System Worked* (Washington, D.C.: Brookings, 1979).

24 Truman, he jibed, "didn't know any more": Doyle, *Inside the Oval Office*, p. 82.

24 "Organization cannot make a genius": Dwight Eisenhower, *Mandate for Change: The White House Years 1953–1956* (Garden City, N.Y.: Doubleday, 1963), p. 114.

24 "Having chosen his Cabinet and staff": Richard M. Nixon, *Six Crises* (Garden City, N.Y.: Doubleday, 1962), p. 140.

24 Eisenhower institutionalized the NSC process: Office of the Historian, Department of State, *History of the National Security Council*, p. 5; Fred I. Greenstein, *The Hidden-Hand Presidency: Eisenhower as Leader* (New York: Basic Books, 1982), p. 124.

24 One pungent example: Merle Miller, *Plain Speaking: An Oral Biography of Harry S. Truman* (New York: Berkley, 1973, 1974), pp. 343–44.

25 "I said to him": Ibid., p. 344.

25 a revisionist view of Eisenhower began to appear: Murray Kempton, "The Underestimation of Dwight D. Eisenhower," *Esquire*, September 1967, p. 108ff.; Garry Wills, *Nixon Agonistes: The Crisis of the Self-Made Man* (Boston: Houghton Mifflin, 1970), esp. Part I, Chapter 6.

25 Nixon recounted among his "six crises": Nixon, *Six Crises*, pp. 73–129, 158–67.

25 "a far more complex and devious man": Ibid., p. 161.

26 "Not shackled to a one-track mind": Ibid.

26 "'Don't worry, Jim'": Eisenhower, *Mandate for Change*, p. 478. A fuller account of the episode, and of the news conference, is in Greenstein, *The Hidden-Hand Presidency*, pp. 68–70.

26 A full-blown revisionist assessment: Greenstein, *The Hidden-Hand Presidency*, pp. 5, 31, 36, 57.

27   "In fact, Eisenhower was actively in command": Office of the Historian, Department of State, *History of the National Security Council.*, p. 6.

27   "Eisenhower took personal charge": Doyle, *Inside the Oval Office*, p. 87.

27   The recently published transcript: Ibid., p. 88.

28   Allen Dulles sent a message via his station chief: Chester L. Cooper, *The Lion's Last Roar: Suez, 1956* (New York: Harper & Row, 1978), p. 181.

28   After the crisis was over, a bedridden Foster Dulles: Selwyn Lloyd, *Suez 1956: A Personal Account* (New York: Mayflower, 1978), pp. 219, 257–58; Christian Pineau, *1956 Suez* (Paris: Laffont, 1976), p. 195.

28   Eisenhower told at least two interlocutors: During the 1967 Middle East crisis, Eisenhower spoke in this vein both to Richard Nixon and to Israeli ambassador Avraham Harman. See Richard Nixon, "My Debt to Macmillan," *The Times* (London), January 28, 1987, p. 16; and author's communication in 1992 with Israeli diplomat Ephraim Evron, who was Harman's deputy chief of mission and was debriefed by Harman after his visit to Eisenhower in Gettysburg before the 1967 war. See sources collected in Peter W. Rodman, *More Precious than Peace: The Cold War and the Struggle for the Third World* (New York: Scribner's, 1994), pp. 84–86, and p. 560 nn.73–78.

29   Astute observers: I. M. Destler, Leslie H. Gelb, and Anthony Lake, *Our Own Worst Enemy: The Unmaking of American Foreign Policy* (New York: Simon & Schuster, 1984), e.g., pp. 179–85.

29   "[o]ccasionally, in the past, I think": President Kennedy, Transcript of Interview for British Television, April 19, 1961.

29   "The Eisenhower concept was": Charles Bartlett, *Chattanooga Times*, early February 1961, quoted in Bromley K. Smith, *Organizational History of the National Security Council During the Kennedy and Johnson Administrations*, monograph written for the National Security Council, September 1988, p. 15.

30   "The parochialism of experts and department heads": Sorensen, *Decision-Making in the White House*, p. 70.

30   The NSC met as a body less often: McGeorge Bundy, "The National Security Council in the 1960's," letter to Sen. Henry M. Jackson, September 4, 1961, in Jackson, *The National Security Council*, pp. 276–78.

30   "essentially a Presidential instrument": Ibid., p. 278; Office of the Historian, Department of State, *History of the National Security Council*, pp. 7–8.

30   Bundy was praised as scrupulously fair: Office of the Historian, Department of State, *History of the National Security Council*, p. 8; Inderfurth and Johnson, *Fateful Decisions*, p. 66.

31   "The first lesson was never": Arthur M. Schlesinger, Jr., *A Thousand Days: John F. Kennedy in the White House* (London: Andre Deutsch, 1965), p. 268.

31   "[T]he White House–NSC group has gradually encouraged": Memorandum for President Kennedy, "Current Organization of the White House and NSC for Dealing with International Matters," June 22, 1961, in *Foreign Relations of the United States, 1961–1963*, Vol. 8: National Security Policy (Washington: Government Printing Office, 1996), Document 31, pp. 107–8.

31   "[t]he State Department has not proved to be as effective": McGeorge Bundy, memorandum to the President in response to John McCone's report of Eisenhower criticism, mid-November 1962, quoted in Bromley Smith, *Organizational History of the National Security Council*, p. 49.

31 A "bowl of jelly": Theodore C. Sorensen, "The President and the Secretary of State," *Foreign Affairs,* vol. 66, no. 2 (Winter 1987–1988).

31 "blood transfusion [at State]": Schlesinger, *A Thousand Days,* pp. 390, 395.

32 "sit quietly by, with his Buddha-like face": Ibid., pp. 384–86.

32 Rusk answered back: Dean Rusk with Richard Rusk and Daniel S. Papp, *As I Saw It* (New York: W. W. Norton, 1990), p. 520.

32 decisions on naval and aircraft movements: Bromley Smith, *Organizational History of the National Security Council,* p. 37.

32 "More than anything else, the Sit[uation] Room": Office of the Historian, Department of State, *History of the National Security Council,* p. 7.

33 But Bundy successfully argued against: Bromley Smith, *Organizational History of the National Security Council,* pp. 45–48.

33 "secrecy and despatch": Alexander Hamilton, "The Federalist No. 70," in *The Federalist* (Introduction by Edward Mead Earle) (New York: Modern Library, n.d.), p. 455.

34 The full extent of the compromise arrangement: For a full summary, see Jim Hershberg, "Anatomy of a Controversy: Anatoly F. Dobrynin's Meeting with Robert F. Kennedy, Saturday, 27 October 1962," Cold War International History Project (CWIHP), *Bulletin,* no. 5 (Spring 1995), pp. 75–80. See also Dobrynin's memoir, *In Confidence: Moscow's Ambassador to America's Six Cold War Presidents* (New York: Times Books, 1995), pp. 87–88. On Sorensen's admission, see Bruce J. Allyn, James G. Blight, and David A. Welch, eds., *Back to the Brink: Proceedings of the Moscow Conference on the Cuban Missile Crisis, January 27–28, 1989* (Lanham, Md.: University Press of America, 1992), pp. 92–93; and John Lewis Gaddis, *We Now Know: Rethinking Cold War History* (Oxford: Clarendon Press, 1997), pp. 271, 381n.65.

34 "Adlai wanted a Munich": The quote about Stevenson came from an unnamed official to two journalists known to be close to the president. See Stewart Alsop and Charles Bartlett, "In Time of Crisis," *Saturday Evening Post,* vol. 235, no. 44 (December 8, 1962).

34 As Walt Rostow has described it: W. W. Rostow, *The Diffusion of Power: An Essay in Recent History* (New York: Macmillan, 1972), p. 358.

35 Johnson convened some 160 Tuesday lunches: Bromley Smith, *Organizational History of the National Security Council,* p. 63; Office of the Historian, Department of State, *History of the National Security Council,* p. 9. See also Henry F. Graff, *The Tuesday Cabinet: Deliberation and Decision on Peace and War Under Lyndon B. Johnson* (Englewood Cliffs, N.J.: Prentice Hall, 1970).

35 "rather conventional and orderly": Rostow, *The Diffusion of Power,* pp. 359–60.

35 In March 1966, a presidential directive: On the SIG/IRG system, see Office of the Historian, Department of State, *Foreign Relations of the United States, 1964–1968 (FRUS),* Vol. 33, Organization and Management of U.S. Foreign Policy; United Nations.

CHAPTER THREE: RICHARD NIXON

36 "Influence of State Department establishment": Henry Kissinger, *White House Years* (Boston: Little, Brown, 1979), p. 43.

37 "Washington is a city run primarily by Democrats": Richard Nixon, *RN: The Memoirs of Richard Nixon* (New York: Grosset & Dunlap, 1978), pp. 352, 355–56.

37 In a campaign radio address: Richard Nixon, address on CBS Radio Network, October 24, 1968, in *Nixon Speaks Out: Major Speeches and Statements by Richard M. Nixon in the Presidential Campaign of 1968* (New York: Nixon-Agnew Campaign Committee, October 1968), pp. 242–43.

37 "When Eisenhower selected Foster Dulles": Nixon, *RN*, p. 340. See also Stephen Hess, *Organizing the Presidency* (Washington, D.C.: Brookings, 1976), pp. 113–14.

38 In 1961 . . . Senator Henry Jackson's national security subcommittee: Sen. Henry M. Jackson, ed., *The National Security Council: Jackson Subcommittee Papers on Policy-Making at the Presidential Level* (New York: Frederick A. Praeger, 1965), pp. 5, 30, 39.

38 Goodpaster took Kissinger along: Kissinger, *White House Years*, pp. 42–46.

38 Goodpaster later recalled: Goodpaster quoted by David J. Rothkopf, *Running the World: The Inside Story of the National Security Council and the Architects of American Power* (New York: Public Affairs, 2005), p. 115.

39 The Kissinger memorandum: Memorandum from the President's Assistant for National Security Affairs-Designate (Kissinger) to President-Elect Nixon, "Proposal for a New National Security Council System" (Tab A of Document 1: "Memorandum on a New NSC System," December 27, 1968) in Office of the Historian, Department of State, *Foreign Relations of the United States (FRUS)*, *1969–1976*, Vol. 2: Organization and Management of U.S. Foreign Policy, *1969–1972*, pp. 1–10. On the drafting of the memorandum, see Morton H. Halperin, "The 1969 NSC System," unpublished paper drafted for the Commission on the Organization of the Government for the Conduct of Foreign Policy (the Murphy Commission), 1974.

39 An innocuous-sounding but very pregnant "note": Kissinger Memorandum to President-Elect, December 27, 1968, in *FRUS, 1969–1976*, Vol. 2, pp. 4–5.

39 The distinguished senior diplomat: U. Alexis Johnson with Jef Olivarius McAllister, *The Right Hand of Power* (New York: Prentice Hall, 1984), pp. 513–14, cited in *FRUS, 1969–1976*, Vol. 2, Editorial Note, pp. 10–11.

40 other NSC subcommittees to be set up: The best account is Chester A. Crocker, "The Nixon-Kissinger National Security Council System, 1969–1972: A Study in Foreign Policy Management," published by the Murphy Commission (June 1975), Vol. 6, Appendix O, pp. 79–99.

40 "I do not believe that Presidential leadership": Richard Nixon, *U.S. Foreign Policy for the 1970's: A New Strategy for Peace,* a report to the Congress (The White House, February 18, 1970), Part I: The National Security Council System, p. 22.

41 "*coup d'état* at the Hotel Pierre": This is the title of Chapter 2 of Roger Morris, *Uncertain Greatness* (New York: Harper & Row, 1977).

41 "important less in terms": Kissinger, *White House Years*, pp. 44, 47.

41 Morton Halperin stresses that it worked that way: Halperin, "The 1969 NSC System," pp. 25, 29.

42 the record of an early meeting of the new NSC Review Group: R. J. Smith, Deputy Director for Intelligence, CIA, "Memorandum for the Record: NSC Review Group Meeting on 13 February," February 13, 1969, in *FRUS, 1969–1976*, Vol. 2, Document 27, pp. 64–65 (paragraph numbers omitted).

43 Nixon never claimed in his campaign: William Safire, *Before the Fall: An Inside View of the Pre-Watergate White House* (Garden City, N.Y.: Doubleday, 1975), p. 48.

43 Kissinger used the term "linkage": Excerpts from the Kissinger background briefing can be found in *FRUS, 1969–1976*, Vol. 1: Foundations of Foreign Policy, 1969–1972, Document 11: Editorial Note.

43 Nixon sent a letter: This discussion of "linkage" draws on Nixon, *RN*, p. 346, and Kissinger, *White House Years*, pp. 128–36.

44 In January 1969, an article written: Henry A. Kissinger, "The Viet Nam Negotiations," *Foreign Affairs* (January 1969), pp. 211–34.

45 Kissinger complained bitterly: Kissinger comments to Haldeman, March 9 and 10, 1969, in H. R. Haldeman, *The Haldeman Diaries: Inside the Nixon White House* (New York: Berkley, 1995), pp. 47–48.

45 The State Department quickly leaked: Kissinger, *White House Years*, pp. 157 and 1478n.18.

46 "Tactics turn into strategy": Kissinger comment to H. R. Haldeman, September 20, 1970, in Haldeman, *Diaries*, p. 234.

46 Kissinger called Attorney General John Mitchell: Editorial Note, in *FRUS, 1969–1976*, Vol. 2: Document 50, pp. 109–11, 115–16.

46 Kissinger met on a Saturday morning with Mitchell: Memorandum from the President's Military Assistant [sic] (Haig) to the President's Assistant for National Security Affairs (Kissinger), "Items to Discuss with the Attorney General, 2:30 p.m., Saturday, July 12, 1969," Document 63, July 12, 1969, in *FRUS, 1969–1976*, Vol. 2, pp. 135–39.

46 Nixon . . . issued a more formal directive: Telegram from President Nixon to Secretary of State Rogers, Secretary of Defense Laird, and Director of Central Intelligence Helms, Document 70, September 1, 1969, in *FRUS, 1969–1976*, Vol. 2, p. 151.

46 NSC staffers later discovered: Memorandum from W. Anthony Lake of the National Security Council Staff to the President's Assistant for National Security Affairs (Kissinger), "Relations with the State Department," November 14, 1969, Document 86, Attachment A: "The Problem and Its Consequences," in *FRUS, 1969–1976*, Vol. 2, pp. 184, 186.

47 leading Nixon to muse in a philosophical vein: Haldeman, *Diaries*, entries for October 9, 11, 13, 15, 27, 1969, pp. 116–20, 123–24.

47 Fifty foreign service officers and two hundred other officials: David E. Rosenbaum, "50 in State Dept. Chided on Letter," *New York Times*, May 21, 1970. The two hundred others included officials from the Agency for International Development and the Arms Control and Disarmament Agency, which were divisions of State.

47 Periodically, Kissinger's staff would pull together: E.g., Memorandum from the President's Military Assistant [sic] (Haig) to the President's Assistant for National Security Affairs (Kissinger), "Continuing Problems with State Department," Document 85, October 29, 1969, in *FRUS, 1969–1976*, Vol. 2, pp. 177–82, and a similar memo from Haig, Document 96, February 21, 1970, in ibid., pp. 213–16.

47 Losing Kissinger would be a "major loss": Haldeman, *Diaries* (Multimedia Edition), entry for September 26, 1970, quoted in Editorial Note, *FRUS, 1969–1976*, Vol. 2, p. 271. See also Haldeman, *Diaries*, entry for March 3, 1971, p. 306.

48 Nixon repeated his instruction to Haldeman: Haldeman, *Diaries*, entry for December 3, 1970, p. 256; Editorial Note, Document 129, in *FRUS, 1969–1976*,

Vol. 2, pp. 277–78, quoting the Multimedia Edition of Haldeman, *Diaries,* and other sources.

48　Nixon later became fond of quoting British statesman William Gladstone: E.g., Richard Nixon, *Leaders* (New York: Warner, 1982), pp. 334–35.

49　Elder statesman Dean Acheson commented: Dean Acheson, "The Eclipse of the State Department," *Foreign Affairs* (July 1971), p. 605.

50　Nixon . . . told Dobrynin he wanted this special channel: Kissinger, *White House Years*, p. 141; Nixon, *RN*, p. 369; Anatoly Dobrynin, *In Confidence: Moscow's Ambassador to America's Six Cold War Presidents (1962–1986)* (New York: Times Books, 1995), p. 199.

50　Nixon sent Kissinger to see Dobrynin: Kissinger, *White House Years*, p. 264.

50　Kissinger warned Dobrynin that Vietnam could become a major obstacle: Nixon, *RN*, p. 391; Kissinger, *White House Years*, pp. 267–68.

51　"Gromyko became very angry": Dobrynin, *In Confidence*, pp. 205–6.

51　A formal negotiation had begun in early 1970: Kissinger, *White House Years*, esp. pp. 805–10, 823–33.

52　Nixon had published an article: Richard Nixon, "Asia After Viet Nam," *Foreign Affairs* (October 1967).

52　one of the first of the new National Security Study Memorandums: Kissinger, *White House Years*, pp. 169–70, 178.

53　delegations of senior State Department diplomats: Ibid., pp. 189–90.

53　"We'll kill this child before it is born": Ibid.

53　In fact there were three sets of briefing books: Winston Lord comments in Ivo H. Daalder and I. M. Destler, moderators, "The Nixon Administration National Security Council," The National Security Council Project: Oral History Roundtables (Washington, D.C.: Center for International and Security Studies at Maryland/University of Maryland, and the Brookings Institution, December 8, 1998), p. 42.

55　The American ambassador to Japan: Armin Meyer, *Assignment Tokyo* (Indianapolis: Bobbs-Merrill, 1974), pp. 133–37.

55　John Lewis Gaddis has acknowledged: John Lewis Gaddis, *The Cold War* (London: Penguin, 2007), p. 172. But see his criticisms of Nixon's allegedly "compulsive" secrecy concerning military and intelligence operations of which he disapproves. Ibid., pp. 172–76.

55　Gaddis is similarly charitable: Gaddis, *The Cold War*. He quotes Nixon's defense of secrecy in *RN*, p. 390.

55　Alexander Haig, briefed Nixon by telephone: Transcript of Nixon-Haig telephone conversation, June 13, 1971, in Editorial Note, Document 154, in *FRUS, 1969–1976*, Vol. 2, p. 323.

55　Nixon and Kissinger also had a conversation that afternoon: Transcript of Nixon-Kissinger telephone conversation, June 13, 1971, 3:09 p.m. (White House Tape WHT-5, Cassette 825, Conversation 5-59), transcribed by National Security Archive.

56　A treatment of the Nixon-Kissinger relationship: Robert Dallek, *Nixon and Kissinger: Partners in Power* (New York: HarperCollins, 2007).

57　Lyndon Johnson's decisions on the Vietnam War: Leslie H. Gelb with Richard K. Betts, *The Irony of Vietnam: The System Worked* (Washington, D.C.: Brookings, 1979).

58　Internal documents show the State Department struggling: E.g., Memorandum from the Executive Secretary of the Department of State (Theodore L. Eliot) to the Under Secretary of State (John N. Irwin),"Your Luncheon Today with Henry Kissinger," October 28, 1970, Document 127, in *FRUS, 1969–1976*, Vol. 2, p. 275.

58 Rogers would sometimes complain bitterly: E.g., Transcript of Telephone Conversation Between Secretary of State Rogers and the President's Assistant for National Security Affairs (Kissinger), September 25, 1970, and Haldeman, *Diaries*, entries for September 25, 26, and 27, 1970, Documents 123 and 124, in *FRUS, 1969–1976*, Vol. 2, pp. 267–71.

58 Haldeman had to go over to the State Department afterward: H. R. Haldeman Diary Entry, May 19, 1971, in *FRUS, 1969–1976*, Vol. 2, Document 148, pp. 310–13 (citing Multimedia Edition of Haldeman, *Diaries*).

59 the departments discovered that they could take hard-line positions: E.g., Henry Kissinger, *Years of Upheaval* (Boston: Little, Brown, 1982), p. 1017.

59 "To everyone's surprise and Nixon's immediate intense relief": Ibid., p. 422.

59 Nixon recounts in his memoirs: Nixon, *RN*, p. 339.

59 Rogers as attorney general in the Eisenhower administration: Richard M. Nixon, *Six Crises* (Garden City, N.Y.: Doubleday, 1962), passim. There is another view, held by a number of Nixon's senior aides, that Nixon felt that Rogers had condescended to him in the Eisenhower period and secretly relished subordinating Rogers now that he was president. See the views of John Ehrlichman and Elliot Richardson quoted in Walter Isaacson, *Kissinger: A Biography* (New York: Simon & Schuster, 1992), p. 196, and Kissinger, *White House Years*, p. 29.

59 "a staff man to the President on foreign policy": Editorial Note, in *FRUS, 1969–1976*, Vol. 2, Document 152, transcript of Oval Office conversation between Nixon and Haldeman, June 12, 1971, pp. 320–21.

61 Nixon mentioned to former President Eisenhower: Nixon, *RN*, p. 289.

61 "There was about him a buoyancy": Kissinger, *White House Years*, pp. 32–33.

62 Laird withdrew his formal objections: Ibid., pp. 44–45. See Memorandum from Secretary of Defense-Designate Laird to the President's Assistant for National Security Affairs-Designate (Kissinger), "Your Memorandum Dated January 3, 1969 Concerning a New NSC System," January 9, 1969, Document 6, in *FRUS, 1969–1976*, Vol. 2, pp. 22–24.

62 "all official National Security Council communications": Editorial Note, Document 16, in *FRUS, 1969–1976*, Vol. 2, p. 42.

62 intended to review, as he reported to Congress: Nixon, *U.S. Foreign Policy for the 1970's*, February 18, 1970, Part I: The National Security Council System, p. 20.

62 He signed a directive in this vein: Memorandum from President Nixon to the Chairman of the Defense Program Review Committee (Kissinger), April 2, 1970, Document 102, *FRUS, 1969–1976*, Vol. 2, p. 224.

64 Rogers and Laird were informed only a few hours before: See, e.g., Memorandum from the President's Assistant for National Security Affairs (Kissinger) to President Nixon, "Interdepartmental Meeting on Fourth Redeployment Increment from South Vietnam, 5:00 p.m., April 13," April 13, 1970, Document 228, in *FRUS, 1969–1976*, Vol. 6: Vietnam, January 1969–July 1970, p. 806; Kissinger, *White House Years*, pp. 479–81.

64 "The maneuvers of Nixon and Laird": Kissinger, *White House Years*, pp. 32–33. See also Dale Van Atta, *With Honor: Melvin Laird in War, Peace, and Politics* (Madison: University of Wisconsin Press, 2008), p. 183.

64 Nixon considered both these operations strategically necessary: Nixon, *RN*, pp. 448–50; Kissinger, *White House Years*, pp. 483–505; and the extensive documentation in *FRUS, 1969–1976*, Vol. 6, especially Documents 215–72, pp. 741–917.

65 "Nixon was determined not to stand naked": Kissinger, *White House Years*, p. 994. See also pp. 502–3.

66 Laird later regaled journalist Seymour Hersh: Seymour M. Hersh, *The Price of Power: Kissinger in the Nixon White House* (New York: Summit, 1983), pp. 207–8. See also Van Atta, *With Honor*, pp. 224, 298.

66 Laird reportedly had advance knowledge of Kissinger's secret trip: Van Atta, *With Honor*, p. 300.

66 the famous Yeoman Charles Radford: United States Congress, Senate, Committee on Armed Services, *Transmittal of Documents from the National Security Council to the Chairman of the Joint Chiefs of Staff, Hearings*, 93rd Cong., 2nd Sess., Part 1 (February 6, 1974), and Part 2 (February 20, 21, 1974); Hersh, *The Price of Power*, pp. 466–70.

67 Kissinger and Haig wanted Moorer fired: Nixon, *RN*, pp. 531–32; Kissinger, *Years of Upheaval*, pp. 806–9; Editorial Note, Document 164, in *FRUS, 1969–1976*, Vol. 2, pp. 334–38. Ehrlichman comments in Hersh, *The Price of Power*, Chapter 33, esp. p. 476.

67 Kissinger trusted Zumwalt: Kissinger, *White House Years*, pp. 722, 810.

67 Zumwalt . . . concluded that the secretive style: Elmo R. Zumwalt, Jr., *On Watch: A Memoir* (New York: Quadrangle, 1976), esp. Chapter 14.

67 Zumwalt disclosed with some satisfaction to JCS historians: Historical Division, Joint Secretariat, Joint Staff, *The Joint Chiefs of Staff and National Policy*, Vol. 10: 1969–1972, p. 9, quoted in Editorial Note, Document 159, in *FRUS, 1969–1976*, Vol. 2, p. 328.

67 "I had my own spies": Isaacson, *Kissinger*, p. 202.

67 In some cases their reporting was oral and informal: Conversation with an individual with direct knowledge.

67 Seymour Hersh's book on Kissinger: Hersh, *The Price of Power*, p. 569. See also pp. 583, 591, 597, 621, 630, 637.

68 David Packard peeked at Moorer's briefing book: Zumwalt, *On Watch*, p. 370.

68 Zumwalt also met frequently: Historical Division, Joint Secretariat, Joint Staff, *Joint Chiefs and National Policy*, in *FRUS, 1969–1976*, Vol. 2, p. 328.

68 he saw it as his mission: Ibid.

68 In Haig's recollection: Alexander M. Haig, Jr., with Charles McCarry, *Inner Circles: How America Changed the World: A Memoir* (New York: Warner, 1992), p. 245n.

69 Nixon as the "puppetmaster": William Safire, "Puppet as Prince," *Harper's*, March 1975.

69 The life of Richard Nixon: A good portrait of Nixon's many layers and contradictions is in Safire, *Before the Fall*, esp. pp. 97–106. See also Henry Kissinger, *Years of Renewal* (New York: Simon & Schuster, 1999), pp. 43–91.

70 "Nixon distrusted his own impulsiveness": Safire, *Before the Fall*, p. 112.

71 Safire observed: Ibid., p. 157.

71 While Kissinger appeared on the cover of *Time*: *Time*, February 14, 1969.

71 Nixon had given strict orders to that effect: Memorandum from the President's Assistant (Haldeman) to the Director of Communication for the Executive

Branch (Herbert G. Klein), March 24, 1969, Document 32, in *FRUS, 1969–1976*, Vol. 2, p. 77.

71 pre-summit trip by Kissinger to Moscow: Kissinger, *White House Years*, pp. 1135–37, 1148; Nixon, *RN*, pp. 587–88. The quote on Vietnam is from an Oval Office conversation between Nixon and Kissinger on April 19, 1972, in *FRUS, 1969–1972*, Vol. 39, *European Security*, p. 274.

72 In the fall of 1972 . . . Le Duc Tho: see Kissinger, *White House Years*, pp. 1347–52; Nixon, *RN*, pp. 691, 700–702.

73 Haig writes with some relief: Haig, *Inner Circles*, p. 345.

73 Some observers have been tempted to speak: E.g., Robert Dallek, "The Kissinger Presidency," *Vanity Fair*, May 2007, and Dallek, *Nixon and Kissinger*, Chapter 16.

74 a characteristically bold Nixon decision: Kissinger, *Years of Upheaval*, pp. 513–15; Haig, *Inner Circles*, p. 412.

74 An event often cited: Dallek, *Nixon and Kissinger*, p. 530.

74 But the truth about the Situation Room meeting is less dramatic: Haig, *Inner Circles*, pp. 415–16; Haig communications with the author, February 27 and April 16, 2008; Henry Kissinger, *Crisis: The Anatomy of Two Major Foreign Policy Crises* (New York: Simon & Schuster, 2003), p. 355.

75 When he wrote his memoirs: Kissinger, *Years of Upheaval*, pp. 432–46.

76 The legendary Arabist bias of the Foreign Service: Robert D. Kaplan, *The Arabists: The Romance of an American Elite* (New York: Free Press, 1993).

76 Another example was Nathaniel Davis: Henry Kissinger, *Years of Renewal* (New York: Simon & Schuster, 1999), pp. 800–809, 827; Nathaniel Davis, "The Angola Decision of 1975: A Personal Memoir," *Foreign Affairs* (Fall 1978).

77 "In the hands of a determined Secretary": Kissinger, *Years of Upheaval*, p. 442.

77 most of the pivotal players on his team: See the observations of Helmut Sonnenfeldt and Winston Lord in Daalder and Destler, "The Nixon Administration National Security Council," pp. 15, 55–56.

77 A conservative critic, Ambassador Laurence Silberman, has written: Laurence H. Silberman, "Toward Presidential Control of the State Department," *Foreign Affairs* (Spring 1979), pp. 888–89.

78 what scholar Graham Allison calls the "rational actor" model: Graham T. Allison, *Essence of Decision: Explaining the Cuban Missile Crisis* (Boston: Little, Brown, 1971).

78 the "madman theory": H. R. Haldeman with Joseph DiMona, *The Ends of Power* (New York: Times Books, 1978), p. 83 (emphasis in original).

78 an intriguing theory of the Watergate scandal: Nicholas von Hoffman, *Make-Believe Presidents: Illusions of Power from McKinley to Carter* (New York: Pantheon, 1978); Nicholas von Hoffman, "Unasked Questions" (review of Bob Woodward and Carl Bernstein, *The Final Days*), *New York Review of Books*, vol. 23, no. 10 (June 10, 1976).

79 Nixon saw all this as a long-overdue reform: Nixon, *RN*, pp. 761–69.

79 Nathan, in contrast, calls it a plan: Richard P. Nathan, *The Plot That Failed: Nixon and the Administrative Presidency* (New York: John Wiley & Sons, 1975). For a calmer assessment of the Nixon administration's restructuring plans, see Hess, *Organizing the Presidency*, Chapter 7.

79 But what this accomplished: Von Hoffman, "Unasked Questions." The number two thousand corresponds to what is today about three thousand.

79 Von Hoffman does not claim: Von Hoffman, *Make-Believe Presidents*, pp. 30–32.

80 The "super-secretaries" . . . proved unworkable: George P. Shultz and Kenneth W. Dam, *Economic Policy Beyond the Headlines*, 2nd ed. (Chicago: University of Chicago Press, 1998), pp. 169–70.

80 The CIA rejected White House efforts: Vernon A. Walters, *Silent Missions* (Garden City, N.Y.: Doubleday, 1978), Chapter 29.

80 "[t]he bureaucracy was fighting back in the way it always does": Von Hoffman, *Make-Believe Presidents*, p. 34.

80 Professor Neustadt agreed: Richard E. Neustadt, *Presidential Power and the Modern Presidents: The Politics of Leadership from Roosevelt to Reagan*, rev. ed. (New York: Free Press, 1990), pp. 203, 226.

81 bureaucracy *should* be independent: On the theory of the "representative bureaucracy," see the work of Norton E. Long and Peter Woll, cited sympathetically in Nathan, *The Plot That Failed*, pp. 89–90.

CHAPTER FOUR: GERALD FORD

82 the newsmagazines had gotten wind: Ron Nessen, *It Sure Looks Different from the Inside* (Chicago: Playboy Press, 1978), p. 156. Most sources refer to a *Newsweek* scoop, but my Brookings colleague Strobe Talbott, then a *Time* correspondent, assures me that *Time* was pursuing the story too.

82 Ford's conversation with Colby: Gerald R. Ford, *A Time to Heal: The Autobiography of Gerald R. Ford* (New York: Harper & Row and Reader's Digest Association, 1979), pp. 328–29. For Colby's account, see William Colby and Peter Forbath, *Honorable Men: My Life in the CIA* (New York: Simon & Schuster, 1978), pp. 8–11.

83 "[G]et that son-of-a-bitch in here": Stephen F. Hayes, *Cheney: The Untold Story of America's Most Powerful and Controversial Vice President* (New York: Harper-Collins, 2007), p. 97.

83 "There is no guile, no convolution": Scowcroft interview in William Doyle, *Inside the Oval Office: The White House Tapes from FDR to Clinton* (New York: Kodansha International, 1999), p. 201.

83 "immune to the modern politician's chameleon-like search": Henry Kissinger, *Years of Renewal* (New York: Simon & Schuster, 1999), p. 30.

83 "left the presidential presence without afterthoughts": Ibid. p. 25.

83 "With Ford, what one saw was what one got": Ibid.

84 "What I wanted in my Cabinet": Ford, *A Time to Heal*, pp. 131–32. On the quality of Ford's cabinet, see David S. Broder, "How Ford's Legacy Still Serves," *Washington Post*, December 28, 2006, p. A27.

84 "A President controls his Administration": Ford, *A Time to Heal*, p. 352.

84 "God, but he is good at this": Hugh Sidey, "Beyond the Facts and Figures," *Time*, February 2, 1976, p. 11, quoted in Doyle, *Inside the Oval Office*, p. 202.

84 Kissinger found that Ford was more interested than Nixon: Kissinger interview, ibid., p. 205.

85 "President Ford came into office with wonderful training": Rumsfeld interview, ibid., p. 220.

85 "extreme collegiality": Ibid., p. 206.

85 There would be no gatekeeper, no Haldeman: Richard B. Cheney, "Forming and Managing an Administration," in Kenneth W. Thompson, ed., *The Ford Presi-*

dency: Twenty-two Intimate Perspectives of Gerald R. Ford, Portraits of American Presidents/Vol. 7 (Lanham, Md.: University Press of America/The Miller Center, University of Virginia, 1988), p. 62.

85 The exigencies of office broke down this idyllic system: Robert T. Hartmann, *Palace Politics: An Inside Account of the Ford Years* (New York: McGraw-Hill, 1980), Chapter 12; James Cannon, *Time and Chance: Gerald Ford's Appointment with History* (New York: HarperCollins, 1994), pp. 356, 369.

85 Yet both Rumsfeld and his successor: John Osborne, *White House Watch: The Ford Years* (Washington, D.C.: New Republic Books, 1977), pp. xxxii–xxxiii.

85 "With Nixon, you had to try": Nessen, *It Sure Looks Different from the Inside,* p. 162.

85 he exulted to Kissinger that he had purchased: Henry Kissinger, *Years of Upheaval* (Boston: Little, Brown, 1982), p. 514. Nixon said something similar to Nelson Rockefeller. See James Cannon, *Time and Chance,* pp. 275–76.

86 Ford appreciated it: Ford, *A Time to Heal,* p. 121; James Cannon, *Time and Chance,* p. 266.

86 "It would be hard for me to overstate": Ford, *A Time to Heal,* p. 129.

86 He made a good impression on the students: Kissinger, *Years of Renewal,* p. 20.

86 Ford as vice president: John Osborne, "White House Watch," *The New Republic,* April 13, 1974, quoted in James Cannon, *Time and Chance,* p. 275. For the description of it as a "late-night, highball-lubricated *Air Force Two* interview," see Thomas M. DeFrank, *Write It When I'm Gone: Remarkable Off-the-Record Conversations with Gerald R. Ford* (New York: G. P. Putnam's Sons, 2007), p. 8.

86 Brent Scowcroft took rough notes: Scowcroft's handwritten notes of these meetings were very sketchy. The typed records now in the archives should not be treated as verbatim transcripts for any purpose. His rough notes, often difficult to read, were deciphered and fleshed out somewhat by a staffer who was familiar with the subject matter but had not been present in the room (usually me) so that they would acquire some clarity and coherence, and then were typed up to be available for reference.

87 Kissinger was such a red flag to the conservatives: Nessen, *It Sure Looks Different from the Inside,* pp. 229–31, 233–34.

87 Meanwhile, I have been told by a Democratic friend: Told to me by an individual who later served in the Carter administration. See also I. M. Destler, Leslie H. Gelb, and Anthony Lake, *Our Own Worst Enemy: The Unmaking of American Foreign Policy* (New York: Simon & Schuster, 1984), p. 23.

88 Ford shot back: "Jim's fight is not with you": Kissinger, *Years of Renewal,* pp. 181–82.

89 Various memoirs attribute this idea: Hartmann, *Palace Politics,* p. 288; Nessen, *It Sure Looks Different from the Inside,* pp. 132–33.

89 Ron Nessen reports: Nessen, *It Sure Looks Different from the Inside,* p. 133.

89 One episode . . . Tulane University: Ibid., pp. 107–9; Hartmann, *Palace Politics,* pp. 321–23; Kissinger, *Years of Renewal,* pp. 534–36.

90 As Robert Hartmann writes: Hartmann, *Palace Politics,* p. 363.

90 "Goddamn it, I don't want any more of this": Nessen, *It Sure Looks Different from the Inside,* p. 162.

90 The fact was, as Ford says: Ford, *A Time to Heal,* p. 355.

90 "But he didn't seem mad": Nessen, *It Sure Looks Different from the Inside,* p. 135.

92 cooperation with France over its nuclear weapons program: See Richard H. Ull-
man, "The Covert French Connection," *Foreign Policy*, no. 75 (Summer 1989).

92 In the indiscreet airborne interview: Osborne, *White House Watch*, pp. 219–20
(reprinting article in *The New Republic* dated November 15, 1975).

92 that Ford himself had to repair: Ford, *A Time to Heal.*, pp. 320–21.

92 Schlesinger had instructed the Joint Chiefs: Ibid., pp. 136, 322–23; Alexander M.
Haig, Jr., with Charles McCarry, *Inner Circles: How America Changed the World:
A Memoir* (New York: Warner, 1992), p. 529.

93 In addition, Ford did not even think: Ford, *A Time to Heal*, pp. 323–24; Hartmann, *Palace Politics*, p. 364.

93 Ford, the most easygoing of men: Ford, *A Time to Heal*, p. 324.

93 Robert Hartmann writes: Hartmann, *Palace Politics*, pp. 364–65.

93 Bryce Harlow, the wise counselor: Ibid., p. 360.

93 Ford decided the time was ripe: Ibid., p. 364.

94 "The only way I could feel comfortable": Ford, *A Time to Heal.*, p. 326.

94 Ford has insisted convincingly: Ibid., pp. 323–28; also Rumsfeld conversation with the author, 2006. See also Ford comments to Bob Woodward in "Ford
Disagreed with Bush About Invading Iraq," *Washington Post*, December 28,
2006.

94 Rockefeller withdrew his candidacy: Ford, *A Time to Heal*, pp. 327–28.

94 Meanwhile, George H. W. Bush: Kissinger, *Years of Renewal*, pp. 842–43; Hartmann, *Palace Politics*, p. 370.

95 Even the sympathetic John Osborne: Osborne, *White House Watch*, p. 217
(reprinting article in *The New Republic* dated November 15, 1975); Hartmann,
Palace Politics, pp. 378–79; Nessen, *It Sure Looks Different from the Inside*,
pp. 159–60.

95 Kissinger told Schlesinger in an awkward telephone conversation: Kissinger,
Years of Upheaval, p. 842.

97 One week later: The "Family Jewels" compendium, with redactions, was declassified by the CIA on June 26, 2007. See www.gwu.edu/~nsarchiv/NSAEBB/
NSAEBB222/family_jewels_full_ocr.pdf.

97 Schlesinger and Colby conferred and agreed: Colby, *Honorable Men*, p. 345.

97 they also sheepishly realized: Ibid., pp. 389–94.

97 In a phone conversation with Kissinger: Kissinger, *Years of Renewal*, pp. 312–13.

98 Ford himself had inadvertently generated the latter excitement: Colby, *Honorable Men*, p. 409.

98 Ford, in the vain hope: Ford, *A Time to Heal*, p. 266.

98 "to develop some criteria": Kissinger, *Years of Renewal*, p. 320.

99 Colby writes that he was "privately delighted": Colby, *Honorable Men*, p. 402.

99 More broadly, Colby considered: Ibid., p. 404.

99 Colby circumvented the order: Kissinger, *Years of Renewal*, pp. 322–23.

99 While the Church Committee had to admit: United States Senate, Select Committee to Study Governmental Operations with Respect to Intelligence Activities, *Alleged Assassination Plots Involving Foreign Leaders, Interim Report*, 94th
Cong., 1st Sess. (Washington, D.C.: Government Printing Office, November 20,
1975), p. 262. The section on Schneider is pp. 225–54.

100 Even Colby deplored it: Colby, *Honorable Men*, p. 433.

100 Particularly egregious in Colby's eyes: Ibid., pp. 434–35.

100 Kissinger was furious at Colby: Ibid., p. 16.

100 In his memoirs Kissinger speculates: Kissinger, *Years of Renewal*, p. 336.

100 perjury indictment of his predecessor: Ibid., p. 343; Richard Helms with William Hood, *A Look over My Shoulder: A Life in the Central Intelligence Agency* (New York: Random House, 2003), Chapters 40, 44; Colby, *Honorable Men.*, pp. 383–87.

100 Ford shared his disappointment: Kissinger, *Years of Renewal*, p. 838.

100 Ford, in turn, treats Colby more gently: Ford, *A Time to Heal*, pp. 265–68, 329.

100 "I did not share the view that intelligence": Colby, *Honorable Men*, p. 404.

101 "totally contrary to the purpose and intent of the NSC": "A Conversation with President Ford," at a 1999 session of a John F. Kennedy Institute of Politics study group, in Aaron Lobel, ed., *Presidential Judgment: Foreign Policy Decision Making in the White House* (Hollis, N.H.: Hollis Publishing, 2000), p. 80. See also DeFrank, *Write It When I'm Gone*, pp. 90–91.

101 But over time, Ford came to the conclusion: Ford, *A Time to Heal*, pp. 325–26.

101 Kissinger . . . carrying the letter still in "draft": Ibid., p. 354; Kissinger, *Years of Renewal*, pp. 839–40, 843.

102 On reflection, Kissinger came to see: Kissinger, *Years of Renewal*, p. 839.

102 Ford later told David Rothkopf: David J. Rothkopf, *Running the World: The Inside Story of the National Security Council and the Architects of American Power* (New York: Public Affairs, 2005), p. 154.

102 Scowcroft describes his role modestly: Ibid., p. 155.

103 A widely read analysis of Kissinger's NSC staff operation: John P. Leacacos, "Kissinger's Apparat," *Foreign Policy*, no. 5 (Winter 1971–1972), p. 19.

103 George P. Shultz gives Kissinger credit: George P. Shultz and Kenneth W. Dam, *Economic Policy Beyond the Headlines*, 2nd ed. (Chicago: University of Chicago Press, 1998), pp. 12, 116.

104 As economist Fred Bergsten has put it: Bergsten quoted in Ivo H. Daalder and I. M. Destler, moderators, "International Economic Policymaking and the National Security Council," The National Security Council Project: Oral History Roundtables (Washington, D.C.: Center for International and Security Studies at Maryland/University of Maryland, and the Brookings Institution, February 11, 1999), p. 38.

105 John Connally, tried to stifle it: Shultz and Dam, *Economic Policy Beyond the Headlines*, pp. 175–76.

106 Kissinger was pulled into the EPB: Roger B. Porter, *Presidential Decision Making: The Economic Policy Board* (Cambridge, U.K.: Cambridge University Press, 1980), pp. 49–55.

106 the Kremlin outsmarted the Agriculture Department: Henry Kissinger, *White House Years* (Boston: Little, Brown, 1979), pp. 1269–73.

106 The upshot was a five-year agreement: Porter, *Presidential Decision Making*, Chapter 5; the quote about Kissinger is on p. 127.

107 "We have to find a way to break the cartel": Kissinger, *Years of Renewal*, p. 669.

107 The second element of U.S. strategy was to split the Third World: Ibid., esp. Chapter 22, as well as pp. 734–36.

108 The aggressive approach was an early test of the EPB: Porter, *Presidential Decision Making*, pp. 49–54.

108 Simon called the shah of Iran a "nut": Kissinger, *Years of Renewal*, p. 670.

110 an outside group (dubbed "Team B"): See Richard Pipes, *Vixi: Memoirs of a Non-Belonger* (New Haven: Yale University Press, 2003), pp. 132–38. See also Strobe

Talbott, *The Master of the Game: Paul Nitze and the Nuclear Peace* (New York: Alfred A. Knopf, 1988), pp. 145–47.

110 A Gallup Poll in early January 1976: Ford, *A Time to Heal*, p. 347.

111 "Under Kissinger and Ford": Quoted in ibid., pp. 373–74.

111 Michael Barone describes: Michael Barone, *Our Country: The Shaping of America from Roosevelt to Reagan* (New York: Free Press, 1990), p. 552.

112 "I cannot judge whether the political impact": Ford, *A Time to Heal*, pp. 380–81.

112 As political analyst Jonathan Martin elaborates: Jonathan Martin, "The Moderates' Last Stand: Gerald Ford and the GOP," *National Review Online* (December 28, 2006).

113 "of stunning proportions": Barone, *Our Country*, p. 533.

113 "over 100 separate prohibitions and restrictions": President Ronald Reagan, "America's Foreign Policy Challenges for the 1980's," address at the Center for Strategic and International Studies, Washington, April 6, 1984.

114 The most recent complete set comprises five volumes: U.S. House of Representatives, Committee on International Relations, and U.S. Senate, Committee on Foreign Relations, *Legislation on Foreign Relations Through 2005*, Vols. 1-A and 1-B (January 2006); *Legislation on Foreign Relations Through 2000*, Vols. 2 and 3 (May 2002); *Legislation on Foreign Relations Through 1996*, Vol. 4 (December 1997); *Legislation on Foreign Relations Through 1988*, Vol. 5 (December 1989).

115 the CIA found itself "equidistant": Robert M. Gates, "CIA and the Making of American Foreign Policy," address at the Woodrow Wilson School of Public and International Affairs, Princeton University, September 29, 1987; Robert M. Gates, "The CIA and American Foreign Policy," *Foreign Affairs* (Winter 1987–1988), p. 225.

115 Cheney said a few years later: Cheney remarks in Thompson, *The Ford Presidency*, p. 64.

115 Decades later, he called the Ford period: Cheney quoted in Kenneth T. Walsh et al., "The Cheney Factor," *U.S. News & World Report*, January 23, 2006.

116 As a young member of Congress Cheney became an outspoken champion: See the contrasting views of Congress's role expressed by Cheney and Gingrich in John Charles Daly, moderator, "Revitalizing America: What Are the Possibilities?," AEI Forum 49, December 9, 1980 (Washington, D.C.: American Enterprise Institute, 1981).

116 The same conviction clearly infused his later actions as vice president: See Hayes, *Cheney*, p. 490; Walsh et al., "The Cheney Factor."

CHAPTER FIVE: JIMMY CARTER

117 Carter in his memoirs says: Jimmy Carter, *Keeping Faith: Memoirs of a President* (New York: Bantam, 1982), pp. 51, 54.

117 In an appearance as president-elect: Carter remarks, November 1976, quoted in Karl F. Inderfurth and Loch K. Johnson, eds., *Fateful Decisions: Inside the National Security Council* (New York: Oxford University Press, 2004), p. 71.

117 Toward the end of his term: Carter, Town Hall appearance, Nashville, Tennessee, October 9, 1980.

118 he came to lament the "inertia": Carter, *Keeping Faith*, pp. 53–54.

118 He later told interviewers from the *Harvard Business Review*: Interview with Jimmy Carter, *Harvard Business Review* (March/April 1988), p. 62, quoted in

William Doyle, *Inside the Oval Office: The White House Tapes from FDR to Clinton* (New York: Kodansha International, 1999), p. 234.

118 "A flaw in our foreign policy during this period": Cyrus Vance, *Hard Choices: Critical Years in America's Foreign Policy* (New York: Simon & Schuster, 1983), p. 27.

119 But there is no doubt that Carter wanted him: Carter, *Keeping Faith,* pp. 53–54.

119 Vance recognized in retrospect: Vance, *Hard Choices,* pp. 15, 35–36.

119 Brzezinski was also given some important substantive assignments: Zbigniew Brzezinski, *Power and Principle: Memoirs of the National Security Adviser, 1977–1981* (New York: Farrar, Straus & Giroux, 1983), p. 536; Brzezinski comments in "A Forum on the Role of the National Security Adviser," co-sponsored by the Woodrow Wilson International Center for Scholars and the James A. Baker III Institute for Public Policy of Rice University, in Houston, Texas, April 12, 2001, reprinted in Inderfurth and Johnson, *Fateful Decisions,* pp. 151–52.

119 State Department officials were extremely bitter: See the account in David J. Rothkopf, *Running the World: The Inside Story of the National Security Council and the Architects of American Power* (New York: Public Affairs, 2005), pp. 187–95. Cf. Brzezinski, *Power and Principle,* Chapter 6. See also Ivo H. Daalder and I. M. Destler, moderators, "China Policy and the National Security Council," The National Security Council Project: Oral History Roundtables (Washington, D.C.: Center for International and Security Studies at Maryland/University of Maryland, and the Brookings Institution, November 4, 1999), esp. pp. 11–16.

120 In an extraordinary letter to *Foreign Affairs:* Jimmy Carter, "Being There," letter to the editor, *Foreign Affairs* (November/December 1999), pp. 164–65; see also Carter, *Keeping Faith,* p. 194, and Brzezinski, *Power and Principle,* pp. 202–6.

120 In December 1978 Carter convened a meeting: Brzezinski, *Power and Principle,* p. 41; Carter, *Keeping Faith,* pp. 59–60.

121 "Carter, quite rightly in my judgment": "The Best National Security System. A Conversation with Zbigniew Brzezinski," *The Washington Quarterly* (Winter 1982), p. 75.

121 Reading between the lines of Carter's memoirs: Carter, *Keeping Faith,* pp. 53–54.

121 Brzezinski, in turn, lamented in his diary: Brzezinski, *Power and Principle,* p. 520.

122 Brzezinski does not conceal his disappointment: Ibid., pp. 23, 525.

122 A senior Carter aide has commented to me: Conversation with former senior Carter national security aide, March 30, 2007.

122 Legend had it that the president was personally managing: Doyle, *Inside the Oval Office,* pp. 227–31.

122 Richard Neustadt was told: Richard E. Neustadt, *Presidential Power: The Politics of Leadership from FDR to Carter,* rev. ed. (New York: John Wiley & Sons, 1980), p. 208.

122 Scowcroft was astounded: Brent Scowcroft, "Ford as President and His Foreign Policy," in Kenneth W. Thompson, ed., *The Ford Presidency: Twenty-two Intimate Perspectives of Gerald R. Ford* (Lanham, Md.: University Press of America/The Miller Center, University of Virginia, 1988), p. 311.

122 "anti-political attitude used to drive me nuts": Mondale quoted in Peter G. Bourne, *Jimmy Carter: A Comprehensive Biography from Plains to Postpresidency*

(New York: Scribner, 1997), p. 419, cited in Doyle, *Inside the Oval Office,* pp. 231–32.

123 "suggestive of a President more unpolitical in some respects": Neustadt, *Presidential Power,* 1980 ed., pp. 215, 276–77n.21.

123 The National Security Council met formally only ten times: Office of the Historian, Department of State, *History of the National Security Council, 1947–1997* (August 1997), p. 12.

123 "favorite meeting of the week": Carter, *Keeping Faith,* pp. 55–56.

123 Carter resisted Brzezinski's suggestion: Brzezinski, *Power and Principle,* p. 68.

123 after an embarrassing foul-up that led to the public retraction: Ibid.; Office of the Historian, Department of State, *History of the National Security Council,* p. 12.

123 a weekly Vance-Brown-Brzezinski luncheon: Brzezinski, *Power and Principle,* p. 70; Vance, *Hard Choices,* p. 39.

123 But Vance remained forever jealous: Vance, *Hard Choices,* p. 37.

123 State Department historians also note glumly: Office of the Historian, Department of State, *History of the National Security Council,* p. 12.

124 Mondale was the first vice president to be given: See the discussion in Event Summary, "The Office of the Vice Presidency," Woodrow Wilson International Center for Scholars, April 26, 2007, at http://www.wilsoncenter.org/index.cfm? fuseaction=events.print&event_id=228842.

124 A close observer has noted the parallels between: William G. Hyland, *Mortal Rivals: Superpower Relations from Nixon to Reagan* (New York: Random House, 1987), pp. 174–75.

125 Vance favored this course: Vance, *Hard Choices,* pp. 48–49.

125 Vladivostok was dismissively branded: Hyland, *Mortal Rivals,* p. 208.

125 Carter and his team instead were attracted: Ibid., pp. 208–10; Carter, *Keeping Faith,* p. 216.

125 Soon after Carter's inauguration, the State Department: Hyland, *Mortal Rivals,* pp. 204–6; Brzezinski, *Power and Principle,* pp. 155–56.

127 William Hyland, the holdover on the NSC staff: Hyland, *Mortal Rivals,* pp. 211–12.

127 *The Washington Post* called it: Editorial, "The Retreat from Moscow," *Washington Post,* April 5, 1977, p. A18.

127 " Had the Soviets moved quickly to consolidate an agreement": Hyland, *Mortal Rivals,* p. 218. See also Vance, *Hard Choices,* p. 54.

128 The Soviets and their allies seemed to be on a roll: On the Soviet geopolitical offensive, see Peter W. Rodman, *More Precious than Peace: The Cold War and the Struggle for the Third World* (New York: Scribner's 1994), esp. pp. 147–52.

129 SALT was "buried . . . in the sands of the Ogaden": Brzezinski, *Power and Principle,* p. 189.

129 His "greatest regret," he admitted a few years later: "The Best National Security System: A Conversation with Zbigniew Brzezinski," p. 79.

129 a speech on the subject at the U.S. Naval Academy: Brzezinski, *Power and Principle,* pp. 320–21; Vance, *Hard Choices,* p. 102; Carter, *Keeping Faith,* p. 229.

130 Brzezinski continued to deplore: Brzezinski, *Power and Principle,* e.g., pp. 42, 520.

130 Carter was torn: Ibid., p. 522.

130 Carter saw it as an augury: Carter, *Keeping Faith.,* pp. 433–34.

130 Carter took the shah aside: Ibid., pp. 436–37.

131 As the domestic unrest within Iran grew to engulf the shah: An excellent account of the crisis is Michael Ledeen and William Lewis, *Debacle: The American Failure in Iran* (New York: Alfred A. Knopf, 1981).

132 he found U.S. policy to be "confusing and contradictory": Mohammad Reza Pahlavi, *Answer to History* (New York: Stein & Day, 1980), pp. 164, 169; Mohammad Reza Pahlavi, "How the Americans Overthrew Me," *NOW!* (London), no. 13 (December 13–17, 1979), p. 34.

132 Henry Kissinger, visiting Iran as a private citizen: This author accompanied Kissinger to Iran.

132 the shah expounded the same theory to visiting *Time* correspondents: Author's conversation with Strobe Talbott, one of the correspondents.

132 Unfortunately the head of French intelligence: Count [Alexandre] de Marenches and David A. Andelman, *The Fourth World War: Diplomacy and Espionage in the Age of Terrorism* (New York: William Morrow, 1992), p. 178.

132 And to his dying day he believed it: Pahlavi, *Answer to History*, p. 165.

132 did not crack down ruthlessly: Vance, *Hard Choices*, p. 324.

132 Brzezinski conveyed the message to him personally: Carter, *Keeping Faith*, p. 439; Brzezinski, *Power and Principle*, p. 365.

133 Carter told Vance on November 10: Carter, *Keeping Faith.*, p. 440.

133 Brzezinski later wrote: Brzezinski, *Power and Principle*, p. 368.

133 Carter continued to reject this: Carter, *Keeping Faith.*, p. 443; Ledeen and Lewis, *Debacle*, pp. 170–71.

133 "There had already been too much violence": The shah quoted in Ledeen and Lewis, *Debacle*, p. 140.

134 "Sullivan reported [that he had told the shah]": Brzezinski, *Power and Principle*, p. 375.

134 The upshot was a complicated cable: Compare ibid., p. 375, with Vance, *Hard Choices*, p. 333.

134 Brzezinski's hope was that it would do so: Brzezinski, *Power and Principle*, pp. 379–82.

135 castigated them for disloyalty and leaking: Ibid., pp. 389–90.

135 Brzezinski thought he was annoying Carter: Ibid., pp. 393, 396–97.

136 Brzezinski argued for a time, after leaving office: Ibid., pp. 533–36.

137 The Senate Foreign Relations Committee: U.S. Senate, Committee on Foreign Relations, *The National Security Adviser: Role and Accountability*, Hearing, April 17, 1980, 96th Cong., 2nd Sess. (U.S. Government Printing Office, 1980), esp. pp. 24–25 (Scowcroft), 29–31 (Neustadt), 147–48 (Goodpaster), 148–49 (Bundy), and 149–50 (Rostow). Brzezinski, too, seems to have had second thoughts about the idea. See his comments in "A Forum on the Role of the National Security Adviser," in Inderfurth and Johnson, eds., *Fateful Decisions*, p. 156.

138 Richard Neustadt asked himself: Neustadt, *Presidential Power*, 1980 ed., pp. 208, 212–14.

138 the "dignified" elements of a constitutional system: Walter Bagehot, *The English Constitution* (Introduction by R. H. S. Crossman) (London: Collins / Fontana Library, 1963), pp. 61–62.

138 "A question troubling Congress": Vance, *Hard Choices*, p. 395.

CHAPTER SIX: RONALD REAGAN

140 "I had an agenda I wanted to get done": Lou Cannon, *President Reagan: The Role of a Lifetime* (New York: Simon & Schuster, 1991), p. 845n.2.

140 He was better suited to leading the nation": Ibid., p. 147.

140 "[T]he whole of Reagan's performance": Ibid., p. 185.

141 Published compilations of his pre-presidential speeches: E.g., Kiron K. Skinner, Annelise Anderson, and Martin Anderson, eds., *Reagan, in His Own Hand* (New York: Free Press, 2001).

141 "principled [and] confident": Douglas Brinkley, ed., *The Reagan Diaries* (New York: HarperCollins, 2007), p. xiii.

141 At the Bonn economic summit: See the Economic Declaration issued by the G-7 economic summit participants in Bonn, May 4, 1985.

141 A famous essay on intellectual history: Isaiah Berlin, *The Hedgehog and the Fox: An Essay on Tolstoy's View of History* (New York: Simon & Schuster/Clarion, 1970).

142 He made a point of never taking his coat off: Michael K. Deaver with Mickey Herskowitz, *Behind the Scenes* (New York: William Morrow, 1987), p. 143.

142 determined to focus on the "big picture": Edwin Meese III, *With Reagan: The Inside Story* (Washington, D.C.: Regnery Gateway, 1992), p. 22. See also Carnes Lord, *The Presidency and the Management of National Security* (New York: Free Press, 1988), p. 24.

142 "ruthlessly geared to preserving his energy": William Doyle, *Inside the Oval Office: The White House Tapes from FDR to Clinton* (New York: Kodansha International, 1999), p. 252.

142 He came into the Oval Office around 9:00 a.m.: Lou Cannon, *President Reagan*, pp. 144–45.

142 Both sides in the administration's internal quarrels: E.g., Lou Cannon, *President Reagan*, Chapter 10; Doyle, *Inside the Oval Office*, pp. 252–55, 265–69; Constantine C. Menges, *Inside the National Security Council: The True Story of the Making and Unmaking of Reagan's Foreign Policy* (New York: Simon & Schuster, 1988), pp. 382–88.

143 He did not usually nap during his "staff time": Lou Cannon, *President Reagan*, p. 146.

143 Donald Regan, who served as chief of staff: Regan interview in Doyle, *Inside the Oval Office*, p. 254.

143 According to William Doyle: Doyle, *Inside the Oval Office*, pp. 254–55.

143 Alexander Haig, who served both Nixon and Reagan: Haig interview in Lou Cannon, *President Reagan*, p. 151.

144 "We wanted our appointees to be the President's ambassadors": Meese, *With Regan*, p. 77.

144 The Reagan team is widely regarded: James Q. Wilson, *Bureaucracy: What Government Agencies Do and Why They Do It* (New York: Basic Books, 1989), pp. 261–62; Lord, *The Presidency and the Management of National Security*, p. 30.

145 Jimmy Carter in his time: Wilson, *Bureaucracy*, pp. 261–62.

145 Reagan welcomed their presence as a buffer: Deaver, *Behind the Scenes*, pp. 124, 128.

145 Alexander Haig . . . was surprised: Alexander M. Haig, Jr., *Caveat: Realism, Reagan, and Foreign Policy* (New York: Macmillan, 1984), pp. 80–81.

145 Richard Allen: In Ivo H. Daalder and I. M. Destler, moderators, "The Role of the National Security Advisers," The National Security Council Project: Oral History Roundtables (Washington, D.C.: Center for International and Security Studies at Maryland/University of Maryland, and the Brookings Institution, October 25, 1999), p. 3.

146 The Reagan presidency can usefully be divided: This useful construct is from Doyle, *Inside the Oval Office*, p. 264.

146 Clark's relationship with his president: Paul Kengor and Patricia Clark Doerner, *The Judge: William P. Clark, Ronald Reagan's Top Hand* (San Francisco: Ignatius Press, 2007).

146 "Nothing ever gets settled": Secretary of State George P. Shultz, "Iran and U.S. Policy," testimony before the U.S. House of Representatives, Committee on Foreign Affairs, December 8, 1986.

147 "a witches' brew of intrigue": James A. Baker III with Thomas M. DeFrank, *The Politics of Diplomacy: Revolution, War and Peace, 1989–1992* (New York: G. P. Putnam's Sons, 1995), p. 26.

148 Watergate special prosecutor Leon Jaworski: Jaworski letter introduced into the record of Haig's confirmation hearing, U.S. Congress, Senate, Committee on Foreign Relations, *Nomination of Alexander M. Haig, Jr.,* Hearings, 97th Cong., 1st Sess. (Washington, D.C.: Government Printing Office, January 1981), Part 1, p. 276. See also Theodore H. White, *Breach of Faith: The Fall of Richard Nixon* (New York: Atheneum, 1975).

148 Ford was outwardly noncommittal: James Cannon, *Time and Chance: Gerald Ford's Appointment with History* (New York: HarperCollins, 1994), p. 357.

149 Haig had also negotiated the text: Haig, *Caveat*, pp. 56–61, 74.

149 Senator Paul Tsongas: U.S. Senate, *Nomination of Alexander M. Haig, Jr.,* Part 2, p. 109.

150 In May and June 1982, for example: For Haig's account, see Haig, *Caveat*, pp. 310–14. For his critics' version, see Lou Cannon, *President Reagan*, pp. 199–205. See also Kengor and Doerner, *The Judge*, pp. 152, 180–85.

151 "Today was the day—I told Al H[aig]": Brinkley, ed., *The Reagan Diaries*, pp. 90–91.

151 Nixon's broad policies were more fully articulated: Nixon's four reports to Congress, all entitled *U.S. Foreign Policy for the 1970's*, were published on February 18, 1970; February 25, 1971; February 9, 1972; and May 3, 1973.

151 On U.S.-Soviet relations, three such directives: NSDDs 66 and 75 can be found, e.g., in Norman A. Bailey, *The Strategic Plan That Won the Cold War: National Security Decision Directive 75* (McLean, Va.: The Potomac Foundation, 1998). For NSDD 75, see also Appendix B to Robert C. McFarlane and Zofia Smardz, *Special Trust* (New York: Cadell & Davies, 1994), pp. 372–80.

152 owed much to the pen of Richard Pipes: Richard Pipes, *Vixi: Memoirs of a Non-Belonger* (New Haven: Yale University Press, 2003), pp. 188–202.

152 William Casey . . . would be in charge: See John O'Sullivan, *The President, the Pope, and the Prime Minister: Three Who Changed the World* (Washington, D.C.: Regnery, 2006), and Peter Schweizer, *Victory: The Reagan Administration's Secret Strategy That Hastened the Collapse of the Soviet Union* (New York: Atlantic Monthly Press, 1994).

153 Casey would collude with Crown Prince Fahd: Schweizer, *Victory,* esp. Chapter 8.

153 the Reagan administration perceived a Soviet vulnerability: Stephen Sestanovich, "Do the Soviets Feel Pinched by Third World Adventures?," *Washington Post*, May 20, 1984, p. B1. Sestanovich was the NSC staff's Soviet specialist
at the time of this article. See also Ronald Reagan, "Freedom, Regional Security,
and Global Peace," a White House document published on March 14, 1986, and
Peter W. Rodman, *More Precious than Peace: The Cold War and the Struggle for
the Third World* (New York: Scribner's, 1994), esp. Chapter 11.

153 The State Department opposed: Interview with Richard Pipes in Kengor and
Doerner, *The Judge*, p. 170.

153 "Is it possible," he wrote: Reagan, *An American Life*, pp. 271–73.

154 "Some of the N.S.C. staff are too hard line": Brinkley, ed., *The Reagan Diaries*,
p. 142.

154 Some liberal critics saw Reagan's policy: E.g., Raymond L. Garthoff, *The Great
Transition: American-Soviet Relations and the End of the Cold War* (Washington,
D.C.: Brookings, 1994).

154 Reagan tried to strike up a correspondence: E.g., the correspondence with
Andropov in Reagan, *An American Life*, pp. 576–82.

155 In a series of candid articles in authoritative journals: See sources collected in
Rodman, *More Precious than Peace*, Chapter 12, and also Peter W. Rodman,
"Reversal of Fortune," in Kiron K. Skinner, ed., *Turning Points in Ending the
Cold War* (Stanford: Hoover Institution Press, 2008), pp. 186–88. Some of the
discussion of Reagan in this chapter is also adapted from *More Precious than
Peace*.

155 Gorbachev explained to his party colleagues: Mikhail Gorbachev, Report to the
Plenary Meeting of the CPSU Central Committee, October 15, 1985, quoted
in *On the New Edition of the CPSU Programme* (Moscow: Novosti, 1986),
pp. 13–15; also in FBIS-SOV-85-200, October 16, 1985, pp. R3, 6.

156 George Shultz in his memoirs: George P. Shultz, *Turmoil and Triumph: My Years
as Secretary of State* (New York: Scribner's, 1993), pp. 265–66, 275–76.

156 The surprise unveiling of Reagan's Strategic Defense Initiative: McFarlane, *Special Trust*, pp. 232–33.

156 In June 1983, with Reagan's blessing: Secretary of State George P. Shultz, "U.S.-
Soviet Relations in the Context of U.S. Foreign Policy," statement to the Senate
Committee on Foreign Relations, June 15, 1983.

158 their president, who saw SDI as a goal in itself: See President Reagan's news
conference, September 17, 1985, and McFarlane, *Special Trust,* p. 234.

158 "more Catholic than the Pope": Colin L. Powell with Joseph E. Persico, *My
American Journey* (New York: Random House, 1995), p. 295.

158 Shultz strongly objected: Shultz, *Turmoil and Triumph*, pp. 578–81.

158 Reagan "thought the leak unnecessary": McFarlane, *Special Trust*, p. 317.

159 "He really disliked personal confrontation": McFarlane interview in Doyle,
Inside the Oval Office, p. 267.

159 "Bud, I know what you're describing": McFarlane interview in Daalder and
Destler, "The Role of the National Security Advisers," p. 42.

160 I was one of those seeking extensive changes: Peter Robinson, the chief draftsman of this speech, tells his account in Peter Robinson, *It's My Party: A Republican's Messy Love Affair with the GOP* (New York: Warner, 2000), pp. 13–18, and in
Peter Robinson, *How Ronald Reagan Changed My Life* (New York: Harper-
Collins, 2003), pp. 101–3.

161 "The boys at State are going to kill me": Robinson, *How Ronald Reagan Changed My Life*, p. 103.

161 thousands of young East Germans clashed with police: Serge Schmemann, "Rallying Cry of East Berliners: 'Gorbachev!,'" *New York Times*, June 10, 1987, p. A7.

161 "We didn't build this wall": Yakovlev quoted in *Tagesspiegel*, January 10, 1989, quoted in Garthoff, *The Great Transition*, p. 602.

161 a "swamp": Shultz, *Turmoil and Triumph*, p. 322.

161 sensitivity to Latin fears of the "Great Colossus": Reagan, *An American Life*, pp. 239–40.

161 It would be "lunacy": As recounted by Shultz at the time to his State Department senior staff (including me).

162 "Those sonsofbitches won't be happy": Lou Cannon, *President Reagan*, p. 337.

162 Thus, when CIA director William Casey came up with: See, e.g., Brinkley, ed., *Reagan Diaries*, pp. 52, 110, Lou Cannon, *President Reagan*, pp. 345–56.

162 standing against "the tide of history": Sen. Christopher J. Dodd, "Democratic Response to President Reagan's Address to Joint Session of Congress," April 27, 1983, News Release, p. 7.

163 This overture got nowhere: The best account of U.S. policy in Central America in this period is Robert Kagan, *A Twilight Struggle: American Power and Nicaragua, 1977–1990* (New York: Free Press, 1996). On the Enders mission, see Chapter 20.

163 "This revolution goes beyond our borders": Speech by Tomás Borge at ceremonies marking the second anniversary of the Nicaraguan revolution, July 19, 1981, in FBIS-LAM-81-139, July 21, 1981, p. P10.

163 Shultz in his memoirs repeatedly accuses Clark: Shultz, *Turmoil and Triumph*, pp. 306–22. Clark says he was "shock[ed]" by the treatment of him in Shultz's memoirs. See Kengor and Doerner, *The Judge*, p. 241.

163 Clark and his staff, in turn: Menges, *Inside the National Security Council*, p. 94.

163 "George, don't be a pilgrim": Shultz, *Turmoil and Triumph*, p. 305.

164 On her trip, one sympathetic U.S. ambassador: Menges, *Inside the National Security Council*, pp. 107–9; Lou Cannon, *President Reagan*, pp. 376–77.

164 Shultz in turn was caught by surprise in July 1983: Shultz, *Turmoil and Triumph*, pp. 310–11.

164 "[S]ince he didn't keep anybody informed": Lou Cannon, *President Reagan*, pp. 380–81.

164 At the end of the lengthy and stormy meeting: An account of the meeting can be found in Kagan, *A Twilight Struggle*, pp. 312–14, and in Rodman, *More Precious than Peace*, pp. 253–54. Strictly speaking it was a meeting of the National Security Planning Group (NSPG), a more restricted forum.

165 With McFarlane's grudging acquiescence: Compare Menges, *Inside the National Security Council*, pp. 126–27, and Shultz, *Turmoil and Triumph*, pp. 415–16.

165 As head of the State Department's Policy Planning Staff: Rodman, *More Precious than Peace*, p. 254.

165 Thomas Enders had barked to NSC staffer: Menges, *Inside the National Security Council*, pp. 105, 113.

165 A key figure in this evolution was Elliott Abrams: Kagan, *A Twilight Struggle*, pp. 419–20; Rodman, *More Precious than Peace*, pp. 410–13.

166 The Tower Board . . . published a thoughtful report: President's Special Review Board, *Report* (Washington, D.C.: Government Printing Office, February 26, 1987).

167 Bud McFarlane was called out of retirement: McFarlane, *Special Trust*, pp. 53–65.

168 a brief shaped by Representative Dick Cheney: U.S. Congress, Senate Select Committee on Secret Military Assistance to Iran and the Nicaraguan Opposition and House Select Committee to Investigate Covert Arms Transactions with Iran, *Report of the Congressional Committees Investigating the Iran-Contra Affair*, S. Rept. No. 100-216/H. Rept. No. 100-433, 100th Cong., 1st Sess. (Washington, D.C.: Government Printing Office, November 1987), Section II: The Minority Report, pp. 431–586.

168 Cheney's vigorous defense of Reagan helped propel him: Stephen F. Hayes, *Cheney: The Untold Story of America's Most Powerful and Controversial Vice President* (New York: HarperCollins, 2007), pp. 197–200.

168 The Tower Board enumerated the many "mistakes": President's Special Review Board, *Report*, p. I-2.

169 All these recommendations were adopted: Paul Schott Stevens, "The Reagan NSC: Before and After," *Perspectives*, vol. 19, no. 2 (Spring 1990), pp. 118–22. Stevens was NSC executive secretary when the reforms were made.

169 The Tower Board is often cited for its conclusion: President's Special Review Board, *Report*, p. V-4.

169 George Shultz took advantage of the opening: Carlucci quoted in Daalder and Destler, "The Role of the National Security Advisers," p. 12.

169 Cyrus Vance, a decade earlier: Zbigniew Brzezinski, *Power and Principle: Memoirs of the National Adviser, 1977–1981* (New York: Farrar, Straus & Giroux, 1983), p. 36.

170 Thus the board, after all its investigation: President's Special Review Board, *Report*, Part V.

170 The debacle occurred because of a policy failure: A good account is in David C. Martin and John Walcott, *Best Laid Plans: The Inside Story of America's War Against Terrorism* (New York: Harper & Row, 1988), pp. 87–153.

170 "no intention or expectation that U.S. Armed Forces": Letters from President Ronald Reagan to Speaker of the House Thomas P. O'Neill on the role of U.S. forces in Lebanon, August 24 and September 29, 1982.

171 In August 1983 he authorized the MNF to stay: Shultz, *Turmoil and Triumph*, p. 222.

171 In December, he agreed to step up: Brinkley, ed., *Reagan Diaries*, pp. 201–2.

172 "We're a divided group": Ibid., p. 201.

173 Cap Weinberger's Pentagon was reluctant: Shultz, *Turmoil and Triumph*, pp. 329, 331, 342–43; Russell Crandall, *Gunboat Democracy: U.S. Interventions in the Dominican Republic, Grenada, and Panama* (Lanham, Md.: Rowman & Littlefield, 2006), pp. 139–40.

173 A frustrated Reagan ordered Poindexter: Conversation with John Poindexter, January 2007; Shultz, *Turmoil and Triumph*, pp. 677, 680–82.

174 "It was precisely our military role in Lebanon": Secretary of State George P. Shultz, "Power and Diplomacy in the 1980's," address to the Trilateral Commission, Washington, April 3, 1984.

174 Caspar Weinberger to respond: Secretary of Defense Caspar Weinberger, "The

Uses of Military Power," address at the National Press Club, Washington, November 28, 1984. Weinberger wanted to deliver his response to Shultz earlier, but the White House delayed it to after the election. See also the discussion in Caspar W. Weinberger, *Fighting for Peace: Seven Critical Years in the Pentagon* (New York: Warner, 1990), pp. 401–2, 433–45.

175   Yet the Pentagon was even more enthusiastic about this mission: Weinberger, *Fighting for Peace*, Chapter 13, esp. pp. 395–97.

175   somehow this convinced him that it was perfectly consistent: Ibid. See also Secretary of Defense Caspar W. Weinberger, *A Report to the Congress on Security Arrangements in the Persian Gulf* (Department of Defense, June 15, 1987).

175   These indictments launched the United States into a political crisis: A good account is in Crandall, *Gunboat Democracy,* Chapter 4.

176   Justice has been known to resist sharing too much information: Nicholas Rostow, "Law Enforcement and Foreign Policy," unpublished draft paper, July 1994, p. 3.

176   At Situation Room meetings, they argued: Shultz, *Turmoil and Triumph*, pp. 1054, 1058; Crandall, *Gunboat Democracy*, p. 194.

177   the Pentagon remained cautious: Powell, *My American Journey*, p. 416.

177   The negotiation fell through: Shultz, *Turmoil and Triumph*, pp. 1058–79.

177   After the al-Qaida attack on the USS *Cole*: National Commission on Terrorist Attacks upon the United States ("9/11 Commission"), *Final Report* (New York: Norton, [2003]), Section 6.3, pp. 190–92.

CHAPTER SEVEN: GEORGE H. W. BUSH

179   covert action program . . . SOUTHCOM: Russell Crandall, *Gunboat Democracy: U.S. Interventions in the Dominican Republic, Grenada, and Panama* (Lanham, Md.: Rowman & Littlefield, 2006), pp. 195–97; James A. Baker III with Thomas M. DeFrank, *The Politics of Diplomacy: Revolution, War, and Peace, 1989–1992* (New York: Putnam's Sons, 1995), Chapter 11.

179   Cheney secured his replacement: Stephen F. Hayes, *Cheney: The Untold Story of America's Most Powerful and Controversial Vice President* (New York: Harper-Collins, 2007), p. 221.

180   Bush decided: "Okay, let's do it": Colin L. Powell with Joseph E. Persico, *My American Journey* (New York: Random House, 1995), p. 425.

181   "China desk officer": comment of NSC staffer Robert Suettinger in David J. Rothkopf, *Running the World: The Inside Story of the National Security Council and the Architects of American Power* (New York: Public Affairs, 2005), p. 291.

181   Bush had found time to chat by telephone: George Bush and Brent Scowcroft, *A World Transformed* (New York: Alfred A. Knopf, 1998), pp. 61–62.

181   "mad dialer": John Bolton, *Surrender Is Not an Option: Defending America at the United Nations and Abroad* (New York: Threshold/Simon & Schuster, 2007), p. 36.

181   "Core Group": Bush and Scowcroft, *A World Transformed*, pp. 41–42.

181   "[W]e made the national security apparatus": Baker, *The Politics of Diplomacy*, p. 22.

181   Gates . . . has a somewhat sharper assessment: Robert M. Gates, *From the Shadows: The Ultimate Insider's Story of Five Presidents and How They Won the Cold War* (New York: Simon & Schuster, 1996), p. 454.

182   Scowcroft was described by a journalist: David Lauter, "The Man Behind the

President," *Los Angeles Times,* October 14, 1990, p. A1, in Karl F. Inderfurth and Loch K. Johnson, *Fateful Decisions: Inside the National Security Council* (New York: Oxford University Press, 2004), p. 203.

182 "It is probably accurate to say": Bush and Scowcroft, *A World Transformed,* p. 36.

183 Scowcroft's ability to "knock heads": Ibid., p. 35.

183 had Tower been confirmed: Rothkopf, *Running the World,* p. 264.

183 In Robert Gates's estimation: Gates, *From the Shadows,* p. 457.

183 By all accounts . . . the disagreements never: Baker, *The Politics of Diplomacy,* pp. 21–24; Hayes, *Cheney,* p. 209.

184 "Operation Just Because": One of the journalists present, Strobe Talbott, recounts the story in Strobe Talbott, *The Great Experiment: The Story of Ancient Empires, Modern States, and the Quest for a Global Nation* (New York: Simon & Schuster, 2008), p. 264.

184 "smothering presence" of Soviet forces: Scowcroft in Bush and Scowcroft, *A World Transformed,* p. 43.

184 Similarly in . . . START, Cheney was doubtful: Ibid., pp. 208–10.

184 as the Soviet Union headed toward breakup: Gates, *From the Shadows,* pp. 529–31.

184 In his first news conference as secretary: Hayes, *Cheney,* pp. 215–16.

184 Later, in the run-up to the Gulf War: Ibid., pp. 234–38; Powell, *My American Journey,* pp. 476–78.

184 But he treated the chairman of the Joint Chiefs: Gates, *From the Shadows,* p. 457; Hayes, *Cheney,* p. 234.

185 Scowcroft reports his unhappiness: Bush and Scowcroft, *A World Transformed,* p. 381; see also pp. 353, 354, 431.

185 it was Cheney's strategy: Baker, *The Politics of Diplomacy,* p. 409.

185 "Dick led the way": Bush and Scowcroft, *A World Transformed,* p. 354; see also Hayes, *Cheney,* pp. 227, 233–34.

185 In July 1989, he appeared before: Secretary of Defense Richard Cheney, "Cost of Congressional Reporting Requirements," Testimony to the House Armed Services Committee, July 1989. The quote is from the related report, Secretary of Defense Dick Cheney, *Defense Management: Report to the President,* July 1989, p. 27 (emphasis in original).

185 In January 1990, his office published: Office of the Secretary of Defense, *White Paper on the Department of Defense and the Congress,* January 1990.

186 "big brother–little brother": Baker, *The Politics of Diplomacy,* p. 19.

186 "[M]ore comfortable with action": Ibid., pp. 38–40.

186 "a series of discrete problems": Ibid., pp. 134–35.

187 "the guy who got elected": Bolton, *Surrender Is Not an Option,* p. 36.

187 "I headed to State assuming that the President": Baker, *The Politics of Diplomacy,* pp. 29–30.

187 Shultz found this rankling: Author's conversations with Shultz during the period.

187 Baker's memoirs contain the all-too-familiar criticism: Baker, *The Politics of Diplomacy,* pp. 31–32.

188 never overcame their initial impression: E.g., John M. Goshko, "Poor Morale, Drift Seen at Baker's State Dept.; Inner Circle Aloof, Bureaucrats Charge," *Washington Post,* March 6, 1989, p. A1.

188 On April 1, 1989, what purported to be: Copy of *"Newsletter"* in author's collection. Note the date.

189 The Bush-Scowcroft memoir notes, more than once: Bush and Scowcroft, *A World Transformed*, pp. 354, 437, 463.

189 "furious" at Baker: Ibid., p. 461. Baker's account, only partially contrite, is in *The Politics of Diplomacy*, pp. 391–95.

189 Thomas L. Friedman . . . wrote: Thomas L. Friedman, "Mideast Tensions; Baker Seen as a Balance to Bush on Crisis in Gulf," *New York Times*, November 3, 1990.

189 Baker devotes a long passage in his memoirs: Baker, *The Politics of Diplomacy*, p. 131.

189 Other journalists reported: *U.S. News & World Report, Triumph Without Victory: The Unreported History of the Persian Gulf War* (New York: Times Books, 1992), p. 104.

189 Robert Gates . . . is on record: Gates, *From the Shadows*, p. 456.

190 Scowcroft, for example, believed: Bush and Scowcroft, *A World Transformed*, pp. 12, 135, 154.

191 Hard-line colleagues in the Kremlin: Raymond L. Garthoff, *The Great Transition: American-Soviet Relations and the End of the Cold War* (Washington, D.C.: Brookings, 1994), p. 367.

191 Inside accounts of the Bush administration: Bush and Scowcroft, *A World Transformed*, pp. 187–88.

191 Baker visited the East German capital: Baker, *The Politics of Diplomacy*, pp. 174–75.

192 the Soviet leader was conflicted: Ibid., pp. 167, 172.

192 "We're going to win the game": Baker, *The Politics of Diplomacy*, p. 230.

192 accepted the U.S. role in Europe: Ibid., pp. 170–71.

192 Baker's team at the State Department: The definitive account of the Two Plus Four process is Philip Zelikow and Condoleezza Rice, *Germany Unified and Europe Transformed: A Study in Statecraft* (Cambridge: Harvard University Press, 1995).

193 Baker phoned the president to complain: Baker, *The Politics of Diplomacy*, p. 70.

193 a speech that Scowcroft's deputy Robert Gates: Ibid., pp. 156–58; Gates, *From the Shadows*, pp. 480–81.

194 At two crucial Oval Office meetings: See Bush and Scowcroft, *A World Transformed*, pp. 541–44; Baker, *The Politics of Diplomacy*, pp. 560–61; Gates, *From the Shadows*, pp. 529–31.

194 As Scowcroft later admitted: Bush and Scowcroft, *A World Transformed*, p. 544.

194 This warning was aimed: Ibid., pp. 515–16.

195 none other than Richard Nixon: See Thomas L. Friedman, "Nixon Scoffs at Level of Support for Russian Democracy by Bush," *New York Times*, March 10, 1992; Marvin Kalb, *The Nixon Memo: Political Respectability, Russia, and the Press* (Chicago: University of Chicago Press, 1994).

195 By early December, opinion polls: Bush and Scowcroft, *A World Transformed*, pp. 427n., 439n.

195 Scowcroft reports that he was "appalled": Ibid., p. 317.

195 Scowcroft . . . sensed the president: Ibid., p. 318.

195 Mrs. Thatcher, too, found Bush resolute: Margaret Thatcher, *The Downing Street Years* (London: HarperCollins, 1993), pp. 817–18, 820.

195 Her famous admonition to Bush: Ibid., pp. 823–24.

196 Bush worked the phones: Bush and Scowcroft, *A World Transformed*, pp. 318–19.

196 "Norm Schwarzkopf, under pressure": Powell, *My American Journey*, p. 492.

196 "Dick was probably ahead of his military": Bush and Scowcroft, *A World Transformed*, p. 354. See also ibid., pp. 353, 381, 431, 477, and Hayes, *Cheney*, pp. 233–34.

197 Powell candidly expressed his concerns: Michael R. Gordon and Gen. Bernard E. Trainor, *The Generals' War: The Inside Story of the Conflict in the Gulf* (Boston: Little, Brown, 1995), pp. 31–34.

197 Scowcroft led off the second NSC meeting: Bush and Scowcroft, *A World Transformed*, pp. 315–24.

197 Powell ventured a question: Powell, *My American Journey*, pp. 464–66.

197 Cheney thenceforth insisted: Ibid., pp. 425–26, 503.

198 "When I finished, Scowcroft asked": Powell, *My American Journey*, pp. 488–89.

198 Margaret Thatcher, for one: Thatcher, *The Downing Street Years*, pp. 821, 827–28; Bush and Scowcroft, *A World Transformed*, pp. 384–87.

199 Baker, as we have noted, was eager: Bush and Scowcroft, *A World Transformed*, pp. 419, 437–38.

199 Bush later defended Baker: Ibid., p. 487.

200 Powell and his military colleagues: Powell, *My American Journey*, pp. 519–22.

200 Baker and his State colleagues: Baker, *The Politics of Diplomacy*, pp. 436–38.

200 Dick Cheney agreed: Hayes, *Cheney*, pp. 249–51.

200 Bush and Scowcroft . . . concede: Bush and Scowcroft, *A World Transformed*, pp. 488–90.

201 "I am a practical man": Quoted in Jon Margolis, "Bush Opens Run as 'Own Man,'" *Chicago Tribune*, October 13, 1987.

CHAPTER EIGHT: BILL CLINTON

203 he interrupted veteran Foreign Affairs Committee chairman: Quoted in David Halberstam, *War in a Time of Peace: Bush, Clinton, and the Generals* (New York: Scribner, 2001), p. 168.

203 David Gergen . . . assessed Clinton thusly: David Gergen, *Eyewitness to Power: The Essence of Leadership: Nixon to Clinton* (New York: Simon & Schuster, 2000), p. 276.

204 "a tendency toward intellectual clutter": Dick Morris, *Behind the Oval Office: Getting Reelected Against All Odds* (Los Angeles: Renaissance, 1996), p. 51.

204 Nor did he want to spend a lot of political capital: Ivo H. Daalder and I. M. Destler, *In the Shadow of the Oval Office: The President's National Security Adviser and the Making of America's Foreign Policy* (New York: Simon & Shuster, forthcoming), Chapter 7.

204 He came into office with a broad vision of a post–Cold War: Strobe Talbott, *The Great Experiment: The Story of Ancient Empires, Modern States, and the Quest for a Global Nation* (New York: Simon & Schuster, 2008), Chapter 15.

205 otherwise critics saw him: Elizabeth Drew, *On the Edge: The Clinton Presidency* (New York: Simon & Schuster, 1994), p. 140.

205 pride in his reliance on the Foreign Service: Warren Christopher, *Chances of a Lifetime* (New York: Scribner, 2001), pp. 80–81.

205 Clinton himself acknowledged the doubts: Bill Clinton, *My Life* (New York: Alfred A. Knopf, 2004), p. 455.

205 there are those who believe: Halberstam, *War in a Time of Peace*, p. 174; Daalder and Destler, *In the Shadow of the Oval Office*, Chapter 7.

206 Lake took a prominent role in articulating: See Anthony Lake, "From Containment to Enlargement," speech at the Johns Hopkins University School of Advanced International Studies, September 21, 1993 (at http://www.mtholyoke.edu/acad/intrel/lakedoc.html).

206 He admitted to being "emotional": Drew, *On the Edge*, p. 143; Halberstam, *War in a Time of Peace*, pp. 283–92.

206 the vice presidency reached another new level of power: Gergen, *Eyewitness to Power*, pp. 295–96.

206 Berger's true talent and focus: R. W. Apple, Jr., "A Domestic Sort with Global Worries," *New York Times*, August 25, 1999, p. A1; Halberstam, *War in a Time of Peace*, pp. 404–9.

207 Clinton's memoirs speak about Berger: Clinton, *My Life,* pp. 737–38.

207 "I don't talk to the military": Drew, *On the Edge*, p. 45.

207 In his memoir he tells the story: Colin L. Powell with Joseph E. Persico, *My American Journey* (New York: Random House, 1995), p. 576.

207 apparent determination by Clinton: Halberstam, *War in a Time of Peace*, pp. 324, 389, 412–14.

207 Powell, indeed, had warned Clinton: Powell, *My American Journey*, pp. 563, 578–80.

208 Lake . . . had co-authored a book: I. M. Destler, Leslie H. Gelb, and Anthony Lake, *Our Own Worst Enemy* (New York: Simon & Schuster, 1984), p. 279.

208 "[U]nlike Bush's team, Clinton's lacked a captain": Daalder and Destler, *In the Shadow of the Oval Office*, Chapter 7.

208 Sandy Berger has commented: Berger interview in David J. Rothkopf, *Running the World: The Inside Story of the National Security Council and the Architects of American Power* (New York: Public Affairs, 2005), p. 381.

209 "There is a comfort you get": Lake interview in Daalder and Destler, *In the Shadow of the Oval Office*, Chapter 7.

209 there are many reports of Clinton's irritation: E.g., Halberstam, *War in a Time of Peace*, pp. 223, 262–65, 272, 279–80, 316–17.

209 Colin Powell . . . was offended: Powell, *My American Journey*, p. 576.

209 he told *Time* magazine: Michael Kramer, "What He Will Do," *Time*, November 16, 1992, p. 31.

209 "This sounded much like": William Doyle, *Inside the Oval Office: The White House Tapes from FDR to Clinton* (New York: Kodansha International, 1999), pp. 304–5.

209 James Woolsey . . . had his own stories to tell: Woolsey interview in Rothkopf, *Running the World*, p. 327.

210 National Economic Council: Kenneth I. Juster and Simon Lazarus, *Making Economic Policy: An Assessment of the National Economic Council* (Washington, D.C.: Brookings, 1997).

211 "The administration continues to coddle China": Gov. Bill Clinton, address at Georgetown University, December 12, 1991.

211 "[t]his is going to be an arm's-length relationship": Berger quoted by Sandra Kristoff in Ivo H. Daalder and I. M. Destler, moderators, "China Policy and the National Security Council," The National Security Council Project: Oral His-

tory Roundtables (Washington, D.C.: Center for International and Security Studies at Maryland/University of Maryland, and the Brookings Institution, November 4, 1999), p. 28.

212   "Rough, somber, sometimes bordering": Christopher, *Chances of a Lifetime*, pp. 238–39.

212   The NEC staff (which had not been significantly involved): Juster and Lazarus, *Making Economic Policy*, pp. 26–27, 44–45.

212   Kantor told the Senate: Mickey Kantor, testimony before the Senate Finance Committee, March 9, 1993, quoted in William G. Hyland, *Clinton's World: Remaking American Foreign Policy* (Westport, Conn.: Praeger, 1999), p. 128.

212   As Jeffrey Garten, under secretary of commerce: Jeffrey E. Garten, *The Big Ten: The Big Emerging Markets and How They Will Change Our Lives* (New York: Basic Books, 1997), p. 141.

213   The State Department—through leaks to the press: E.g., Daniel Williams and Clay Chandler, "U.S. Aide Sees Relations with Asia in Peril," *Washington Post*, May 5, 1994.

213   Again, the NEC staff joined with the NSC: Juster and Lazarus, *Making Economic Policy*, pp. 37, 44.

213   Said one senior official: David E. Sanger, "At the End, U.S. Blunted Its Big Stick," *New York Times*, June 30, 1995, p. A9.

213   Robert Rubin took the lead: A good account of Rubin's role in the Mexican crisis is in Rothkopf, *Running the World*, pp. 358–62.

214   A testimony to Rubin's personal stature: Ibid., p. 361.

214   "I don't think five people could repeat": Clinton, *My Life*, p. 504. Talbott's account is told in Strobe Talbott, *The Russia Hand: A Memoir of Presidential Diplomacy* (New York: Random House, 2002).

215   Nixon told Talbott: Talbott, *The Russia Hand*, p. 46; see also Clinton, *My Life*, pp. 505, 593.

216   the initial high hopes for both Russian democracy: Hyland, *Clinton's World*, pp. 85–90.

217   Clinton had harshly criticized George H. W. Bush: E.g., "Statement by Gov. Bill Clinton on the Crisis in Bosnia," July 26, 1992.

218   "all the verve of a solicitor": Raymond Seitz, *Over Here* (London: Phoenix, 1998), p. 329.

218   A coalition of the unwilling: See Halberstam, *War in a Time of Peace*, pp. 224–31; Rothkopf, *Running the World*, pp. 364–66.

218   "[The president] is going south on this": Drew, *On the Edge*, pp. 157–58.

218   In his memoirs, Clinton attributes: Clinton, *My Life*, pp. 525–26.

218   Yet at the time, Clinton's discomfort: Evan Thomas et al., *Back from the Dead: How Clinton Survived the Republican Revolution* (New York: Atlantic Monthly Press, 1997), p. 1.

218   immortalized in the book and film: Mark Bowden, *Black Hawk Down: A Story of Modern War* (Berkeley: Atlantic Monthly Press, 1999); the film *Black Hawk Down*, 2001, produced by Jerry Bruckheimer and Ridley Scott and directed by Scott.

219   They repeatedly sought guidance from the White House: Halberstam, *War in a Time of Peace*, p. 259.

219   At his hotel on a visit in San Francisco: Drew, *On the Edge*, pp. 317–18, 335. See the similar assessment of blame in Clinton, *My Life*, pp. 550–53.

219 Then came Haiti: On the *Harlan County* episode, see Drew, *On the Edge*, pp. 333–34; Halberstam, *War in a Time of Peace*, pp. 267–72. Drew estimates the number of Haitians on the dock at forty to sixty, Halberstam at "more than one hundred."

220 he personally reviewed the plan at the Pentagon: Clinton, *My Life*, pp. 616–19.

220 At the White House it was suspected: Steve Coll, *Ghost Wars: The Secret History of the CIA, Afghanistan, and bin Laden, from the Soviet Invasion to September 11, 2001* (New York: Penguin, 2004), pp. 497–501, 533–34.

220 "They keep trying to force me": Morris, *Behind the Oval Office*, p. 245.

221 memos by Madeleine Albright: Rothkopf, *Running the World*, p. 366.

221 Meanwhile at Defense: Ivo H. Daalder, *Getting to Dayton: The Making of America's Bosnia Policy* (Washington, D.C.: Brookings, 2000), pp. 105, 169–70.

221 In June, Clinton responded to allied pleas: Ibid., pp. 66–67.

221 "the position of leader of the free world is vacant": Chirac quoted in Michael Dobbs, "Bosnia Crystallizes U.S. Post–Cold War Role; As Two Administrations Wavered, the Need for U.S. Leadership Became Clear," *Washington Post*, December 3, 1995.

221 One July evening around 7:00 p.m.: Bob Woodward, *The Choice* (New York: Simon & Schuster, 1996), pp. 260–61; Halberstam, *War in a Time of Peace*, pp. 316–17.

221 "The United States can't be a punching bag": Woodward, *The Choice*, pp. 262–63.

222 American diplomats sympathetic to Croatia: Daalder, *Getting to Dayton*, pp. 120–22; Richard Holbrooke, *To End a War* (New York: Modern Library, rev. ed., 1999), pp. 72–73.

222 "rooting for the Croatians": Clinton, *My Life*, pp. 166–67.

222 Holbrooke recounts a Principals meeting: Holbrooke, *To End a War*, pp. 144–46.

223 Holbrooke had no direct contact with Clinton: Morris, *Behind the Oval Office*, p. 261.

223 Defense . . . successfully blocked: Holbrooke, *To End a War*, p. 277.

223 While his national security team told him optimistically: Adm. Vern Clark quoted in Bob Woodward, *State of Denial* (New York, Simon & Schuster, 2006), p. 61. See also Ivo H. Daalder and Michael E. O'Hanlon, *Winning Ugly: NATO's War to Save Kosovo* (Washington, D.C.: Brookings, 2000), p. 91ff.

223 "We're just gerbils": Daalder and O'Hanlon, *Winning Ugly*, p. 71; Daalder and Destler, *In the Shadow of the Oval Office*, Chapter 7.

224 Clark developed his own regular contact with Sandy Berger: Steven Lee Myers and Eric Schmitt, "Crisis in the Balkans: The Leadership," *New York Times*, May 30, 1999.

224 Clark wanted to attack "strategic" targets: Gen. Wesley K. Clark, *Waging Modern War: Bosnia, Kosovo, and the Future of Combat* (New York: Public Affairs, 2001), esp. pp. 236–38, 265–66, 271.

224 Secretary Cohen consistently opposed: Ibid., pp. 269, 285, 332.

224 Public hints of planning for a ground war: Ibid., p. 405; Daalder and O'Hanlon, *Winning Ugly*, pp. 184, 203–4.

224 Clinton in his memoir is adamant: Clinton, *My Life*, pp. 851, 859. But see Daalder and O'Hanlon, *Winning Ugly*, pp. 156–61.

225 Cohen was often uncommunicative: Clark, *Waging Modern War*, pp. 98–99, 106.

225 Clark wondered if this was consistent with the intent: Ibid., pp. 288, 319.

225 The conflicting pressures on Clark: For this paragraph, see Halberstam, *War in a Time of Peace*, pp. 441–43.

226 The president . . . seems not to have known: Halberstam, *War in a Time of Peace*, pp. 478–79.

226 a paradoxical effect on alliance relations: This point is expanded upon in Peter W. Rodman, *Drifting Apart? Trends in U.S.-European Relations* (Washington, D.C.: Nixon Center, June 1999), pp. 64–67 (at http://nixoncenter.org/publications/monographs/drifting.pdf).

227 Carter's legacy as a reputation for incompetence: Halberstam, *War in a Time of Peace*, pp. 175, 280.

228 to, among others, former President Gerald Ford: Thomas M. DeFrank, *Write It When I'm Gone: Remarkable Off-the-Record Conversations with Gerald Ford* (New York: G. P. Putnam's Sons, 2007), pp. 148, 164.

228 he authorized Carter to go: Clinton, *My Life*, pp. 602–3.

228 Carter telephoned Colin Powell: Powell, *My American Journey*, pp. 597–98.

229 "desperately wanted to avoid": Clinton, *My Life*, p. 617.

229 the president approved a draft that read: George Stephanopoulos, *All Too Human* (Boston: Little, Brown, 1999), p. 313; Halberstam, *War in a Time of Peace*, p. 280.

229 Carter contacted the administration: Holbrooke, *To End a War*, pp. 121, 147–50.

229 William Hyland sums up: Hyland, *Clinton's World*, p. 202.

229 Schlesinger saw in Bill Clinton: Arthur M. Schlesinger, Jr., "The Ultimate Approval Rating," *New York Times Magazine,* December 15, 1996. See also the fuller analysis in Arthur M. Schlesinger, Jr., "Rating the Presidents: Washington to Clinton," *Political Science Quarterly*, vol. 112, no. 2 (1997), p. 188.

230 forcefully articulated the danger that was thought to be posed; See, e.g., President Clinton's address to the Joint Chiefs of Staff and Pentagon staff, at the Pentagon, February 17, 1998.

CHAPTER NINE: GEORGE W. BUSH

232 Bush liked to see himself as "the decider": He used this formulation notably in April 2006 in reply to a barrage of press questions on whether he was considering firing Secretary of Defense Donald Rumsfeld: "I'm the decider, and I decide what is best." See "President Bush Nominates Rob Portman as OMB Director and Susan Schwab for USTR," White House press release, April 18, 2006.

232 *The Washington Post* once mischievously published: Alasdair Roberts, "The Bush Years, in a Word," *Washington Post*, January 1, 2007, p. A13. See also David Rose, "Neo Culpa," *Vanity Fair* (January 2007), p. 85; David J. Rothkopf, *Running the World: The Inside Story of the National Security Council and the Architects of American Power* (New York: Public Affairs, 2005), pp. 406, 415, 436; Glenn Kessler and Peter Slevin, "Rice Fails to Repair Rifts, Officials Say," *Washington Post*, October 12, 2003, p. 1.

233 Some were criticizing a reputed "cabal": Lawrence B. Wilkerson, "The White House Cabal," *Los Angeles Times*, October 25, 2005.

233 Others were referring: See, e.g., Rose, "Neo Culpa," pp. 85, 90 (Richard Perle), 90, 144 (Frank Gaffney).

233 Team Bush: The title is borrowed from Donald F. Kettl, *Team Bush: Leadership Lessons from the Bush White House* (New York: McGraw-Hill, 2003).

233 White House speechwriter David Frum: David Frum, *The Right Man: The Sur-*

prise Presidency of George W. Bush (New York: Random House, 2003), pp. 28, 146, 272–77. In a later book, Frum expressed more disappointment in Bush's performance. David Frum, *Comeback: Conservatism That Can Win Again* (New York: Doubleday, 2008), Chapter 1.

234   a needed change from Bill Clinton: Kettl, *Team Bush*, p. 149.

234   one of the lessons taught: Thomas Lifson, "GWB: HBS MBA," *American Thinker*, February 3, 2004.

234   the dilemma of the statesman: Henry A. Kissinger, *Nuclear Weapons and Foreign Policy* (New York: Harper & Bros., 1957), p. 424.

235   "I'm not a textbook player": Bob Woodward, *Bush at War* (New York: Simon & Schuster, 2002), pp. 136–37, 145, 168, 342.

235   Conservative writer: Richard Brookhiser, "Close Up: The Mind of George W. Bush," *The Atlantic* (April 2003).

235   "[T]he vision thing matters": Woodward, *Bush at War*, p. 341.

235   According to many accounts, Bush's model of leadership: See esp. Lou Cannon and Carl M. Cannon, *Reagan's Disciple: George W. Bush's Troubled Quest for a Presidential Legacy* (New York: Public Affairs, 2008).

235   Bush considered that he had a mandate: Bob Woodward, *Plan of Attack* (New York: Simon & Schuster, 2004), pp. 28, 410; Charles O. Jones, "Governing Executively: Bush's Paradoxical Style," in John C. Fortier and Norman J. Ornstein, eds., *Second-Term Blues: How George W. Bush Has Governed* (Washington, D.C.: American Enterprise Institute and Brookings, 2007), pp. 123–24.

235   "He very much believes": Quoted in Dick Kirschten, "Bush as Boss: The Leadership Style of the Man Who Could Be Government's Next CEO," *Government Executive* (July 2000).

235   "uncanny ability": Dana Milbank, "Dispelling Doubts with the Rangers," *Washington Post*, July 25, 2000. See also Fred I. Greenstein, "George W. Bush: The Man and His Leadership," in Fortier and Ornstein, *Second-Term Blues*, p. 43.

236   "[A] president has got to be the calcium": Woodward, *Bush at War*, p. 259. See a similar observation by Bush in an interview in Robert Draper, *Dead Certain: The Presidency of George W. Bush* (New York: Free Press, 2007), pp. x–xi.

236   Woodward tells the story of a moment: Woodward, *Bush at War*, pp. 260–63.

236   Military experts know this resolve: Eliot Cohen, "What Combat Does to Man: Private Ryan and Its Critics," *The National Interest*, 1998–1999 (Winter). Cohen mentions a scene in the film *Saving Private Ryan* in which Tom Hanks's character, Capt. John Miller, seeks refuge in a solitary shell hole when he is about to crack with grief and doubt, determined that his men not see him, knowing how much they depended on confidence in his strength.

236   "a good executive": Remarks by Bush on announcing three new cabinet appointments, January 2, 2001.

237   in his 1995 memoir: Colin L. Powell with Joseph E. Persico, *My American Journey* (New York: Random House, 1995), p. 608.

238   "empower the desks": Ben Barber, "Bush Welcomes Sharon Victory, Fresh Start to Peace," *Washington Times*, February 8, 2001, p. A10. On the "special envoys," see Richard Boucher, State Department spokesman, Daily Briefing, March 12, 2001, p. 10.

238   Karl Rove clashed with Powell: Woodward, *Plan of Attack*, p. 127.

238   As Powell said in his confirmation hearing: U.S. Senate, Committee on Foreign Relations, *Nomination of Colin L. Powell to Be Secretary of State*, Hearing, Janu-

ary 17, 2001, 107th Cong., 1st Sess., p. 97 (exchange with Senator Chris Dodd, Democrat of Connecticut).

238 "You do cover": John Bolton, *Surrender Is Not an Option: Defending America at the United Nations and Abroad* (New York: Threshold/Simon & Schuster, 2007), pp. 47, 54.

239 International Criminal Court: Ibid., pp. 85–87.

239 "axis of evil": Ibid., pp. 103–4.

239 Powell was later criticized by liberals: E.g., Karen De Young, *Soldier: The Life of Colin Powell* (New York: Alfred A. Knopf, 2006).

240 during the transition, Powell had been briefed: Charles L. Pritchard, *Failed Diplomacy: The Tragic Story of How North Korea Got the Bomb* (Washington, D.C.: Brookings, 2007), p. 73.

240 The president himself called Rice: Elisabeth Bumiller, *Condoleezza Rice: An American Life: A Biography* (New York: Random House, 2007), pp. 145–47.

240 "got a little too far forward on my skis": Powell interview, May 14, 2001, with Andrea Koppel of CNN, quoted in Bolton, *Surrender Is Not an Option*, p. 102.

240 "There existed a distance": Woodward, *Bush at War*, p. 13.

241 later declared himself satisfied: Powell interview in Rothkopf, *Running the World*, p. 409.

241 a "cabal" of the vice president and secretary of defense: Wilkerson, "The White House Cabal."

241 "thumb on the scales": Rothkopf, *Running the World*, pp. 389, 407.

241 "Powell is a diplomat": Woodward, *Bush at War*, p. 342. See also the *Time* cover story, "Where Have You Gone, Colin Powell?," September 10, 2001, alleging his declining stock in the White House, discussed by Woodward, p. 14.

241 "Somebody got to the President": Interview with Lawrence Wilkerson in Yoichi Funabashi, *The Peninsula Question: A Chronicle of the Second Korean Nuclear Crisis* (Washington, D.C.: Brookings, 2007), p. 142. I heard a close friend of Powell's give the same account in a conversation in November 2007.

242 Colin Powell, when he was Reagan's: Powell, *My American Journey*, p. 338.

242 His friend Newt Gingrich: Rowan Scarborough, *Rumsfeld's War: The Untold Story of America's Anti-Terrorist Commander* (Washington, D.C.: Regnery, 2004), p. vii.

242 He had the president's explicit mandate: President-elect Bush's announcement nominating Rumsfeld, December 28, 2000. See also candidate Bush's speech, "A Period of Consequences," at The Citadel, South Carolina, September 23, 1999.

244 Marc Grossman . . . is on record: Quoted in Rothkopf, *Running the World*, p. 410. Grossman is incorrect, however, in claiming to Rothkopf that the Office of the Secretary of Defense had superior numbers of people.

244 The White House, for its part: Favorable comments on Feith's work by deputy national security adviser Stephen Hadley are reported in Bob Woodward, *State of Denial* (New York: Simon & Schuster, 2006), p. 208.

245 Carter treated Mondale: Woodrow Wilson International Center for Scholars, "The Role of the Modern Vice President," *Centerpoint* (June 2007), summarizing a Center Director's Forum on the topic held on April 26, 2007 (at http://www.wilsoncenter.org/index.cfm?fuseaction=events.print&event_id=228842).

245 Carter's attorney general: Griffin B. Bell with Ronald J. Ostrow, *Taking Care of the Law* (New York: William Morrow, 1982), pp. 22–36.

245 Leon Fuerth . . . "a very major player": Daniel Poneman, NSC staffer, quoted in Ivo H. Daalder and I. M. Destler, moderators, "The Clinton Administration National Security Council," The National Security Council Project: Oral History Roundtables (Washington, D.C.: Center for International and Security Studies at Maryland/University of Maryland, and the Brookings Institution, September 27, 2000), p. 4.

245 some experts believe Cheney's staff : Bradley H. Patterson, Jr., quoted in David Nather, "The Vice Presidency: An Office Under Scrutiny," *CQ Weekly Online,* June 11, 2007, p. 17ff.

245 "considerably more time with the president": Rothkopf, *Running the World,* p. 423.

245 The accusation often made: This is the thesis set forth, for example, in ibid., Chapter 12.

246 The attempt to assert broad presidential powers: Jack Goldsmith, *The Terror Presidency: Law and Judgment Inside the Bush Administration* (New York: W. W. Norton, 2007).

246 shared by other senior White House officials: Conversation with former senior Bush White House official.

246 subsequent accounts suggest the relationship between them: E.g., Bumiller, *Condoleezza Rice,* pp. 159–60, 177–78, 217–19; Bolton, *Surrender Is Not an Option,* pp. 69–70, 76.

247 Rice took her and Powell's concerns: Bumiller, *Condoleezza Rice,* pp. 189–90

247 White House insiders scoffed: Conversation with several senior Bush White House officials.

247 "Cheney was certainly a powerful figure": Frum, *The Right Man,* p. 62.

248 "She threw a fit": Bumiller, *Condoleezza Rice,* pp. 136–37.

248 Rice saw the first role as the most important: Ibid., p. 134.

248 "On a typical day": Rothkopf, *Running the World,* p. 393.

248 Rice came to be accused of being weak: E.g., Karl F. Inderfurth and Loch K. Johnson, "Crucial flaw demands immediate reform," *Chicago Tribune,* June 20, 2004.

248 "acceleratron": Bumiller, *Condoleezza Rice,* p. 134.

248 she has been criticized harshly: Ivo H. Daalder and I. M. Destler, *In the Shadow of the Oval Office: The President's National Security Adviser and the Making of America's Foreign Policy* (New York: Simon & Schuster, forthcoming), Chapter 8.

249 Henry Kissinger considered it: E.g., Henry Kissinger, *White House Years* (Boston: Little, Brown, 1979), p. 31.

249 He did not want to referee every dispute: Conversations with two former senior officials, one in the White House and the other on the NSC staff.

250 Hadley was heard saying more than once: Author's conversation in August 2007 with a former White House official. See also Woodward, *State of Denial,* pp. 244–45.

252 The president reportedly sided: Connie Bruck, "Exiles: How Iran's Expatriates Are Gaming the Nuclear Threat," *The New Yorker,* March 6, 2006, pp. 53–54.

252 he wanted a North Korea policy "180 degrees" different: Bolton, *Surrender Is Not an Option,* p. 105.

253 Bush told Bob Woodward: Woodward, *Bush at War,* p. 340.

253 Powell's "accidental" meeting . . . in Brunei: Pritchard, *Failed Diplomacy,* p. 31.

253 On at least two other occasions: Ibid., pp. 31–32, 57–58.

253 to build a nuclear weapon via highly enriched uranium (HEU): The facts of the North Korean HEU program, and of the North Koreans' admission of it, are not

disputed. See the convergent accounts of two men on opposite sides of the policy debate: John Bolton, in *Surrender Is Not an Option*, Chapter 4, and Charles Pritchard, in *Failed Diplomacy*, Chapter 2. Pritchard was part of Kelly's delegation in Pyongyang, as was a member of my staff.

254 "A trained monkey": Kelly quoted in Funabashi, *The Peninsula Question*, p. 162.

254 The State Department felt passionately: This is one of the main themes of Pritchard, *Failed Diplomacy,* esp. Chapter 11.

254 would have to abandon its harsh rhetoric: Ibid., esp. pp. 9–21, 140–41.

254 a Democratic senator called Armitage: Funabashi, *The Peninsula Question*, p. 164; Nicholas D. Kristof, "Secret, Scary Plans," *New York Times*, February 28, 2003, p. 25.

255 Within two years, however, U.S. diplomats: This is the assertion of Pritchard, *Failed Diplomacy,* pp. 109–12.

255 U.S. policy in New York toughened: Bolton, *Surrender Is Not an Option*, pp. 299, 300, 304, 310.

255 A spate of press articles: E.g., Elaine Shannon, "How Rice's Posse Struck Back," *Time*, March 19, 2007, p. 28; Matthew Lee, "Diplomats Reclaim Foreign Policy Roles," Associated Press, August 22, 2007.

255 "Rice telephoned Bush": Karen DeYoung and Glenn Kessler, "Policy Successes—or U-Turns; Views Differ on Bush Moves on Iran, N. Korea, Mideast," *Washington Post*, March 11, 2007. See also David E. Sanger and Thom Shanker, "Rice Is Said to Have Speeded North Korea Deal," *New York Times*, February 16, 2007.

256 U.S. diplomats considered the Berlin setting: Pritchard, *Failed Diplomacy*, pp. 158–59.

256 meet, in the Waldorf Towers in New York: Ibid., p. 185.

256 Bush had second thoughts: Conversations in 2007 and 2008 with three senior sources in the Executive Branch who had heard the president on the subject.

258 The president's decision to go to war, made finally in January 2003: This is the assessment of Woodward, *Plan of Attack*, p. 254.

258 an unprecedented degree of transparency and communication: Powell was struck by the preeminent role of the CENTCOM commander and the reduced role of the chairman of the JCS, compared with his experience in the 1991 Gulf War. See De Young, *Soldier,* pp. 394–95. Probably this will vary in the future, depending on personalities and geography. The chairman is chief military adviser to the president, but the combatant commander is the chief planner and is in the chain of wartime command. Both have a claim on being included.

258 Powell . . . spent more than two hours with the president: Woodward, *Plan of Attack*, pp. 149–53; De Young, *Soldier*, pp. 401–2.

258 Powell also had private conversations . . . with Franks: Woodward, *Plan of Attack*, pp. 80, 125–26; De Young, *Soldier*, pp. 396, 426.

258 Rumsfeld sent Bush his own memo: Douglas J. Feith, *War and Decision: Inside the Pentagon at the Dawn of the War on Terrorism* (New York: Harper, 2008), pp. 332–35.

259 George Tenet, then CIA director: George Tenet with Bill Harlow, *At the Center of the Storm: My Years at the CIA* (New York: HarperCollins, 2007), pp. 307–8.

259 Bush admitted this: Woodward, *Plan of Attack*, pp. 251–52.

259 "I know of one way": Dwight D. Eisenhower, Columbia University Oral History

Interview, July 20, 1967, uncorrected transcript, quoted in Greenstein, "George W. Bush: The Man and His Leadership," pp. 65, 69n.36.

260 French sabotage of the second resolution: An authoritative account is Charles Cogan, *French Negotiating Behavior: Dealing with La Grande Nation* (Washington, D.C.: United States Institute of Peace Press, 2003), pp. 186–214.

260 The Executive Steering Group . . . chafed: Woodward, *State of Denial*, pp. 108–10.

260 the White House asked Rumsfeld to delay: Feith, *War and Decision*, pp. 316–17.

261 Rumsfeld made a misstep that seriously embittered: Rajiv Chandrasekaran, *Imperial Life in the Emerald City: Inside Iraq's Green Zone* (New York: Vintage, 2007), p. 37; Feith, *War and Decision*, pp. 386–89.

261 The "planning order" sent by the chairman: See the timeline in the Joint Staff briefing, "Operation Iraqi Freedom: Strategic Lessons Learned," August 29, 2003, in Scarborough, *Rumsfeld's War*, pp. 175–77.

261 For a considerable period, however, General Franks seemed to believe: Feith, *War and Decision*, pp. 291–93, 317–18, 349–50, in answer to Woodward, *State of Denial*, pp. 91, 144–45. See also Michael R. Gordon and General Bernard E. Trainor, *COBRA II: The Inside Story of the Invasion and Occupation of Iraq* (New York: Pantheon, 2006), pp. 68, 70, 138.

261 On December 19, an updated "planning order": See the timeline in Joint Staff briefing, "Operation Iraqi Freedom: Strategic Lessons Learned," in Scarborough, *Rumsfeld's War*, p. 178.

262 a post-Iraq "lessons learned" assessment: Ibid.

262 Rumsfeld signed a directive: DoD Directive 3000.05, "Military Support for Stability, Security, Transition, and Reconstruction (SSTR) Operations," November 28, 2005.

262 A memorandum I wrote to Rumsfeld on this subject: Feith, *War and Decision*, Appendix 7 ("Who Will Govern Iraq?" Rodman Memo, August 15, 2002), pp. 546–48. See also the discussion in ibid., pp. 252–57, 497–501.

263 The president's decision was spelled out in unusual detail: Ibid., pp. 406–8.

263 Bremer concluded that a multiyear U.S. occupation: His account is in Ambassador L. Paul Bremer III with Malcolm McConnell, *My Year in Iraq: The Struggle to Build a Future of Hope* (New York: Simon & Schuster, 2006), pp. 43–49, and also in L. Paul Bremer III, "Facts for Feith," *National Review Online*, March 20, 2008 (at http://article.nationalreview.com/print/?q=NDIwN2MzOTlj OTNlODdiMDIzZWQ5Zm7jZ).

263 By October, Bremer was persuaded to agree: Chandrasekeran, *Imperial Life in the Emerald City*, pp. 218–19; Feith, *War and Decision*, pp. 455–66.

263 Bremer's charter: Presidential letter of appointment, May 9, 2003.

264 there was a flood of tendentious leaks: E.g; Jonathan S. Landay and Warren P. Strobel, "Postwar U.S. Plan for Iraq Called Flawed," *Miami Herald*, July 12, 2003; Peter Slevin and Dana Priest, "Wolfowitz Concedes Iraq Errors," *Washington Post*, July 24, 2003; James Fallows, "Blind into Baghdad," *Atlantic Monthly*, January/February 2004; David Rieff, "Blueprint for a Mess," *New York Times Magazine*, November 2, 2003. Other leaks, criticizing the conduct of the war, came from military sources. On, e.g., the allegation that the State Department had a significant planning effort that was suppressed, see Gordon and Trainor, *COBRA II*, p. 159; and Bremer, *My Year in Iraq*, p. 25. On the Pentagon's alleged plan to install Chalabi, see Feith, *War and Decision*, pp. 279, 383, 487–90.

264 Senior White House officials made calls: Conversation with former senior White House official, December 2007.

264 Thereby, they not only conceded much: Feith, *War and Decision*, pp. 474–77, 491–93.

264 Democratic candidate John Kerry: E.g., Sen. John Kerry, Remarks to the American Legion Convention, September 1, 2004. Kerry also raised some of these points directly with Bush in the debates on September 30 and October 8, 2004.

264 The *New York Times* reported: Douglas Jehl, "U.S. Intelligence Shows Pessimism on Iraq's Future," *New York Times*, September 16, 2004.

264 the *Times* cited prewar intelligence: Douglas Jehl and David E. Sanger, "Prewar Assessment on Iraq Saw Chance of Strong Divisions," *New York Times*, September 28, 2004.

264 a senior CIA Middle East analyst was reported: Robert Novak, "Is CIA at War with Bush?; A National Intel Officer Tells of Secret, Unheeded Warnings of War in Iraq," *Chicago Sun-Times*, September 27, 2004.

264 A second senior intelligence officer: Dana Priest, "CIA Officer Criticizes Agency's Handling of bin Laden," *Washington Post*, November 9, 2004.

265 In October, the Knight Ridder/Tribune chain: Warren P. Strobel, Jonathan S. Landay, and John Walcott, "CIA Review Finds No Evidence Saddam Had Ties to Islamic Terrorists," Knight Ridder/Tribune News Service, October 5, 2004, cited in Hayes, *Cheney*, pp. 456–57.

265 Patrick Lang, a retired Defense intelligence analyst: Lang quoted in Robert Dreyfuss, "The Yes-Man; President Bush Sent Porter Goss to the CIA to Keep the Agency in Line. What He's Really Doing Is Wrecking It," *The American Prospect*, November 2005.

265 The CIA's supposed prediction: Gordon and Trainor, *COBRA II*, pp. 570–71. On the CIA's assessment of the Iraqi police and other lapses, see ibid., pp. 136, 161, 202–3, 212–13, and 466.

265 the unclassified summary . . . of an NIE: National Intelligence Council, "Iran: Nuclear Intentions and Capabilities," National Intelligence Estimate: Key Judgments, November 2007. For critical comments, see, e.g., Henry A. Kissinger, "Misreading the Iran Report: Why Spying and Policymaking Don't Mix," *Washington Post*, December 13, 2007, and John R. Bolton, "Our Politicized Intelligence Services," *Wall Street Journal*, February 5, 2008.

266 Bush and his closest colleagues: Bumiller, *Condoleezza Rice*, pp. 299–302; David E. Sanger, Michael R. Gordon, and John F. Burns, "Chaos Overran Iraq Plan in '06, Bush Team Says," *New York Times*, January 2, 2007; Michael Abramowitz and Peter Baker, "Embattled, Bush Held to Plan to Salvage Iraq," *Washington Post*, January 21, 2007.

267 General George Casey . . . firmly resisted: See Casey quoted in Sanger, Gordon, and Burns, "Chaos Overran Iraq Plan in '06."

268 Hadley's answer was: yes, but only if the military recommended it: Conversation with senior NSC staff member.

268 "What I want to hear from you": Sanger, Gordon, and Burns, "Chaos Overran Iraq Plan in '06."

268 "thoughtful and sensitive" in his handling of the military: Fred Barnes, "How Bush Decided on the Surge," *The Weekly Standard*, February 4, 2008, p. 23.

268 As scholar Eliot Cohen has shown: Eliot A. Cohen, *Supreme Command: Soldiers, Statesmen, and Leadership in Wartime* (New York: Free Press, 2002).

269 As Hadley told: Conversation with a senior NSC staffer with whom Hadley spoke.

269 made his decision to relieve Donald Rumsfeld: Bumiller, *Condoleezza Rice*, pp. 298–300.

269 Bush made the surprising comment: Peter Baker, "As Democracy Push Falters, Bush Feels like a 'Dissident,'" *Washington Post*, August 20, 2007, p. A1.

270 On Iran as well, State's policy under Rice: Bruck, "Exiles," pp. 62–63.

271 Gates deftly shifted to support the president: Gates's early view may be found in Michael Abramowitz and Thomas E. Ricks, "Pentagon Chief Talks of Further Iraq Troop Cuts," *Washington Post*, September 15, 2007, p. A1. Compare with the president's remarks at Camp Arifjan, Kuwait, after meeting with Gen. David Petraeus and Ambassador. Ryan Crocker, January 12, 2008, and Gates's revised position as reported in Lolita C. Baldor, "Gates Hopes to Continue Iraq Drawdown," Associated Press, February 22, 2008.

CHAPTER TEN: LESSONS LEARNED

272 Justice Louis Brandeis: Brandeis dissent in *Myers v. United States*, 272 U.S. 293 (1926).

272 Richard Neustadt, reaffirming in 1990: Richard E. Neustadt, *Presidential Power and the Modern Presidents: The Politics of Leadership from Roosevelt to Reagan*, rev. ed. (New York: Free Press, 1990), Preface, p. xvii.

272 The Communists thought they had the solution: E.g., Milovan Djilas, *The New Class. An Analysis of the Communist System* (New York: Praeger, 1957), and Zbigniew K. Brzezinski, *The Permanent Purge: Politics in Soviet Totalitarianism* (Cambridge: Harvard University Press, 1956).

273 "The truth . . . is": Bernard Crick, *In Defense of Politics* (London: Pelican, 1964), p. 199.

274 politicization of the role of U.S. attorneys: The accusations made are summarized in Karen Tumulty and Massimo Calabresi, "Inside the Scandal at Justice," *Time*, May 21, 2007, pp. 44–49.

274 Jimmy Carter even proposed during his 1976 campaign: Griffin B. Bell and Ronald J. Ostrow, *Taking Care of the Law* (New York: William Morrow, 1982), p. 28.

274 "involuntarily equidistant": Robert M. Gates, "CIA and the Making of American Foreign Policy," address at the Woodrow Wilson School of Public and International Affairs, Princeton University, September 29, 1987; Robert M. Gates, "The CIA and American Foreign Policy," *Foreign Affairs* (Winter 1987–1988), p. 255.

274 Retired intelligence officer Paul Pillar: Paul R. Pillar, "Intelligence, Policy, and the War in Iraq," *Foreign Affairs* (March/April 2006), p. 27.

275 The controversies over intelligence in the Iraq War were thoroughly investigated: U.S. Senate, Select Committee on Intelligence, *The U.S. Intelligence Community's Prewar Intelligence Assessments on Iraq, Report*, S. Report 108-301, 108th Cong., 2nd Sess., July 9, 2004; The Commission on the Intelligence Capabilities of the United States Regarding Weapons of Mass Destruction (Laurence S. Silberman and Charles S. Robb, co-chairmen), Report to the President of the United States, March 31, 2005. Both inquiries found that prewar intelligence analysis on Iraq was not skewed by policy or political pressures from elsewhere in the administration.

280 The Eisenhower precept: Dwight D. Eisenhower, Columbia University Oral History Interview, July 20, 1967, uncorrected transcript, quoted in Fred I. Greenstein, "George W. Bush: The Man and His Leadership," in John C. Fortier and Norman J. Ornstein, eds., *Second-Term Blues: How George W. Bush Has Governed* (Washington, D.C.: American Enterprise Institute and Brookings, 2007), pp. 65, 69n.36.

281 "Presidents assume that their task": W. W. Rostow, *The Diffusion of Power: An Essay in Recent History* (New York: Macmillan, 1972), p. 368.

282 Zbigniew Brzezinski in his memoir: Zbigniew Brzezinski, *Power and Principle: Memoirs of the National Security Adviser, 1977–1981* (New York: Farrar, Straus & Giroux, 1983), pp. 533–37.

282 Henry Kissinger, having become secretary of state: Henry Kissinger, *Years of Upheaval* (Boston: Little, Brown, 1982), p. 434.

283 "Cabinet members cannot successfully compete": Stephen Hess, *Organizing the Presidency* (Washington, D.C.: Brookings, 1976), p. 193.

283 McGeorge Bundy, who . . . was fervently of the view: McGeorge Bundy, *The Strength of Government* (Cambridge: Harvard University Press, 1968), pp. 39–40. See also Hess, *Organizing the Presidency*, pp. 187–88.

284 Indeed it has been suggested: Laurence H. Silberman, "Toward Presidential Control of the State Department," *Foreign Affairs* (Spring 1979), pp. 888–89.

285 Dean Acheson conceded this point: Dean Acheson, "The Eclipse of the State Department," *Foreign Affairs* (July 1971).

286 "a Goldwater-Nichols Act for the interagency process": See, e.g., the joint testimony of Secretary of State Condoleezza Rice and Secretary of Defense Robert Gates before the House Armed Services Committee, on "Building Partnership Capacity and Development of the Interagency Process," April 15, 2008; Hans Binnendijk, "At War but Not War-Ready," *Washington Post*, November 3, 2007, p. A19; and Kenneth R. Dahl, "New Security for New Threats: The Case for Reforming the Interagency Process," unpublished paper, May 30, 2007, for the Twenty-first Century Defense Initiative of the Brookings Institution.

286 Various reform proposals have been put forward: A radical proposal for reform of the State Department's structure may be found in the U.S. Commission on National Security/21st Century (Hart-Rudman Commission), "Road Map for National Security: Imperative for Change," Phase III Report, March 15, 2001, pp. 52–63; more modest reforms were proposed by Frank C. Carlucci, chair, "State Department Reform," Report of an Independent Task Force Cosponsored by the Council on Foreign Relations and the Center for Strategic and International Studies, 2001.

286 A broader reform agenda: Donald Rumsfeld, among others, has been a strong advocate of this. See Donald Rumsfeld, "The Smart Way to Beat Tyrants Like Chavez," *Washington Post*, December 2, 2007, p. B3.

287 as writers like Thomas Ricks have pointed out: Thomas E. Ricks, *Making the Corps* (New York: Scribner's, 1997).

287 Both these problems raise profound issues that may loom larger: See Richard H. Kohn, "Coming Soon: A Crisis in Civil-Military Relations," *World Affairs* (Winter 2008), pp. 68–80.

INDEX